LATIN AMERICA'S QUEST FOR GLOBALIZATION

The International Political Economy of New Regionalisms Series

The International Political Economy of New Regionalisms Series presents innovative analyses of a range of novel regional relations and institutions. Going beyond established, formal, interstate economic organizations, this essential series provides informed interdisciplinary and international research and debate about myriad heterogeneous intermediate level interactions.

Reflective of its cosmopolitan and creative orientation, this series is developed by an international editorial team of established and emerging scholars in both the South and North. It reinforces ongoing networks of analysts in both academia and think-tanks as well as international agencies concerned with micro-, meso- and macro-level regionalisms.

Latin America's Quest for Globalization

The Role of Spanish Firms

Edited by

FÉLIX E. MARTÍN
Florida International University, USA

PABLO TORAL
Beloit College, USA

ASHGATE

Published by
Ashgate Publishing Limited
Gower House
Croft Road
Aldershot
Hants GU11 3HR
England

Ashgate Publishing Company
Suite 420
101 Cherry Street
Burlington, VT 05401-4405
USA

Ashgate website: http://www.ashgate.com

British Library Cataloguing in Publication Data
Martín, Félix E.
    Latin America's quest for globalization : the role of
    Spanish firms (The international political economy of new regionalisms series)
    1. Investments, Spanish - Latin America   2. Corporations,
    Spanish - Latin America 3. International business
    enterprises - Spain 4. International business enterprises -
    Latin America
    I. Title II. Toral, Pablo
    338.8'894608

Library of Congress Cataloging-in-Publication Data
Latin America's quest for globalization : the role of Spanish firms / edited by Félix
E. Martín and Pablo Toral.
    p. cm. -- (The international political economy of new regionalisms series)
    Includes index.
    ISBN 0-7546-4342-5
   1. Investments, Spanish--Latin America. 2. Corporations, Spanish--Latin America. 3.
International business enterprises--Spain. 4. International business enterprises--
Latin America. I. Martín, Félix E. II. Toral, Pablo. III. Series.

   HG5160.5.A3L37 2005
   338.8'894608--dc22

2005017278

ISBN 0 7546 4342 5

Printed and bound by Athenaeum Press Ltd, Gateshead, Tyne & Wear.

Contents

List of Figures

List of Tables

List of Contributors

JAMES R. BARTH is the Lowder Eminent Scholar in Finance at Auburn University and a Senior Fellow at the Milken Institute. His research has focused on financial institutions and capital markets, both domestic and global, with special emphasis on regulatory issues. He has authored more than 100 articles in professional journals and has written and edited several books, including *The Great Savings and Loan Debacle* and *The Reform of Federal Deposit Insurance: Disciplining the Government and Protecting Taxpayers*.

ÁLVARO CALDERÓN is Researcher on Economic Affairs at the Unit of Investment and Business Strategies, Division of Productive and Business Development of the UN Economic Commission for Latin America and the Caribbean (ECLAC-CEPAL) in Santiago de Chile. He also worked as a researcher at the Institute of Europe-Latin America Relations (IRELA) in Madrid. He has published extensively on foreign direct investment in Latin America, especially on European and Spanish investment, in the area of banking.

GUSTAVO DE LAS CASAS is a doctoral fellow in the Political Science Department at Columbia University. His research interests are international relations theory, bargaining, cooperation across economic and security issue-areas, and decision-making theory. Recently, his research on interstate bargaining was featured at the 100th Annual Meeting of the American Political Science Association in 2004. Gustavo also taught international political economy at Florida International University, and worked as a financial analyst in the private sector.

JUAN JOSÉ DURÁN is Professor of Economics and Director of the Centro Internacional Carlos V, at Universidad Autónoma de Madrid. His research interests include business economy, globalization and international finance. He is one of Spain's leading experts in the study of Spanish multinational enterprises. He has published numerous books and articles on these topics, including *La moneda en Europa. De Carlos V al euro*, *Multinacionales españolas en Iberoamérica*, *Economía y dirección financiera de la empresa*, and *La diversificación como estrategia empresarial. El conglomerado multinacional*.

FERNANDO GALLARDO is Associate Professor at Universidad Autónoma de Madrid. He teaches international finance and corporate finance. He also works as a consultant in the fields of telecommunications, information society, finance and banking. Before he began his academic career, he worked for Telefónica de España for twelve years, in the areas of Economic Studies and Strategic Planning. He was involved in the preparation of a Strategic Plan for Telefónica and its subsidiaries, international relationships, assessments of foreign direct investments, studies on regulation and international analysis. He has been a member of the Board of Directors of the International Telecommunications Society (ITS) since 1996.

JAVIER MAESTRO is Professor in the Department of History of Social Communication, School of Journalism, at Universidad Complutense in Madrid. His research and teaching are related to the history of political and social thought, the history of contemporary Spanish political institutions and the history of social movements. He also teaches American Politics and American Government at the Institute for American Studies at Universidad de Alcalá. His most recent publications include "European Peripheries in Interaction: The Nordic Countries and the Iberian Peninsula" (2002), and "The Late Nineteenth Century Scientific Impact on American and Spanish Intellectuals" (2003).

HARRY M. MAKLER is Professor of Sociology, Emeritus, at the University of Toronto and Visiting Scholar at Stanford University. His research, supported by the National Science and Ford Foundations, focuses on bank transformation in the Americas and its implications for public policy, entrepreneurship, the development of industrial leadership and institutional transformation. His recent publications include: "Financial Institutions in Economic Development," *International Encyclopedia of Social and Behavioral Sciences;* and "Bank Transformation in Brazil: Financial Federalism and Some Lessons About Bank Privatization," *Quarterly Review of Economics and Finance.*

FÉLIX E. MARTÍN is Assistant Professor of International Relations at Florida International University. He has taught at the Instituto Universitario de Estudios Norteamericanos of the Universidad de Alcalá in Madrid, Spain, and Hunter College (CUNY) in New York City, Rutgers University in Newark, and Saint Peter's College in Jersey City. Dr. Martín has published his work in *Foro Internacional, Revista Quórum* and, more recently, contributed a chapter to *Entre votos e botas: as forces armadas no laberinto latino-americano do novo milênio.*

WALTER L. NESS, JR. is Associate Professor of Administration at the Pontifical Catholic University of Rio de Janeiro in Brazil. He has published various articles and books on topics related to financial institutions and capital markets. He is also a partner in SR Rating, a Brazilian rating agency. He has taught at the Stern School of Business of New York University and was Director-Superintendent of the Brazilian Capital Markets Institute (IBMEC). He has worked and consulted on financial system development in Nigeria, Pakistan, the Central American Common Market, Trinidad and Tobago, Argentina, and Ghana.

MARIA-ANGELS OLIVA works as an economist at the European Central Bank in Frankfurt. Previously, she held positions at World Economic Forum's Global Competitiveness Programme and the European School of Management (ESCP-EAP) in Paris. Ms Oliva held a post-doctoral fellowship at the MIT Sloan School of Management, and was a visiting scholar at Columbia University and Université de Montréal. She specializes in trade and international finance. She is coauthor of *International Trade: Theory, Strategies, and Evidence*. She has published numerous articles on trade and international finance in various journals and books.

MICHAEL H. PERIU, JR. is the founder of Proximo International, a strategic consulting firm specializing in Hispanic and interactive marketing and co-founder of Posip, a leading provider of revolutionary internet-based Point of Sale and Customer Relationship Management Systems in Latin America. Mr Periu has also served as a consultant to leading banks, telecommunications companies and other utilities in Latin America, Europe and Africa through the International Finance Corporation. He also writes a weekly personal finance column for a leading Spanish-language newspaper. Recently, he was profiled on the front page of *The Wall Street Journal*, the front page of *The Standard* (Switzerland) and on *RTE Television* (Europe).

TRIPHON PHUMIWASANA is a researcher at the Milken Institute. His research focuses on banks, non-bank financial institutions, capital markets, banking regulation and economic development with special emphasis on global issues. Prior to joining the institute, he taught international finance at Claremont Graduate University. Phumiwasana has regularly co-authored a number of Milken Institute publications, including Policy Briefs and Milken Institute Review. His research also featured in the Office of Comptroller of the Currency working papers on Financial Markets, Institutions and Instruments.

LUIS A. RIVERA-BATIZ is Director of the Center for Business Research and Academic Initiatives at the University of Puerto Rico-Río Piedras. His research interests include international trade, economic policy, finance and development. He is the co-author of *International Finance and Open Macroeconomics and International Trade: Theory, Strategies and Policies*. He has taught at McGill University, Columbia University, Universitat Pompeu Fabra, and University of Florida-Gainesville. He has also served at the IMF, the IDB and several public and private organizations.

JOAQUÍN ROY is Jean Monnet Professor of European Integration, founding Director of the European Union Research Institute, and Senior Research Associate of North-South Center, of the University of Miami, and Co-Director of the Miami European Union Center. He is the author of over two hundred articles and reviews and twenty-five books, among them *The Reconstruction of Central America: the Role of the European Community*, *The Ibero-American Space/El Espacio Iberoamericano*, and *Cuba, the U.S. and the Helms-Burton Doctrine*. His over 1,100 columns and essays have been appearing in newspapers and magazines in Spain, the United States and Latin America.

SEBASTIÁN ROYO is an Assistant Professor in the Government Department at Suffolk University in Boston and affiliate and co-chair of the Iberian Study Group at the Minda de Gunzburg Center for European Studies at Harvard University. Royo has published articles and reviews on Southern European and Latin American politics. His recent publications include *From Social Democracy to Neoliberalism: The Consequences of Party Hegemony in Spain, 1982-1996*; *A New Century of Corporatism? Corporatism in Southern Europe*; and he is the co-editor of *Spain and Portugal in the European Union: the First Fifteen Years*.

CARLOS SEIGLIE is Associate Professor of Economics at Rutgers University. His research interests include finance, defense economics, law and economics, macroeconomics, international economics and industrial strategies, Cuban economic reform, the transition from centrally-planned to market-oriented economies in Russia and Eastern Europe and the interaction between economic practices and development performance in Latin America. His articles have been published in scholarly journals such as *Economica, Economic Inquiry, Journal of Conflict Resolution* and *Economics and Politics*, amongst others. He currently serves on the editorial board of numerous journals, including *Peace Economics, Peace Science and Public Policy, Pax Economica, Review of Economics of the Household*, and *Defence and Peace Economics*. Currently, he is a Managing Director at Analytica, Inc, an economic and management-consulting firm specializing in management strategies and the valuation of damages.

PABLO TORAL is Mouat Junior Professor of International Studies at Beloit College. He has published articles about Spanish multinational enterprises and their activities in Latin America, regional integration in the Americas, and nationalism, education and identity in Spain. He is the author of *The Reconquest of the New World. Spain's Multinational Enterprises and Direct Investment in Latin America*. He also serves as a consultant. Before becoming an academic, Toral worked as a journalist in Latin America, the United States and Europe.

GLENN YAGO is Director of Capital Studies at the Milken Institute. He specializes in financial innovations, financial institutions and capital markets, public policy and its relation to high-yield markets, initial public offerings, industrial and transportation concerns, and public and private sector employment. Yago has worked on financial innovations transfer and privatization projects in the Middle East since 1996, primarily in Israel, Jordan and in cooperation with the Palestinian Authority. In the area of Environmental Finance, Yago's work focuses on developing financial innovations that monetize environmental goods and services. He teaches at the Tel Aviv University Recanati School of Business Administration. The author of five books including *Restructuring Regulation and Financial Institutions*, and *Beyond Junk Bonds*, Yago's work has been widely published in edited volumes and scholarly journals such as the *Journal of Applied Corporate Finance, Urban Affairs Quarterly*, and *Journal of Contemporary Studies*.

Foreword

Without question, the subject of foreign investment and its relationship to the ongoing process of globalization is one of the most compelling topics of the early 21ˢᵗ century. Within this rubric, the dramatic expansion of investment by Spanish firms in Latin America provides one of the potentially most fruitful examples for study from which both empirical and conceptual research can be derived. Anybody who has traveled in Latin America in recent years will know exactly of what I speak, if from no other source than the proliferation of prominent signs advertising the presence of Spanish companies. The increasingly more important role that Miami and Southeast Florida play as an *entrepôt*, or nexus, for European-Latin American commerce, finance, and travel, as part of this globalization process, is particularly interesting, not merely for a local point of view, but as a case study in globalizing communities and regions. From this point of view, we conceived of a conference that would bring together both academic specialists and business people to think about how these globalizing linkages manifest themselves and why they occur in this way and in this place, from the perspective both of the scholar and the practitioner.

Thus, this volume results from a conference on "Spanish Investment in Latin America", held in Coral Gables, Florida, on 18-19 October 2002, which drew scholars with expertise on the subject from Spain, Latin America, and the United States to investigate the topic. Representatives of major Spanish firms and others with extensive business experience in the region from various sectors served as commentators on the presentations. The conference was part of a series entitled "The European Union and the Americas", which was funded by the European Commission through its program of European Union Centers and, specifically, the Miami European Union Center (MEUC). The MEUC is a consortium of the University of Miami (co-director: Professor Joaquín Roy) and Florida International University and, like all such centers, engages in a broad range of initiatives designed to address trans-Atlantic issues through curriculum development, outreach activities, and scholarly research.

The MEUC is grateful to H.E. Javier Rupérez, Ambassador of Spain to the United States at that time, for his active participation in the conference, and to the Honorable Javier Vallaure, Consul General of Spain in Miami, for his longstanding support of the MEUC in general and for his efforts as regards this conference in particular. Likewise, the Miami office of the Spanish Trade Commission provided guidance and contacts for the organizers. Ambassador Ambler Moss, Miguel Rabay, Juan A. Yañes, Pedro Freyre (and the firm of Akerman Senterfitt) and Eduardo G. Del Valle gave generously of their time and expertise. We are especially grateful that Professors Félix E. Martín and Pablo Toral have undertaken to bring the rich content of the conference presentations forward in published form.

The organizers would like to thank the staff of the Political and Academic Affairs Section of the European Commission Delegation in Washington, DC, for their support of the MEUC over the years. Jonathan Davidson, Bill Burros, and Helen Henderson in particular guided us through the EU's administrative rules and regulations and provided encouragement and advice as regards the development of the MEUC's programs.

Ralph S. Clem
Director, Center for Transnational and Comparative Studies
Florida International University, and
Co-Director, Miami European Union Center
Miami, Florida
March 2005

Preface

As Latin America and the Caribbean make their way into the twenty-first century, the countries of the region are grappling with the consequences of very significant decisions regarding the structure of their economies and the pace of democratization. Throughout the hemisphere, countries opted for a strategy that unilaterally opened economies and implemented significant structural reform policies that were only later to be dubbed the Washington Consensus by the World Bank's John Williamson. Depending on the point of view, the impact of these policy decisions has been either negative or positive or mixed. A sound analysis of their impact would probably conclude that the record has indeed been quite mixed and that the results are neither as good as its proponents had claimed nor as bad as the vast number of detractors now claim. In any event, for better or for worse, these reforms have fundamentally transformed the region.

One of the most important dimensions of this transformation has been the return of the Spaniards, this time as investors in a wide range of industries, including telecommunications, energy, banking, and tourism. The Spanish presence spans the hemisphere as their ventures can be found in nearly every country of the region. In this wonderful collection of essays edited by Professors Félix Martín and Pablo Toral, the underlying concern is to explain why Spanish investment opted for Latin America and the Caribbean, especially when the very nature of globalization allowed private firms, individuals and state enterprises to invest anywhere in the world. The answer put best and succinctly by Toral's chapter is in a nutshell, that "market knowledge" provided the essence of the decision to invest in the region. This is probably the most unique set of chapters available in English on the motivations that drove Spanish investment in the 1990s and the early part of this century.

This book also provides a good analysis of the impact of this investment pattern on the Americas. As is the case with the evaluations of market oriented reforms, an assessment of the impact of Spanish investment presents a mixed record. This volume will perhaps shed some light on the current very controversial debate in many parts of Latin America regarding the impact of this investment. In some countries, Spanish investment in key public enterprises has come under attack from social activists and others who see all foreign direct investment, especially in public sector companies, as bad economic policy. This is clearly a debate that will not be decided by the authors in this volume; however, their insights offer valuable contributions to a better understanding of the problem.

The Latin American and Caribbean Center at Florida International University was proud to have co-sponsored the conference where these essays were first presented. It is with greater pride that LACC is pleased to present the results in this edited volume. I am particularly thrilled to see the concrete results of a great collaborative effort between Félix E. Martin, a member of FIU's department of international relations, and Pablo Toral, one of our own former students and now an assistant professor at Beloit College. Our gratitude is also extended to Professor Ralph S. Clem, the Director of FIU's Center for Transnational and Comparative Studies for conceiving the original idea and guiding all of the participants through the process of putting the conference together and editing this volume.

Eduardo A. Gamarra
Director, Latin American and Caribbean Center
Florida International University
Miami, Florida
March 2005

Acknowledgements

This book is an international collaborative effort to study the economic globalization of Latin America. Over the course of three years academics and business professionals from several countries have engaged actively in an exchange of ideas to make this book a better product. Our continuous requests for changes, revisions, omissions, and updates were heeded scrupulously by all of the contributors to this volume. Needless to say, we appreciate their work.

We would also like to acknowledge the institutional support that we have received from the Miami European Union Center, the Center for Transnational and Comparative Studies (TCS), the Latin American and Caribbean Center (LACC), the International Relations Department at Florida International University and the Trade Commission of Spain in Miami. The kernel of this project originated from a conference organized in October 2002 by the Miami European Union Center and LACC; and their respective Directors, Ralph S. Clem, Eduardo Gamarra and Joaquín Roy encouraged us to turn the presentations into a book. Begoña Cristeto and María Gracia Moreno, from the Trade Commission of Spain in Miami, also provided invaluable advice to help us organize the conference. We also appreciate the participation in the conference of managers from some of the firms included in this study: BBVA, Endesa, Telefónica, and Unión Fenosa. Ziulyn Chan, Judith Rassoletti, and especially Myriam Ríos, from TCS, as well as Liesl Picard (LACC) did most of the work to make sure the conference went well.

The support of the Political Science Department at Beloit College was also very valuable. As we dedicate this book to all of our students at Florida International University and Beloit College, we would like to extend our special appreciation for their editorial help to Eloisa López, Robert Markum, Frances Spiegle from Florida International University and Scott G. Weber from Beloit College. Last but not least, we would also like to thank our editors at Ashgate, especially Carolyn Court and Kirstin Howgate, for their patience and support. While a lot of people have provided valuable input to improve the quality of this book, all of its shortcomings rest entirely on our shoulders.

Félix E. Martín
Florida International University
Miami, Forida
April 2005

Pablo Toral
Beloit College
Beloit, Wisconsin
April 2005

List of Abbreviations

ADR	American Depositary Receipt
ADSL	Asymmetric Digital Subscriber Line
AECI	Spanish Agency for International Cooperation
ANCAP	Administración Nacional de Combustibles, Alcohol y Portland
AOL	America on Line
AT&T	American Telephone and Telegraph
BANESPA	Banco do Estado de São Paulo
BBV	Banco Bilbao Vizcaya
BBVA	Banco Bilbao Vizcaya Argentaria
BCH	Banco Central Hispanoamericano
BIT	Bilateral investment treaty
BS	Banco de Santander
BSCH	Banco Santander Central Hispano
BT	British Telecom
CAP	Common Agriculture Policy of the EU
CDBs	certificates of bank deposits
CDIs	certificates of interfinancial deposits
CEO	Chief Executive Officer
CEPAL	United Nations Commission for Latin America and the Caribbean (Spanish acronym)
CESCE	Compañía Española de Seguro de Crédito a la Exportación
CLEC	Competitive Local Exchange Carriers
COFIDES	Spanish Development Financial Corporation
DGEITE	Directorate General of International Trade and Overseas Transactions (Spanish Ministry of Trade)
DJ	Dow Jones Utility Index
EBITDA	Earnings before interest, taxes, depreciation and amortization
EC	European Community
ECLAC	see CEPAL
ECSC	European Coal and Steel Community
EEC	European Economic Community
EFTA	European Free Trade Association
EMS	European Monetary System
EMU	European Monetary Union
ENASA	Engenharia, SA
ERM	European Exchange Rate Mechanism
EU	European Union
Euratom	European Atomic Energy Community
EUROSTAT	Bureau of Statistics of the European Union

FDI	Foreign Direct Investment
FNA	Financial Network Association
FTAA	Free Trade Area of the Americas
GATT	General Agreement on Tariffs and Trade
GCI	Growth Competitiveness Index
GDP	Gross Domestic Product
GNI	Gross National Income
GSM	Global System for Mobile Communications
GTE	wireline and wireless communications company
HSBC	Hong Kong Shanghai Banking Corporation
ICEX	Spanish Instituto de Comercio Exterior
ICO	Spanish Instituto de Crédito Oficial
IDB	Inter-American Development Bank
IDP	International Development Path
IMF	International Monetary Fund
INI	Instituto Nacional de Industria (National Institute of Industry)
INH	Instituto Nacional de Hidrocarburos
IPAB	Mexican Instituto de Protección del Ahorro Bancario
ISI	Import Substitution Industrialization
ITT	International Telephone and Telegraph
JNI	Joint Network Initiatives
LDCs	Less Developed Countries
LIS	Lines in Service
MENA	Middle East and North Africa
MERCOSUR	Mercado Común del Sur
MIGA	Multilateral Investment Guarantee Agency
MNEs	Multinational Enterprises
NAFTA	North American Free Trade Agreement
NATO	North Atlantic Treaty Organization
OAS	Organization of American States
ODA	Official Development Aid
OECD	Organisation for Economic Co-operation and Development
OLI	Ownership-Location-Internalization
PACI	Annual International Cooperation Plans
P&L	Profit and Loss
RBOC	Regional Bell Operating Company
R&D	Research and development
SCH	see BSCH
SEA	Single European Act
SEC	Securities and Exchange Commission
SECIPI	Spanish Directorate for International Cooperation and for Latin America
SEAT	Spanish Automobile Company
SMEs	Small And Medium Enterprises
SOCAL	Standard Oil of California

TASA	Telefónica de Argentina, S.A.
TMT	telecommunications sector
TPI	Telefónica Publicidad e Información
TdE	Telefónica de España
UNCTAD	United Nations Commission on Trade and Development
UPC	Universitat Politecnica de Catalunya
VAT	Value added tax
WB	World Bank
WIDER	World Institute for Development Economics Research
WTO	World Trade Organization
YPF	Yacimientos Petrolíferos Fiscale

To our students

Introduction

The Role of Spanish Firms in Latin America's Structural Reforms: 1989-2005

Félix E. Martín
Pablo Toral

Introduction

International capital flows in the form of foreign direct investments (FDI) have been fundamental to the evolution of the modern international economic system since the seventeenth century. Ever since early precursors like the Dutch East India Company (Vereenigde *Landsche Ge-Oktroyeerde Oostindische*), the Massachusetts Bay Company, and other international merchants established a permanent position outside their home countries through the purchase of existing enterprises and/or by establishing new ones through Greenfield investments, FDI has been an important corporate strategy, an effective tool of statecraft, and a major contributing factor to the expansion of the global market economy. This has been particularly evident since the collapse of the Soviet Union in 1989 and the simultaneous embracing of liberal economic policies worldwide.

As the mid-1990s approached, the process of economic globalization achieved unprecedented levels as a record number of companies became involved in multinational business operations, governments actively sought or promoted international investments and the volume of FDI increased significantly. Indicative of this trend at the height of the Cold War in 1970, the world's FDI total volume in millions of 2004 constant U.S. dollars was approximately $27,189. A decade later it increased to $108,660. By 1995 it jumped dramatically to $693,969 and the tendency has continued throughout the first four years of the new millennium at an annual average of $16,402,202 (see Table I.1) (UNCTAD, http://stats.unctad.org).

Closely mirroring international economic trends, Spain's total volume of FDI increased steadily from a low of $265 million in 1970 to $10,361 million in 1995 and, subsequently, to $92,198 million in 2000. At this juncture, Spain's FDI outflows surpassed inflows for the first time since the end of the Spanish-American War of 1898. Also, in the first few years of the new century, Spain has maintained a significant presence among the leading investors in the world economy, with an annual average of $674,285 million.

Table I.1 Foreign Direct Investment Trend in the World and Spain, 1970-2003

Region	Indicator	1970	1980	1990	1995	2000	2001	2002	2003
World	FDI inflows	13,032	54,986	208,646	335,734	1,387,953	817,574	678,751	559,576
	FDI outflows	14,157	53,683	242,057	358,235	1,186,838	721,501	596,487	612,201
	Total	27,189	108,669	450,703	693,969	2,574,791	1,539,075	1,275,238	1,171,777
Spain	FDI inflows	222	1,493	13,984	6,285	37,523	28,005	35,908	25,625
	FDI outflows	43	311	3,522	4,076	54,675	33,093	31,512	23,373
	Total	265	1,804	17,506	10,361	92,198	61,098	67,420	48,998

Source: UNCTAD (http://stats.unctad.org)

The bulk of Spanish FDIs have been made in Latin America. Partly as a result of the implementation of structural reforms by the governments of Latin America, the investments of Spanish firms in this region grew significantly since the early 1990s, when they purchased many of the state-owned firms put out to tender. These investments made Spain the second largest home market of FDI for Latin America and the Caribbean, behind the United States. In 1999 and 2000, the FDI flows from Spain to Latin America and the Caribbean even surpassed those coming from the United States. In 1999, Spanish FDI into Latin America and the Caribbean was $26 billion, US FDI was $20 billion, FDI from the European Union (EU) – except Spain – was $9 billion, and Japanese FDI was $5 billion. In 2000, Spanish FDI was $21 billion, US FDI was 20 billion, EU FDI was $14 billion, and Japanese FDI was $5 billion (Eurostat and U.S. Department of Commerce).

Indeed, the 1990s was the decade of the strongest rapprochement between Spain and Latin America and the Caribbean since the 1820s. Although this rapprochement began in the 1980s, with the consolidation of democracy in Spain and the transitions to democracy in Latin America, the growth of economic relations between Spain and Latin America and the Caribbean in the 1990s added a new dimension to the relationship. Since the independence of its Latin American colonies, Spain had not been a major economic player in the new world. But this changed radically since the 1980s. Spain's rapid and aggressive investment drive influenced profoundly Latin America's quest for economic globalization. Spanish firms purchased newly privatized state enterprises and some private companies. They injected desperately needed finance capital in the region, revamped and modernized business operations in different sectors of the economy, and helped improve the economic, political, and social prospects of a region that since the 1970s had been mired in economic crises and political instability. As the result of this investment process, Spain managed to transform fundamentally its self-perception and international image. Spaniards felt generally proud of the renewed economic and political role played by Spanish multinational enterprises in the world. In addition, Spain shed off significantly part of its backward and traditional economic, political and social image in the international state system.

Origins of the book

Thus, motivated to analyze and explain the multifaceted nature and consequences of this momentous international economic development in Iberoamerica, we organized a seminar on Spanish FDI in Latin America and the Caribbean and on Spain's role as a major economic actor in this region. This conference was attended by scholars and business practitioners from Latin America, the Caribbean, Spain and the United States, including representatives of Spanish firms BBVA, Endesa, Telefónica and Unión Fenosa.

The conference, funded by the Miami European Union Center, was held in Miami in October 2002. It was divided into five sections. The first section provided some historical and theoretical background to approach the topic. The second section analyzed the role of Spanish firms in the banking sector, the third concerned with the telecommunications sector, the fourth with the energy and public utility sector, and the fifth provided an analysis of the socio-political circumstances that surrounded the participation of Spanish firms in Latin America's quest for globalization. With this setup we tried to analyze in depth the main industries in which the largest investments by Spanish firms took place.

We solicited contributions from a number of scholars who had analyzed the FDIs of Spanish firms in Latin America and the Caribbean, as well as from others who studied Spain's foreign policy in Latin America and the Caribbean. Those who presented at the conference were James Barth, Álvaro Calderón, Juan José Durán, Fernando Gallardo, Eduardo Gamarra, Prosper Lamothe, Javier Maestro, Félix E. Martín, Harry Makler, Walter Ness, Michael Periu, Luis Rivera-Batiz, Joaquín Roy, Sebastián Royo, Carlos Seiglie, Andrés Serbín, and Pablo Toral. Their presentations were later developed into chapters for this book. Prosper Lamothe and Andrés Serbín decided not to submit their presentations to this book project, so we asked Gustavo de las Casas for an additional chapter to strengthen the energy section.

This group included scholars from different fields, such as sociology, literature, law, political science and international relations, and economics, as well as consultants. We also invited representatives of the Spanish firms that made the largest investments in Latin America and the Caribbean, including BBVA, Endesa, Iberdrola, Repsol-YPF, SCH, Telefónica and Unión Fenosa (Iberdrola, Repsol-YPF and SCH turned down our invitation), representatives of competing firms from the United States and Europe, and government officials and diplomats of some of the host countries, as well as diplomats of the countries of the European Union. The goal was to provide a multidisciplinary approach that would allow us to analyze critically the FDIs of Spanish firms in Latin America and the Caribbean and to understand their contribution to the globalization of the economies of Latin America and the Caribbean. The conference was attended by a hundred people, including also journalists and practitioners. This diverse audience provided a very interesting background and helped generate stimulating and lively discussions.

This book analyzes the political, economic, social and institutional circumstances in Latin America, the Caribbean, Spain and in the European Union that led to Spanish firms becoming such important players in Latin America. This book is important for those who want to understand the structural reforms implemented by the Latin American governments and their consequences, the international impact of the economic reforms of the European Union, the internationalization of the Spanish economy and the role played by the Spanish government in such endeavor.

The authors adopt different levels of analysis, from the global to the domestic. By looking at the domestic level, they seek to understand the conditions in each country that led governments to implement the reforms that opened the door to the Spanish firms. At the international level, they look for the constraints from the international system that governments face, including pressures by international institutions such as the World Bank and the International Monetary Fund, other governments and multinational enterprises, among others. By looking at bilateral relations between Spain and Latin America and the Caribbean, they shed some light on the motivations on both sides of the Atlantic that provided the context for the FDIs of Spanish firms, including state goals as articulated through their foreign policies. A look at the specific conditions in each industrial sector and each of the main Spanish firms that made the FDIs is necessary to understand the motivations that led them to invest. These motivations include technological developments, international competition, concentration of ownership in many sectors, the pressures of liberalization, etc.

The book brings all of these issues together by looking at the goals, motivations, strategies and gains and losses from the FDIs of the governments of Latin America, the Caribbean and Spain, the Spanish firms making the direct investments and the social sectors on both sides of the Atlantic Ocean that were directly affected by and reacted to these investments.

The main issue that this book addresses is the role of the Spanish firms in the new development strategy adopted by the Latin American governments under the auspices of the "Washington consensus". In this sense, the authors provide a normative assessment of the results of the reforms. Further, the work examines the contribution of the Spanish firms to the development of the Latin American countries in which they invested. The author explore the relationship between foreign direct investment and economic growth, and try to assess whether the Spanish firms contributed something different from firms from other regions, such as the United States.

The emergence of firms from a late developer like Spain is a recent phenomenon of the 1990s that has not been researched thoroughly by academics and specialists in this field. This book focuses on the emergence of Spanish multinational enterprises in Latin America, a region that shared a lot of similarities with Spain in the sectors analyzed in this book. The focus is on the economic relations between Spain and Latin America. Relations between both regions had focused on the analysis of democratic transitions and studies of political culture. The book takes a multidisciplinary perspective.

The book also analyses the sociological and political consequences of these investments. It explores the response of political and social actors in Spain and in

Latin America and the Caribbean to these investments. The Argentinean crisis that erupted in December 2001 is taken as a test case for the Spanish firms. The crises that affected Latin America and the Caribbean in the 1980s deterred many firms with prior experience in the region from making investments there again during the implementation of the structural reforms in the 1990s. Some analysts from the United States and Western Europe believed that the Spanish firms, which had not been exposed to Latin America before, were engaging in a very risky enterprise there, by making such substantial investments.

This issue is important because the economies of Latin America and the Caribbean had limited the access of foreign firms to their markets by way of imports, direct investments or both. This is also important because Spanish firms had never made such sizeable direct investments outside of Spain. This book analyzes the conditions that have led Spanish firms to make these large investments in Latin America. It reviews the processes of liberalization undertaken on both sides of the Atlantic. On the one hand, the elimination of national restrictions within the European Union in a number of sectors that were operated under conditions of monopoly by a single (sometimes state-owned) firm (banking, telecommunications, public utilities, and oil and natural gas), and the structural reforms implemented by the governments of Latin America, on the other, provided the appropriate incentives on both sides for the investments of the Spanish firms in Latin America. This work thus takes a close look at the main economic areas in which the Spanish enterprises have become leading players in the Latin American and Caribbean economies. This study sheds light on the cultural, historical, economic, political, and social forces that have shaped the globalization of international capital. Rather than presenting globalization as an unstoppable process of international integration, the contributors to this book demonstrate that there are still powerful forces at work that constrain the internationalization of capital and economic activities.

This book challenges the interpretation according to which the elimination of technological and political constraints to the internationalization of capital flows is allowing multinational enterprises to expand freely around the globe. Contrary to this prediction, this book shows that the internationalization of capital is constrained by the experiences of the managers of the multinational enterprises, who are bound by the particular setting in which they learned to conduct business. This setting is the result of a series of political, economic, historical, and social conditions in which they operate. Although globalization is opening up opportunities for investment around the world, the decision-makers may move only into the markets that they "know" better.

Structure of the book

The book follows the structure of the conference. It is divided into three sections: frameworks for analysis of the expansion of Spanish multinational enterprises abroad, analysis of the sectors, and the politics of Spanish investment in Latin

America and the Caribbean. The chapters of the first section review the history of Spanish FDI in Latin America and the Caribbean and propose some theoretical models to analyze the characteristics of Spanish firms and their competitive advantages in Latin America and the Caribbean. Juan José Durán analyses the attainment of multinational status by Spanish companies in Latin America from the early 1960s to the present, in line with current theory on international direct investment. The article argues that two circumstances emerged that were vital to an understanding of the preference of Spanish firms for Latin America. The first one was a series of competitive advantages for Spanish companies operating in Latin America, especially in the service industries, which were bolstered by deregulation and internationalization in the 1990s: telecommunications, energy, transport and financial services. The second was a series of factors encouraging business location in Latin America due to changes in economic attitudes and models, and the mostly favorable environment in recent years for flows of capital into emerging economies.

Pablo Toral proposes a social theory approach to study the direct investments of Spanish firms in Latin America. He argues that the Spanish firms had an advantage in Latin America, "market knowledge", which led them to make these investments. This advantage resulted from a process of learning by doing in Spain since the 1970s, which was embodied in the firms' internal organization and external relations, to best adapt to the environment, especially in the provision of basic infrastructure services like finance, telecommunications, and energy. The institutional context in which they operated was characterized by processes of transition from conditions of monopoly to open competition, privatization of state-owned firms, modernization of infrastructure, rapid expansion of services, frequent interactions with the government, and heavy regulation. To adapt to these conditions, the managers organized the firms' internal processes and their external relations with the market forces and the government in ways to best satisfy the demands of the market. The reproduction of similar conditions in Latin America in the 1990s led them to invest there, transplanting to the new markets the internal and external institutional settings that they had developed in Spain earlier.

The purpose of Sebastián Royo's chapter is to examine some of the *push factors* that led Spanish firms to expand in Latin America, and to propose a model to examine the impact of institutions on the behavior of actors. It analyzes how the transformation of the Spanish economy influenced the explosion of Spanish FDI towards the region, and the impact that the process of European integration had on the Spanish economy. In the 1990s the Spanish economy reached a new level of development that propelled a wave of FDI abroad. From a theoretical standpoint his chapter shows that a major shortcoming of the existing literature has been the failure to explain how institutions affect the behavior of economic agents. How do institutions hinder or facilitate firm-level adjustment to international competition and lead firms to invest abroad? How do they influence the success – or failure – of firms' strategies? Royo concludes the paper outlining an analytical framework to examine the impact that existing institutional frameworks have on the operations of firms.

Javier Maestro reviews Spanish Latin America policy. He argues that Spanish foreign policy has been rather stable over time regardless of the type of regime or administration. The main focus of the Spanish rulers were its geographic and cultural neighbors, mainly Mediterranean Europe, North Africa and Latin America and, since the outset of the Cold War, the United States. The preference ordering of these regions varied along the years on the basis of changes in the world order. Within this context, this article reviews the evolution of relations between Spain and Latin America, mainly since the 1940s, with special emphasis on the principles guiding their interactions, and how the investments made by Spanish firms in Latin America since the early 1990s put the Latin American region on the top of the list.

The articles in the second section of the book analyze the role of Spanish firms in Latin American and Caribbean banking, telecommunications, public utilities and oil and natural gas, with special emphasis on their participation in the process of opening and structural reforms undertaken since the 1980s by the Latin American and Caribbean governments. James R. Barth, Triphon Phumiwasana and Glenn Yago assess the recent and dramatic change that occurred in the structure of banking markets in Latin America, an important aspect of the free-market model now common in the region, as a result of the striking penetration of foreign banks, particularly Spanish. The authors review the wide disparity in the size of the banking sectors for different countries, as well as differences in output structures and their implications for the allocation of credit. They also analyze differences in structure, scope and independence of bank supervision in these countries, and conclude with a study of the performance of foreign-owned and domestic-owned banks. The analysis focuses on the six largest countries, Argentina, Brazil, Chile, Colombia, Mexico, and Venezuela.

Harry M. Makler and Walter L. Ness, Jr. argue that with the substantial investment of Banco Santander Central Hispano and Banco Bilbao Vizcaya Argentaria, two leading Spanish banks in Latin America, Spanish banks have become major players in Latin American financial systems, even in countries such as Brazil, which had no tradition of Spanish banking. This study compares the extent to which these banks conform to lending and investment practices of foreign banking in Brazil, the extent to which these practices reflect the prior strategies of the banks that they acquired, or whether these banks impose their own strategies. The relation of credit allocation activities to regional integration concludes this essay.

Álvaro Calderón argues that in a context of rapid change in the banking and financial industries, the strategy of internationalization followed by the main Spanish banking institutions in Latin America generated great debates. In Latin America, in Spain and in the United States, the political and economic authorities, business people, investors, and the clients of these institutions, responded very differently to rapid expansion of Spanish banks in the region. He addresses these issues, emphasizing the central role played by the Spanish banks in the processes of liberalization and financial deregulation, as well as in the modernization of the Latin American financial systems. He also analyzes the strategies followed by the banks, which went through an early period of market-seeking investments to gain entry into new countries, a second period of renewal of the infrastructure of the banks taken over, a third period of rationalization of investments, reducing expenses in the less profitable markets, and a fast process of amortization of goodwill in consolidation.

In the next chapter, Fernando Gallardo addresses the internationalization strategy of the telecommunications operators and analyzes the case of Telefónica in Latin America. The first section examines, from a historical perspective, the causes, phases and strategies that telecommunications operators used in their internationalization strategies. The case of Telefónica and Terra are then discussed. The study ends with an analysis of the financial crisis that is affecting the telecommunications, media, and technology sectors and its implications for Telefónica.

Michael Periu, Jr. analyzes the critical importance of the telecommunications industry for economic development in Latin America, emphasizing the role played by Telefónica in its modernization. First, he examines how, through financial investment and knowledge transfers, Telefónica brought much-needed improvements in efficiency, quality and competitive pricing throughout the region. Then he explains that, by fostering the development of telecommunications, Telefónica provided a key pillar of further investment and development in derivative and complementary sectors which require an established telecommunications infrastructure to operate.

Gustavo de las Casas explains patterns of liberalization in the Latin American energy sector by using a model grounded on realist theory. He questions the liberal argument that Latin American states are discarding ideology for the clear benefits of liberalization. Using a deductive approach, this study builds an alternative explanation incorporating key realist premises, with one premise – that of rational-egoist states – qualified to account for societal preferences. A model is then produced to show the relationship between two variables: a state's power status and its degree of resource nationalism; and a state's sensitivity to foreign investment in its energy sector. The model is compared against Argentinean oil policies during the 20th century and Repsol-YPF's FDIs in Latin America. De las Casas shows that there is a negative correlation between Argentina's power status fluctuations in its oil sector and its openness to foreign investment. When Argentina's power status was low, it cooperated with foreign firms out of necessity. When its status was high, it curtailed this cooperation. Repsol's reserves in Latin American states also reflect the dynamic between power status and foreign investment. The more powerful and wealthier states cooperated the least with Repsol, while the weaker cooperated the most, presumably out of necessity. He concludes by examining the prospects for Repsol-YPF in Latin America and the Caribbean.

Carlos Seiglie presents an overview of Spanish foreign direct investments in the Latin American energy sectors. He analyzes how the capital markets reacted to these investments, to conclude that some of them were not completely successful. He looks at the Argentine crisis to explain the risks inherent to these investments when deteriorating economic conditions lead host governments to enact policies that are not market-friendly. In the last section of his chapter, he also reviews the distributional impact of privatization, paying attention to the relation between social attitudes toward greater regulation and government reaction to political dissatisfaction.

The articles in the third section explore the role of politics in promoting the investments and their social impact. Félix E. Martín analyzes the extent to which socio-political factors played a role in the Spanish direct investments process in Latin America. He argues that national origin of multinational firms and the concomitant socio-political milieu of the home and host countries are crucial causal variables for the analysis of the international behavior of companies. In an attempt to gauge whether socio-political motivations are important, he focuses on home-based societal factors and on the socio-political, and economic dimensions of the trilateral relations, linking Spain, the U.S., and Latin America. The author executes an internet-based, tri-continental survey of the public perceptions and opinions of the people of Spain, Latin America, and the U.S.A. In addition, he controls the Spanish sample by measuring the public opinion of the people through a random telephone survey of 600 subjects in three mid-size cities. He finds strong public convictions on both sides of the Atlantic regarding possible cooperation and collusion between the Spanish government and multinational enterprises. He concludes that the results corroborate indirectly the role of socio-political factors in the Spanish investment process in Latin America.

Joaquín Roy analyses how the large investments of Spanish firms in Latin America changed the perception that Latin American and Spanish citizens had about each other. On the one hand, Latin Americans stopped regarding the Spanish as those poor emigrants that left Spain to look for a better living standard, to regard them as bossy and pretentious neocolonialists. On the other, the Spanish came to think of Latin America as a region of underdeveloped and corrupt people.

Luis A. Rivera-Batiz and Maria A. Oliva conclude that foreign direct investment in Latin America has gone from the boom of the 1990s to stagnation and collapse during 2000-2003. Their chapter reviews FDI strategies based on market potential and those based on production sharing in a scenario characterized, except for Chile, by opacity, institutional weakness, and macroeconomic vulnerabilities. The analysis suggests that market potential works best only if growth is reinstated in the long run, which in turn depends on strengthening institutions, propping up governance, and establishing adequate macroeconomic policy, debt management and a reliable exchange rate regime.

Chapter 1

Spanish Direct Investment in Latin America, 1960-2002

Juan José Durán

Introduction

From the end of the Civil War (1936-39) to 1959, Spain underwent a period of autarky. The country was virtually cut off from the rest of the world. In 1959, a decree was launched underlying the conditions for a gradual opening of the Spanish economy to the outside. In 1960, a flow of inward foreign direct investment (FDI) began and, to a lesser extent, some outward Spanish FDI. In terms of capital flow Spain was a net recipient of FDI until the second half of the 1990s, at which point the net investment position (outward less inward) was positive.

The growth and development of the Spanish economy since 1960 can only be understood in light of the special role played by multinational enterprises (MNEs). Outward and inward FDI and a series of economic and institutional factors influenced Spanish economic development. In 2005, Spain could be classified as an advanced country (Durán and Ubeda, 2002). Latin American countries – to a certain extent the main recipients of Spanish FDI – were at earlier stages of development. This chapter provides a context for the attainment of multinational status by Spanish companies in Latin America from the early 1960s to the present, in line with the current theory of the international investment development path.

The main statistical sources for Spanish FDI used in this chapter are produced by the Spanish Secretariat of State for Trade. These sources do not regard loans (intra-group finance) as direct investment, nor do they account for investment in real estate. Since 1993, there exists the Registry of Direct Investments for projects that were carried out (as opposed to merely authorised, as was previously the case). Balance-of-payments figures, however, do include intra-group finance and real estate investments. In addition, this chapter uses data contributed by Moreno Moré (1975), Aguilar (1985) and Durán and Muñoz (1981), and compiled by Campa and Guillen (1996), besides some other sources or developed by the author in other papers or research projects.

The investment development path

The process of economic development involves a succession of structural changes that relate systematically to the direct investment received or issued by the country or region in question (Lall, 1996). On that basis, one can say that the kind of multinational company that a country is able to attract or generate depends on that country's degree of economic and institutional development. This is the context for the International Development Path (IDP). Initially, four stages were defined (Dunning, 1981): the first three stages comprise less developed countries, while the fourth applies to a small number of countries representing the most advanced economies. However, a high degree of international interdependence began to emerge in the late 1980s and early 1990s, when the term 'globalization' was coined, and this gave rise to a distinction between two stages of development in advanced countries: a fourth and fifth phase (Dunning, 1993; Dunning and Narula, 1996).

Economies at the first stage are practically excluded from FDI. Only natural resources (fisheries, agriculture and mining) are able to attract foreign capital. The next stage includes economies that offer potential markets and have created structural and institutional conditions to attract FDI in mature technologies (light manufacturing, metallurgy, industrial chemicals). At this stage, the country lacks companies that compete internationally, although it does have companies that make FDIs abroad in activities relating to natural resources, often financed or supported by their respective government. Such countries are clearly net recipients of FDI. Countries at the third stage offer an attractive market and have competitive assets in mid-level technological industries (automobile, electronics and machine tools). They generate outward FDI associated with advantages based on intangible assets, which largely emerge in sectors penetrated by foreign capital. Nonetheless, these countries still receive more FDI than their own MNEs send abroad. These countries' outward FDIs focus mostly on countries at earlier stages of economic development, although they also invest in more advanced countries seeking markets and strategic assets. Third-stage countries are characterized by government policy that focuses on education and innovation, bringing about significant structural changes.

Finally, the last stages comprise developed countries. The fourth stage includes countries that still lag behind the most prosperous economies in terms of technology or institutions. This gap is evident in the balance of trade and technology, but also in the type of inward and outward FDI (Durán and Úbeda, 2002). The theory stipulates that a country may move to the fourth stage when its stock of outward FDI is greater than the stock of inward FDI, that is to say, when the country's net investment position in positive. However it has been proved (Durán and Úbeda, 2004) that the main feature of countries in the fourth phase is the shape of its outward FDI and not the weight of inward FDI in the net investment position. These countries showed an exponential function of outward FDI independent of the heterogeneous function of inward FDI.

The fifth stage includes developed countries with the most knowledge-intensive assets (technology, comercial capital and management know-how). Their firms compete globally for the same markets and sectors, and there is pressure for gradual convergence of inward and outward volumes of FDI. In theory there is a tendency towards a zero net investment position. Government policy is especially important in the process of structural transformation that enables an economy to progress through the various stages. In fourth- and fifth-stage countries, government policy focuses on creating appropriate institutional conditions to achieve knowledge-intensive assets with a differentiating value, thus assuring the international competitiveness of the country's businesses. There are several kinds of intervention to improve the firms' competitiveness (Dunning, 1996): creation of an appropriate framework for business so as to reduce producers' and consumers' transaction costs (public services, roads, airports, telecommunications networks), macroeconomic stability (interest rates, exchange rate, tax laws, inflation...), influence on the economic and corporate climate with regard to the attitudes, values and ethics of economic agents. To these categories I would add the following: fostering the creation and improvement of intangible assets (technological capital, commercial capital – such as brand-names – and management know-how).

The necessary condition for a firm to become a multinational enterprise (to make a FDI) is to have some proprietary-specific assets (to have competitive advantages) that can be transfered abroad within the boundaries of the firm, in order to be efficiently combined with location-specific advantages of countries or geographical areas. This competitive advantage of firms can be named "specific economic capital" (physical, technological, comercial and managerial) (Durán, 2004).

The multinationalization process of the firm is a combination of three types of variables: ownership advantages (0), locational advantages (L) and internalization advantages (I) (Dunning, 1988, 1993). The MNE can be seen as an entity with a stock of specific knowledge that can be transfered abroad within the boundaries of the firm or to independent companies based upon the cost to replicate that knowledge, both taught and codifiable (Kogut and Zander, 1933). In fifth-stage countries, because the economies are relatively similar (i.e., convergent), structural variables have less explanatory value than business variables (competitiveness and advantages of each specific firm) (Dunning and Narula, 1996; Narula, 1996; Úbeda, 2001).

The Spanish investment development path

There are two levels of analysis for the empirical evidence supporting the core hypothesis of the investment development path. On the one hand, attention has been paid to the functional relationship between a country's development and the entry and exit of FDI for a cross-section of countries (Dunning, 1981, 1986; Dunning and Narula, 1996; Narula, 1996, Durán and Ubeda 2002). On the other, each specific country has been analyzed in a similar way.[1] This chapter will use the case of Spain to show that there exists a functional relationship between the inward and outward of accumulated per capita FDI and gross domestic product (GDP) per capita for the period 1960-1990. This allows us to model the relationship with a fourth-degree polynomial equation. Figure 1.1 shows the relationship between the two economic facts and offers a graphical picture of the equation. Thus the R squared of 97.89 enables one to say that the core IDP hypothesis holds in the case of Spain.

Having shown that a functional relationship holds between net direct investment and GDP per capita, we will set out the basic features of the various stages of the IDP. We will look closely at the nature of Spanish outward FDI. In the period 1959-1977, Spain underwent the second stage of the IDP. The end of the period coincides with an international economic crisis and the political transition in Spain. This accounts for a slowdown in the rate of entry of FDI, to some extent, as shown in Figure 1.2. During this period, Spain received significant FDI in chemicals, heavy machinery and electricity. FDI also rose notably in automobile production. All of this may be viewed as the first signs of the Spanish economy's progress into the third stage. In the 1970s, the automobil industry was the prime recipient of FDI.

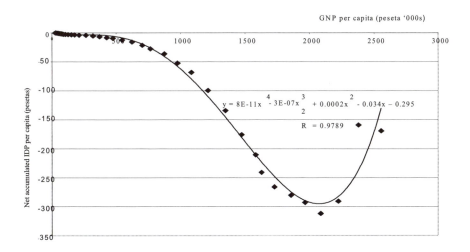

Figure 1.1 Functional relationship between net accumulated foreign direct investment per capita in the Spanish economy and gross domestic product per capita, 1960-2000

Source: The author, based on data from the Spanish Secretariat of State for Trade

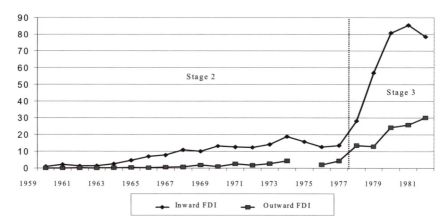

**Figure 1.2 Inward and outward foreign direct investment in Spain,
             1978-1996 (peseta billion)**
Source: The author, based on data from the Spanish Secretariat of State for Trade

Outward FDI began to rise virtually as soon as 1959, when a decree regulating
FDI came into effect. However, it rose very slowly because of the low
competitiveness and development of the Spanish economy at the time (see Figure
1.2). It was not until 1973 that any specific law regulating Spanish outward FDI
specifically was approved, although such investment had become by then fairly
significant. Up to that time, FDI was based on legislation passed in 1939 to
regulate exchange control (this law also authorized the acquisition of assets and
rights abroad), and in 1965, requiring Spanish MNEs to notify the Spanish
Secretariat of State for Trade. After the firm notified the government, the
competent authority would then authorize the investment as appropriate. Spanish
banking investments were reported by the Bank of Spain and authorized by the
Spanish Foreign Currency Institute. The Cabinet was in charge of approving
external investment through the Instituto Nacional de Industria (a holding company
that brought together state-owned enterprises).

The growing importance of both inward and outward FDI required a clearer
and more precise legal framework. Above all, for the sake of efficiency, it seemed
best to bring all of the responsibilities regarding FDI under a single decision-
making body. This was implemented through the laws enacted in 1978 and 1979,
essentially liberalizing FDI by replacing the need for prior authorization with
verification of reported FDI operations and *post facto* monitoring by the Ministry
of Trade. However, liberalization did not extend to investments made by
companies whose purpose was to hold foreign shares, such as the acquisition,
ownership or exploitation of real estate, investment funds and companies and

creation of bank branches abroad. Inward FDI, on the other hand, was regulated since 1952. The regulatory framework was completed with laws enacted in 1959, 1974, 1978 and in later years (1985, 1986, 1992 and 1999), with a consistent trend towards greater liberalization and investment protection.

In the early 1970s, the Spanish economy was prospering. Growth in 1973 was 8 percent in real terms. Involuntary unemployment was 2% of the working population[2] and the central bank accumulated an unprecedented level of foreign currency reserves, exceeding $6 billion (García Delgado, 1990). High oil prices in 1973 and the period of political instability between that year and 1977 caused a serious economic downturn. At that time, a national political agreement was reached for political and economic stability, thus laying down the basis for initiating structural reforms. Between the mid-1970s and 1985 – the year prior to Spain's entry into the European Community – Spain was at the third stage of development. Inward FDI grew strongly (see Figure 1.2), mainly to differentiated Smithsonian sectors, seeking economies of scale and scope in assembly processes. Examples include the car industry and electronics. From that time on Spain became a world leader in the market of automobile production. Exports of automobiles had a notable impact on the Spanish trade balance. Automobile companies were among the main exporters and importers in the country. Their balance of trade showed either negative or positive ratios (Durán, 1994). This can be viewed as a sign of intracompany trade as well as an indicator of intra-industry trade (Martín and Velázquez, 1993) and vertical and inter-company specialization (Durán, 2001). FDI inflows into the service sector also grew tremendously, especially in the food industry, banking and insurance.

In the early 1980s, the Spanish government introduced policies to restructure and rationalize the economy (unemployment had grown to over 10%) and began negotiating entry into the European Economic Community. Structural change became more rapid during the first phase of integration (1986-1991), with significant spending on infrastructure, education, health and research and development[2]. In addition, there was considerable modernization within Spanish companies (and the industries in which they operated) due to the climate of growing competition.

As shown in Figure 1.1, from 1990 onwards sustained growth in the outflows of Spanish FDI really came into its own – thus allowing us to classify the country as being at stage 3/4, i.e., with sufficient structural development to join stage-four countries. Entry into stage four can be dated at 1997, when outflows of FDI exceeded inward FDI (see Figure 1.4). However, in terms of stock, a fourth-stage economy may also have negative net direct investment position, as shown in Figure 1.1. Capital stock associated with FDI, accumulated over a long period of time, buffered the strong rise of Spanish direct outward investment that occurred since the mid-1990s (Durán and Úbeda, 2004).

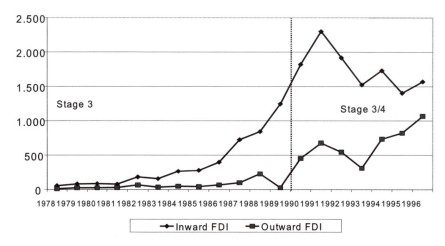

Figure 1.3 Inward and outward FDI in Spain, 1978-1996 (peseta billion)

Source: The author, using data from the Spanish Secretariat of State for Trade

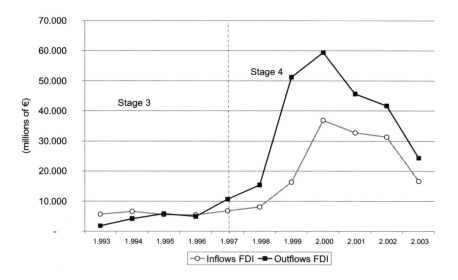

Figure 1.4 Inward and outward FDI in Spain, 1994-2001

Source: The author, using data from the Spanish Secretariat of State for Trade

Table 1.1   Development of Spain and the Latin American countries along the foreign investment development path

Year	1975	1980	1985	1990	1997
Stage 4					SPAIN
Stage 3	SPAIN 2/3	SPAIN	SPAIN Uruguay	SPAIN (STAGE 3/4) Uruguay Chile	Argentina Mexico Chile Brazil
Stage 2		STAGE 2/3 Chile Colombia Costa Rica Uruguay Argentina Mexico Brazil Venezuela	Stage 2/3 Peru Chile Venezuela Brazil Mexico	Stage 2/3 Costa Rica Peru Ecuador Venezuela Mexico Brazil	Stage 2/3 Venezuela
	Ecuador Colombia Costa Rica Peru Chile Venezuela Mexico	El Salvador Honduras Guatemala Nicaragua Dom. Rep. Ecuador Peru	Guatemala Nicaragua Dom. Rep. Costa Rica	El Salvador Nicaragua Paraguay Guatemala Bolivia Colombia	Colombia Ecuador Nicaragua Paraguay Dom. Rep. Costa Rica Uruguay Peru
Stage 1	Dom. Rep. Nicaragua Honduras				Honduras Guatemala El Salvador

Source: Ubeda (2000)

The greater volume of outward FDI involved significant quantitative and qualitative changes at the industry level, resulting from the interaction of two processes: technological and institutional changes on the one hand, and the gradual accumulation of international capabilities by Spanish corporations, on the other. In this regard, the elimination of natural monopolies in certain public services, the deregulation and privatization of certain activities that traditionally had been protected and the modernization of the Spanish financial system, among other sectors, encouraged the multinationalization of a range of companies, such as BBVA, Banco Santander, Telefónica, Repsol-YPF, Aguas de Barcelona, Endesa, and more. Furthermore, industries in which the Spanish economy was already competitive in the 1980s benefited from increased strategic assets (technology, brand names and management know-how), and this led to the emergence of a number of important Spanish multinationals such as Freixenet, Pescanova, Chupa-Chups, Nutrexpa, Borges, Torres, Obsborne, Acerinox, Tubacex, Campofrío, Zara, Mango, Puig, Cortefiel, Sol-Meliá, Barceló, Kelme, etc.

Evidence on the impact of the technological development of Spanish firms (as measured by research and development – R&D – and patents indicators) and the extent of their multinationalization shows us that, at the sector level, there is very little bearing of one upon the other (Molero, 1998; Casado and Granda, 1998). In this regard, Durán and Úbeda (2002) have examined the importance of tacit (non-codified) knowledge, such as technological capability, as one of the factors explaining the process of multinationalization of Spanish firms. It is worth pointing out the relative backwardness of the commercial capital of Spanish firms, as gauged by a review of internationally known brands. Although there are no large international Spanish brands, some are leaders in certain sectors (Durán 2002).

The first wave of Spanish multinationals in Latin America, 1959-1978

Structural change in the Spanish and the Latin American economies can help us gain an understanding of their FDI flows. Table 1.1 shows the relationship between the development of Spain and the Latin American countries and their foreign investment development path. Spain has clearly progressed to the fourth stage. Some Latin American countries had progressed to the third stage by 1997, such as Argentina, Mexico, Brazil and Chile. Other countries, however, have suffered a step back in their development, such as Venezuela, Peru, Ecuador and Uruguay.

Table 1.2   Distribution of Spanish outward foreign direct investment,
             1963-1978 (percentages)

REGION	1963-69	1970-78	1963-78
Europe	42.8	30.4	31.4
Latin America	46.7	47.2	47.1
United States	2.0	4.9	4.6
Africa	7.5	8.3	8.3
Asia	0.4	4.7	4.4
Pro memoria (peseta millions)	4,705	52,454	57,159

Source: J.J. Durán and M.P. Sánchez (1981, pp. 168-171)

As shown in Table 1.2, Spanish outward FDI between 1963 and 1978, when the Spanish economy was at stage 2, chiefly targeted Latin America and Europe (mostly France and Portugal). Lagging far behind were North Africa and the

United States. Throughout the entire period, and up until Spain joined the European Economic Community in 1986, Latin America was at all times the main destination. Until the debt crisis of 1982, Latin American governments followed a policy of import substitution industrialization (ISI) that allowed for strong growth. The goal of this policy was to attain a degree of economic independence (Bruton, 1998). ISI was primarily implemented through import duties, exchange control and manipulation (central-bank intervention) of foreign exchange rates. As a result, there was a reduction in imports but exports were also discouraged (due to over-valued home currencies, among other reasons) and so it became unavoidable to import capital goods and intermediate goods.

Until the 1980s, Spanish FDI in Latin America targeted the manufacturing industry mainly (transformation of metals, precision mechanics) and to a lesser extent, the financial sector, fisheries, farming and food and construction. By contrast, FDI in Europe mostly focused on the trading sector, in order to support exports (Durán and Sánchez, 1981). Tables 1.1 and 1.3 show the distribution by sector of FDI in the 1960s and 1970s. In Table 1.2, which concerns the period 1959-1973, the main issue is the relatively high number of projects and the significant investment in banking (28%), trade (25%) and industry (22%), followed by FDI in the primary sector (15%), chiefly mining. In the period 1974-78, certain differences arose, mainly an increase of FDI in the industrial sector, which accounted for 33% of total FDI. The service sector attracted almost 45% of total FDI for the period, finance 30% and trade 13.5%.

Table 1.3   Spanish outward foreign direct investment, both authorized by government or liberalized, by target sector, 1959-1973

SECTORS	NUMBER		VALUE	
	Units	Percent	Dollar '000s	Percent
Agriculture, forestry, fisheries	16	1.7	5.06	1.8
Mining and quarrying	15	1.6	35,549	13.0
Electricity, water, gas and sanitation	3	0.3	120	0.1
Manufacturing	199	22.0	61,075	22.3
Construction	45	5.0	9,861	3.6
Trade	432	47.9	69,424	25.4
Banking	79	8.7	77,743	28.3
Transport, warehousing and communications	36	4.0	4,606	1.7
Services	74	8.2	9,756	3.6
Unclassified	4	0.4	978	0.4
TOTAL	903	100	274.181	100

Source: Moreno Moré, J.L., (1975, p. 93)

**Table 1.4   Spanish outward foreign direct investment, both authorized by
government or liberalized, by target sector, 1974-1978**

	1974-1978	
Sectors	*Peseta millions*	*%*
Primary	**6758.1**	**16.4%**
Agriculture, livestock	4471.3	10.8%
Energy and water	2286.8	5.5%
Manufacturing	**16,097.9**	**39.0%**
Services	**18,452.0**	**44.7%**
Construction	1129.4	2.7%
Trade	5576.8	13.5%
Transport	621.7	1.5%
Financial and insurance institutions	11,114.3	26.9%
Other services	9.8	0.0%
Total	**41,308.0**	**100.0%**
Total in € millions	**248.3**	*

Source: The author, using data from the Spanish Secretariat of State for Trade

The geographic and sectoral distribution of Spanish FDI during the time in
which Spain was at the second stage of the IDP bears a fair resemblance to the
model for the first wave of multinationals from less developed countries (Dunning,
Hoesel and Narula 1999). There is a strong concentration in nearby countries
(France and Portugal) or countries with a sister culture, such as Latin America. As
pointed out above, from the standpoint of sectoral distribution, FDI in the
European Union is markedly biased towards trade, as a corollary of companies'
export activities. However, investment in Latin America concentrated mostly in the
low-tech industry.

The emergence of Spanish multinationals in Latin America

In the 1980s, the debt crisis, hyperinflation and structural problems in Latin
America led to a reduction in per capita production. In addition, Spain's entry into
the European Union also helps to explain why there was a sharp rise in the volume
of Spanish capital departing from Latin America. Table 1.5 shows the distribution
by country and sector of Spanish FDI from 1981 to 2000, each period being further
divided into two sub-periods. In the pre-EEC period (1981-85), Latin America was
still a bigger recipient of Spanish FDI than EEC countries (manufacturing being
the main target, at 41.2% of the total). This contrasts with the first phase of
integration with Europe: the EU received 54% of the total, while Latin America
received only 9.4%.

In 1986-90, Spanish FDI in the European Union (EU) exceeded its counterpart in Latin America across all sectors. However, from 1989 Latin American governments began to implement new policies. They began vigorously to open up, with privatization and deregulation (liberalization) programs. Policy worked towards assuring property rights and achieving balanced budgets, all within a democratic political framework. By way of example, whereas import duties reached 24.1% in the period 1986-90, they fell to 11.1% for the period 1996-1999. This new environment led to far more Spanish FDI in the region throughout the 1990s. Another highlight was the relative importance (56%) of investment in the industrial sector in the EU, which can be viewed as one of the outcomes of the improved international competitiveness of Spanish firms (Durán and Úbeda 2002).

Table 1.5   Distribution of Spanish outward FDI by region and sector, 1981-2000

| | PRIMARY | | SECONDARY | | SERVICES | | | | | | % TOTAL | |
| | | | | | Trade | | Transport and Communications | | Finance | | | |
	1981-1985	1986-1990	1981-1985	1986-1990	1981-1985	1986-1990	1981-1985	1986-1990	1981-1985	1986-1990	1981-1985	1986-1990
EU	10.3	30.6	29.5	60.9	35.2	48.1	55.6	43.4	16.6	56.2	21.4	53.8
USA	31	31.1	7.2	8.3	28.8	10	1.6	5.4	14.6	6.7	16	9.5
Eastern Europe	0	0	0	2.8	0	0.6	0	0	0	0	0.2	0.4
Latin America	23.3	7.9	41.2	15.1	12.7	14.9	9.2	1.9	29	7.2	29.1	9.4
Other	35.4	30.4	22.1	12.9	23.3	26.4	33.6	49.3	39.8	29.9	33.3	26.9
%Total	6.83	8.93	19.76	17.14	13.94	8.90	1.36	1.43	54.21	62.25		

	PRIMARY				SECONDARY				SERVICES			
	1993-96		1997-00		1993-96		1997-00		1993-96		1997-00	
	% of FDI 4%		% of FDI 14%		% of FDI 9%		% of FDI 6%		% of FDI 87%		% of FDI 80%	
	$ '000s	%	$ '000s	%	$ '000s	%	$ '000s	%	$ '000s	%	$ '000s	%
European Union	250.839	28,4	1.176.668	4,2	1.184.925	56	7.073.083	56,6	8.015.882	41,2	72.150.528	45,4
Rest developed countries	30.751	3,5	98.067	0,4	254.937	12,2	1.379.447	11	2.698.765	13,9	17.166.595	10,8
OECD	281.590	31,9	1.274.734	4,6	1.439.862	69,1	8.452.531	67	10.714.647	55,1	89.317.121	56,2
Eastern Europe	2.461	0,3	519	0,0	136.378	6,5	261.755	2	65.560	0,3	1.648.697	1
Latin America	445.017	50,4	26.008.293	93,7	543.957	26,1	3.365.718	27,0	6.6287.527	34,1	5.852.649	36,8
North Africa	1.902	0,2	6.232	0,0	59.787	2,9	244.003	2,0	40.138	0,2	312.551	0,2
Asia (except Japan)	-	0,0	323.741	1,2	23.871	1,1	119.590	1.0	70.717	0,4	176.144	0,1
Total	883.111		27.750.479		2.083.538		12.487.662		19.453.355		158.864.431	

Source: Figures based on data from the Spanish Ministry of the Economy, Secretariat of State for Trade

Table 1.6 shows the distribution by sector of Spanish FDI in Latin America and the European Union in the period 1993-2001. Spanish companies invested in Latin American countries mainly in the service sector (banking and insurance, transport and communication), followed by the primary sector (electricity, gas, water, oil) and manufacturing. A significant point is the large amount accounted for by FDI in holding companies. The table also shows the relative distribution of Spanish FDI in Latin America in comparison with FDI worldwide. Close to 84% of FDI in the primary sector was made in Latin America, which was also the top destination for FDI in publishing and graphic arts, construction, telecommunications and financial services, followed at a fair distance by the food and beverages industry, trade, real estate and hotels-catering. Spanish FDI in the European Union is different in the perior 1993-2003, due to the fall of FDI in Latin America and the growth of Spanish FDI in the Europea Union between 1998 and 2002 (see Figure 1.5), just when the new monetary integration begun. About 52% of FDI in manufacturing took place in the European Union, and 53% in the service sectors, especially in real estate and trade. FDI in holding firms was also relevant.

Table 1.6 Distribution by sector of Spanish FDI in Latin America, 1993-2000

	Distribution by Sector €'000 Iberoamérica		Percent of total DI (%) UE		Percentage Distribution worlwide	Sectorial shares of the investment in Latin American	UE's sectorial shares
	(million euros)	percentage	(million euros)	percentage			
PRIMARY	**23.090,65**	**20,1%**	**2.454,26**	**1,5%**	**8,1%**	**83,5%**	**8,9%**
Agricultural, Livestock and Fishing	363,09	0,3%	133,75	0,1%	0,2%	45,6%	16,8%
Electricity, gas and water	7.847,46	6,8%	1.798,65	1,1%	3,0%	76,6%	17,6%
Mining	14.880,09	12,9%	521,84	0,3%	4,9%	89,6%	3,1%
SECONDARY	**10.291,77**	**8,9%**	**25.743,05**	**15,2%**	**14,5%**	**20,7%**	**51,9%**
Food and beverage	3.460,81	3,0%	2.991,84	1,8%	2,7%	37,0%	32,0%
Textiles	137,35	0,1%	821,90	0,5%	0,3%	12,3%	73,6%
Paper, publ. and arts	1.304,85	1,1%	3.826,09	2,3%	3,2%	12,0%	35,2%
Chemical	1.516,73	1,3%	6.015,38	3,6%	2,3%	19,7%	78,2%
Other manufacturing	3.872,01	3,4%	12.087,82	7,2%	6,0%	18,8%	58,6%
SERVICES	**81.648,88**	**71,0%**	**140.649,81**	**83,3%**	**77,4%**	**30,9%**	**53,3%**
Construction	805,80	0,7%	165,82	0,1%	0,3%	73,3%	15,1%
Trade	3.094,34	2,7%	6.453,69	3,8%	3,2%	28,2%	58,7%
Hotels	807,05	0,7%	646,29	0,4%	0,6%	40,3%	32,3%
Transport and comm.	18.819,36	16,4%	7.436,84	4,4%	9,3%	59,4%	23,5%
Financial & insurance brokering	23.750,86	20,6%	10.751,54	6,4%	13,3%	52,3%	23,7%
Real state	5.632,19	4,9%	34.670,32	20,5%	13,0%	12,7%	77,9%
Holding	24.627,75	21,4%	77.434,69	45,9%	34,9%	20,7%	65,1%
Other services	4.111,51	3,6%	3.090,58	1,8%	2,7%	44,3%	33,3%
TOTAL	**115.031,31**	**100,0%**	**168.847,12**	**100,0**	**100,0**	**33,7%**	**49,5%**

Source: Based on data from Directorate General of International Trade and Overseas Transactions (DGEITE), Ministry of the Economy

The rationale for the outward FDI is the search for natural resources, created assets (strategic factors), markets and efficiency. Taking this rationale in conjunction with the business activities of Spanish MNEs (Durán, 1996), we have drawn up Table 1.7. In the table we have not taken into account the search for strategic assets (technology, commercial and management know-how), but it is nonetheless clear that Spanish FDI in Latin America has given rise to experiences that have in turn led to gains in competitiveness, through the advantages inherent to business diversification and multi-nationality.

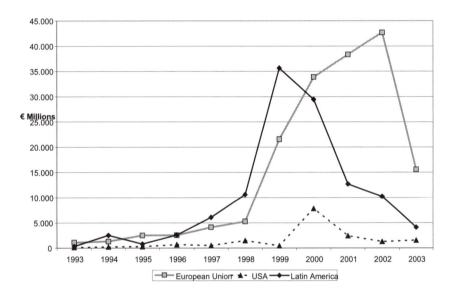

Figure 1.5   Development of Spanish FDI by region 1993-2001 (€ millions)

Source: Based on data from the Spanish Ministry of the Economy, Secretariat of State for
Trade

Figure 1.6 shows the geographic distribution of Spanish FDI in Latin America between 1993 and 2001. The leading FDI recipient was Argentina, followed by Brazil, Mexico and Chile. Almost two thirds of FDI was made in Mercosur countries. From the standpoint of location, however, it is important to note the proximity of the regions north of Panama to the United States, as well as the great influence of US foreign policy promoting trade and FDI (Reinhart and Peres, 2000) helps to explain US FDI in that area and perhaps also accounts for the presence of some Spanish companies, for which being close to the US market is a location factor.

Table 1.7 Rationale of Spanish Direct Investment in Latin American countries

Main causes of FDI	Primary	Manufacturing	Services
Natural Resources-seeking	*Petroleum and gas:* Venezuela, Colombia, Argentina, Barbados • Repsol-YPF • Gas Natural *Minerals:* Chile, Argentina, Peru. *Agriculture, fisheries:* Chile • Pescanova • Torres		
Market-seeking		*Automotive:* Mercosur *Chemicals:* Brazil *Agro-industry:* Argentina, Brazil and Mexico • Freixenet • Torres • Chupa Chups *Electronics:* Mexico, Caribbean Basin. • Indra	*Financial Services:* Brazil, Mexico, Chile, Argentina. • BBVA • SCH • Mapfre *Telecommunications:* Brazil, Peru, Chile, Argentina. • Telefónica *Electricity:* Colombia, Brazil, Argentina, Central America • Endesa • Iberdrola • Soluziona *Tourism:* Caribbean Basin, Mexico • Sol Meliá • Barceló
Efficiency-seeking		*Automotive:* Mercosur, • Ficosa • Antolín Irausa • Mondragon *Apparel:* Caribbean basin, Mexico	

Source: Author

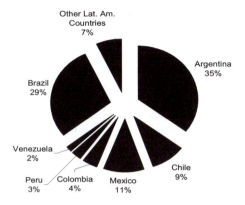

Other Lat. Am.
Countries
7%

Argentina
35%

Brazil
29%

Venezuela
2%

Chile
9%

Peru
3%

Colombia
4%

Mexico
11%

Figure 1.6   Geographic distribution of Spanish FDI in Latin America, 1993-2003

Source: Based on data from the Spanish Ministry of the Economy. Secretariat of State for Trade

On aggregate, Latin America received 11% less FDI flows in 2001 than in 2000, which was 13% lower than in 1999. It was expected that 2002 figures would show a 27% fall in FDI in the region (UNCTAD, 2002). The drop in FDI was especially sharp in Argentina and Brazil, where in terms of distribution by industry there was a very significant drop of FDI in the telecommunications sector. However, Mexico (which together with Brazil became one of the main FDI hosts in Latin America) and Chile saw an increase in FDI in general, including FDI from Spanish firms. The economic crisis that affected Mexico in 1995, followed by Argentina (from 1997) and Brazil (1998) slowed down growth in Latin America (with the exceptions of Mexico and Chile) and reduced FDI inflows. Spain's FDI flows to Latin America started to fall in 1999. At that point, Spanish FDI in the European Union, the United States, and to a significant degree Brazil, began to rise (see Figure 1.5).

Although there are many Spanish firms with subsidiaries in Latin America, the larger corporations, such as Telefónica, Repsol-YPF, BSCH, BBVA, Mapfre, Endesa, Iberdrola, Aguas de Barcelona, Iberia and Sol Meliá, are the most prominent. During the 1990s, they made the largest FDIs in Latin America. These companies had great weight on the Spanish stock exchange, making up a fundamental part of the operative and financial fabric of the Spanish economy. Their activities had a 'pull' effect on smaller Spanish firms that also became MNEs in Latin America. Therefore, their large investments in Latin America to some extent, linked the Spanish economy with the economies of the host countries, and bound it directly to Latin American economic progress, as was evident during the crisis of 2000-2003, in terms of results (with some losses) and stock-market capitalization.

In general, these large companies were former state-owned firms, privatized by the Spanish government, and operated in heavily regulated industries. They made FDIs in Latin American firms that were also formerly state-owned (Durán, 2004) and began to play leading roles in their sector in some of the countries of Latin America. For instance, Telefónica led the telecommunications sector in Latin America, while Endesa and Repsol-YPF were the largest foreign producers of electricity and oil and gas, respectively, in the region (CEPAL, 2000, 2001). Although in general terms, Spanish FDI in Latin America had a clear strategic value – reflected in the higher market value of Spanish multinationals (Durán, 1999) – there has been great risk (financial, economic and legal), as shown by the impact of the Argentine crisis and, in some other countries, recession and political risk. These circumstances generated losses for some Spanish-owned subsidiaries, exacerbated by the devaluation of some Latin American currencies. Thus, some experts argued for divestment. However, before any such decision is made, Spanish companies should assess the real options open to them for their Latin American subsidiaries and they should implement effective risk management.

Conclusions

Since 1959, when the Spanish economy opened up to the rest of the world, there are four distinct phases in the process of Spain's integration with the global economy: 1960-85 was the first wave of Spanish multinationals; 1986-92 was the period of integration with the European Economic Community and the European Interior Market (Europeanization of Spanish companies); 1993-98 was the expansion into Latin America and non-OECD countries; and from 1999 until 2005, integration in the European Monetary Union and consolidation in Latin America.

Latin America has been a prime host region for Spanish outward FDI. Throughout the period examined here, there was a change in the sectoral distribution of FDI and also a revitalization of FDI flows as a result of developmental factors and structural and institutional changes. In the first stage, from 1960 to 1985 – the year before Spain joined the European Union – the sectors that received more Spanish FDI in Latin America were industry, the primary sector and financial services. During the period of "Europeanization", there was a significant rise in trade and FDI between Spain and EEC countries, as might be expected from the standpoint of economic-integration theory and in view of earlier experiences. Companies were restructured and sectors were rationalized, sometimes involving mergers and acquisitions with Spanish and foreign firms. Furthermore, there was considerable spending on economic and social infrastructure (education, health, housing, etc.), the economy was deregulated and rationalized, and there was significant modernization and strengthening of public institutions. This was a key period, in which government policy aimed to support the internationalization of Spanish businesses, while Spanish companies improved their competitiveness and became more active in the international arena.

The second phase of the process began in 1992, involving a strong rise in FDI and further multinationalization of Spanish companies. Medium-size and smaller firms continued to extend their international operations. However, the most distinctive feature of this period was the very large FDIs made by leading firms that were traditionally engaged in providing public services (telecommunications, transport, energy) and were privatized in the 1980s and 1990s. The internationalization of these sectors was coupled with the deregulation and privatization process that characterized recent economic history in Spain. In less than two years (1997-98), the privatization of the five largest Spanish state-owned enterprises, which had begun at an earlier stage, was brought to full completion: thus Repsol, Telefónica, Endesa, Tabacalera and Argentaria (now a part of BBVA) became wholly private. These companies later proved highly competitive.

The competitiveness of a company is the outcome of a gradual, cumulative process that requires time. In Spain, such competitiveness came into being more clearly from the 1980s onward. Parallel to the internationalization and deregulation of the Spanish economy, there was strong investment in infrastructure and some increase in research and development spending. The large corporations mentioned above, as well as other firms that achieved notable transnational presence through FDIs, benefited greatly from this larger investment in facilities. The most successful Spanish MNEs were those in banking, insurance, construction, the automobile-parts industry and other manufacturing businesses, hotels, publishing and agro-business. Some firms had already made considerable FDIs abroad in earlier periods, but since 1960, FDI became all the more vigorous and reached unprecedented levels. The banking sector was a particularly good example of this.

In this context, two circumstances emerged that are vital to an understanding of the preference of Spanish firms for Latin America. First, the competitive advantages of Spanish companies operating in Latin America, especially in the service industries, which were bolstered by deregulation and internationalization in the 1990s: telecommunications, energy, transport and financial services. Secondly, factors encouraging business locations in Latin America due to changes in economic attitudes and models, and the favorable environment in recent years for FDI flows into emerging economies.

Spanish firms made good use of these two factors. They sought not only markets and production factors (hydrocarbons), but especially the strategic value of gaining a foothold in markets that were then starting to be deregulated and privatized. This may help to explain the excessive price that some Spanish firms seemed to have paid for a number of acquisitions, and the considerable risk incurred in terms of political instability and flaws in the regulatory frameworks of certain Latin American countries in which the Spanish firms made FDIs.

Cultural aspects also influence business operations in some ways, such as management styles and decision-making processes. National culture has an impact on the economy and the conduct of international business. People from different cultural backgrounds can perceive a message in very different ways. Likewise, culturally determined attitudes to life and one's worldview can affect negotiations, including the pace at which they are conducted and their final outcome. Culture also affects the organization and control of activities abroad, as the value system of the host country must be combined with the culture of the company itself, based mostly on the culture of the home country. It is an undoubted fact that international business operations are all the more expensive and difficult the greater the difference of cultures. Conversely, cultural similarities between the home country and the host country make for easier relations between parent and subsidiary and, consequently, facilitate the creation and business operations of that subsidiary. The transfer of technology and organizational and management know-how becomes easier when countries are culturally similar (Kogut and Singh, 1988), i.e., the less the cultural divergence, the lower the cost of conducting business.

FDI is a decisive factor in economic development (Durán and Úbeda, 2002, 2004). It supplements domestic investment and it is a catalyst for growth. In order to attract FDI, a potential host country must have a domestic corporate fabric with some degree of technological capability and enough human capital to learn new skills and know-how, so that the economy may benefit from any opportunities arising from the presence of MNEs.

In less developed countries, the structure of the economy and the role of the government are important for economic growth. Governments play a key role in designing and implementing proactive industrial policies and in making use of public and quasi-public assets so as to foster the creation of the right conditions for industrial development (Ramos, 2000; Katz, 2001). The introduction of a differential import substitution policy can boost the corporate advantages of a country. In this context, however, government policy in Latin American countries does not seem to have had the desired effect (Narula, 2002).

Notes

[1]   Country specific studies can be found in de Dunning and Narula (1996) for the United Kingdon, U.S.A., Sweden, Japan, New Zealand, Spain, Mexico, Taiwan, Indonesia, India and China. For Portugal, see Buckley and Castro (1998) and for Australia, Bellak (2001).

[2]   In the preceding decade there had been a significant outflow of Spanish emigrants, chiefly to other European countries.

References

Aguilar Fernández-Hontoria, E. (1985), "Cinco años de liberalización de las inversiones españolas en el exterior, 1980-1984", *ICE*, August-September, pp. 51-70.
Bellak, C. (2001), "The Austrian investment development path", *Transnational Corporation*, vol 10, no. 2, pp. 107-134.

Bruton, H. (1998), "A Reconsideration of Import Substitution", *Journal of Economic Literature*, vol. 36, pp. 903-36.

Buckley, Peter J. and Francisco B. Castro (1998), "The investment development path: the case of Portugal", *Transnational Corporation*, vol 7, no. 1, pp. 1-15.

Campa, Jose M. and Mauro F. Guillen, (1996), "Spain: a boom from economic integration", in J.H. Dunning and R. Narula, (eds), *Foreign Direct Investment and Governments*, Routledge, London.

CEPAL (2001), *La Inversión Extranjera en América Latina y El Caribe*, United Nations, Santiago de Chile.

Chudnovoky, D., B. Kosacoff and A. López (1999), *Las multinacionales Latinoamericanas: sus estrategias en un mundo globalizado*, Fondo de Cultura Económica, Mexico, D.F.

Dunning, J.H. (1981), "Explaining the international direct investment position of countries: towards a dynamic or developmental approach", *Weltwirtshaftlicher Archive*, 119, pp. 30-64.

Dunning, J.H. (1986), "The investment development cycle revisited", *Weltwirtshaftlicher Archive*, no. 122, pp. 667-77.

Dunning, J.H., and N. Rajnesh (ed) (1996), *Foreign Direct Investment and Governments*, Routledge, London.

Dunning, J., R. Van Hoesel and N. Rajnesh (1998), "Third world multinational revisited: new and theoretical implications", in J.H. Dunning (ed), *Globalisation, Trade and Foreign Direct Investment*, Pergamon, Oxford, pp. 255-286.

Durán, J. J., (1999), *Multinacionales españolas en Iberoamérica, Valor Estratégico*, Pirámide, Madrid.

Durán, J. J. and Sánchez, P. (1981), *La internacionalización de la empresa española. Inversiones españolas en el exterior*, Ministerio de Economía y Comercio, Madrid.

Durán, J.J. and F. Úbeda (2001), "The investment development path: a new empirical approach and some theoretical issues", *Transnational Corporations*, August.

Durán, J.J. and F. Úbeda (2005), "A dynamic analysis of the inward and outward direct investment of the newly developed countries", forthcoming.

García Delgado, J.L. (1990), *Economía Española de la transición y la democracia*, C.I.S., Madrid.

Katz, J. (2001), "Structural Reforms and Technological Behaviour. The sources and Nature of Technological change in Latin America in the 1990s", *Research Policy*, vol. 30, pp. 1-19.

Kogut, B. and H. Singh (1988), "The Effect of National Culture on the Choice of Entry Mode", *Journal of Internacional Business Studies*, 3, pp. 411-432.

Kogut, B. and U. Zander (1993), "Knowledge of the Firm and the Evolutionary Theory of the Multinational Corporation", *Journal of International Business Studies*, 24/4, pp. 625-46.

Lall, S. (1996), "The investment development path: some conclusions" In J.H. Dunning and R. Narula (ed), *Foreign Direct Investment and Governments*, Routledge, London.

Martín C. and J. Velázquez (1996), "Factores determinantes de la inversión directa en los países de la OCDE: una especial referencia a España", *Papeles de Economía Española*, 66, pp. 209-219.

Molero, J. (1998), "Patterns of internationalization of Spanish innovatory firms", *Research Policy*, 27, pp. 541-558.

Moreno Moré, J.L. (1975), "Quince años de inversiones españolas en el exterior", *Información Comercial Española*, 499, Marzo, pp. 91-107.

Narula, R. (1996), *Multinational Investment and Economic Structure. Globalisation and Competitiveness*, Routledge, London.

Narula, R. (2002), "Switching from import substitution to the 'New Economic Model' in Latin America: A case of not learning from Asia", unpublished.

Ramos J. (2000), "Directions for the New Economic Model in Latin América", *World Development*, vol. 28, pp. 1703-17.

Reinhardt, N. and W. Peres (2000), "Latin America's New Economic Model: Micro Responses and Economic Restructuring", *World Development*, vol.28, 9, pp. 1543-66.

Toral, P. (2001), *The Reconquest of the New World. Multinational Enterprises and Spain's Direct Investment in Latin America*, Ashgate, Aldershot.

Úbeda, F. (2001), "Análisis dinámico de la senda de la inversión directa exterior en los países desarrollados", Working Paper, Centro Internacional Carlos V. Universidad Autónoma de Madrid.

Chapter 2

The Advantage of Spanish Firms in Latin America, 1990-2002

Pablo Toral

Introduction

Since the Spanish government gradually eliminated the restrictions on foreign direct investments (FDI)[1] by Spanish enterprises between 1977 and 1992,[2] Spanish FDI reached important proportions, making Spain the twelfth home country for FDI in the world in 2000 by "stock". The "position" or "stock" of Spanish FDI abroad grew from $1.931 billion in 1980, to $15.652 billion in 1990, and to $160.202 billion in 2000 (see Table 2.1). This meant an increase of 8,294% in this period of twenty years, the fifth largest percent growth among the top home economies in the world (see Table 2.2).[3]

Although the growth in amount of Spanish FDI abroad in this short period of time was very large, what made these investments even more interesting was the fact that they were very highly concentrated in two geographic areas, the European Union and, especially, Latin America (see Figure 2.1), where Spanish FDI flows surpassed those coming from the United States in 1999 and 2000. The United States was the main home to inward FDI in Latin America since the mid-twentieth century (see Figure 2.2).[4]

By the turn of the century, the seven Spanish firms included in this chapter (BBVA, SCH, Telefónica, Endesa, Iberdrola, Unión Fenosa and Repsol-YPF) had assets worth $283 billion and 128 million customers in Latin America, and they had become prominent actors in the economies of the region.[5] For the Latin American societies, the Spanish FDI since the 1990s was very important, not only because the amounts of money that came into the economies were large, but also because new firms came in, from a country that until the 1990s had not been present in Latin America through FDIs. These firms brought with them their own business culture, and were located especially in infrastructure sectors, mainly in banking, insurance and financial services, electricity, oil, and telecommunications. All of these firms had a direct impact on the individual economies of many Latin Americans, because in most cases they operated in activities that were deemed as basic public services. For this reason, and because the entry of many of these firms occurred through the privatization of state-owned enterprises, their arrival was very visible, acquiring social and political significance.[6]

Table 2.1   FDI outward stock, by home country, in 2000, in US$ million

Country	1980	1990	2000
United status	220,178	430,521	1,244,654
United Kingdom	80,434	229,294	901,769
France	23,599	120,179	496,741
Germany	43,127	148,457	442,811
Hong Kong China	148	11,920	384,732
Belgium and Luxembourg	6,037	40,636	339,644
The Netherlands	42,135	102,608	325,881
Japan	19,610	201,440	281,664
Switzerland	21,491	66,087	232,045
Canada	23,777	84,829	200,878
Italy	7,319	57,261	176,225
Spain	**1,931**	**15,652**	**160,202**
Sweden	3,721	49,491	115,574
Australia	2,260	30,507	83,220
Singapore	3,718	7,808	53,216
Finland	737	11,227	53,046
Taiwan Province of China	97	12,888	49,187
Denmark	2,065	7,342	46,111
Norway	561	10,888	44,133
South Africa	5,722	15,027	33,557
China	39	2,489	27,212
Korea, Republic of	127	2,301	25,842
Argentina	6,128	6,105	20,189

Source: United Nations, *World Investment Report* (New York, 2001), 307-311

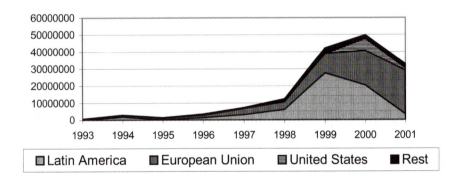

Figure 2.1 Flows of Spanish FDI by destination, 1993-2001 (US$million)

Source: Spanish Ministry of the Economy (Dirección General de Comercio e Inversiones, Secretaría de Estado de Comercio y Turismo)

Table 2.2   Position or stock of FDI by country of origin, first twenty-two home economies, percent variation, 1980-2000

Country	% Variation
Hong Kong China	259,954
China	69,774
Taiwan Province of China	50,708
Korea, Republic of	20,348
Spain	**8,296**
Norway	7,866
Finland	7,197
Belgium and Luxemburg	5,626
Australia	3,682
Sweden	3,105
Italy	2,407
Denmark	2,232
France	2,104
The Netherlands	1,738
Japan	1,436
Singapore	1,431
United Kingdom	1,121
Switzerland	1,079
Germany	1,026
Canada	844
South Africa	586
United Status	565
Argentina	329

Source: United Nations, *World Investment Report*, New York, 2001, 307-311

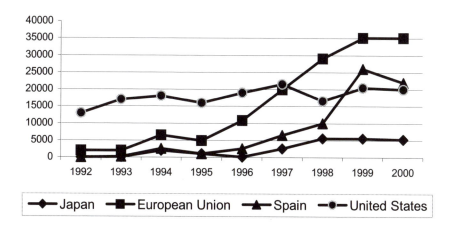

Figure 2.2   Inward FDI flows in Latin America and the Caribbean, 1992-2000 (US$ million)

Source: EUROSTAT and U.S. Department of Commerce

For instance, the Spanish firms were prominent in some infrastructure sectors, thereby having a direct impact on many firms in the region, through the provision of credit, energy, or telecommunication systems.[7] In other words, the competitiveness of many of the Latin American enterprises came to depend, to a certain degree, on the competitiveness of the products and services that the Spanish firms provided to them. These Spanish firms became direct participants in the new strategies of economic development based on the opening of markets, which replaced strategies based on import substitution industrialization (ISI) since the late 1990s.[8]

From the Spanish point of view, the FDI of Spanish firms in Latin America was an important phenomenon too, economically mainly and, to a lesser extent, politically and socially.[9] Spanish FDI in Latin America was 0.96% of Spain's gross domestic product (GDP) in 1997, rose to 1.63% in 1998, 4.62% in 1999, and 3.97% in 2000 and then dropped precipitously to 0.48% in 2001. This rapid increase made the Governor of the Bank of Spain, Luis Ángel Rojo, warn about the risks that a general Latin American crisis could have, not only on the stability of these firms in the stock exchange, but on the Spanish economy too. In fact, his worst predictions seemed to come true with the Argentinean crisis of December 2001, because the value of the Spanish firms that had made some of the largest investments in that country fell, especially Repsol-YPF, since 40% of its assets were in Argentina. However, their stocks grew again little by little in 2002. In general, the behavior of Spanish firms in the stock exchange was not very different from that of non-Spanish firms that operated in the same sectors but had not made sizeable investments in Latin America. This makes it hard to conclude that the investors punished the Spanish firms for their exposure in Latin America (Banco de España, *Balanza de pagos de España* and *Boletín estadístico*, 2002; Dirección General de Comercio e Inversiones, 2002; and M.Á. Cortés, 2002).

In this chapter I will provide an explanation for these foreign direct investments. It is divided into two sections. I will first review the existing literature on multinational enterprises and how it has been applied to the study of Spanish firms in Latin America. Most of the theorists have applied John E. Dunning's OLI theory (ownership-location-internalization). In reviewing the literature, I will expose some of the limitations of the existing models, many of them developed to explain the internationalization through direct investments of U.S. firms, Central and North European firms, and Japanese firms, mostly operating in manufacturing activities. By emphasizing the concept of "advantage" in service-sector industries, I will argue that most of these models take the concept for granted, failing to explain how the advantage is developed in the home market and how it is applied in the host markets. In the last section, I will claim that the Spanish firms derived their advantage from operating in institutional frameworks in Spain that were very similar to those they found in Latin America in the 1990s. I will then provide a model to study the FDIs of Spanish firms in Latin America between 1990 and 2002.

Theoretical approaches

Since the 1990s, there have been a lot of analyses of different aspects of Spanish FDI in Latin America.[10] Many are based on John E. Dunning's theories (Dunning, 1974, 1993, 2000), including his OLI paradigm. According to this model, FDI is the result of three factors: ownership of an asset, tangible or intangible, by one firm; location considerations like, for instance, proximity or not to the market where its products and services will be sold; and the efficiency of the firm as organizers of transactions, above the markets, due to the existence of imperfections that lead the managers of the firms to internalize the activities that they could contract with other firms freely in the market if there were not such imperfections.

Juan José Durán Herrera (Durán, 1996, 1997, 1999) has studied the FDI of the Spanish firms since the 1970s. Following Dunning's model, he argued that the Spanish FDI in Latin America was due to three factors. First, the existence of factors and location economies in Latin America that became important in the 1990s. Secondly, deregulation and technological advances which allowed for the internationalization of firms through FDIs, especially in telecommunications, energy, banking and insurance. The third aspect was the capacity of the Spanish firms to generate resources and capacities in the 1980s. The new international setting, more open for FDI in the 1980s, led the managers of the firms to internationalize these advantages through direct investments.

William Chislett wrote one of the few books in English on this subject. He also followed John H. Dunning's OLI model, emphasizing especially the location advantages that existed in Latin America in the 1990s, such as the processes of privatization, market access and acquisition of market share, expectations of population growth, change of regulatory system, and similarity of macroeconomic environment between Spain and Latin America in the 1980s and 1990s (Chislett, 2003). Also focusing on location advantages in Latin America, José Antonio Alonso analyzed the direct investments of Spanish firms in Latin America in the aftermath of the Southeast Asia crisis of 1997. He concluded that macroeconomic stability, trade and financial opening, liberalization and deregulation of economic activities, the privatization of state-owned enterprises, and regional integration worked as important pull factors into the region.

José Manuel Campa and Mauro F. Guillén (Campa and Guillén, 1996a, 1996b), and Cristina López-Duarte and Estaban García Canal (López-Duarte and García Cañal, 1997), followed the "investment development path" (IDP) model developed by Dunning and Rajneesh Narula (Dunning and Narula, 1996), which analyzes the relationship between economic development and FDI. They treated Spain as a late investor. Mikel Buesa and José Molero (Molero and Buesa, 1992; Buesa and Molero, 1998) applied this model to the industrial sector and emphasized the technological transfers from Spain. Yolanda Fernández (Fernández, 2000) underlined the ownership advantages (common culture and oligopolistic situation) and location advantages (growth potential in Latin America).

Adolfo Gutiérrez de Gandarilla Saldaña and Luis Javier Heras López (Gutiérrez and Heras, 2000) applied the gradualist theory of the Scandinavian School. This theory posits that the enterprises of small countries begin to make FDIs once they have developed their national markets, even though they may still be small. FDI is an independent decision of incremental expansion. Firms expand their international operations gradually as a logical process of firm growth. These authors recognize that the Scandinavian model can only explain some of the cases of FDI by some Spanish firms, but not all.[11]

Several authors follow the theory of international trade. They explore the relationship between exports and FDI. María Teresa Alguacil Mari and Vicente Orts Ríos (Alguacil and Orts, 1998), María Teresa Alguacil Mari, Óscar Bajo Rubio, María Montero Muñoz and Vicente Orts Ríos (Alguacil, Bajo, Montero and Orts, 1999), Eduardo Cuenca García (Cuenca, 2001), and Carlos Rodríguez González (Rodríguez, 2001) concluded that Spanish FDI in Latin America was the result of the substitution of trade by investment.[12]

There are important studies in the field of strategic management. Francisco Mochón and Alfredo Rambla (Mochón and Rambla, 1999) see the Spanish FDI just as a strategic move by the managers of the firms to add value to their companies. They proposed that the managers see market niches that need to be filled in Latin America. Their strategies are based on a clear definition of the targets, the strategy to follow, and the results. In other words, they emphasized the transparency of their operations in order to gain the trust of the investors and thus increase the value of their companies in the stock exchange. Miguel Ángel Gallo and José Antonio Segarra (Gallo and Segarra, 1987) emphasized the importance of the team of managers. The managers must have a clear vision and choose FDI as a strategy to make their business grow, either because they perceive business opportunities abroad, or because their domestic market shrinks. Their analysis is based on a small group of family-owned small and medium enterprises (SMEs).

Other authors use a historical analysis. For Ramón Casilda Béjar (Casilda, 2002), Spanish FDI in Latin America was the result of several factors, firm-specific, sectoral, and cultural. On the one hand, the Spanish firms had a set of managerial assets that varied from firm to firm. Based on these assets, they developed a strategy of geographic diversification of their investments to grow. At the sectoral level, there was a process of gradual liberalization of the Spanish market. The Spanish market was characterized by a high degree of competition. Finally, the cultural and linguistic similarity between Spain and Latin America made the Spanish managers choose this region in their international expansion.

Using historical analysis too, Santos S. Ruesga and Julimar S. Bichara (Ruesga and Bichara, 1998-1999), Rafael Pampillón and Ana Raquel Fernández (Pampillón and Fernández, 1999), and Guillermo de la Dehesa (Dehesa, 2000) showed that Spanish FDI was the result of two factors that came together in the 1990s. On the one hand, there was a push factor, the economic consolidation of Spain, which generated capital for the Spanish firms and, on the other, there was a pull factor, the change of policies in Latin America. José Antonio Alonso and J. Manuel Cadarso (Alonso and Cadarso, 1982) also underlined the importance of culture and language. Both claimed, in the early 1980s, that the cultural similarity between Spain and Latin America was an important pull factor for the Spanish firms in Latin America. María Teresa Fernández (Fernández, Fernández, 2000) studied another pull factor, the links that exist between the Spanish subsidiaries of non-Spanish service firms settled in Spain and some Spanish firms, through contracts and services. The Spanish firms decided to make FDIs at some point, to follow the international operations of the parent companies of the foreign firms with which they work in Spain, so that they can sell them their goods or services in new markets.

In the 1990s, the adoption of a single currency by the European Union and the gradual elimination of restrictions to the mobility of firms within generated great interest in the study of the impact of the European integration process on the Spanish firms. Many academics concluded that FDI was one of the most intelligent options for the Spanish firms to face the competition generated by the integration process. Juan Velarde, José Luis García Delgado y A. Pedreño (Velarde, García and Pedreño, 1991), and Álvaro Calderón (Calderón, 1999a, 1999b) followed this type of analysis.

From a sociological perspective, Mauro Guillén (Guillén, 2001) believed that the Spanish FDI (mainly, but not only, in Latin America), was the result of the evolution of a group of firms that operated in a particular institutional context, the Spanish one. In his analysis, he compared the cases of Argentina, South Korea, and Spain. He concluded that globalization was not forcing the convergence of the organizational models of firms and countries. In other words, the practices of those firms and countries that had proven more successful were not being imitated across the board by other firms and countries. Instead, firms and countries were being pushed to take advantage of their unique economic, political, and social advantages. The result was a diverse array of development models.

One of these models was the Spanish, which he called "pragmatic-modernizing" (as opposed to the nationalist-populist model of Argentina, and the nationalist-modernizing model of South Korea). The Spanish model was characterized by the great degree of competition that exists in the market, due to the presence of many imported products and many subsidiaries of foreign firms (competing closely with Spanish small and medium enterprises – SMEs – and with a small number of very large Spanish oligopolistic firms), and by its openness, because it promoted exports and FDI. The cooperative character of the unions facilitated the negotiation of the development model between the government, the Spanish and foreign businesses, and the workers.

Cristina López Duarte (López-Duarte, 1997) based her analysis on industrial organization theory, developed by Stephen Hymer (Hymer, 1976), who argued that, to make FDIs, a firm must have an advantage from which it can generate an income stream, and it must apply it in new markets. However, theorists of the firm showed in the 1980s that, even though having an advantage may be a necessary condition for FDI, it is not the only one. Oliver Williamson (Williamson, 1975, 1979) explained that the existence of imperfect markets leads the company that has the advantage to exploit it itself instead of licensing it through a franchise or instead of selling it. The result is that the firm decides to "internalize" the markets. That is, the firm itself develops all of the operating units that it needs to produce the goods and services derived from its advantage in new markets and makes the FDI. Duarte tested this theory with an analysis of a group of Spanish industrial firms.[13]

A model to explain the emergence and application of an advantage

In this chapter, I conclude that the Spanish firms that made FDI in Latin America, especially in the 1990s, had an advantage. I find this advantage in a series of institutional factors. Subsequently, I will explain how the Spanish firms developed this advantage, and how they applied it in the markets where they invested. I will focus on seven companies that operate in the sectors that generated the largest amounts of FDI in Latin America, banking, telecommunications, public utilities, and oil and natural gas. These sectors generated more than half of the Spanish FDI in Latin America.

The firms on which I base my conclusions are Telefónica in telecommunications, Banco Bilbao Vizcaya Argentaria (BBVA) and Banco Santander Central Hispano (SCH) in banking, Endesa, Iberdrola, and Unión Fenosa in public utilities, and Repsol-YPF (Yacimientos Petrolíferos Industriales) in oil and gas. The companies were selected because they made the largest share of FDIs in their sectors. It is impossible to determine, based on the official statistics, how much money each of them invested, because the Spanish authorities do not provide this information in order to protect the privacy of the investments. Nevertheless, these firms were the largest in Spain in terms of market capitalization during the period of analysis.[14] While in the early 1980s these sectors absorbed hardly half of the Spanish FDI in Latin America, mostly in banking, in the 1990s they concentrated almost 70% (including "holding societies"), and the total amount was more evenly distributed among energy (which includes the public utilities and the oil and natural gas sectors), telecommunications, and banking, (see Table 2.3).

I base my conclusions on several sources, including interviews, annual reports, and other archival documents from the firms, as well as academic and specialized publications. I include the results of interviews with senior executives of the Spanish firms. These interviews were based on a questionnaire with thirty-four questions. Some executives answered the questions verbally in personal interviews conducted by me, some chose to answer them in writing. Through the words of the executives and managers, I show how they believed that their firms had an advantage in new markets in Latin America and the Caribbean and thus decided to invest there.

In the annual reports, each firm explains the reasons for their investments in Latin America, as well as the strategies, the types of businesses in which they engaged, their goals, targets, results, and expectations, etc. Because all of these firms are publicly traded, their managers want analysts and potential investors to know the state of their accounts and operations. For this reason, their reports are quite complete, because they are important tools of communication. My primary sources also include speeches by the top executives of the firms, as well as opinion articles that they published in specialized and academic publications. I also used reports and analyses by analysts, state agencies, like the Bank of Spain and the Ministry of the Economy, and international organizations like the United Nations Commission for Latin America and the Caribbean (CEPAL), the Inter-American Development Bank, the OECD, UNCTAD, and academic studies.

Table 2.3 Sectoral allocation of Spanish FDI in Latin America, 1980-2000[15]

	1980-1984	*1985-1989*	*1990-1994*	*1995-2000*
Energy	0.12	0.23	9.20	22.70
Communication	0.73	2.26	25.14	5.84
Banking and finance	48.86	57.48	40.29	13.17
Holding[16]			17.09[17]	27.33
Total[18]	49.71	58.8	53.93 (69.82[19])	41.71 (69.04[20])

Source: Dirección General de Comercio e Inversiones, Secretaría de Estado de Comercio y Turismo, Spanish Ministry of the Economy.

If this were a sectoral advantage, only firms from one specific sector would have invested in Latin America. If it had been a firm-specific advantage, there would not have been such large flows of investment from so many different sectors. Therefore, since the investments came from different sectors, I argue that there was a Spain-specific advantage, which was especially important in the four sectors analyzed here.

With this theoretical endeavor, I try to fill the gap that exists in analyses of FDI, because it is quite common among the students of multinational enterprises to take the concept of "competitive advantage" at face value. They assume that firms have a competitive advantage that they decide to apply in other markets. However, to be able to draw theoretical conclusions, it is necessary to apply a model that allows to explain how the advantage is developed, how the decision to make FDIs is based on the ownership of this advantage and, finally, how the advantage is put to work in the host markets, in the daily activities of the firm, for the generation of value added for the firm, and with what results.

Subsequently, I will propose a model to explain the creation and the application of an advantage, using the empirical case of the Spanish firms mentioned above. The advantage of Spanish firms in Latin America was their "knowledge of the market". Their managers believed that they knew very well the needs of the Latin American markets, and thought that their firms had what was needed to provide the services and products that the markets required. Therefore, they decided to make FDIs there.

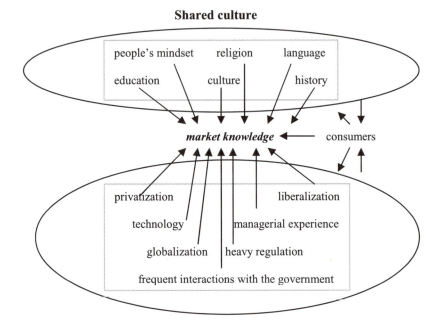

Figure 2.3 Development of the advantage

This knowledge of the market was the result of two factors (see Figure 2.3). On the one hand, a shared culture between Spain and Latin America. The strong historical contact that existed for centuries between Spain and Latin America left its mark in the Latin American culture, making it very similar to the Spanish. The managers of the Spanish firms interpreted that the common language, the predominantly Catholic religion, in both Spain and Latin America, and the similar educational systems, based on the same principles and similar values, generated similar mindsets among the people on both sides of the Atlantic. Therefore, they concluded that it would be easier for them to operate in this cultural environment.

Moreover, the linguistic and cultural similarity would also facilitate the interactions with the employees of their potential Latin American subsidiaries, and it would make it easier to move employees between the parent and the subsidiaries. For all of these reasons, they concluded that transactions would be easier and less onerous, and that the environment in which they would have to operate would be appropriate (*El Exportador*, 2003: 61). This is an important thesis, because it emphasizes a human aspect that is sometimes ignored by many disciplines. In other words, businesses are conducted by people. The impact of cultural differences in business has generated a great number of studies from an anthropological perspective.[21]

On the other hand, knowledge of the Latin American market, in the more technical aspects, came out of the shared institutional experiences that were similar to Spain and Latin America, in each sector. That is to say, the institutional context in which Spanish firms operated was very similar to the one the managers believed they found in Latin America. The markets had several characteristics:

- Privatization: many of the Spanish firms had been state-owned and went through processes of privatization in the 1990s (with the exception of the two large banks). With the structural reforms implemented in Latin America, many state-owned firms were going to be privatized, opening the door to the entry of Spanish firms. The Spanish managers were certain about their knowledge of the processes of internal reform and about the external relations needed to make the transition from a state-owned firm to a private firm.[22]

- Liberalization: in Spain, the firms included in this study had been operating under conditions of monopoly in telecommunications, oil and public utilities, but in the 1990s, the Spanish government lifted gradually the restrictions to the entry of new firms into the market. The Latin American countries went through a similar situation in the 1990s. In some Latin American countries and sectors, the process of liberalization even preceded that of Spain, and the managers of the Spanish firms took this as an opportunity to learn how to operate in a new competitive environment.[23]

- Technology: the Spanish firms in this study had to improve and modernize their services, technologies, and products very rapidly since the 1980s, due to the quick growth of demand in Spain. For this reason, they made large investments, fueled by the fast growth of the Spanish economy. The growth expectations in Latin America in the 1990s were very attractive to the Spanish managers, who deemed it necessary to undertake a similar process of technological improvement quickly, like the one they had gone through in Spain in the previous years (Buesa and Molero, 1998; Molero and Buesa, 1992; and Durán, 1996, 1997).

- Managerial experience: by operating in this context, the managers were forced to adjust the internal organization of their firms to the new characteristics of the market, testing different organizational patterns until they adopted the organizational arrangements that were more successful in the pursuit of their goals. This learning process gave them knowledge of how to act in this kind of environment, and the managers decided to put their knowledge to work in new markets, where the conditions were conducive to the application of their knowledge (Vázquez, 1995; and Durán, 1995).

- Globalization: the deregulation of markets, especially in the European Union, led the Spanish managers to ask themselves what would happen when the national restrictions to the operation of foreign firms in Spain were lifted, in each one of their sectors of operation. They feared to lose market share and came to the conclusion that, due to the liberalizing trend in the market, which they defined as "globalization", the best strategy to guarantee the survival of their firms was to leave Spain to grow in new markets. They thought that only the large firms would survive in each sector, thereby deciding to grow by pursuing an aggressive strategy of expansion overseas through direct investments, in order to become some of the largest firms in their sectors by European standards (Dehesa, 2000).

- Heavy regulation: in spite of the privatization of state-owned firms and the liberalization of the sectors in which they operated under monopolistic conditions, liberalization did not mean the elimination of legislation. In fact, the Spanish government generated a lot of laws to establish the new rules of the game in each sector, trying to smooth the transition from situations of monopoly to competition, in order to prevent the emergence of oligopolistic behavior among firms. An analogous situation occurred in Latin America, with the privatization of state-owned firms and the elimination of monopolies (Ariño 1999, 2000).

- Frequent interactions with the government: due to the production of a heavy legal corpus in each of the sectors, the managers of the firms were forced to continue to interact with the governments on a regular basis, lobbying to try to get the new legislation to be as conducive as possible to the pursuit of their own interests. A similar situation occurred in Latin America (Ariño, 1999, 2000).

These conditions created a particular institutional and cultural context in which the Spanish firms found themselves in the 1990s. When they adjusted to them, their managers decided to adopt the internal organizational processes that were more suited to the pursuit of their businesses. These organizational processes constituted the internal organization of the firm. They also developed a web of external relations with the regulators and with the government to lobby.

Both internally and externally, the firms adopted a "ruled" behavior, that is to say, behavior based on a series of organizational rules or rules of internal behavior (internal organization) and external behavior (their relations with regulators), which institutionalized their advantage and coerced their employees to adapt their behavior on the basis of the products and services that their managers wanted (or "had") to produce. This institutionalized behavior, externally and internally, constituted the normative framework or organizational culture of the firms.

Here I use the rule-oriented constructivist approach developed by Nicholas Onuf. In proposing a mode of analysis for the social sciences, he tackled the agency-structure debate and explained that agents and institutions (he prefers to use this term instead of structures) co-constitute each other. That is, the agents construct the social institutions in which they operate and these institutions, in turn, constrain agency. In other words, they constitute one-another. To understand this process of co-constitution, Onuf looked at social rules, which mediate between agents and institutions. The institutions are sets of rules that tell agents how to behave in a given setting. In our case, we regard the firm as an institution, governed by a series of rules created by its own employees (the agents). Outside of the firm, the market is the institution and the firm becomes the agent. The rules of the market are determined by the regulating agents and by the firms that operate in them (Onuf, 1989).

When the executives of the Spanish firms included in this study considered the possibility of making FDIs, they saw that many other regions of the world were going through the same processes of privatization and liberalization, including Latin America, Central and Eastern Europe, and Africa. They came to the conclusion that, although the institutional framework in which they had to operate was similar in all of these three regions, the Latin American cultural framework was also similar to Spain's. This led them to make FDIs in Latin America (see Figure 2.4).

Figure 2.4 Application of the advantage

It is hard to determine whether the fact that Portuguese was the language spoken in Brazil influenced the investment decision of the managers of the Spanish firms in that country. First, the institutional conditions in Brazil were similar to those of the rest of the Latin American countries, from the perspective of the Spanish managers. Therefore, based on this criterion, Brazil should not have been a different case. However, Brazil received the Spanish FDIs a few years later, especially in the second half of the 1990s. However, this may have happened because the privatization of Brazilian state-owned firms and the elimination of restrictions to the entry of FDI in Brazil did not occur until then.

Would the Spanish firms have invested in Brazil earlier if the opening of its market had taken place earlier? The Spanish managers interviewed for this study explained that it was not hard to find within their own firms qualified employees who spoke Galician, who could therefore operate comfortably in a Portuguese-speaking environment. In this case, the answer to the question would be yes, because Portuguese would not have been serious enough a deterrent to make the Spanish managers perceive Brazil as a very different cultural environment.

However, this cannot be confirmed with empirical evidence, because of the institutional impediments that existed in Brazil, as discussed above. Methodologically, it is difficult to take the Brazilian case apart from the rest of Latin America. On the one hand, if we look at the fact that Telefónica developed an alliance with Portugal Telecom for its expansion in Brazil, it would seem that language may have been an entry barrier, and it would be hard to determine to what extent the similarity of institutional experiences between Spain and Brazil, as well as the size of the Brazilian market, may have weighed more than the linguistic barrier in the investment decisions of the Spanish managers.

The following quotes, taken from some of the top executives of each one of the seven Spanish firms included in this study, are examples of their reasoning. They believed they had an advantage in Latin America and decided to invest there.

"In Latin America, our group's strategy is based on a long-term commitment to consolidate a regional franchise, which already has great value, in which the entrepreneurial model, the automation, and the systems platforms that our business units have in Spain, are in an advanced stage of implementation" (BBVA 1999: 5-6).

Emilio Ybarra, Chairman of BBVA in 1999

"The processes of privatization, concentration and liberalization that we went through in Spain in the last twenty or twenty-five years were a great learning experience for Banco Santander and facilitated our internationalization in Latin America" (Luzón, 2002).

Francisco Luzón, CEO, SCH

The presence of Endesa abroad is "a purely entrepreneurial decision to search for new business opportunities, in which Endesa and its group of firms could capture the benefits of all of the knowledge that we had accumulated since our creation in 1944; the availability of experienced human resources that could apply adequately and efficiently their skills, as well as financial resources that could be invested profitably in countries that were going through deep processes of opening and sociopolitical change" (Miranda, 1998/99: 117).

Rafael Miranda, CEO, Endesa

"The expansion in new markets, in other business areas, and in other countries is vital if Iberdrola is to grow profitably in the future. This is a strategy designed to take the maximum advantage of our competitive advantages and to transfer the experience, management, and technological capacity of our Group to markets that have a great growth potential, with the goal of getting the return that we are looking for" (Oriol, 1997: 4).

Íñigo de Oriol Ybarra, Chairman of Iberdrola

"To be able to improve management it is essential to undertake a transfer of knowledge and experiences. It is necessary to enrich the capacity of the people and, with the experience accumulated in other projects, to take them to the belief that they have to break routines and that they have to be open to change. (...) This is the orientation that Unión Fenosa wanted to give initially to its international activity: a consulting job to modernize management and to share knowledge with professionals from other countries. The solutions that we proposed were the same that already existed in our own firm, and they could be appropriately tested and experimented by the professionals of the firms for which we worked" (Reinoso, 1998: 65).[24]

Victoriano Reinoso, Vice-Chairman of Unión Fenosa

"South America is an emerging area in the world economic stage, with an energy market in fast expansion, where we believe we have clear competitive advantages" (Cortina, 1996: 3).

Alfonso Cortina de Alcocer, CEO, Repsol-YPF

"The internationalization of Telefónica was established on the basis of the competitive advantages that Telefónica had vis-à-vis the American and European operators. It was based on the ability to undertake important investment programs in short periods of time. In the decade of the 1980s, and especially in its last years, Telefónica faced a crisis of demand for telephones and telephone services in Spain. In this period, Telefónica had close to one million demands to install a telephone. This crisis forced Telefónica to develop efficiently large investment programs quickly. This know-how, which some characterized as "trench technology", was very useful and extraordinarily attractive to satisfy the demands of the countries that needed an urgent expansion of their telephone systems, given the high demand of the people for telephones waiting to be installed. There was a coincidence, that the countries with these problems were involved in a process of privatization of the state-owned firms that provided the telecommunication services under condition of monopoly" (Santillana, 1997: 94).

Ignacio Santillana, CEO of Telefónica Internacional, S.A., 1990-1996

Once in Latin America, the Spanish firms applied in their subsidiaries the same organizational culture that they had developed for their business in Spain. Their managers believed firmly that the conditions in which they had to operate would require the same products and services that they had developed in the Spanish market in the 1980s and 1990s. For this reason, the normative framework that they developed in Spain was transplanted to their Latin American subsidiaries. However, over time they found out that, in spite of the cultural and institutional similarities, there were also important differences in each country (the regulations

were different in each country and the demands of each market also varied, depending on the tastes and preferences of the customers). This forced them to change their normative models on the basis of the peculiarities of each market. This experience, as well as the need to adjust, represented a learning process for them, with new knowledge that was incorporated to the organizational culture of the firms. From this perspective, the organizational culture of each firm is not a static phenomenon. It undergoes a permanent process of change, due to the adaptation to the context in which it operates, which is, in turn, the result of the practices of the firms in a given institutional setting,[25] (see Figures 2.4 and 2.5).

To test the limits of my approach, however, it would be interesting to undertake a comparative study of the FDI of the Spanish firms in Latin America and the FDIs of firms from other countries, in order to see if this model applies in different contexts and institutional settings. A good case would be that of the Portuguese firms, because there exist many important similarities between the Portuguese and the Spanish cases, not only in their economic histories, institutional models, and their belonging in the European Union, but also in the fact that Brazil could be a similar pull factor for the Portuguese firms, attracting their FDIs because of its linguistic, cultural, and institutional similarities.

Moreover, this study would provide new insights to understand the case of the Spanish firms in Brazil, as discussed above. It would also be important to take a case from outside the European Union, for instance, the United States, the main home for FDIs going to Latin America in the second half of the twentieth century. Why did the firms from the United States not invest in Latin America as much as Spanish firms did in the sectors analyzed in this study? The case of U.S. firms would allow me to test whether my approach applies only to firms from late developing countries, like Spain.

The case of Chile would also be important, because some Chilean firms made important FDIs in the 1990s, and some of these firms even participated in the privatization processes of state-owned enterprises in other Latin American countries. Lastly, it would also be interesting to include the case of China, whose outward FDI grew substantially since the 1990s. China, with its different political and economic framework, would be a very useful case to test the limitations of our model.[26]

	BBVA	BSCH	Endesa	Iberdrola	Repsol-YPF	Telefónica	U. Fenosa
Argentina	■	■	■		■	■	
Bahamas		■					
Bolivia	■	■		■	■		■
Brasil	■	■	■	■	■	■	■
Islas Caimán	■	■	■				
Chile	■	■	■		■	■	
Colombia	■	■		■	■	■	■
Costa Rica	■						■
Cuba	■						
República Dominicana	■	■	■				■
Ecuador	■				■		
El Salvador	■					■	■
Guatemala	■			■		■	
México	■	■		■		■	
Nicaragua	■						■
Panamá	■	■				■	
Paraguay	■	■				■	
Perú	■	■	■		■	■	
Puerto Rico	■	■				■	
Trinidad y Tobago					■		
Uruguay	■	■				■	■
Venezuela	■	■			■	■	

Figure 2.5   Geographic distribution of Spanish foreign direct investment in Latin America and the Caribbean by host country in 2002

Source: Annual reports of the companies

Notes

[1]   The difference between direct investment (foreign or not) and portfolio investment (foreign or not) depends on whether the party making the investment gains "control" over the management of the firm in which s/he invested. If the investor gains control, the investor intends to remain involved in the firm in the long run and, through "control", will participate in the management and development of the entrepreneurial culture of the firm. Portfolio investments are speculative. The investor takes over a number of shares because s/he believes that the value of the firm will go up (s/he may

not even know much about the business in which the firm operates). For statistical purposes, the more general criterion is to assume that when a party owns 10% or more of a firm, there is direct investment. Any acquisition below 10% of the total capital of the firm is regarded as portfolio investment.

This criterion was initially adopted by the Commerce Department of the United States and eventually taken by the International Monetary Fund. Since then, it was also applied by the members of the Organization for Economic Cooperation and Development (OECD). However, in reality, this criterion does not necessarily allow to set the direct investments apart from portfolio investments, because in a small firm, a party can own 49% of the capital and still not have control over management decisions, because another party may own 51% of the firm's capital. In the large firms, where capital is very spread out, it could be the case that a single party owns less than 10% of the capital, and still be the largest investor, with control over management.

Moreover, since it became possible to make investments through the Internet, the capacity of governments to track down every one of the investments has disappeared. According to Elena Martín Tubía, Technical Advisor of the Dirección General de Comercio e Inversiones of the Spanish Ministry of the Economy, the amount of money invested across borders that governments cannot keep track of could be as high as 10% of all of the transactions taking place. Therefore, these statistics have to be taken as indicators of trends, rather than as the final amounts. Source: E. Martín, 2001. For more information on the difference between direct investment and portfolio investment, see S. Hymer, 1976; R. Caves, 1996; F. Merino and M. Muñoz, 2002.

[2]   To prevent capital flight, the government of Francisco Franco required all Spanish investments overseas to be approved by the Council of Ministers. In 1977, Royal Decree 1087 of 14 of April reduced the need to go through the Council of Ministers for investments of more than 50 million pesetas, while investments lower than that, only had to be approved by the Minister of Trade and Tourism, as well as by the Director General of Foreign Transactions. In 1979, Royal Decree 2236 authorized Spanish citizens to own assets denominated in foreign currency, although those who made investments overseas still had to notify the Dirección General de Comercio e Inversiones. Royal Decree 2374 of 1986 introduced some conceptual modifications, although the spirit of the law remained the same. Royal Decree 672 of 1992 reduced the types of investments subject to verification by the Dirección General de Comercio e Inversiones to those higher than 250 million pesetas, as well as those made in fiscal havens (these were regulated by Royal Decree 1080 of 1991) and those in holding societies. Royal Decree 664 of 1999 and a ministerial order of 28 May 2001 introduced a series of conditions for the submission of information on FDI to the Dirección General de Comercio e Inversiones in order to compile the official statistics. However, these regulations respected the liberalizing character of the law of 1992. Source: *ICE*, 1979; *ICE*, 1981; *ICE*, 1994; and F. Merino and M. M, 2002.

[3]   The economies of Hong Kong, China, and Taiwan, the three with the greatest growth, were more and more interrelated. A great amount of the FDI moving in that triangle originates within. The percent growth of Spanish FDI abroad between 1990 and 2000 was 1,023%, the forth highest in the group of the twenty-two largest homes to FDI. Ahead of Spain were Hong Kong China (3,227%), the Republic of Korea (1,123%), and China (1,093%). Source: UNCTAD, 2001: 307-311.

[4]   Investment flows measure the amount of money that leaves the parent company and is invested in the acquisition of a subsidiary in a different country. For statistical purposes, it is calculated annually. The position or "stock" measures the flows, plus the earnings reinvested by the subsidiaries in activities related to their business or in the

development of new ventures in the host country. Therefore, position figures incorporate an important variable that does not show up in the flow figures, such as the reinvested earnings. Position figures are also provided annually, although it is more difficult to quantify. However, it is a better measurement of the amount of FDI, because flows vary a lot from year to year. It could be that in a given year, the investment flows from one country to another grow by 500%, due to a large single operation by a large firm. If in the following year there are no such large investments, the FDI flow figures for that country will fall again. The result is a graph with ups and downs. If no firm from a particular sector of economic activity makes investments abroad, the FDI flows may be zero, or even negative, if there is repatriation of profits. However, this does not mean that the multinational enterprises left the country. In other words, the statistics may lead to the wrong conclusions. That is why the position or "stock" figures are more stable, because they include the value of the FDI made every year, as well as the investments made by the subsidiary with the earnings generated in the host country. This means that, even if in a particular year there are no FDI flows (meaning that FDI flow figures may be zero or even negative, if there is repatriation of earnings) the position figures may be similar to those of the previous year, or even higher, if the subsidiary reinvested some of its earnings. Unfortunately, the Spanish Ministry of the Economy and the Bank of Spain do not provide position figures. Therefore, in some cases I will have to base my analysis on flow figures.

[5] Figures for Repsol-YPF and Telefónica refer to foreign assets in 1999, not only Latin America. However, most of their assets outside of Spain were concentrated in this region. Source: UNCTAD, 2001. Figures for BBVA are 2001, for the rest, 2002. Source: BBVA, 1999: 22; BBVA, 2001: 120; BBVA, 2002: 17; SCH, 2002: 5, 22; Endesa,:2002, 9, 110; Iberdrola, 2002: 101-104; and Unión Fenosa, 2002: 63-64.

[6] Two good examples of this the work of Maura de Val (2001) and Horacio Verbitsky (1991). De Val denounces the entry of Spanish firms into Latin America in the processes of privatization of state-owned enterprises, because she believes that this was part of a scheme to alienate the national productive, financial, and economic systems of each Latin American country. This process of alienation was, in turn, part of the general process of transnationalization of the instruments of economic and political control (the main characteristic of "globalization" for this author). In Latin America, these processes were not transparent and, in her opinion, they were probably corrupt.
To denounce corruption was precisely the goal of Verbitsky's work. He believes that the acquisition of several Argentinean state-owned firms was the result of a plan by the government of Carlos Ménem in Argentina, on the one hand, and, on the other, by the administration of Felipe González in Spain and the top executives of a group of Spanish firms that were interested in participating in acquiring the Argentinean firms. It is important to keep in mind that none of these pieces is academic, because the authors did not support their claims with references.
There are, however, many academic pieces that analyze the contribution of FDI to economic growth. Among the more recent ones, there are A. Rodríguez-Clare (1996), J. Markusen and A. Venables (1997), R. Caves (1999), J. Markusen, T. Rutherford and D. Tarr (2000), P. Loungani and A. Razin (2001) and A. Balcão (2001). UNCTAD has also published extensively on this topic. See UNCTAD, 2001 and 2002.

[7] Some authors have studied the concentration of the Spanish FDI abroad, geographically (in the European Union and Latin America) and by sector (petrochemical, trade, and finance). See C. López-Duarte, 1998 and J. M. Delgado, M. Ramírez and M.A. Espitia, 1999.

8   John Williamson coined the term "Washington consensus" when he worked for the World Bank to refer to a set of ten policies, on which the Latin American reforms were based: fiscal discipline; different use of public funds, by reducing subsidies and increasing investments in health, education, and infrastructure; fiscal reform to increase state revenue; free allocation of interest rates in the market; free allocation of exchange rate by the market; trade liberalization; liberalization of investment flows; privatization of state-owned enterprises; deregulation of economic activities to foster competition; and strengthening of property rights (J. Williamson, 1990). For an analysis of the model based on the "Washington consensus", also called orthodox or neoliberal, as well as the alternative heterodox model, see L.C. Bresser Pereira, J.M. Maravall, and A. Przeworski (1992). For a detailed analysis of the first wave of reforms, see S. Edwards (1995). For an analysis of the privatization processes in Latin America, with the entry of foreign MNEs, see M.R. Agosin (1995), M.H. Birch and J. Haar (2000), W. Glade and R. Corona (1996), J.A. Ocampo and R. Steiner (1994), R. Ramamurti (1996) and G. Vidal (2001).

9   In spite of this, several journalistic works have analyzed the economic reforms implemented by the administrations of Felipe González in the first half of the 1990s, as well as the administrations of José María Aznar after his ascension to power in 1996. These works denounced the lack of transparency in the processes of privatization of several Spanish state-owned enterprises, including some of the firms that made the largest investments in Latin America. The journalists also concluded that some of the investments in Latin America were pushed by the political agreements between the governments of Spain and those from the Latin American countries that wanted to privatize their state-owned enterprises. However, these journalists do not provide references, so it is impossible to verify the validity of their accusations. See J.D. Herrera and I. Durán (1996) and J. Mota (1998 and 2001).

10   Even though there are many studies that analyze the Spanish FDI in some specific sectors, in this section I concentrated exclusively on the analyses of FDI in general.

11   For the Uppsala School, see J. Johanson and J.E. Vahlne, (1977).

12   For the international trade theory, see J.R. Markusen, (1995) and J.R. Markusen and A.J. Venables, (1998).

13   For industrial organization theory, as developed by Stephen Hymer, see S.H. Hymer, (1976). For internalization theory, see O.E. Willliamson, (1975 and 1979).

14   Spanish Ministry of the Economy.

15   These categories derive from the ones used in Spanish official statistics. Until 1993, there was a category for "energy and water", another one for "transport and communications", and another for "financial institutions, insurance, services provided for enterprises and rents". Since 1993, "energy and water" was divided into two, "production/distribution of electric energy, gas and water", and "extractive industries, oil refining, and processing of hydrocarbons"; and "transport and communications" was broken up, so after 1993 there was a separate category for "telecommunications". I added the data for "production/distribution of electric energy, gas and water", to the data from "extractive industries, oil refining and processing of hydrocarbons" because this study comprises firms from both categories, and this will allow me to make comparisons among different years. However, I did not add the data for "telecommunications" and "transport" since 1993 because the transport sector firms are not included in this research. Because of the ambiguity of the definitions, it is possible that all of the money included in each category may not correspond to the firms analyzed in this study. However, the firms included in it generate the largest amount of

FDI in their sectors, and therefore the figures included are indicative of their investment trends.

Since 1993, a new category appeared in the Spanish official statistics, "management of societies and holding societies". Until then, the data for these firms were included in "financial institutions, insurance, and services provided to enterprises and rents". I included them here because some, if not all of the firms in this study, channel part of their FDI to Latin America through these societies. For this reason, it is possible that a large part of the amounts included in this category end up in one of the sectors of this study. However, it is impossible to determine to what extent, due to the policy of protection of privacy of the investments of the Dirección General de Comercio e Inversiones.

Another important aspect to keep in mind when reading these statistics is that the Spanish government passed a law in the mid-1990s to eliminate the payment of taxes on dividends and capital gains generated abroad for firms based in Spain. The firms that could benefit from this policy were those based in Spain whose social goal was to manage firms outside of Spain. These firms could not be speculative and their capital gains or dividends should have paid taxes before. The Spanish government passed this law to facilitate the FDIs of the large Spanish enterprises through societies based in Spain, thus preventing them from channeling their investments through third countries (mainly fiscal havens). In fact, it is impossible that the percentage included in "communication" dropped in the second half of the 1990s (as seen in the table) because Telefónica made important investments in Latin America in that period of time. This means that Telefónica channeled many of its Latin American investments through holding societies. In 2000, this law was extended to non-Spanish holding societies. For this reason, the Spanish FDI figures since then include the FDIs channeled through Spain by non-Spanish firms.

When reading these statistics, it is important to keep in mind that the amounts included in them are revised periodically and retroactively, when the Spanish authorities have new data. If the Spanish Ministry of the Economy were to find out in 2005 new investment data for 1997, the figures for 1997 would be revised to incorporate the new information. Therefore, these statistics must be taken as indicators of trends, rather than as final figures (Abril and Jiménez, 2003 and Dirección General de Comercio e Inversiones).

[16] Since 1993, Spanish official statistics included a new category, "holding and other". It is likely that many of the investments made by the firms from the sectors included in this work may have been channeled through holding societies, but it is impossible to determine how much of the total amount included in this category belongs to them.

[17] 1993 and 1994 only.

[18] The figures in parenthesis are the summation of all of the sectors included in the study plus "holding and other".

[19] Including holding societies.

[20] Including holding societies.

[21] Two of the main scholars in this field are Edward Hall, a pioneer in the study of the influence of culture in business, and Geert Hofstede. See E. Hall (1960) and G. Hofstede (1980). For a compilation of the main studies of the importance of culture in business, see J. L. Graham (2001).

[22] For an analysis of the processes of privatization in Spain, see Á. Cuervo, (1998); L. Mañas (1998); E. Rivas (1998); and L. Gámir (1999). For privatizations in Latin America, see J. A. Ocampo and R. Steiner (1994); M.R. Agosin (1995); W. Glade and

R. Corona (1996); R. Ramamurti (1996); M.H. Birch and J. Haar (2000); and G. Vidal (2001).

[23] For Latin America, see S. Edwards (1995). For Spain, Instituto de Estudios Económicos, 1994; G. Ariño (1999 and 2000); and P. Arocena and F. Castro(2000).

[24] He was referring here to the initial period in which Unión Fenosa began to operate in Latin America as a consulting firm.

[25] For an analysis of the activities of the governments of the host countries to attract inward FDI, see J.A. Ocampo and R. Steiner (1994); M.R. Agosin (1995); W. Glade and R. Corona (1996); R. Ramamurti (1996); M.H. Birch and J. Haar (2000); and G. Vidal (2001). There are no detailed studies about the contribution of Spanish firms to economic development in Latin America.

[26] It is especially important to compare cases from different parts of the world. In part, I base this assertion on the fact that Spanish FDI in Latin America has generated great surprise in academic and business circles, in Latin America as well as in the United States. I sensed this feeling of surprise from the comments and questions when debating Spanish FDI in conferences in both regions. It is worth conducting a study to see on what assumptions these comments and expressions of surprise are based.

References

Abril, F. (2002), "Iberoamérica y las empresas españolas. La experiencia de Telefónica", presentation at seminario "Iberoamérica y las empresas españolas", Universidad Internacional Menéndez Pelayo, Santander, Spain, August 19-20 (F. Abril was Telefónica's CEO in 2002).

Abril, I. and M, Jiménez (2003), "España se convierte en un "paraíso fiscal" para atraer a las grandes multinacionales", *5 días.com* (observed 8 May 2003).

Agosin, M.R. (ed.) (1995), *Foreign Direct Investment in Latin America*, Inter-American Development Bank, Washington, D.C.

Alguacil, M., O. Bajo, M. Montero and V. Orts (1999), "¿Existe causalidad entre exportaciones e inversión directa en el exterior? Algunos resultados para el caso español", *ICE*, 782, Nov-Dec, pp. 29-34.

Alguacil, M., M.T. Orts and V. Orts (1998), "Relación dinámica entre inversiones directas en el extranjero y exportaciones: una aproximación VAR al caso español, 1970-1992", *ICE*, 773, Sept-Oct, pp. 51-63.

Alonso, J.A. and J.M. Cadarso (1982), "La inversión directa española en Iberoamérica", *ICE*, 590, Oct-Nov, pp. 105-121.

Álvarez, C. (2001), interview, Corporate Development Manager (gerente de desarrollo corporativo), Telefónica, Madrid, July 31.

Ariño, G. (ed.) (1999), *Privatizacion y liberalización de servicios*, Universidad Autónoma de Madrid and Boletín Oficial del Estado, Madrid.

--- (2000), *Liberalizaciones*, Comares S.L., Granada.

Arocena, P. and F. Castro (2000), "La liberalización de sectores regulados" *BICE*, 2640, Jan. 10-23, pp. 27-36.

Balcão, Ana (2001), "On the Welfare Effects of Foreign Direct Investment", *Journal of International Economics*, 54 (2), August, pp. 411-427.

Banco de España (2003), *Balanza de pagos de España*, www.bde.es (observed 5 May 2003).

--- (2003), *Boletín estadístico*, www.bde.es (observed 5 May 2003).

BBV (1996-1998), *Informe anual*, Madrid.

BBVA (1999-2002), *Informe anual*, Madrid.

BCH (1995-1998), *Informe anual*, Madrid.

Birch, M.H. and J. Haar (eds.) (2000), *The Impact of Privatization in the Americas*, North-South Center Press, University of Miami, Coral Gables.

Bresser, L.C., J.M. Maravall and A. Przeworski (eds.) (1992), *Economic Reforms in New Democracies. A Social-Democratic Approach*, Cambridge University Press, Cambridge.

BS (1994-1998), *Informe annual*, Madrid.

Buesa, M. and J. Molero (1998), *Economía industrial de España. Organización, tecnología e internacionalización*, Civitas, Madrid.

Calderón, Á. (1999a), "El boom de la inversión extranjera directa en América Latina y el Caribe: el papel de las empresas españolas", *Economistas*, 81, Sept, pp. 24-35.

--- (1999b), "Inversiones españolas en América Latina: ¿una estrategia agresiva o defensiva?", *Economía Exterior*, 9, Summer, pp. 97-106.

Campa, J.M. and M. Guillén (1996a), "A Boom from Economic Integration", in J.H. Dunning and R. Narula (eds.), *Foreign Direct Investment and Governments*, pp. 207-239.

--- (1996b), "Evolución y determinantes de la inversión directa en el extranjero por empresas españolas", *Papeles de Economía Española*, 66, pp. 235-247.

Caves, R.E. (1996), *Multinational Enterprise and Economic Analysis*, Cambridge University Press, New York.

--- (1999), "Spillovers From Multinationals in Developing Countries: The Mechanisms at Work", Working Paper 247. Prepared for the William Davidson Institute Conference on The Impact of Foreign Investment on Emerging Markets, University of Michigan, Ann Arbor, June 18-19.

Chislett, W. (2003), *Spanish Direct Investment in Latin America: Challenges and Opportunities*, Real Instituto Elcano de Estudios Internacionales y Estratégicos, Madrid.

Conthe, M. (2002), "La significación internacional de la inversión española en el exterior". Presentation at "seminario Iberoamérica y las empresas españolas", Universidad Internacional Menéndez Pelayo, Santander, Spain, August 19-20 (M. Conthe was Vice-Chairman of the World Bank in 2002).

Cortés, M.Á. (2002), opening speech at "Seminario Iberoamérica y las empresas españolas", Universidad Internacional Menéndez Pelayo, Santander, Spain, 19-20 August (M.Á. Cortés was Spain's Secretary of State for International Cooperation and for Latin America in 2002).

Cuenca, E. (2001), "Comercio e inversión de España en Iberoamérica", *ICE*, 790 (Feb-March), pp. 141-162.

Cuervo, Á. (1998), "La privatización de las empresas públicas, cambio de propiedad, libertad de entrada y eficiencia", *ICE*, 772, July-August, pp. 45-57.

Dehesa, G. (2000), *Comprender la globalización*, Alianza, Madrid.

--- (2000), "La inversión directa española en Latinoamérica", *Boletín del Círculo de Empresarios*, 65 *Iberoamérica y España en el umbral de un nuevo siglo*, pp. 201-241.

Delgado, J.M., M. Ramírez and M.A. Espitia (1999), "Comportamiento inversor de las empresas españolas en el exterior", *ICE*, 780, Sept., pp. 101-112.

Díaz, J. and I. Durán (1996), *El saqueo de España*, Ediciones Temas de Hoy, Madrid.

Dirección General de Comercio e Inversiones, Secretaría de Estado de Comercio y Turismo, Ministerio de Economía español, www.mcx.es/polco/InversionesExteriores/estadisticas (observed 5 May 2003).

Dunning, J.H. (1974), *Economic Analysis and the Multinational Enterprise*, Praeger Publishers, New York.

--- (1993a), "Trade, Location of Economic Activity and the Multinational Enterprise: a Search for an Eclectic Approach", in J.H. Dunning (ed.), *The Theory of Transnational Corporations*, pp. 183-218.

--- (ed.) (1993b), *The Theory of Transnational Corporations*, vol. 1, United Nations Library on Transnational Corporations, Routledge, New York.

--- (2000), "The eclectic paradigm as an evelope for economic and business theories of MNE activity" *International Business Review* 9, pp. 163-190.

Dunning, J.H. and R. Narula (1994), *Transpacific FDI and the Investment Development Path: the Record Assessed*", University of South Carolina Essays in International Business, no. 10, May.

--- (eds.) (1996), *Foreign Direct Investment and Governments: Catalysts for Economic Restructuring*, Routledge, London.

Durán, J.J. (1995), "Estrategia de localización de la empresa multinacional española", *Economía Industrial*, 306, pp. 15-26.

--- (ed.) (1996), *Multinacionales españolas I. Algunos casos relevantes*, Pirámide, Madrid.

--- (ed.) (1997), *Multinacionales españolas II. Nuevas experiencias de internacionalización*, Pirámide, Madrid.

--- (1999), *Multinacionales españolas en Iberoamérica. Valor estratégico*, Pirámide, Madrid.

Edwards, S. (1995), *Crisis and Reform in Latin America. From Despair to Hope*, Oxford University Press for the World Bank, Oxford.

El Exportardor (2003), "El español como recurso económico", p. 61, Feb., www.el-exportador.com (observed May 14, 2003).

Endesa (1996-2002), *Informe anual* (Madrid).

Fernández, Y. (2000), "España como inversor en América Latina", *Análisis Financiero Internacional*, 98, Feb.-March, pp. 41-50.

Fernández, M.T. (2000), "Presencia y efectos de arrastre de las filiales extranjeras de servicios a empresas en España", Universidad de Alcalá, Documento de trabajo no. 1.

Gallo, M.Á. and J.A. Segarra (1987), "La tendencia en la internacionalización de la empresa", *ICE*, 643, March, pp. 87-90.

Gámir, L. (1999), *Las privatizaciones en España*, Pirámide, Madrid.

García, I. (2001), interview, Head of the Office of Relations with Investors, SCH, Madrid, June 29.

Glade, W. and R. Corona (eds.) (1996), *Bigger Economies, Smaller Governments. Privatization in Latin America*, Westview Press, Boulder.

Gomis, A. (2002), "Iberoamérica y las empresas españolas. La experiencia de Repsol", presentation at "Seminario Iberoamérica y las empresas españolas", Universidad Internacional Menéndez Pelayo, Santander, Spain, August 19-20 (A. Gomis worked at Repsol's External Relations Department in 2002).

Graham, J.L. (2001), "Culture and Human Resources Management" in A.M. Rugman and T.L. Brewer (eds.), *Oxford Handbook of International Business*, pp. 503-536.

Guillén, M. (2001), *The Limits of Convergence. Globalization and Organizational Change in Argentina, South Korea, and Spain*, Princeton University Press, Princeton.

Gutiérrez, A. and L.J. Heras (2000), "La proyección exterior de las empresas españolas: de la teoría gradualista de la internacionalización", *ICE*, 788, Nov., pp. 7-17.

Hall, E. (1960), *The Silent Language*, Anchor Books, New York.

Hofstede, G. (1980), *Culture's Consequences*, Sage, Beverly Hills.

Hymer, S. (1976), *The International Operations of National Firms: a Study of Direct Foreign Investment*, MIT Press, Cambridge.

Iberdrola (1995-2002), *Informe anual* (Bilbao).

ICE (1979), 1661, 1 Febrero, pp. 349-350.

--- (1981), 1765, 29 Enero, pp. 382-383.

--- (1994), 2415, 6-12 Junio, p. 1403.

Instituto de Estudios Económicos (1994), *La necesaria liberalización de los servicios en España*, Madrid.

Johanson J., and J. E. Vahlne (1977), "The Internationalization Process of the Firm – A Model of Knowledge Development and Increasing Foreign Market Commitments", *Journal of International Business Studies*, vol. 8.

Lema, G. (2001), interview, Director of Investment Analysis (director de análisis de inversiones), Unión Fenosa Internacional, Madrid, July 27.

López-Duarte, C. (1997), "Internacionalización de la empresa española mediante inversión directa en el exterior. 1988-1994", *Economía Industrial*, 318, pp. 141-150.

--- (1998), "Evidencias empíricas sobre las inversiones directas en el exterior realizadas por las empresas españolas", *Revista Asturiana de Economía – RAE*, 13, pp. 131-149.

López-Duarte, C. and E. García (1997), "La inversión directa realizada por empresas españolas: análisis a la luz de la teoría del ciclo de desarrollo de la inversión directa en el exterior", papeles de trabajo de la Universidad de Oviedo, doc. 146/97.

Loungani, P. and A. Razin (2001), "How Beneficial Is Foreign Direct Investment for Developing Countries?" *Finance and Development* 38 (2), International Monetary Fund, Washington, D.C., June.

Luzón, F. (2002), "La experiencia de Santander Central Hispano", presentation at "Seminario Iberoamérica y las empresas españolas", Universidad Internacional Menéndez Pelayo, Santander, Spain, August 19-20 (F. Luzón was CEO of SCH in 2002).

Mañas, L. (1998), "La experiencia de una década de privatizaciones", *ICE*, 772, July-August, pp. 145-175.

Markusen, J.R. (1995), "The Boundaries of Multinational Enterprises and the Theory of International Trade", *Journal of Economic Perspectives*, vol. 9, no. 2 (Spring), pp. 169-189.

Markusen J.R., and A.J. Venables (1997), "Foreign Direct Investment as a Catalyst for Industrial Development", Working Paper 6241. National Bureau of Economic Research, Cambridge, October.

--- (1998) "Multinational Firms and the New Trade Theory", *Journal of International Economics*, vol. 46, no. 2 (Diciembre), pp. 183-203.

Markusen, J.R., T.F. Rutherford and D. Tarr (2000), "Foreign Direct Investments in Services and the Domestic Market for Expertise", Policy Research Working Paper 2413. World Bank, Washington, D.C., August.

Martín, E. (2001), interview, Technical Counselor of the Department of Spanish Investments Overseas, Spanish Ministry of the Economy (Consejera Técnica del Departamento de Inversión Española en el Exterior del Ministerio de Economía), Madrid, 24 junio 2001.

Merino, F. and M. Muñoz (2002), "Fuentes estadísticas para el estudio de la inversión directa española en el exterior", *BICE*, 2751, Dec. 9-15, pp. 5-15.

Miranda, R. (1998), "La experiencia de Endesa en Mercosur", *Economía Exterior*, 7, 1998/99, pp. 117-122.

Mochón, F. and A. Rambla (1999), *La creación de valor y las grandes empresas españolas. Los casos de BBV, Banco de Santander, Endesa, Iberdrola, Repsol y Telefónica*, Ariel Sociedad Económica, Barcelona.

Molero, J. and M. Buesa (1992), "La expansión internacional de la empresa española: posibilidades y limitaciones hacia Iberoamérica", *Economía Industrial*, 283, Jan.-Feb., pp. 25-41.

Montejo, S. (2002), "Iberoamérica y las empresas españolas. La experiencia de Endesa", presentation at "Seminario Iberoamérica y las empresas españolas", Universidad Internacional Menéndez Pelayo, Santander, Spain, August 19-20 (S. Montejo was Secretary of Endesa's Board in 2002).

Mota, J. (1998), *La gran expropiación. Las privatizaciones y el nacimiento de una clase empresarial al servicio del PP*, Ediciones Temas de Hoy, Madrid.

--- (2001), *Aves de rappiña. Cómo se han apoderado los populares de empresas, medios de comunicación y organismos independientes*, Ediciones Temas de Hoy, Madrid.

Ocampo, J.A. and R. Steiner (eds.) (1994), *Foreign Capital in Latin America*, Inter-American Development Bank, Washington, D.C.

Ontiveros, E. (2002), "Las empresas españolas en Iberoamérica", presentation at "Seminario Iberoamérica y las empresas españolas", Universidad Internacional Menéndez Pelayo, Santander, Spain, August 19-20.

Onuf, N. (1989), *World of Our Making. Rules and Rule in Social Theory and International Relations*, University of South Carolina Press, Columbia.

Pampillón, R. and A.R. Fernández (1999), "Comportamiento reciente y perspectivas de la inversión española en América Latina", *Economía Exterior*, 9, Summer, pp. 58-70.

Panizo, F. (2002), interview, Director General of Coordination of Projects in Europe (Director general de coordinación y control de proyectos en Europa), Telefónica Móviles, S.A., Madrid, 6 March.

Ramamurti, R. (ed.) (1996), *Privatizing Monopolies. Lessons from the Telecommunications and Transport Sectors in Latin America*, The Johns Hopkins University Press, Baltimore.

Reinoso, V. (1998), "Oportunidades del nuevo entorno energético internacional. La experiencia de Unión Fenosa en los mercados emergentes", *Economistas*, 76, Feb., pp. 62-68.

Rejón, L. (2001), interview, Head of the Department of Relations with Investors (Jefa de Sección del Departamento de Relaciones con Inversores). Repsol-YPF, Madrid, July, 19.

Repsol (1995-1998), *Informe anual*, Madrid.

Repsol-YPF (1999-2002), *Informe anual*, Madrid.

Rivas, E. (1998), "Valor de la empresa y privatizaciones" *ICE* 772, July-August, pp. 99-108.

Rodríguez, C. (2001), "Un estudio preliminar de la relación por países entre las inversiones directas españolas en el exterior y las exportaciones", *BICE*, 2683, February 26 to March 4, pp. 7-14.

Rodríguez-Clare, A. (1996), "Multinationals, Linkages, and Economic Development", *American Economic Review*, 86 (4), Sept., pp. 852-73.

Rugman, A.M. and T.L. Brewer (2001), *Oxford Handbook of International Business*, Oxford University Press, New York.

Santillana, Ignacio (1997), "La creación de una multinacional española. El caso de Telefónica", *Economistas*, 73, pp. 90-99.

SCH (1999-2002), *Informe anual*, Madrid.

Telefónica (1990-2002), *Informe anual*, Madrid.

UNCTAD (2001), *World Investment Report 2001: Promoting Linkages*, New York.

--- (2002), *World Investment Report 2002: TNCs and Export Competitiveness*, New York.

Unión Fenosa (1996-2002), *Informe anual*, Madrid.

Val, Maura de (2001), *La privatización en América Latina. ¿Reconquista financiera y económica de España?*, Editorial Popular, Madrid.

Vázquez, C.J. (1995), "Estrategias de internacionalización de un negocio", *Economía Industrial*, 304, pp. 101-117.

Velarde, J., J.L. García and A. Pedreño (eds.) (1991), *Apertura e internacionalización de la economía española. España en una Europa sin fronteras*, Colegio de Economistas de Madrid, Madrid.

Verbistsky, H. (1991), *Robo para la corona: los frutos prohibidos del árbol de la corrupción*, Planeta, Buenos Aires.

Vidal, G. (2001), *Privatizaciones, fusiones y adquisiciones: las grandes empresas en América Latina*, Anthropos, Barcelona.

Williamson, J. (1990), *Latin American Adjustment. How Much Has Happened?*, Institute for International Economics, Washington, D.C.

Willliamson, O.E. (1975), *Markets and Hierarchies*, The Free Press, New York.

--- (1979), "Transaction Cost Economics: The Governance of Contractual Relations", *Journal of Law and Economics*, vol. 22, pp. 233-261.

Chapter 3

The Transformation of the Spanish Economy and FDI in Latin America. Towards a New Theoretical Framework

Sebastián Royo

Introduction

Since the 1980s, Spain has emerged as a major economic actor and player in Latin America. Between 1992 and 2002, Spain invested $96,000 million in Latin America, accounting for half of the European Union investment in the region. This was a dramatic development. Until very recently Spain had been a net importer of capital. The modernization of the Spanish economy, a process that started in the late 1950s and culminated with the accession of Spain to the European Union, was the starting point. It led to a surge in the inflow of inward foreign direct investment (FDI), technology transfers, and increases in the domestic savings rate, which contributed to the transformation of the economy. Therefore, the timing was not accidental. It coincided with the transformation of the Spanish economy that followed access to the European Union and the economic reforms in Latin America after the "lost decade" of the 1990s.

The nature of this investment has been strategic for Spanish firms and the Spanish government. Spain has contributed significantly to strengthen the political and institutional framework in these countries, has provided economic assistance and has fostered economic integration. Yet, the operation of Spanish firms has also generated new tensions in many Latin American countries, which have hindered their strategies. Nevertheless, despite recurring crisis (i.e. the Argentine collapse in 2001), Spanish firms have refused to withdraw from the region.

Spanish FDI has also been a factor in the modernization of the economic structures of Latin American countries. While Spanish FDI investment in the region contributed to economic recovery and modernization, Latin America is once again at a crossroad. Despite the profound political, institutional and structural changes that transformed these economies over the last decade these countries still face important challenges in the new millennium. Given the commitment of Spanish firms to stay in the region, it is important to explore the challenges that they face in the context of increasing tensions and socio-economic problems in these countries.

From a theoretical standpoint this chapter will highlight a major shortcoming of the existing literature, namely, the fact that institutional economists frequently ignore the fact that companies operate and structure their relationships within an institutional framework of incentives and constraints (see North, 1990; Alston, Eggertsson and North, 1996). I will examine the *push factors* that contributed to the decision of Spanish firms to invest in Latin America. While there is a substantial literature on the determinants of MNEs engaging in FDI, there is little analysis on the impact that existing institutional frameworks have on the operations and competitiveness of firms. When examining the actions of Spanish firms, it is glaring to observe that they did not consider how the existing institutional framework in Latin American countries would affect their operations in the region. While they looked at particular institutions (and in many cases they contributed to reform them), they did not systematically examine how institutional frameworks influence their strategies and operations. The chapter will outline a research proposal to consider this issue in a systematic way.

The chapter is structured in three main sections. In the first section of the chapter, I describe the pattern of Spanish FDI in Latin America and outline briefly the motives and determinants of multinationals. In the second part, I examine the *push factors* that contributed to Spanish firms' decision to engage in FDI in Latin America. The process of European integration and the simultaneous transformation of the Spanish economy cannot be separated from the explosion of Spanish investment in Latin America, therefore in this section of the paper will look at the impact of European integration on the modernization of the Spanish economy. I close the chapter with a proposal for a new research agenda that focuses the impact of the institutional framework on firms' strategies and competitiveness.

Spanish FDI in Latin America

Following the independence of its Latin American colonies throughout the 19th century, Spain played a very limited economic role in Latin America. Britain, during the first half of the 20th century, and the United States since World War II, became the major economic players. However, during the last decade Spain has become the second largest investor in Latin America after the United States. This was a dramatic departure from previous decades. In the 1960s and 1970s Spain's outward investment only accounted for 0.1% of worldwide FDI flows.

In contrast, between 1992 and 2001, Spain invested $96,000 million (the US $117 billion) and became the world's eighth-largest net home of direct investment (Chislett, 2003: 19). The process of opening to international trade, improved potential for growth, falling production costs (lower wages), and the lower risk premium in response to the brighter macroeconomic outlook associated with economic reforms help account for the increase. Between 1986 and 1993, Spanish FDI in Latin America averaged $310 million a year led by the telephone company, *Telefónica*, and the main Spanish banks. During the following five years, Spanish FDI to the region exploded, averaging $9,700 million a year, and representing close to 10% of GDP by 2000. The reasons for the decline in 2001 and 2002 were linked to the worldwide economic crisis, the slowdown of the privatization processes and the growing risk premium of investing in Latin America.

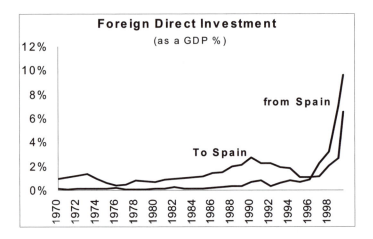

Figure 3.1 Inward and outward FDI in Spain, 1970-2000
Source: Bank of Spain

Table 3.1　Inward and outward FDI flows in Spain, 1990-2002

($ bn)	1990-95*	1996	1997	1998	1999	2000	2001	2002
Inflows	10.7	6.6	7.7	11.8	15.7	37.5	28.0	21.1
Outflows	3.5	5.4	12.6	18.9	42.0	54.7	33.0	18.5

* Annual Average

Source: *World Investment Report 2003* (UNCTAD)

Table 3.2　Leading Spanish MNEs in Latin America

Company	Sector	Investment, 1997-2000 ($ Million)
Telefónica	Telecommunications	30,449
SCH	Banking	12,930
BBVA	Banking	6,848
Repsol-YPF	Energy	17,252
Endesa	Electricity	7,226
Iberdrola	Electricity	1,806
Union Fenosa	Electricity	850

Source: CEPAL, Unidad de Inversiones y Estrategias Empresariales

The increase in Spanish FDI has been one of the contributing factors behind the recovery of the Latin American economy in the 1990s. Latin American countries have undergone a profound transformation over the last decade. As a result of the combined processes of fiscal discipline and liberalization, macroeconomic fundamentals were restored. The rate of inflation declined from 872% in 1993 to 6% in 2001, the budget deficit was reduced to an average of 3.5%, and per capita income rose 55% in the 1990s. FDI also contributed to the increasing dynamism of the corporate sector in Latin America. More than 100 Latin American companies are listed in the New York Stock exchange and Nasdaq (Chislett 2003, 28). From a political standpoint, a region that has been historically characterized by military coups and authoritarian regimes underwent sweeping democratic reforms that led to the establishment and consolidation of their democratic regimes. Cuba is the only Latin American country with a totalitarian regime. All of these developments contributed to make Latin America an attractive FDI destination. However, while the overall outcome of these investments has been positive both for Spanish firms and the host countries, significant problems remain (See Figure 3.2). In Argentina, for instance, Spanish firms became some of the main targets of local anger when the economy crashed in 2001, and in other countries like Chile, hostile takeovers from Spanish firms have led to contentious reactions among local governments and business leaders.

- Intensification of critical attitudes in local countries: Nationalism
- Concerns over the operation of local markets and prices
- Problems associated with methodology: privatization processes tainted by corruption
- Spanish public firms (SEPI-Aerolíneas) involved in local conflicts
- Inadequate regulation of new sectors: Regulatory vacuums generate uncertainties
- Visibility of the consumer service sectors
- Concentration and lack of competition
- Conflict over further investment to improve services and increase capacity
- Dependency on Latin America: Vulnerability
- Tarnished image of Spain

Figure 3.2 Risks associated with Spanish FDI in LA

Determinants of FDI

There is substantive literature explaining the determinants on firms engaging in FDI (Dunning, 1996; Caves, 1996). Most scholars differentiate between FDI that seeks to increase the competitive advantage of the MNE (*asset-seeking* FDI) or investment designed to add value to existing advantages (*asset-exploiting* FDI).

I. Policy Framework For FDI:	III. Principal Economic Determinants
Economic, political and social stability	A. *Market-seeking:*
Entry and operating rules	Market size and per capita income
Treatment of foreign affiliates	Market growth
Competition and M&A policies	Access to regional/global markets
International agreements on FDI	Country consumer preference
Privatization policy	B. *Resource/Asset seeking:*
Trade policy	Raw materials
Tax policy	Low cost labor
	Skilled labor
II. Business Facilitation:	Technological assets (brand name)
Investment promotion (i.e. image building, services)	Physical infrastructure
Investment incentives	C. *Efficiency-seeking:*
Hassle costs (corruption, administrative efficiency)	Costs of resources and assets
Social amenities (schools, quality of life)	Other input costs (transport, communications)
After-investment services	Membership of a regional integration agreement to establish regional corporate networks

Figure 3.3   Host country determinants of FDI
Adapted from Dunning (2001, Table 3.16, p. 64)

Spain's interests in the region were also rooted in historical and cultural links. The FDIs of Spanish MNEs were largely motivated by their desire to strengthen their competitiveness in face of increasing competition at home and abroad, through the acquisition of assets in countries which had a similar culture. These cultural synergies were strengthened by the learning experiences of Spanish firms, which had to adjust to the liberalization of the Spanish economy throughout the 1980s. In addition, the former state owned firms also had to learn how to compete and operate in open markets following their own privatization processes. These institutionalized learning processes led them to conclude that they had an additional competitive advantage in the region (Toral, 2001). This helps account for the geographical concentration of FDI directed to Latin America (see Figure 3.3).

Finally, the profound transformation of the Latin American economies over the last decade, which culminated with the restoration of macroeconomic fundamentals through the implementation of fiscal discipline and liberalization, also contributed to make Latin America an attractive FDI destination and increased the dynamism of the corporate sector in Latin America.

In summary, Spanish FDI in Latin America was driven by factors that pertained to changes within the Spanish economy and market that provided new challenges and opportunities to Spanish firms (*push factors*), as well as changes within Latin American countries that made them more attractive for Spanish firms to invest in the region (*pull factors*) (see Figure 3.4).

1. Imperatives of technological development
Spanish firms were motivated by the need to upgrade their technology to better meet the demands of the global marketplace and to confront the competitive challenges of a globalized economy.

2. The Growing costs of innovative activities
The expansion of Spanish firms was also influenced by the need to secure finance and knowledge capital to finance the growing costs of innovation. Most of the sectors in which the MNEs operated are very technologically intense and therefore the cost of innovation is very large.

3. To take advantage of economies of scale, product, and process innovation
Expansion in Latin America also offered MNEs the opportunity to increase their economies of scale, and tap into potentially large markets to sell their products and services.

4. To increase global resources and capabilities
Latin America offered Spanish firms a natural market to increase their resources to satisfy their desire to become global players.

5. Liberalization of markets
The expansion was driven by the liberalization of the Latin American economies that followed the "lost decade" of the 1980s. The Mexican default of 1982 sparked a debt crisis throughout the region, plunging these countries into recessions. This crisis led to the collapse of many authoritarian regimes and the election of democratic governments in most Latin American countries. Throughout the 1990s these new democratic governments undertook deep processes of reform to modernize their economies and restore their macroeconomic balance. The liberalization of previously closed markets was a key factor that fostered the Spanish firms' drive into the region.

6. Privatization of large state-owned enterprises
The expansion of Spanish firms in the 1990s was largely motivated by the desire to acquire indigenous state-owned firms at very competitive prices. Spanish firms took advantage of the privatization processes that took place throughout Latin America in the 1990s. Therefore most of these acquisitions concentrated in infrastructure sectors such as telecommunications, utilities, and energy. Spanish and Portuguese firms participated in all but one of the privatization processes that took place between 1997-99 in Latin America, accounting for 67% of all purchases.

7. Removal or reduction of restrictions on inward FDI and foreign takeover of local firms
The elimination of protectionist policies that sought to shield domestic monopolistic firms allowed the inflow of FDI into Latin American countries.

8. Mature host market
As a consequence of the liberalization of the Spanish economy that followed the accession to the European Union, Spanish firms faced increasing competition in their home market, which was already mature for most firms. This situation was putting strong pressure on profit margins. Expansion to Latin America offered the opportunity to expand to new markets and increase their market share.

9. Pivotal Role of Latin America as the back door to the United States
Spanish firms investing in Latin America are seeking to exploit the proximity to the United States. *Repsol* is developing a project to supply energy to California, the banks want to compete for the fees of the remittances that Latin Americans in the US send to their families, and *Telefónica* seeks to tap into the lucrative roaming fees that Latin Americans pay when they travel to the US and call home.

Figure 3.4   Firm-based factors that contributed to FDI in Latin America
Sources: Toral (2001) and Dunning (2001)

Push Factors	**Pull Factors**
Economic growth	Privatizations
Increasing business revenues	Structural reforms
Favorable financing conditions	Opening of the economy
Access to capital	Deregulation
External competitive pressures	Macroeconomic stability
Mature markets in utilities and financial services	Growth potential
Technological changes	Population growth
Deregulation and liberalization	Less competition intensity
Economies of scale	Liberalization

Figure 3.5 Pull and push factors behind the Spanish FDI in Latin America
Sources: Adapted from Dunning (2001)

The transformation of the Spanish economy

The internationalization of the Spanish economy and the consequent expansion to Latin America has to be examined in the context of the dramatic transformation that the Spanish economy undertook over the last two decades.[1] The integration of Spain in the European Community (EC) was the catalyst for the final conversion of Spain into a modern Western-type economy. Indeed, one of the key consequences of its entry into Europe has been that membership has facilitated the modernization of the Spanish economy.[2] This is not to say, however, that membership was the only reason for this development. The economic liberalization, trade integration, and modernization of the Spanish economy started in the 1950s and 1960s and Spain became increasingly prosperous over the two decades prior to EC accession.

In this section, I will address the macroeconomic effects of membership in the EC, which started long before accession. The Preferential Trade Agreement (PTA) between the EC and Spain (1970) resulted in the further opening of European markets to Spanish products, which paved the way for a model of development and industrialization that could be based on exports. At the same time, the perspective of EU membership acted as an essential motivational factor that influenced the actions of policymakers and businesses. Henceforth, Spain took unilateral measures in preparation for accession including increasing economic flexibility, industrial restructuring, the adoption of the VAT, and intensifying trade liberalization. Through the European Investment Bank, Spain also received European aid since 1981 to mitigate some of the expected adjustment costs.

Economic conditions in Spain in the second half of the 1970s and first half of the 1980s were not buoyant. The world crisis caused by the second oil shock in the late 1970s and the lack of adequate response from the collapsing authoritarian regime intensified the structural problems of the economy. The economic crisis of the late 1970s and the first half of the 1980s had devastating consequences and made any additional adjustments caused by the accession to the EC a daunting prospect. High unemployment levels, reaching 22 percent in 1986, suggested that any additional adjustment cost would have painful consequences.[3] In addition, the country was unprepared for accession – i.e., Spanish custom duties remained on average five times higher than the EC's and EC products faced a major disadvantage in the Spanish market because of Spain's compensatory tax system and restrictive administrative practices that penalized harder imported products.4 Slow license delivery was common, and manufacturers who sold vehicles in the country did not have import quotas to introduce cars into Spain from abroad. Finally, when Spain knocked on the door of the EC for accession in 1977, protectionist institutions – which were incompatible with EC rules – were still fully operative. For instance, the Spanish government controlled through the I.N.I (National Institute of Industry) a considerable size of the economy, and subsidized public enterprises such as the auto making companies (SEAT, ENASA), as well as the metallurgic, chemical, ship building and electronic sectors. This situation provided a considerable advantage for Spanish manufacturers.

April 18, 1951	Six European countries (Belgium, the Federal Republic of Germany, France, Italy, Luxembourg and the Netherlands) sign the Treaty of Paris establishing the European Coal and Steel Community (ECSC).
March 25, 1957	The Six sign the Treaty of Rome establishing the European Economic Community (EEC) and Euratom.
July 21, 1959	Seven countries (Austria, Denmark, Norway, Portugal, Sweden, Switzerland and the United Kingdom) create the European Free Trade Association (EFTA).
April 8, 1965	Merging of the ECSC, EEC and Euratom into the European Community (EC).
July 1, 1968	Culmination of the customs union and enactment of the Common Agriculture Policy (CAP).
January 1, 1973	Denmark, Ireland and the United Kingdom join the EEC.
March 13, 1979	European Monetary System (EMS) takes effect.
January 1, 1981	Greece joins the EC.
January 1, 1986	Portugal and Spain join the EC.
January 1, 1987	Enactment of the Single European Act (SEA).
June 29, 1989	Spain joins the Exchange Rate Mechanism (ERM).
July 1, 1990	Stage I of EMU begins.
October 3, 1990	Reunification of Germany and incorporation of the German Democratic Republic (GDR) to the EC.
November 1, 1993	Treaty on European Union (Maastricht Treaty) comes into force. EU.
January 1, 1994	Stage II of EMU begins.
January 1, 1995	Austria, Finland and Sweden join the EU.
March 26, 1995	Schengen Agreement comes into force. Spain is one of the members.
October 1997	Treaty of Amsterdam signed.
January 1, 1999	Stage III of EMU begins. Euro launched in twelve EU Member States, including Spain.
May 1, 1999	Treaty of Amsterdam comes into force.
January 1, 2002	Euro notes and coins replaced national currencies in twelve of the 15 countries of the European Union (Belgium, Germany, Greece, Spain, France, Ireland, Italy, Luxembourg, the Netherlands, Austria, Portugal and Finland).
February 3, 2003	Treaty of Nice comes into force
May 1, 2004	Estonia, Latvia, Lithuania, Poland, Czech Republic, Slovakia, Hungary, Slovenia, Malta, and Cyprus join the EU.

Figure 3.6   European integration and Spanish membership

The prospect of EC membership led the political and economic actors to adopt economic policies and business strategies consistent with membership in the *acquis communautaire* (which included the customs union, the VAT – value added tax –, the Common Agriculture and Fisheries Polices, and the external trade agreements; and later the Single Market, the ERM, and the European Monetary Union). Membership also facilitated the micro and macro economic reforms that successive Spanish governments undertook throughout the 1980s and 1990s. In a context of strong support among Spanish citizens for integration, membership became a facilitating mechanism that allowed Spanish governments to prioritize economic rather than social modernization and, hence, to pursue difficult economic and social policies (i.e., to reform their labor and financial markets), with short-term painful effects. Moreover, the decision to comply with the EMU Maastricht Treaty criteria led to the implementation of macro and microeconomic policies that resulted in fiscal consolidation, central bank independence, and wage moderation. Finally, under the terms of the accession agreement signed in 1985, Spain had to undertake significant steps to align their legislation on industrial, agriculture, economic, and financial polices to that of the European Community. The accession agreement also established significant transition periods to cushion the negative effects of integration. This meant that Spain had to phase in tariffs and prices, and approve tax changes (including the establishment of a VAT) that the rest of the Community had already put in place. This process also involved, in a second phase, the removal of technical barriers to trade. These requirements brought significant adjustment costs.

Since 1986, the Spanish economy has undergone profound economic changes. EU membership has led to policy and institutional reforms in the following economic areas: monetary and exchange rate policies (first independent coordination, followed by accession to the ERM, and finally EMU membership); reform of the tax system (i.e. the introduction of the VAT, and reduction of import duties); and a fiscal consolidation process. These changes have led to deep processes of structural reforms aimed at macroeconomic stability and the strengthening of competitiveness of the productive sector. On the supply side, these reforms sought the development of well-functioning capital markets, the promotion of efficiency in public services, and the enhancement of flexibility in the labor market. As a result, markets and prices for a number of goods and services have been deregulated and liberalized; the labor market has been the subject of limited deregulatory reforms; a privatization program was started in the early 1980s to roll back the presence of the government in the economy and to increase the overall efficiency of the system; and competition policy was adapted to EU regulations. In summary, from an economic standpoint the combined impetuses of European integration and economic modernization have resulted in the outcomes listed in Figure 3.6.

For Spanish manufacturers accession to the Community resulted in increasing competition. Since Spanish nominal tariffs averaged 10-20% before EC entry, and generally speaking manufacturing EC products were cheaper and more competitive, membership resulted in an increase of imports from the EC and therefore, on a worsening in the balance of current account (and the closure of many industrial enterprises in Spain). The intensity of the adjustment, however, was mitigated by the behavior of exchange rates and by the dramatic increase in the levels of investment. Spain has been an attractive production base since it offered access to a large market of 40 million people, and a well educated and cheap – compared with the EC standards – labor base. In the end, the transitional periods adopted in the treaty to alleviate these adjustment problems and the financial support received from the EC played a very important role minimizing the costs for the sectors involved.

Integration into the Europe and the world economy Decentralization Institutional reforms Fiscal reforms Increasing openness of the Spanish economy Financial liberalization Privatization Inward and outward FDI Infrastructure improvements	Limited labour market reforms Increasing competitive pressures Industrial restructuring Deregulation Macroeconomic consolidation Nominal and real convergence Internationalization of firms Higher efficiency and competitiveness Deregulation

Figure 3.7 The Spanish economic transformation

An additional factor that contributed to the Spanish success was the new pattern of investment, which brought about important *dynamics effects*. Spain had a number of attractions as a production base including good infrastructure, an educated and cheap labor force and access to markets with a growing potential. In addition, EC entry added the incentive of further access to the EC countries for non-EC Iberian investors – i.e. Japan or the U.S. – As expected, one of the key outcomes of integration has been a dramatic increase in FDI, from less than 2% to more than 6% of GDP over the last decade. This development has been the result of the following processes: economic integration, larger potential growth, lower exchange rate risk, lower economic uncertainty, and institutional reforms. A secondary effect of FDI has been the transfer of technology, which has also contributed to the transformation of the industrial fabric of the country and increased its competitiveness.

EU integration has also allowed the Spanish economy to become integrated internationally and to modernize, thus securing convergence in nominal terms with Europe. One of the major gains of financial liberalization, the significant decline in real interest rates, has permitted Spain to meet the Maastricht convergence criteria. Indeed in 1999 Spain became a founding member of EMU. As late as 1997, Spain was still considered an outside candidate for joining the euro-zone, but in the end, it fulfilled the inflation, interest rates, debt, exchange rate, and public deficit requirements established by the Maastricht Treaty.

Table 3.3   Compliance of the EMU convergence criteria for Spain, 1993-1997

Year	Inflation rate	Long-term interest rate	Public sector deficit (as % of GDP)	Government debt (as % of GDP)
1993	4.6	10.2	6.9	60.0
1994	4.7	10.0	6.3	62.6
1995	4.7	11.3	7.3	65.5
1996	3.6	8.7	4.6	70.1
1997	1.9	6.4	2.6	68.8

Source: Commission and EMU Reports, March 1998

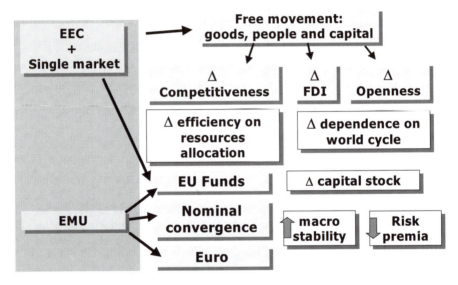

Figure 3.8   The effects of trade liberalization and monetary integration
Source: Sebastián (2001, p.4)

The impetus of lower trade barriers, the introduction of the VAT, the suppression of import tariffs, the adoption of economic policy rules (such as quality standards, or the harmonization of indirect taxes), and the increasing mobility of goods, and factors of production that coincide with greater economic integration, boosted trade and enhanced the competitiveness of the economy.

After 1999, this development has been fostered by the lower cost of transactions and greater exchange rate stability associated with the single currency. For instance, imports of goods and services in real terms as a proportion of GDP rose sharply in Spain (to 13.6% in 1987 from 9.6% in 1984), while the share of exports shrank slightly (to 15.8% of GDP from 16.6% in 1984, and from 17.1% of real GDP in 1992 to 27% in 1997). As a result, the degree of openness of the Spanish economy has increased sharply over the last eighteen years. Henceforth, changes to the production structure and in the structure of exports, indicators of the degree of competitiveness of the Spanish economies (i.e., in terms of human capital skills, stock of capital, technological capital), show important improvements, although significant differences remain in comparison to the leading developed economies (which confirms the need to press ahead with more structural reforms). These achievements verify that in terms of economic stability Spain is part of Europe's rich club. Its income levels, however, remain behind the EU average.

I will now turn to the microeconomic impact of EU ascension. A significant dynamic effect has been the strengthening of the competitive position of Spanish firms. In a country where small firms have increased from 95.1% of firms in 1978 to 98.1% in 1989, economic reforms, which resulted in the development and expansion of local stock markets, have changed the financial landscape for small and medium enterprises and have facilitated their access to capital. Furthermore, Spanish producers gained access to the European market, which provided additional incentives for investment and allowed for the development of economies of scale, resulting in increasing competitiveness.

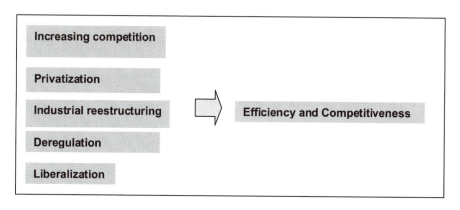

Figure 3.9 Sources of increasing competitiveness

By the 1980s, Spain was already facing increasing competition for their main exports – clothing, textiles, leather – from countries in the Far East and Latin America, which produced all these goods at a cheaper cost, exploiting their low wages. As a result, the latter countries were attracting FDIs in sectors where traditionally Portugal and Spain had been favored. This situation convinced the Spanish business people that the country had to shift toward more capital-intensive industries requiring greater skills in the labor force, but relying on standard technology – e.g. chemicals, vehicles, steel and metal manufacturers . Entry to the

EC facilitated this, because Spain gained access to the EC market, thus attracting investment that would help build these new industries. Finally, Spain also benefited from the EU financial assistance programs – i.e., the European Regional Development Fund, the Social Fund, the Agriculture Guidance and Guarantee Fund, and the newly created Integrated Mediterranean Program for agriculture, and later on from the Cohesion Funds .

The EU policy to reduce regional disparities is built on **four structural funds**:
- The European Regional Development Fund;
- The European Social Fund;
- The section of the EU's common agricultural fund devoted to rural development;
- Financial support for fishing communities as part of the common fisheries policy (CFP).

Allocation of Funds
Disadvantaged regions in all EU countries can benefit from the four structural funds according to certain criteria or objectives.
*Objective 1: 70% of funding goes to so-called Objective 1 regions where GDP is below 75% of the EU average (22% of the EU population). These funds seek to improve basic infrastructure and encourage business investment.
*Objective 2: Another 11.5% of regional spending goes to Objective 2 regions (areas experiencing economic decline because of structural difficulties) to help with economic and social rehabilitation (18% of the EU population live in such areas).
*Objective 3: focuses on job-creation initiatives and programs in all regions not covered by Objective 1. 12.3% of funding goes towards the adaptation and modernization of education and training systems and other initiatives to promote employment.

Figure 3.10   The EU structural funds
Source: European Union

I will now turn to examine the contribution of the EU's Structural and Cohesion Funds for Spanish modernization. Art. 2 of the Treaty of Rome established that the common market would "promote throughout the Community a harmonious development of economic activities" and therefore lower disparities among regions. While regional disparities of the original EC members were not striking (with the exception of Southern Italy), successive enlargements increased regional disparities in terms of per capita income, employment, education, productivity and infrastructure, motivating the creation of EC structural policies. The election of Jacques Delors in 1985 as president of the Commission was very important because he pushed for the establishment of new cohesion policies that were enshrined in the 1986 Single European Act (SEA). The SEA introduced new provisions making economic and social cohesion a new EU common policy. These funds would disburse $255 billion, or roughly one third of total EU spending, between 2000 and 2006 for the poorer regions. An additional $21.6 billion was allocated to the Cohesion Fund, set up in 1993 to finance transport and environment infrastructure in member states with a GDP below 90% of the EU average at the time.

Since the late 1980s, the structural funds became the second largest EU budgetary item. These funds have had a significant impact in relation to the investment needs of poorer EU countries and have made an impressive contribution to growth in aggregate demand in these countries (see Tables 3.2 and 3.3).

Table 3.4 Change in GDP, employment, productivity and population in Objective 1 regions, 1994-2001

	GDP	Employed	GDP/Employed	Population	GDP/capita
All Objectives 1	3.0	1.4	1.6	0	2.8
PT and EL	3.5	1.2	2.3	0.4	3.1
IE	9.3	5.0	4	1.0	8.2
ES Objective 1	3.4	2.9	0.5	0.4	3.0
ES non-Objective 1	3.6	2.5	1.0	0.4	3.2
DE Objective 1	1.7	-0.3	2.0	-0.5	2.2
DE non-Objective 1	1.6	0.8	0.8	0.3	1.3
IT Objective 1	1.9	0.3	1.6	0	1.9
IT non-Objective 1	2.1	1.2	0.9	0.3	1.8
Other Objective1	2.4	1.7	0.6	0.1	2.2
EU15	2.5	1.3	1.2	0.3	2.2

Source: Eurostat, Regional accounts and DG REGIO calculations

Table 3.5 Impact of EU structural aid on GDP growth in the cohesion countries

	Greece	Ireland	Spain	Portugal
1993	4,1	3,2	1,5	7,4
1996	9,9	3,7	3,1	8,5
2006	7,3	2,8	3,4	7,8
2010	2,4	2,0	1,3	3,1

Note: Deviation from a scenario without European Funds.
Source: European Commission, estimations based on HERMIN model (2000)

Indeed, the structural and cohesion funds have been the instruments designed by the EU to develop social and cohesion policy within the European Union. These funds intended to compensate for the efforts that countries with the lowest per capita income relative to the EU (Ireland, Greece, Portugal and Spain) would need to make to comply with the nominal convergence criteria. These funds, which amount to just over one-third of the EU budget, have contributed significantly to reduce regional disparities and foster convergence within the EU. As a result, major infrastructural shortcomings have been addressed and road and telecommunication networks have improved dramatically both in quantity and quality. These additional expenditures in education and training have contributed to the upgrading of the labor force, improving the competitiveness and the growth potential of the least developed regions of Spain.[5]

The main focus of the structural funds has been in 3 areas: improvement of the production system, support for research, development and innovation (RTDI), and industry modernization (particularly addressed SMEs – 34.5% of the resources –); the strengthening of human capital (33%); regional integration (mainly transport and communication infrastructure – 25% –); and infrastructure (7%). During the 1994-1999 period, EU aid accounted for 1.5% of GDP in Spain. EU funding has allowed rates of public investment to remain relatively stable since the mid-1980s. The percentage of public investment financed by EU funds has been rising since 1985, reaching an average of 15% in Spain. Moreover, the European Commission has estimated that the impact of EU structural funds on GDP growth and employment has been significant.

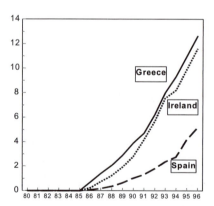

Figure 3.11 Percentage of public investment financed via structural funds

Figure 3.12 Percentage of public capital stock financed with European funds

Source: Sebastián 2001, pp. 25-26

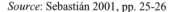

The structural funds (infrastructure development, strengthening of human resources, support for investment in R&D and industry modernization) have contributed to stimulate competitiveness and regional integration and to improve the life quality in Objective 1 regions. According to EU calculations, GDP in Spain increased more than one additional percentage point during the 1994-1999 period thanks to these funds. Investment in infrastructure and human resources will increase productivity, stimulating GDP growth estimated at half a percentage point per year until 2010. From a socio-economic standpoint, income per capita in Objective 1 regions increased by 18.38% and reached 68.7% of the EU average between 1995 and 2000.

Economic development, liberalization and FDI

The transformation of the Spanish economy, catalyzed by the integration into the EU, led to the growth of inward and outward FDI in Spain. According to Durán Navarro, Spain fits neatly into the model developed by Dunning and Narula (Dunning and Narula, 1994) that relates the increase of FDI with the level of economic development (see Toral, 2001: 92-94). In other words, the increase in Spanish outward FDI abroad is a reflection, on the one hand, of the increasing internationalization of markets and, on the other, of the degree of development reached by the Spanish economy, which has led Spanish firms to seek out new markets with potentially higher returns.

The Spanish government played a critical role in the increase of outward FDI (see Toral, 2001: 92-107). One of the most significant steps was the liberalization of financial markets. Prior to the mid-1970s, Spanish firms who wanted to invest abroad needed permission from the government. Royal Decree 1087 (1977) modified this situation. Only investment abroad over 50m pesetas would have to be approved by the Council of Ministers. In 1979 new legislation allowed Spanish citizens to own equity and assets in foreign currency. EC membership accelerated the process of financial liberalization. On the one hand, the prospect of integration forced the government to move faster and prepare the financial sector for competition. On the other hand, EC membership, as we have seen, had a tremendous impact on economic activity and led to massive inflows of foreign capital and rapid rates of economic growth (Pérez 1997, 151-52). In addition, membership stimulated Spanish exports and led Spanish firms to develop distribution networks across Europe to promote and sell their products. This development led to a sharp increase of Spanish FDI into the EC. In 1992 Royal Decree 672 set up new regulations for FDI: only investment over 250 million pesetas, in fiscal havens or in societies to hold stock had to be approved by the General Director of External Transactions. This reform completed the process of liberalization of FDI.

European integration also had an important impact on tax policies. In 1990 the European Union approved Directive 435 to prevent double taxation, allowing member states to deduct the taxes already paid in another EU country. This general criterion against double taxation was applied by Spain to other countries. In 1995, a Corporate Tax Law granted a credit for underlying taxes paid by subsidiaries. Finally, the government allowed Spanish firms to deduct 25% of the tax on their export-related FDI and advertising abroad.

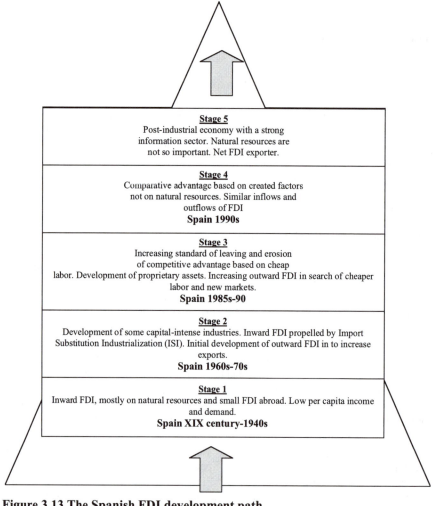

Figure 3.13 The Spanish FDI development path

Based on Durán (1995, pp. 37-38). Adapted from Dunning and Narula (1994).

In addition, the Ministry of Trade and the Institute of Foreign Trade (ICEX), the government created two institutions (ICO, and COFIDES) to channel funds to finance Spanish FDIs and promote exports. In 1997, the government created a new fund of $570 million to promote the FDI of SMEs. Other multilateral institutions (like the European Investment Bank, the Inter-American Development Bank, or the European bank for Reconstruction and Development) supplemented these programs with additional credit.

The effort to promote FDI and exports was furthered by the development of insurance mechanisms provided by institutions such as the Compañia Española de Seguro de Crédito a la Exportación (CESCE), or the Multilateral Investment Guarantee Agency (MIGA), to insure credit for exports and outward FDI. This was coupled with the negotiation of multilateral and bilateral agreements to create a positive investment climate for Spanish MNEs (Toral, 2001: 103-105).

While the overall impact of Spanish FDI in Latin America has been positive, there are still significant problems in these countries. The exacerbation of nationalistic feelings that followed the economic crisis in many countries has intensified the difficulties for Spanish firms operating in the region. These problems have been compounded by the election of new governments with a more populist stance (i.e. Néstor Kirchner in Argentina), as well as the increasing tensions among neighboring countries over long-standing conflicts (i.e. between Chile and Bolivia over access to the Pacific, or Argentina and Chile over gas).

Economic conditions in the region are still dire. The traditional challenges that have affected Latin America (external debt, insufficient legal security, capital flight, corruption) remain largely unresolved. Consequently, the average regional GDP has not changed much since the 1980s (per capita GDP was $3,730 in 1980 and 3,952 in 2000), poverty levels have not decreased much (the average for the 18 countries was 46% of the population in 1980 and 42.2% in 2001) and the absolute numbers of people living below the poverty line increased (190 million in 1990 and 209 in 2001). Income disparities have remained (the Gini Index was 0.554 in 1990 and 0.580 in 1999, and Latin America is the region with the highest levels of inequality in the world).[6] In 15 Latin American countries, (out of 18) over 25% of the population live below the poverty line, and in seven of them this number is over 50%. Infant malnutrition affects more than 5% of the children in 16 of the countries, and illiteracy rates reached over 20% of the population 15 years of age or older in 14 of the countries.

The jury is still out in terms of the economic consequences of FDI in the region. While the quality of the services has improved, the prices have also increased significantly, leading to social problems and political tensions. In addition, Spanish firms are experiencing serious difficulties operating in new regulatory contexts. For instance, the difficulties increasing prices have led many firms to limit their investments in these countries, deteriorating their relationship with the governments. Sometimes Spanish firms botched their investment (i.e. the Spanish national carrier, Iberia, made a mess of running Aerolíneas Argentinas), and Telefónica had a chaotic start in Brazil. In other cases, changes in the regulatory framework led to tensions. Argentina, after the election of president

Néstor Kirchner, established a 20% surcharge to gas exports, which affected particularly the Spanish firm Repsol-YPF (a merged company that resulted from the privatization of the Argentinean YPF), and the government inflamed tensions, accusing foreign firms (and particularly Spanish ones) of extortion (because of their refusal to invest), and blaming them for the ongoing energy crisis. Following the devaluation of the peso, Endesa, Gas Natural, and Telefónica initiated an international arbitration case against Argentina, accusing the government of breaking unilaterally the concessions that they gained during the 1990s, and of violating the law by freezing the tariffs of the services that they offer. In Chile, the negotiations between Spanish firms and the government over tariff increases led to an escalating verbal dispute in which President Ricardo Lagos accused Spanish firms of disrespecting him ("*querer tomarle el pelo*"), and his finance minister, Nicolás Eyzaguirre, declared that Spanish firms have the country's doors open to leave whenever they want.

These problems reflect a shortcoming in the strategies of Spanish firms, namely, their failure to take into account the impact of their actions on social changes. In a region in flux, with a large proportion of the population living below the poverty line, the investment of foreign firms with profound consequences for the people and the markets in which they operate is bound to cause tensions. In the 1990s increasing popular unrest, rising unemployment, and widening income inequalities intensified upheaval and uncertainty in the region. Therefore, it should not be surprising that according to *Latinobarómetro* most Latin Americans believe the free market reforms of the past decade have done little to improve their living standards, and have lost trust on their political leaders and institutions. According to this survey, only 16% of Latin Americans are fully satisfied with the market economy as a model. This development helps explain the rise of populist politicians in the region, exemplified by the elections of Néstor Kirchner in Argentina and Luiz Ignácio Lula da Silva in Brazil.

Generally speaking, MNEs investing in Latin America (and Spanish ones in particular) have focused on the business side and have not paid sufficient attention to the social and political dimension of their FDIs. Only 22% of the respondents to the *Latinobarometro* survey thought privatizations of public services had benefited their country (compared with 46% in 1998).[7] This, in turn, affected Spain's reputation in the region. Indeed, the experience over the last decade illustrates that the foreign policy of a country is no longer the monopoly of the foreign ministry. Other actors, particularly firms, are also policy agents. The conflicts mentioned above show the need to synchronize the economic policies of Spanish firms with the foreign policy of Spain.

In addition, there is a mismatch between the perception of Spanish products and technology and their objective quality. As we have seen, over the last two decades Spain has become one of Europe's most dynamics economies and investment has transformed the competitiveness and quality of Spanish products. Yet Spanish products are perceived as cheap and of limited quality. To overcome this negative perception will require a concerted effort by the Spanish government and firms to fight these clichés. While Spanish firms have become the country's foremost ambassadors, they have not always behaved diplomatically. The arrogance of some Spanish managers has intensified the negative impression of Spanish FDI as the return of the 'conquistadores' and this has fueled popular anger against Spanish firms. This reputation has been intensified by the predominance of Spanish firms in former state-owned utilities, which makes them an obvious target for social discontent when economic conditions deteriorate. The behavior of the Spanish enterprises, accused of monopolistic practices, the repatriation of high profits and corruption has intensified the negative perception against these companies and has contributed to the strengthening of the "black legend" linked to the reconquest. While the Spanish government has intensified efforts to promote Spanish companies abroad through state institutions like the Institute of Foreign Trade, companies have to invest more to promote their image. This has led to the development of initiatives, such as the project "Brand Spain" to raise the profile of Spanish products and strengthen Spanish brands in the region. This effort will have to be sustained in the long term and it needs to be tailored to specific markets.[8]

Becoming accepted and assimilated by the markets, authorities, customers, and citizens of Latin American countries will be the main challenge for Spanish firms. They have to be viewed not as Spanish enterprises but instead as local companies. This will imply a higher awareness about the importance of perceptions, dialogue, democracy and diversity. Latin America is, once again, at a crossroad. In a region in which many countries, including Ecuador, Venezuela, Argentina, Peru, Bolivia, and Brazil, are flirting with populism and anti market reforms, the challenge will be to advance a new agenda that incorporates solutions to the social and political problems. Otherwise they will bear responsibility for the loss of Latin America.

Although economic prospects in the region seem to have improved (it is estimated that in 2004 it grew between 2-4%), FDI is still in a free fall. According to CEPAL, in 2003 FDI inflows into the region decreased for a fourth year in a row (19% in 2003). In 1999, FDI to Latin American countries reached $88,000 million. By 2003 this figure had decreased to $36,500 million.[9] This decline has been caused in part by the collapse of the Argentinean economy in 2002, and the disputes in the negotiations between firms and governments over tariffs and regulatory frameworks. Increasing competition from other regions, particularly China, has also been a factor (particularly for Mexico). To shift this tendency it will be necessary to address the obstacles to FDI, which include those listed in Figure 3.14.

This list confirms that there are serious concerns on the part of European firms about the Latin American institutional frameworks in which they operate. Inadequate and unstable institutions are central to this list of obstacles. There seems to be consensus on the fact that the weakness of institutions continues to drag down the economies of the Latin American countries. However, while there is extensive literature that has sought to explore the relationship between the quality of institutions and economic growth (North, 1990), a major shortcoming of this literature has been the failure to explain how institutions affect the behavior of economic agents. How do institutions hinder or facilitate firm-level adjustment to international competition? How do they influence the success – or failure – of firms' strategies? Which institutional frameworks should Spanish firms pursue in Latin American countries to enhance their competitiveness and support their strategies in these countries? How did the institutional framework in Spain influence the decision of Spanish firms to invest in Latin America?

Political instability
Local regulation and bureaucracy
Legal judicial insecurity
Corruption
Fear of devaluation
Violence
Problems with repatriation of profits/capital
Level of local taxation
Underdeveloped infrastructure
Labor legislation
Social problems/poverty
Lack of qualified human resources
Local safety, health and environmental standards
Underdeveloped local capital markets
Cultural differences

Figure 3.14   Perceived obstacles to FDI in Latin America by European firms

Source: Dunning, 2001, p.67.

Conclusion: Towards a new theoretical framework. Institutions, FDI, and business competitiveness

Basic factor endowments such as labor, land or capital influence economic and business strategies and condition managerial decisions. Their role has been analyzed by the literature (Porter, 1990; Kotler et al., 1997; Fairbanks, Lindsay and Porter, 1997). Institutional factors also hinder or facilitate the strategies of governments and firms. However, the major focus of the political economy literature has been on cross-national patterns of economic policy and performance (Hall, 1998; Iversen, 1999), and institutional theories have focused on the analysis of organizational change (Powell and Dimaggio, 1991). Institutional economists have explained how institutions and institutional change affect the performance of national economies (North, 1990; Alston, Eggertsson and North, 1996).

At the same time, the field of political economy has been separated from the theoretical work developed in business schools and, although institutional reform has been a focus for policy-makers since the mid-1990s, the study of political structures and practices is still an uncharted territory in many areas. For instance, institutional economists frequently ignore the fact that companies operate and structure their relationships within an institutional framework of incentives and constraints. In fact, a major shortcoming of this literature has been the failure to explain how institutions affect the behavior of economic agents. These theoretical deficiencies are particularly evident when firms try to adapt to a rapidly changing economic environment characterized by low inflation, increasing integration of economies, keen competition and rapid trade liberalization. Indeed, there is a lack of understanding of how institutional settings hinder or facilitate firm-level adjustment to international competition and why they may determine the success or failure of their strategies (Hall and Soskice, 1999). At the aggregate level, the performance of national economies is also determined by institutional arrangements (Milgron and Roberts, 1992).

From a company standpoint, the most important institutions that influence the firms' micro behavior and performance are (Soskice, 1999):

1. *Industrial relations institutions*: i.e. wage determination, collective bargaining, and in-company industrial relations.
2. *Education and training systems*: i.e. vocational training, industry training linkages, research programs, universities-companies linkages.
3. *System of company financing*: i.e. shareholder systems, banking-industry linkages, public financing.
4. *Corporate governance and rules governing inter-company relationships*: i.e. technology transfer, standard setting, competitive policy, corporate accountability and the role of boards, the relationship between corporations and financial markets.

Indeed, different institutional frameworks influence companies´ strategies because they allow for cooperative or uncooperative behavior between them (Hall and Soskice, 1999). For instance, financial systems permit short- or long-term financing of companies; industrial relations systems may allow for cooperative industrial relations within firms and coordinated wage bargaining across companies (or deregulated labor markets that facilitate unilateral control by managers). In addition, the educational and training system may foster training for young people or incremental skill acquisition, in which firms may be closely involved. Lastly, the inter-company system may enable technology and standard setting cooperation among companies (or strong competition).

For example, access to capital is a central challenge to Latin American firms. While the larger Latin American companies have been able to raise money in international markets by issuing depository receipts, small and medium enterprises have had enormous difficulties raising capital in these countries. Indeed, Mexico and Brazil – helped by the strength of its manufacturing exports – have benefited in recent years from strong inflows of capital from US companies relocating southwards. Yet, in these countries small firms still face significant constraints accessing capital. This development has a lot to do with the way that international and domestic capital markets have developed.[10] The expansion of stock markets in Latin American countries in the 1990s has stalled in recent years as a result of uncertain returns, which in turn has provoked less enthusiasm from portfolio investment about these emerging markets and the decline of their local stock markets. This challenge has been compounded by the listing of local subsidiaries in New York and Europe, which has had devastating consequences for local financial markets and has diminished their liquidity. This development was further aggravated by capital market reforms. For instance in Chile, the development of private pension funds, generally restricted from investing abroad, has forced up the price of local assets, thus making them relatively expensive, and further reducing liquidity. These challenges have been compounded by the fiscal restraint of Latin American governments, which has made small and medium enterprises increasingly dependent in local banks that are loath to lend to them, and have left them with no other source of finance. How can Spanish financial institutions in the region address this problem? What kind of institutional framework should they promote?

Institutions set the "rules of the game." They determine the capacity of coordination among businesses and consequently, their competitive advantage in world markets. Also, in an interdependent global economy, institutional structures provide support for particular types of inter- or intra-firm relations, and therefore, the reduction of uncertainty levels while rendering commitments more credible (Hall and Soskice 1999). Since institutions are responsible for establishing standards and setting rules, and also for monitoring, rewarding and/or sanctioning behavior (depending on the case), firms should be able to address coordination failures in order to correct the potential adverse effects of cooperation (Soskice, 1999).

Differences across countries in the quality and configuration of these institutional frameworks contribute to explain disparities in firms' behavior and performance. It is therefore essential to construct a theory of "comparative *institutional* advantage" (Soskice, 1999; Porter, 1990) and apply it to the analysis of developing countries. A research agenda on this subject should pursue four main objectives. First, to review the literature in the institutional field and try to explain the ways in which institutions affect the behavior of economic agents in Latin America. For instance, it would be important to analyze how factors such as vulnerability to takeovers, sensibility of capital investors to profitability, capacity for long-term contracts with employees, and the degree to which networks provide an informal coordination capacity all affect firms' behavior in these countries. Furthermore, since companies are the locus of wealth creation, it becomes crucial to understand how local contexts and institutional settings could enhance their competitiveness and foster markets for ideas, capital, and people (Hamel, 2000).

Moreover, at a time when Spanish firms are investing heavily in Latin American countries, it will be important to examine the impact that different institutional settings have on Spanish business activities and strategies. Thus, a cross-country analysis should help to answer key questions such as: What kind of institutions favor enhanced competitiveness and promote entrepreneurship? How can firms exploit to their advantage the institutional setting in which they are operating? How can multinational firms enhance their competitive position by modifying local institutional configurations? How much change is possible? Can the knowledge and experience accumulated during institutional reforms in industrialized countries be used in developing regions?

Third, the political economy literature has mostly focused on the study of industrialized countries. Southern European and Latin American countries do not easily fit into the categories developed for advanced economies. The institutional frameworks of these countries are substantially different and their impact over the behavior of micro economic actors has to be explained, particularly at a time in which the level of economic integration in these countries has intensified as a result of economic liberalization and foreign investment. Therefore, such a research project should study how the level of economic, political and social development determines the level of institutional development in Latin America and Spain and vice versa. It should also analyze how the institutional settings in these countries impact the behavior and performance of economic actors.

The final objective should be to use the empirical analysis to develop a model of *comparative institutional advantage* that can be useful to enhance firms' competitiveness, and to explore the obstacles that will crop up when a reform aims to transform institutional settings.

In summary, a new research agenda should seek to shed light on how institutional frameworks affect strategies and business performance in Iberoamerica. Such a comprehensive analysis will describe the linkages among institutional factors and facilitate policy-making to increase competitiveness. It will also illustrate the ways in which these countries respond to the pressures of international interdependence and technological change. Finally, the analysis of these institutional factors will provide the instruments and data necessary to develop a comprehensive and systemic framework of analysis of institutional sources of competitiveness in developing countries.

Notes

[1]   This section draws from Royo, 2003, and Royo, 2004.

[2]   See Tovias, 2002.

[3]   Hine, 1989, p. 7.

[4]   For example, EC vehicles imported to Spain paid a custom duty of 27% to 30,4% plus a compensatory tax of 13%. See Couste, 1980, p. 129.

[5]   See Sebastián, 2001.

[6]   Dante Caputo (ed.), El Desarrollo Democrático en América Latina, New York: Programa de Naciones Unidas para el Desarrollo, New Cork, 2003. See also, Joaquín Estefanía, "El Desarrollo de América latina," El País, July 28, 2002.

[7]   See "People in Latin America Lose Faith in Free Market Reforms," Financial Times, November 1st, 2003, p.2.

[8]   See "Spanish Brands Seek More Sparkle," Financial Times, January 6th, 2003.

[9]   This decrease has been the result of the sharp decline of FDI in Mexico and Brazil, which represent the destination of 55% of the funds invested in the region. In 2003,

FDI to Mexico and Brazil fell 30% and 52% respectively. See "La Inversión Extranjera en América Latina Cae por Cuarto Año Consecutivo," *El País*, May 22nd, 2004.
[10] See Richard Lapper, "A Mixed Harvest", *Financial Times*, August 23rd, 2000, p. 12.

References

Albert, M. (1992), *Capitalism Against Capitalism*, Whurr, London.
Alston, L. J., T. Eggertsson and D.C. North (1996), *Empirical Studies in Institutional Change*, Cambridge University Press, New York.
Audretsch, D.B. and S. Klepper (2000), *Innovation, Evolution of Industry and Economic Growth*, Edward Elgar Publishing, Williston.
Benavente, J. and P. West (1992), "Globalización y Convergencia: América Latina frente a un mundo en cambio," *Revista de la CEPAL*, no. 47, Santiago de Chile.
Berger, S. and R. Dore (eds.) (1996), *National Diversity and Global Capitalism*, Cornell University Press, Ithaca.
BID (1993), *Progreso económico y social de América Latina. Informe 1992. Tema especial: Recursos Humanos*, Banco Interamericano de Desarrollo, Washington, D.C.
Boyer, R. and D. Drache (eds.) (1996), *States Against Markets*, Routledge, New York.
Boyer, R. and W. Streeck (eds.) (1997), *The Political Economy of Modern Capitalism*, Sage, London.
Buigues, P., A. Jacquemin and J.F. Marchipont (eds.) (2000), *Competitiveness and the Value of Intangible Assets*, Edward Elgar Publishing, Williston.
Cardoso, E. and A. Helwege (1992), *Latin America's Economy: Diversity, Trends and Conflicts*, MIT Press, Cambridge.
Caves, Richard E. (1996), *Multinational Enterprise and Economic Analysis*, Cambridge University Press, New York.
CEPAL (1990), *Transformación productiva con equidad*, Santiago de Chile.
Chislett, W. (2003), *Spanish Direct Investment in Latin America: Challenges and Opportunities*, Real Instituto Elcano, Madrid.
Coase, R. (1967), "The nature of the firm" in *Economica*, 4, November, pp. 386-405.
Coase, R. (1972), "Industrial Organization: A proposal for research", in *Policy issues and research opportunities in industrial organization*, V.R. Fuchs (ed.), pp. 59-73.
Dosi, G. (2000) *Innovation, Organization and Economic Dynamics*, Edward Elgar Publishing, Williston.
Dunning. J.H. (1993), *Multinational Enterprises and the Global Economy*, Addison-Wesley, Boston.
Dunning, J.H. (2001), "European Foreign Direct Investment in Latin America," in Z. Vodusek (ed.), *Foreign Direct Investment in Latin America: The Role of European Investors*, Inter-American Bank, pp. 43-85.
Dunning, J.H. and R. Narula (1994), "Transpacific Foreign Direct Investment and the Investment Development Path: the Record Assessed", *South Carolina Essays in International Business,* 10, May 1994.
Durán, J.J. (1995), "Factores de Competitividad en los Procesos de Internacionalización de la Empresa," *ICE*, 735, 1995.
Edquist, C. and M. Mckelvey (eds.) (2000), *Systems of Innovation. Growth, Competitiveness and Employment*, Edward Elgar Publishing, Williston.
Eichengreen, B. (1997), "Institutions and Economic Growth after World War II," in N. Craft and G. Toniolo (eds.), *Economic Growth in Europe Since 1945*, pp. 38-65.

Fairbanks, M., S. Lindsay and M.E. Porter (1997), *Plowing the Sea: Nurturing the Hidden Sources of Growth in the Developing World*, Harvard Business School Press, Cambridge.

French-Davis, R. (2000), *Reforming the Reforms in Latin America: Macroeconomics, Trade, Finance*, St. Martin's Press, New York.

Franko, P. (1999), *The Puzzle of Latin American Economic Development*, Rowman & Littlefield, New York.

Freeman, C. (1995), "The National System of Innovation in Historical Perspective". *Cambridge Journal of Economics*, 19: pp. 5-24.

Gereffi, G. and D.L. Wyman (1990), *Manufacturing Miracles: Paths of Industrialization in Latin America and East Asia*, Princeton University Press, Princeton.

Goldthorpe, J.A. (ed.) (1984), *Order and Conflict in Contemporary Capitalism*, Oxford University Press, New York.

Guillen, M.F. (1994), *Models of Management*, The University of Chicago Press, Chicago.

Gwyne, R.N. and C. Kay (1999), *Latin America Transformed: Globalization and Modernity*, Oxford University Press, New York.

Hall, P.A. (1999), "The Political Economy of Europe in an Era of Interdependence," in H. Kitschelt et al., (eds), *Change and Continuity in Contemporary Capitalism*.

Hall, P.A. and D. Soskice (eds.) (2001), *Varieties of Capitalism: The Institutional Foundations of Comparative Advantage*, Oxford University Press, Oxford.

Hamel, G. (2000), *Leading the Revolution*, Harvard Business School Press, Cambridge.

Hamel, G. and C.K. Prahalad (1996), *Competing for the Future*, Harvard Business School Press, Cambridge.

Hollingsworth, J.R. and R. Boyer (eds.) (1997), *Contemporary Capitalism: the Embededdness of Institutions*, Cambridge University Press, New York.

IDB (1996), *Economic and Social Progress in Latin America. 1996 Report. Special Section: Making Social Services Work*, Inter-American Development Bank, Washington, D.C.

Iversen, T. (1999), *Contested Economic Institutions*, Cambridge University Press, New York.

Katz, J.M. (1993a), "Falla del mercado y política tecnológica," *Revista de la CEPAL*, 50.

Katz, J.M. (1993b), *Organización industrial, competitividad internacional y política pública. En El Desafío de la Competitividad. La industria Argentina en transformación*, CEPAL/Alianza Editorial, Buenos Aires.

Keasey, K., S. Thompson and M. Wright (eds.) (1999), *Corporate Governance*, Edward Elgar Publishing, Willisnton.

Keohane, R.O. and H.V. Milner (eds.) (1996), *Internationalization and Domestic Politics*, Cambridge University Press, New York.

Kitschelt, H., P. Lange, G. Marks and J. Stephens (eds.) (1999), *Change and Continuity in Contemporary Capitalism*, Cambridge University Press, New York.

Kotler, P., S. Jatusripitak, S. Maesincee and S. Jatusri (eds.) (1997), *The Marketing of Nations: A Strategic Approach to Building National Wealth*, Free Press, New York.

Kuwayama, M. (1992), "América Latina y la internacionalización de la economía mundial", *Revista de la CEPAL*, 46.

Marting, B.R. and P. Nightingale (2000), *The Political Economy of Science, Technology and Innovation*, Edward Elgar Publishing, Williston.

Milgrom, P. and J. Roberts (1990), "The Economics of Modern Manufacturing Technology, Strategy and Organization," *American economic Review*, 80, pp. 511-528.

Milgrom, P. and J. Roberts (1992), *Economics, Organization and Management*, Prentice Hall, New York.

Milgrom, P. and J. Roberts (1995), "Complementarities and Fit: Strategy, Structure, and Organizational Change in Manufacturing", *Journal of Money, Credit and Banking*, vol 19, pp.179-208.

North, D.C. (1990), *Institutions, Institutional Change and Economic Performance*, Cambridge University Press, New York.

O'Donnell, G. (1988), "Introduction to the Latin American Cases" in G. O'Donnell, P. Schmitter and L. Whitehead (eds.), *Transitions from Authoritarian Rule: Latin America*, Johns Hopkins University Press, Baltimore, pp. 3-19.

O'Donnell, G., P. Schmitter and L. Whitehead (eds.) (1988), *Transitions from Authoritarian Rule: Latin America*, Johns Hopkins University Press, Baltimore.

Pérez, S. (1997), *Banking on Privilege*, Cornell University Press, Ithaca.

Porter, M. (1990), *The Competitive Advantage of Nations*, The Free Press, New York.

Powell, W.W. and P.J. Dimaggio (1991), *The New Institutionalism in Organizational Analysis*, Chicago University Press, Chicago.

Royo, S. (2003), "The 2004 Enlargement: Iberian Lessons for Post-Communist Europe," in *South European Society & Politics*, Summer/Autumn, vol. 8, no. 1-2, pp. 287-313.

Royo, S. (2004a), "From Authoritarianism to the European Union: The Europeanization of Portugal", *Mediterranean Quarterly*, vol. 15, no. 3, pp. 95-129.

Royo, S. (2004b), "Entre Libre Comercio y Objetivos Sociales: La Integración Regional en la Península Ibérica y México," in J. Roy, A. Chanona and R. Domínguez (eds.), *La Unión Europea y el TLCAN: Integración Regional Comparada y Relaciones Mutuas*, pp. 523-545.

Royo, S. and P.C. Manuel (2003a), "Some Lessons from the Fifteenth Anniversary of the Accession of Portugal and Spain to the European Union," *South European Society & Politics*, Summer/Autumn, vol. 8, no. 1-2.

Royo, S. and P.C. Manuel (eds.) (2003b), *Spain and Portugal in the European Union: The First Fifteen Years*, Frank Cass, London, pp. 1-30.

Ruiz, J.J. (2004), "Latin America's Seven Mortal Sins: Myth, Reality, and Consequences", Working Paper from Real Instituto Elcano, June.

Sabel, C.F. (1995), "Learning by Monitoring: The Institutions of Economic development," in N. Smelser and R. Swedberg (eds.) *Handbook of Economic Sociology*, pp. 137-165.

Sebastián, M. (2001), "Spain in the EU: Fifteen Years May not be Enough", paper presented at the conference *From Isolation to Europe: 15 Years of Spanish and Portuguese Membership in the European Union*, Minda de Gunzburg Center for European Studies, Harvard University, November 2-3.

Shonfiled, D. (1965), *Modern Capitalism*, Oxford University Press, New York.

Soskice, D. (1990a), "Wage Determination: the Changing Role of Institutions in Advanced Industrialized Countries," in *Oxford Review of Economic Policy* 6, 4, pp. 36-61.

Soskice, D. (1990b), "Reinterpreting Corporatism and Explaining Unemployment: Coordinated and Non-coordinated Market Economies," in R. Brunetta and C. Dell'Aringa (eds.) *Labour Relations and Economic Performance*, Macmillan, London, pp. 170-214.

Soskice, D. (1991), "The Institutional Infrastructure for International Competitiveness: A Comparative Analysis of the U.K. and Germany," in A.B. Atkinson and R. Brunetta, (eds.), *The Economics of the New Europe*, pp. 45-66.

Soskice, D. (1999), "Divergent Production Regimes: Coordinated and Uncoordinated Market Economies in the 1990s," in H. Kitschelt, P. Lange, G. Marks and J. Stephens (eds.) *Change and Continuity in Contemporary Capitalism*, pp. 101-134.

Stephan, P.E. and D.B. Audretsch (2000), *The Economics of Science and Innovation*, Edward Elgar Publishing, Williston.

Streeck, W. (1992), *Social Institutions and Economic Performance*, Sage, Beverly Hills.

Tavares, M.C. and Fiori J.L. (1993), *Ajuste Global e Modernizaçâo Conservadora*, Editorial Paz e Terra, Río do Janeiro.

Thelen, K. (1995), "Beyond Corporatism: Toward a New Framework for the Study of Labor in Advanced Capitalism", *Comparative Politics*, vol 27(1), pp.107-124.

Toral, P. (2001), *The Reconquest of the New World: Multinational Enterprises and Spain's Direct Investment in Latin America*, Ashgate, Aldershot.

Vogel, S. (1996), *Freer Markets, More Rules*, Cornell University Press, Ithaca.

Williamson, O. (1975), *Markets and Hierarchies*, Free Press, New York.

Wynia, G.W. (1990), *The Politics of Latin American Development*, Cambridge University Press, New York.

Zysman, J. (1983), *Governments, Markets and Growth*, Cornell University Press, Ithaca.

Zysman, J. (1996), "How Institutions Create Historically-Rooted Trajectories of Growth," in *Industrial and Corporate Change*, vol. 3, no. 1, pp. 243-283.

Chapter 4

Spanish Foreign Policy in Latin America

Javier Maestro

Introduction

Spanish foreign policy and Spanish FDI in Latin America were very closely related in the 1980s, but not so much thereafter. The reason is that many Spanish firms that made FDIs in the 1980s and early 1990s in Latin America were partially or totally state-owned monopolies, as Telefónica or Iberia.[1] In the 1990s these firms were gradually privatized and thus their link to the state was weakened. This is also a reason why high-ranking officials in the Spanish Foreign Ministry underlined in 2005 that a clear difference should be outlined between Spanish foreign policy guidelines and the decisions taken by privately-owned Spanish firms operating in Latin America, even if the foreign policy agenda aims to nourish and promote Spanish interests abroad through bilateral and multilateral agreements. Before providing a detailed analysis of Spanish foreign policy in Latin America, I will discuss the economic and political context in which it took place.

Globalization and regionalism have acquired a new dimension and profile since the end of the Cold War. The impetus provided by the World Bank, the International Monetary Fund and the GATT/WTO to implement free-market reforms have spread liberalization worldwide. The new neoliberal paradigm subsequently set aside the previous economic strategy based on import substitution industrialization (ISI) – vigorously recommended by ECLAC, as sketched since the 1930s – based on structuralism and dependency theory.

The implementation of these new market-led prerequisites exacted in the late 1980s and early 1990s far-reaching economic reforms in most countries, was called structural adjustment programs (SAPs). If duly accomplished, predictions stated that a competitive worldwide free-market system would in the long run (and in the best possible way) enable all nations to meet the challenges of globalization. Due above all to the effects of the new communication technologies, facilitating capital movements and allocation, the general, very accurate perception, was that both space and time were undergoing unprecedented deep changes in the context of the globalized world economy.

The world's financial and monetary institutions envisaged liberalization as applicable to all countries, although developing countries – by then heavily indebted, especially in Latin America – had to endure the worst scenario. Indeed the need to alleviate the upcoming social negative impact that reforms had in many cases needed to be tackled simultaneously as they were all too visible. This was true in unemployment indices, growing uneven distribution of income, erosion of social provisions, gender inequality, and persistent extreme poverty (BID, 1998: 1-9). The new economic paradigm was often postponed because of political and social constraints. However, Latin American governments gradually endorsed liberalization policies as a necessary and unavoidable worldwide trend, and as the best possible way to solve persistent indebtedness, legitimized by the "lack of an alternative" argument. Thereafter, and all too often, the liberalization process was not followed by the required institutional reforms aimed at gradually guaranteeing transparency. Privatizations were not sufficiently shielded from malpractices.

The new economic policy, which came with a political transition towards democracy, favored rapid export growth, privatizations, and reductions in government spending, paralleled by growing extra- and intra-regional trade as well as by capital inflows from firms and banks. Nevertheless, evidence proved that an increasing asymmetry still prevails between the core and the periphery (CEPAL, 2001: 14), because, as new-dependency theory supporters claim, "within the peripheral or dependant countries a few have succeeded in achieving remarkable and consistent high rates of economic growth over the past three or four decades, as well as improvements in equity. By 1978, per capita income in core countries of the world economy was five times that of the highest income economies and 12 times that of the lowest income economies of Latin America. By 1995, however, the ratio had increased to almost 7 and 30 times respectively" (Gwynne and Kay, 1999: 5).

In terms of regional distribution of aggregate long-term net resource flows, Latin America received in the 1980s and 1990s comparatively the highest amount of international resources channeled to developing countries (LDCs). In 1999 Latin America attracted 36.88% of the flows, followed by 30.36% to Far East Asia and the Pacific, 15.5% to Eastern Europe and Central Asia, 6.84% to the MENA countries, and 6.02% to Sub-Saharan Africa. The developed countries – the tri-polar bloc – stood for 85% of FDI outflows and were also host to 60% of these inflows.

Spain had accomplished a modernization/liberalization pattern that by the early 1990s provided the country with one of the world's most open economies. Significant FDI flows[2] and EU Structural and Cohesion Funds as well as the entry of significant MNEs fuelled the Spanish economy in the 1990s, re-structuring the production system through widespread privatizations, takeovers, and mergers made Spanish firms competitive enough before the European Single Market and Monetary Union were established in the late 1990s. By 2001 Spain managed to rank eighth in the world in terms of GDP, twenty-sixth in GDP per capita, and the seventh as a source of FDI outflows (5.67% of world's total, three times higher than Spain's nearly 2% of world trade share). All this implies that within a forty-year period Spain's GDP increased fourteen times, most notably during the 1980s and 1990s. This remarkable development made Spain much a model to be followed in Latin America.[3]

Most countries in Latin America went through a similar process of modernization and liberalization in the 1990s. Accordingly, Argentina and Chile became by the end of the 1990s the advanced free-market scenario, while the rest followed at different rhythms and with varying outcomes. By then, FDI in Latin America was much demanded, as it became a precondition to accomplish the reforms. Spanish MNEs took the risk (Toral, 2001: 173; Alonso and Cadarso, 1982), while previously hegemonic US firms adopted a much more cautious standpoint especially having in mind the prior negative experiences they had had during the debt crisis of the 1980s. This is also the main reason – though there are many other reasons – why Spanish MNEs became the second main sources of FDI, after US firms, in Latin America, especially within Mercosur, where Spanish MNEs acquired a leading position. Another reason was that Spain shared with Latin America in the 1980s, the hardships of the debt crisis and became the first country interested in finding and later endorsing developmental solutions. This attitude favored a friendly relationship (Spanish Foreign Ministry, 2000: 3). Another strong argument holds to the rationale of comparative advantages: Spanish firms were neither sufficiently modernized nor technologically suited to compete in the European single market – except in Portugal, as was the case – or in rather alien markets for Spanish firms. The cultural affinity with the Latin American market became the unique opportunity for Spanish firms to expand in time and thereby develop a global competitive dimension (Barcela, 2002).

Subsequently a flow of optimism – making virtue of necessity – channeled the bulk of Spanish FDI flows in the 1990s towards Latin American countries, especially in the 1996–2000 year period. The risky situation turned out to be a fabulous success story of profit-making in economies that provided a decade of promising economic growth rates. Many regarded the Spanish FDIS as a "Spanish reconquest of Latin America." But since the international financial crisis began striking Southeast Asia and Russia in 1998 and Latin America in 1999, enthusiasm increasingly turned into pessimism amidst the troubled waters of the worldwide economic slowdown. Disinvestment and possible drawbacks were therefore visible (a 38% drop of Spanish FDI to Latin America in 2000 as compared to 1999),[4] although a wait-and-see policy prevailed for the time being. Steady declines occurred until mid-2003 – with Latin America as the worst performer of all world regions, particularly Argentina and Brazil. – Most economic indicators were reversed in 2004, although, comparatively, the average inflows of FDI were small. FDI inflows to South America fell from $27 billion in 2002 to $21 billion in 2003, and Latin America's FDI share among developing countries declined from 27% to 11%. FDI inflows in 2004 were expected to reach $35 billion after a four-year steady decline. However, in the coming years, global FDI flows to developing countries will mainly be allocated in Asia and Central and Eastern Europe, "with a dampening effect on investor confidence levels in South America, basically because the region's inequality undermines competitiveness and limits FDI potential"[5] (43% of the region's population still lives in poverty). Globalization shows thus how national economies are interdependent more than ever before.

Current FDI in Latin America lacks the appeal of the 1990s when most of these countries accomplished widespread economic reforms together with the world's highest privatization rate[6] of strategic economic sectors such as infrastructure, banking, services, telecommunications, aviation, and energy while leaving aside the previous state-led ISI developmental patterns. Notwithstanding the present challenging economic situation, these countries are obliged in the future to ensure economic growth in order to avoid debt overhang, political instability, and social unrest. How to solve this problem remains unpredictable since conventional wisdom that relates export growth and FDI with automatic commensurate income gains does not seem to apply for the time being.[7] In fact, LDCs trade more but gain less. Probably, the rationale of comparative advantages in conjunction with risk-appraisals will have the last word. As an illustrative sample, Spanish foreign policy guidelines are promoting FDI in other areas such as Asia and the Pacific, mainly considering the growth potential of China after joining the WTO in 2001. Indeed Spanish internationalized firms can no longer remain solely present in Latin America as world competitiveness is basically cradled in SE Asia, China and India.

However, UNCTAD reported that FDI flows in 2001 were less than half of the figure in 2000. The FDI turndown affected the developed countries (-59%) and less significantly in LDCs (-14%). In Latin America, FDI inflows dropped 50%. While FDI inflows (2000/2001) in Argentina decreased dramatically from roughly $11 billion to $3 billion and less intensely in Brazil and Venezuela, inflows to Bolivia, Colombia, and Uruguay remained fairly unchanged, and inflows to Peru, Chile, Ecuador, and Paraguay roughly doubled in volume.

Politics have likewise changed both in Europe and Latin America. Spain's foreign policy since 1986 complies to a large extent with the EU's external policy, framed primarily by means of intergovernmental decisions. Still each country within the EU develops its own foreign policy strategies and priorities as long as these are congruent with the EU's general foreign policy guidelines. This means that EU member states behold considerable leeway when outlining their foreign policy as long as the EU is still enmeshed with weak common foreign policy rulings (Morata, 2000). When Portugal and Spain became EU full-members in 1986, both countries – as well as France and Italy – managed to lobby hard to redirect the EC's attention towards Latin America (Grugel, 1995: 191-198, 205). Until then the European Union had kept to the margins in the EC's external relations. A long-standing cultural and historical affinity with all Latin America was voiced by Portugal and Spain as an opportunity for the EC/EU to broaden its sphere of influence. Political and economic interests interplayed, especially the much demanded democratization of Latin American political life as it was believed to go hand in hand with economic liberalization, though some authors remark that evidence in that sense is at best contradictory.

The successive Spanish governments (1982-1996) headed by Felipe González – also leader of the Socialist International, by then influential in Latin America –

established a solid alliance with Germany and France inside the EU (Barbé, 1999). And, as a result, both an Euro-Mediterranean partnership and closer relations with Latin America were agreed on and put into practice. Spain courted most Latin American countries purporting itself as a paradigm of peaceful and successful transition from dictatorship to democracy and from state protectionism to economic modernization and liberalization. The similarities between Spain and Latin America enhanced the idea of an Ibero-American Community as a way to reinvigorate mutual "special relations" (Morán, 1980: 398)[8] or, as Benny Pollack (Pollack, 1987: 81) puts it:

> Spanish Latin American policies have of course been influenced by what could be called the post-colonial syndrome. Spain owes a special allegiance to the former colonies, and vice versa. Their common culture, religion, and shared historical development for several centuries make it natural for a "special relationship" to exist, irrespective of particular junctures at any given time, such as changing political circumstances, diverse development levels, or relative importance as national states.

The transition of many Latin American countries towards democratic governance in the 1980s and 1990s improved cooperation as Spanish and EU development programs were conditioned to the democratic clause. The EU became in the late 1990s a leading cooperation and trading partner with Mercosur and an influential actor in the rest of Latin America. At present, the European Union's trading policies compete with the United States in the Western hemisphere especially regarding the shape of free-trade blocs (Casilda and Stotelsek, 2001).

Spain expanded vigorously its foreign policy relations with Latin America, creating new overtures for enhanced overall cooperation. The Ibero-American Summit meetings, beginning in 1991, acted as an important policy coordinating springboard to this end (Arenal, 2000). In 1992, the 500th Anniversary of America's discovery was commemorated as the Encounter of Two Worlds followed by the second Ibero-American Summit. Both events reinforced Spanish-Latin American relations, but domestic events diverted Spain's attention in the years ahead from the American hemisphere. The economic recession of 1993-1994 that hit dramatically Spain's economy at a time when the government was trying in vain to clear its way through a storm of political scandals led eventually to new elections in 1996 and the appointment of a new conservative-liberal government. In spite of this, huge FDI inflows pumped the Spanish economy back into shape by 1995. Between 1996 and 2000, Latin America witnessed an avalanche of unprecedented Spanish FDI inflows, later metaphorically described as the arrival of the "new Conquistadores," the "new Spanish Armada", and similar expressions drawn from historical experiences.

The world crisis that began in the spring of 2000 and deepened as a result of the attacks of September 11 brought the battle against world terrorism to the forefront. As a result, common security issues acquired undeniable prominence, at times at the expense of developmental concerns. FDI flows and most economic indicators fell. Latin America's developmental perspectives have consequently been heavily affected (Marín, 2002: 91-92; and Medina, 2002: 65). This coincided also with the decision of Aznar's government to prioritize a closer alliance with the Bush administration to focus on the struggle against world terrorism after September the eleventh 2001. Such a decision jeopardized Spain's relations with both the core EU countries, the Arab world and Latin America, most of which were skeptical about, if not outright opposed to, Bush's doctrine of unilateralism and preemptive strike. The elections held in Spain immediately after the terrorist attacks of the March 11, 2004, in Madrid resulted in a Socialist government, the withdrawal of Spanish troops from Iraq and a stronger alliance with the leading EU and Latin American countries[9].

Spanish foreign policy has over time remained rather unchanged. The priorities revolve around Spain's geographic and cultural neighborhoods and/or influence areas, that is, Mediterranean Europe, North Africa, and Latin America. A special relationship has developed with the US since the outset of the Cold War period. The order and intensity of these priorities have been subject to changes in conjunction with the altering world order. EU-membership has nevertheless strengthened Spain's "Europeanness", simultaneously tilting it towards Atlanticism or Continentalism, or rather a changing blend of the two.

Spanish foreign policy in Latin America until 1975

Spanish foreign policy towards Latin America can be characterized as discontinuous in time. During most of the 19th century, starting with the collapse of the Spanish American Empire in 1821, the relationship with the new Latin American republics was not a priority. Sixty years of indifference and detachment lapsed before they were recognized by Spain as independent republics (Carr, 1966: 145-146). Decision-making to that end dragged from 1836-1894 as recognition was based on a country-by-country basis.

What remained was a relationship based on common kinship, pulled by two opposite driving forces. Spain and its colonies Cuba, Puerto Rico and the Philippines were, on the one hand, regarded by Latin American republican governments with suspicion, as an oppressive empire ready to re-conquer its former status (Filippi, 1986: 99-148). Spain, on the other hand, even if full of imperial nostalgia, was pushed to the margins by the prevailing world powers in the international system, remaining through most of the 20th century as a second rate power, practically removed from world politics. In 1898 the outcome of the Spanish-American War meant total defeat and the loss of Spain's colonial empire in America. This came to be known in Spain as *El Desastre* (the Disaster) and discredited the country's international prestige, making Spain more inward-looking than ever before. It also meant a loss of 20-30% of the country's total foreign transactions. A closer analysis provides nonetheless some promising new departures as a result of 1898, notably: massive repatriation of capital assets in conjunction with a renewal of FDI in Spain, consolidation of an articulated national economy and the emergence of mixed banking and corporate industries (García, 1999). According to Raymond Carr, "in financing hydro-electric schemes, public utilities, and private industry, the large banks began the process of 'nationalization' – in the sense of establishing Spanish as against foreign financial control – which was to be such a feature of the economy after 1940 (..) Bank finance drove on a process of industrial and financial concentration which, as might be expected, was particularly marked in the production of the raw materials of industry: coal, iron and electricity" (Carr, 1966: 412). Protectionism gained adherents and from 1891 the economic triangle Bilbao-Barcelona-Valladolid determined economic decisions. As a result thereof, tariffs moved increasingly upwards until Spain in 1906 reached the highest tariff walls within a protectionist Europe. Peculiar to Spain was the intensity with which self-sufficiency was pursued in a still predominantly agricultural society relying on weak peripheral industrialization. The insignificance of Spain's foreign trade worked in favor of nourishing a protected domestic market until the 1960s.

Spain experienced a longstanding international isolation in relative disconnection with former Spanish America, mainly due to unsolved Spanish domestic matters related to democratization and industrialization. This resilient isolation produced mutual resentfulness, a sort of hate/love relationship. Nevertheless during the first decades of the 20th century domestic reflections on the maladies of the "Disaster of 1898" and the way they were later applied in terms of policy "regeneration", alongside a continuous flow of Spanish immigrants to Latin America between 1875-1960, spurred reconciliation, trade and increased cultural bonds. The Spanish Civil War was echoed deeply in Latin America and was reinforced by the diaspora of Spanish republican exiles. Notwithstanding this, Spanish influence in Latin America was decreasing during the Civil War years as most Latin American countries found Roosevelt's enlightened international cooperation a departure from previous American interference and intervention, creating thus hopes of progress, social justice and modernization. Spain was in consequence pushed aside by the US in the American hemisphere until the late 1950s. The outcome of the Spanish Civil War also affected how the still hollowed liberal idea of "Hispanism" – in competition with US "Pan-Americanism" and French/Italian "Latin-Americanism" – should be understood. For Francisco Franco's Spain "Hispanism" had primarily the utilitarian self-interest value to counteract the regime's utter initial international isolation, by generating brotherhood and solidarity from the Latin American countries.

In addition, the idea was ideologically in tune with the "imperial" aspirations of the Falange, the influential fascist party that initially enjoyed ideological supremacy and political exclusiveness within the dictatorship, though the party – later coined "movement" – lost gradually momentum and tempo in the following decades. This kind of "Hispanism" was outright reactionary in the sense that it cultivated Spanish "essentialism" as equivalent to Imperial Spain and simplified *ad absurdum* the country's historical decadence making the Enlightenment and Liberalism the main culprits. Such a message, mostly wrapped in ideological rhetoric, claimed nothing less than a chauvinistic messianic restoration of Imperial

Spain with catholic and racial overtones. To that end the Council of Hispanity, linked to the Foreign Ministry as a consulting agency, began operating in 1940 on behalf of the regime and the Axis powers as an influential propaganda agency (Arenal, 1994: 34-37) to secure a sphere of influence in Latin America. In 1945, the institution was re-labeled Institute of Hispanic Culture, focusing mainly on the idea of a Hispanic Brotherhood Community in spiritual and cultural terms, while dropping former "anti-yankeeism" and expressions such as "Hispanic race", "imperial Spain" and the like, nothing less than an accommodation to the outcome of the Second World War. Even if Franco's regime declared its neutrality during the war, the Allied intervention in Spain to re-establish democracy remained a looming threat. To make things worse, most Latin American countries backed Mexico's proposition at the UN's General Assembly in 1946 to reject Spain's UN membership and later that year the recommendation to recall ambassadors in Spain. The great exception to the rule was Juan Perón's Argentina that provided Spain food and money between 1947 and 1949, an Argentinean-styled Marshall Plan for a poor and isolated country with economic annual growth rates that hardly surpassed 1%, insufficient to ensure bare domestic reconstruction. But this Spanish-Argentinean honeymoon came to a halt in 1949. It was also an exception to the "subdued neutrality" rule that framed Spanish Latin American policies before and some years after Franco.

However, the Cold War and Franco's staunch anti-communism eventually reconciled his regime with the United States and with most Latin American countries by 1950. Ambassadors returned gradually to Madrid and, in 1953, the United States signed military pacts with Franco's Spain followed by an estimated military and economic aid amounting to more than a billion dollars between 1953 and 1963. Franco became internationally legitimized as a Western ally and everything returned almost to normalcy after Spain's admission to the UN in 1955, IMF and WB in 1958 and OECD a year later.

Hispanism was after 1957 reframed with a nationalist-technocratic ethos in line with the recent technocratic government reshuffle and was provided with a more practical outlook at a point when Spain recovered economic indicators prior to the Civil War – with average high economic growth rates of 5% (1949-1959) – within a framework for slowly deregulating autarchy (González, 1999: 652).[10] The resulting effects were rather meager: double nationality status could be applied by Latin Americans, cultural and economic relations were enhanced, though crippled by a changing political situation in Latin America from the late 1950s onwards that ousted the previously authoritarian rulers, either following the Cuban revolutionary pattern or through an always entangled democratization process in a sub-region where oligarchic rule, usually plastered into populism amidst a widely de-politicized population, hardly ever fainted (Silva, 1999).

The prevailing disparate ideologies and political regimes in Latin America deideologized Franco's Spanish foreign policy towards Latin America, at times searching autonomy *vis-à-vis* US policy in the region as was the case, amongst others, with Cuba and Chile. Moreover, the Hispanity ideal of a Hispanic Commonwealth of Nations was temporarily set aside as a priority as Spain's application for membership to the European Economic Community became an obsessive goal. However, the ideal of Hispanity was never relinquished, it was thought to crystallize later through a proposed – and never seriously considered – Ibero-American Common Market. This was probably the most ambitious project to materialize the idea of making Spain act as a bridgehead between Europe and Latin America. Meanwhile negotiations with EEC and NATO dragged from the early 1960's eventually resulting in a Preferential Trade Agreement with EEC in 1970 – re-negotiated in 1973 along with EEC's enlargement from six to nine member-states – while membership to EEC and NATO were denied on democratic grounds.

Trade with Latin America developed significantly (Tamames, 1968: 38) in the 1960s (17% of total Spanish exports in 1966) as a result of Spain's dynamic economic development (7% GDP average annual growth between 1961 and 1974 (García, 1987: 180), while FDI inflows in Spain bounced remarkably from $16 million in 1959 to $335 in 1973, of which a gross 50% were of US origin), but no planned overseas trade policy was implemented. It was mostly improvised, leading to trade deficits. Spanish FDI in Latin America increased likewise vigorously during the 1960's amounting to 28.4% of total $247 million Spanish FDI (Fernández, 1972: 152), and the Inter-American Development Bank received $20 million as Spain's contribution to Latin American development. Spanish officials visited also all the more frequently different Latin American countries and Spain applied for the status of member or observer to the different regional organizations (OAS, Andean Community, IDB, etc,) as a way of being more actively involved in the regional integration patterns. But Spain's preferential agreements with the EEC and the oil crisis that erupted in 1973 acted as a backlash that led to diminished trade transactions with Latin America (Ruiz, 1976; Erice, 1978). The conflict-ridden final years of Franco's regime that brought international isolation, foreign policy stalemate and queries about post-Franco Spain also affected economic indicators negatively. In spite of this, between 1974 and 1979 50% of total Spanish FDI outflows – still comparatively low- went to Latin America.

Spanish society changed deeply in the 1960s and 1970s to the extent that the political regime could no longer muster the all too obvious domestic contradictions that authoritarianism set off in its opposition to the demands of the emerging civil society – mostly a silent majority – that increasingly pled for modernization and democratization, emulating Western Europe (the GDP per capita differential with Western Europe was roughly 60/100). The opposition became very strong, so that the transition towards democracy was ultimately a question of connecting civil society with the widespread opposition. All other political bridges lay shattered except the role of the hesitant armed forces wherein the civil war syndrome still acted vividly. Franco died in 1975 and with him the plans to perpetuate Francoism.

Spanish Latin American policy in the transition period (1975-1982)

During Francoism the acknowledged expertise of the Spanish foreign civil service was awarded considerable autonomy as the center of foreign policy design formulation and implementation. It was probably the most 'open' sphere, reflecting another contradiction: the divorce between internal and external policy-making. Consequently, though domestic politics underwent crucial changes towards democracy, the foreign policy guidelines and structure remained in these years rather unchanged even if subject to debate and stricter accountability to parliament, the media, public opinion and pressure groups, circumvented though by the aloofness of Spanish public opinion in foreign policy matters and the often sensitive nature of international relations. Nonetheless the demands for an increased multilateral policy were to force in the coming years important organizational changes in the Spanish Foreign Service, enhancing inter-ministerial cooperation and intra-ministerial team work in foreign affairs spurring economic and informal diplomacy as well as building up new agencies in charge of development aid and cooperation.

Moreover, the transition period towards democracy exacted, more than in any other policy sphere, consensus, keeping in mind the different appraisals the parliamentary multi-party system nourished about the bi-polar world structure as related to Spain's national interests. By then Spain no longer had colonies – Morocco achieved independence in 1961, Equatorial Guinea in 1968, Sidi Ifni was transferred to Morocco in 1969 and Sahara was left alone in 1976 subject to a still embattled self-determination procedure under Morocco's protectorate – excepting the two North African enclaves of Ceuta and Melilla, claimed by Morocco, especially in recent times. Gibraltar and the future of US military bases in Spain – since 1970 under co-ownership – were the remaining main contentious issues that affected Spanish national sovereignty.

Spanish pro-Arabism still included the non-recognition of Israel (accomplished in 1986), while the detente period of the 1970s led to the establishment of diplomatic relations with China and East Germany in 1972 and consular relations with the USSR and the East European countries. Diplomatic relations with Mexico and the USSR were re-established later in 1977 as well as with the rest of the Eastern European countries. In other words, Spanish foreign policy managed to broaden significantly during these years the scope of its bilateral diplomatic relations, very much as they remain today.

Further attachment to the Western global defense and security system came about in 1976 when the Spanish-American military pact was re-negotiated, this time as a treaty, linking Spain closer to NATO-membership. Spain received thereafter a billion dollar loan during King Juan Carlos official visit to the United States in June 1976, signaling US support to Spain's democratic transition. Simultaneously official applications were forwarded for full-membership status to the EC, Council of Europe and NATO. A high priority issue then was to fix democratic Spain's new global foreign policy. The goal was to adopt new coordinates and give them relative continuity in a bi-polar context. These coordinates dismissed neutralism and incorporated democratic credentials. The implications were the end of isolationism, recovered international prestige and recognition as well as the Westernization and 'Europeanization' of Spain's foreign policy.

This new foreign policy consensus prevailed as far as membership to the European Community and the Council of Europe was concerned, but not as regards to NATO. However, Spain became a member of NATO in 1982, a decision taken by a weak minority government that soon after had to resign and call for elections. The Spanish Socialist Party won a landslide election in 1982 and froze NATO membership on constitutional grounds – as the party promised to do in its electoral program – until a referendum was held in 1986. The issue polarized the electorate, but the people ratified NATO membership under special conditions, soon later dropped off. Negotiations for EC membership became more cumbersome, complex and time-consuming than expected (1977-1985), but in 1986 Spain, together with Portugal, attained full membership status (Jones, 2000). Further economic modernization ensued in the years following Spain's ascension.

Meanwhile relations with Latin America in the 1973-1977 period amounted to little more than reassuring visits of good will in 1976 by King Juan Carlos and Prime Minister Adolfo Suárez. Both carried the message of Spain's vigorous support for democracy, progress, social justice and human rights in Latin America. Active developmental cooperation and the idea of a Latin American Community of Nations were advanced as one of the future major Spanish foreign policy aims. This new approach to Latin America was no doubt a significant departure from a previous hollow non-ideological policy. But the implementation of this new Atlantic approach was hardly operational as long as the Spanish economy was affected by an increasing public debt, high inflation rates and foreign and domestic disinvestment in connection with domestic political uncertainties and social unrest. This state of affairs was reversed in 1977 once general macroeconomic agreements were reached between all the social agents and the government through the so-called "Moncloa Deal".

Spain's difficult transition to democracy and weakened economic position were not the only reasons for improved Spanish-Latin American relations. Argentina, Uruguay and Chile were obviously not responsive to Spain's emphasis on democratization and human rights. Hence most Spanish political overtures were by exclusion mainly directed to Mexico, Central America and the Andean Community (Peru, Bolivia, Ecuador, Colombia and Venezuela). These countries, plus Costa Rica and the Dominican Republic, endorsed in 1979 the Caracas Declaration and, some months later, the Quito Declaration, both supporting democratization, human rights and mutual international cooperation to promote development in Latin America. While relations with military dictatorial regimes in Argentina, Chile, Brazil, Paraguay and Uruguay were politically stiffened, insurgency situations in Guatemala and El Salvador together with the "contra"-challenged Sandinista government in Nicaragua entangled relations with Central American states due to Spain's active involvement and mediation through conflict-resolution policies. In the Caribbean, a "special interest" policy with Cuba had been built up in the previous decades coupled with important Spanish economic interests and investment, especially in the tourist sector. It was also to become a sensitive issue, especially with regard to the US embargo. This challenging and heterogeneous Latin American scenario became the stepping-stone towards furthering Spanish involvement in the region in political, economic and cultural terms in the 1980s and 1990s.

Spanish Latin American policy in the 1980s

During the post-war period, 1950-1980, the average annual growth of GDP in Latin America, 5.5%, was the world's highest. In the 1980s the debt crisis reversed this trend. Between 1980 and 1985 net capital flows declined 40%, private net flows from international banking fell 80% and net flows from bilateral loans 50%. Average GDP growth slipped down to 1.2% from 1980 to 1990. As opportunities for bilateral loans – mainly from the United States – were restrained, the needed external financing was only feasible through multilateral financial institutions such as the IMF and the WB. But further lending came with strings attached. The structural reforms recommended called for an export-led strategy (Ffrench-Davis, 1999: 79-94). FDI inflows to Latin America increased gradually and rapidly in the late 1980s. They appeared as a better alternative for long-term investment and growth than previous borrowing strategies (Sánchez-Robles, 1995) (see Table 4.1). But, as the World Bank remarks, "while FDI has been traditionally viewed in a more favorable light than debt flows, the recent boom has raised new concerns regarding its desirability and effects" (World Bank Group, 2002).

Table 4.1 FDI inflows to selected Latin American countries, 1985-1991

	1985	*1986*	*1987*	*1988*	*1989*	*1990*	*1991*
Argentina	919	574	-19	1,147	1,028	2,008	2,439
Brazil	1,267	177	1,087	2,794	744	236	Na
Chile	114	116	230	141	184	249	576
Colombia	1,016	642	293	159	547	484	433
Ecuador	62	70	75	80	89	82	85
Mexico	491	1,160	1,796	635	2,648	2,548	4,742
Peru	1	22	32	26	59	41	-7

Source: IMF, January 1993

Global FDI flows had also radically altered their allocation strategy as a result of the changing economic policy of the US in 1980. Increased interest rates and the strengthened dollar value in the 1980-85 period contracted US FDI from 47% to 19%; in turn the US became host to 50% of FDI. The EC and Japan took a combined leading role standing respectively for 50% and 10% of global FDI. In the 1985-1990 period, increased global competitiveness speed up liberalization patterns that deeply re-structured the economies of the developed countries. Takeovers and mergers in all economic sectors were transforming the production system introducing capital-intensive technology and new adequate flexible organizational structures to adopt the far-reaching technological innovations, together with new distribution and marketing techniques. Therefore, developed countries stood for 98% of global FDI and were simultaneously hosts to 90% of inflows (the United States received 26.2% and the European Community 51.5%; while FDI inflows to Latin America dropped from 9.8% in 1980-1985 to 2.2% in 1985-1990).

Spanish trade relations with Latin America plummeted in turn 35% in the 1980-1986 period to the extent that Spanish exports to Latin America accounted for only 3.6% of total Spanish exports. Efforts were made to reverse this situation in the coming years, particularly through the internationalization of Spanish firms. Spanish foreign policy towards Latin America underwent a noteworthy breakthrough in the 1980s supporting democracy, human rights and development cooperation, very much in tune with the Spanish Socialist Party's political standpoints. With an initial absolute majority support of the electorate the first two Spanish Socialist governments (1982-1988 and 1988-1994) were strong enough to reshape in intensity and implement effectively cooperation policies with Latin America. Prime Minister Felipe González took in this respect an active and personal stance relating the European Union to Latin America. The Ibero-American Community of Nations was outlined as the general framework to reach that aim, through proper governmental action and upgraded cooperation programs.

Foreign policy matters related to democratization and human rights in Latin America were conducted with certain autonomy and intensity avoiding as far as possible confrontation with the strong policy against insurgency in Latin America of Ronald Reagan's Administration. Thus while Reagan's foreign policy gravitated on a rehearsal of the Cold War confrontation, Felipe González's governmental policy took the acute social and economic inequalities to be the factors leading to violence, conflict and open warfare in many Latin American countries, especially in Central America. Different perceptions led to different solutions. Spanish foreign policy opted for peace and conflict-resolution, reinforced by development cooperation and aid programs of a non-discriminative political nature. Accordingly the Spanish government joined in 1983 the "Contadora Group" formed by Mexico, Panama, Colombia and Venezuela as an inter-Latin American peace-keeping and conflict-resolution group setting forth arbitration measures in the Central American crisis and supporting democratization and human rights. Spanish Central American policy attained thereby greater credibility as peace initiatives were thereafter decided by neighboring states. Spanish foreign policy in the region won further support in the European Council and the European Union once Spain acquired full membership in 1986.

Emphasis on democratization and human rights was equally prevalent in Spain's foreign policy in the South Cone. These countries were not only much larger, they were also divested of the acute socio-economic unequal structure of Central America. And Spanish interests spelled here, as in Mexico, considerably more. Consequently the Spanish government pursued a less active involvement and ideological stance, even in matters related to human rights. As democratic regimes replaced gradually most military dictatorships by 1985, friendly supportive relations were reestablished with all the Southern Cone countries with the exception of Chile, where transition towards democracy only took place after 1990.

The most outstanding changes in Spanish Latin American policy guidelines were associated to the prominent role that development-cooperation policies would acquire in the coming years.[11] Significantly, the Hispanic Culture Institute was re-labeled Ibero-American Cooperation Center in 1977 and as the Ibero-American Cooperation Institute in 1979, an institution that was to coordinate cooperation for development policies in Latin America in connection with the Foreign Ministry and other governmental agencies.

As Spain joined in 1976, the Inter-American Development Bank a Development Aid Fund (FAD) was created and in 1977 the first FAD-loans were released, coordinated by the recently appointed Inter-Ministerial Commission for Development Aid. The Official Development Aid (ODA) was also operational delivering a growing amount of ODA (Mier, 1996)[12], mostly channeled to Latin America (a gross 63.4%). ODA boomed from an insignificant amount of $164 million in 1979 to $958.7 million in 1990 and $1.24 billion in 1991, of which roughly 50% was released as FAD-loans. However the ratio ODA/GDP (0.13% in 1982 and 0.24% in 1991) remained still far below the average of other European countries (0.39% in 1991), nonetheless it involved an important Spanish development-cooperation effort throughout the 1980s having in mind that the starting point was close to nothing. In 2004, the newly elected Socialist government tried to revamp cooperation policies so that the ratio ODA/GDP attained 0.5% by 2008, still below the 0.7% demanded by NGO's.

As too many governmental agencies were operating and overlapping development plans, in 1985 a Directorate for International Cooperation and for Latin America (SECIPI) was established to coordinate and rationalize all development aids in connection with the Foreign Ministry, together with the support of the Inter-Ministerial Cooperation Commission, entrusted with the release of Annual International Cooperation Plans (PACI). More re-arrangements were introduced to line up Spanish development cooperation schemes with those prevailing in the EC. Shortly after an autonomous agency – the Spanish Agency for International Cooperation (AECI) – was created through SECIPI, and integrating the Ibero-American Cooperation Institute (ICI) as its main geographic working unit (Alonso, 1993), advisory technical development-cooperation offices were established in different Latin American countries. In 1988 the Development Financial Corporation (COFIDES) was created to promote and channel FDI inflows, mainly to Latin America.

Development cooperation on a bilateral basis was strongly activated by means of Global Cooperation and Friendship Treaties, all of which included an Economic Protocol and a "democratic clause". The first treaty, in force for a four-year period, was signed with Argentina in 1988, followed by similar treaties with Chile, Colombia, Mexico, Uruguay, Venezuela, Bolivia, Ecuador, Honduras and Brazil. The financial and economic scope of these treaties – all followed roughly the same blueprint – can best be illustrated looking closer at the provisions established by the first treaty subscribed with Argentina. Of the $3 billion total amount, $1 billion was to be directly administered by the Argentinean government with the provision that 50% had the nature of FAD-loans and the remaining 50% were loans subject to OECD conditions. The remaining $2 billion were to be channeled to the private sector, that is, to Spanish firms, mixed Spanish/Argentinean firms or entirely Argentinean firms. Spanish trade and FDI flows to Latin America were in a way directly related to the side-effects of the increasing volume of development-cooperation programs in the late 1980s.

Multilateral cooperation increased significantly after Spain's ascension to the European Community in 1986. Accordingly, in 1993 60% of total Spanish development-cooperation aid was multilateral and 40% bilateral. The increasing impact of multilateral development aid related necessarily Spanish development-cooperation programs to the complex network of EC's external relations with Latin America.

EC-Spain Latin American policy

Spain's EC-membership Treaty managed to include an addendum that expressed the common interest to develop and strengthen relations with all the Latin American countries. In 1987, the EC's Council of Foreign Ministers adopted accordingly a first document expressly referred to Latin America: "EC's new guidelines for Latin America". Since then Latin America began to be considered as a specific area of the European Community's external relations. But there was still a clear imbalance between the political commitment of the European Community to democracy and human rights in Latin America and further economic involvement. The European Community's initial reluctance to broaden these relations assuming further economic commitments was altered in 1989 following Spain's EC presidency. In 1990 the European Community's Council of Ministers adopted a new document, "New Guidelines for cooperation with Latin America and Asia in the 1990s", that included financial provisions for cooperation and development. For the period 1991-1995 a total amount of Ecu 2.75 billion – a 75% increase in comparison with the previous program covering the period 1976-1990 – was to be released as development aid, of which 35-40%, equivalent to one billion Ecu, were earmarked for Latin America (plus another 1.5 billion Ecu in humanitarian aid). In addition to these amounts, Latin America received further development aid stemming from bilateral agreements with the EC's member-states. During 1988-1989, EC's total development aid to Latin America – including multilateral and bilateral agreements – was estimated to account for 46% of the total amount of aid delivered to Latin America, whereas the US provided 25% and Japan 9%. In 1995 the EU's total development aid bypassed 50%. Though the European Community and its member states became the main aid donors to Latin America, this amount only represented 15% of European Community's aid to LDCs. Since 1990 the European Community was to become further involved in Latin America through bilateral cooperation agreements with Mexico and Chile, while multilateral agreements had previously been reached with the Andean Community, Central America and the Rio Group.

EU and Spain's Latin American policy in the 1990s

The European Community's external relations expanded throughout the 1990s. The end of the Cold War and the subsequent political and economic transition of East European countries towards democratization and economic liberalization were exposed to uncertainties and ups and downs until 1995. As events unfolded, previous political and economic borders were gradually eliminated, embracing most Eastern European countries in the global economy. The European Community embarked soon after on an Eastern enlargement policy that in a first stage comprised negotiations with Austria, Finland and Sweden, all of which became EU members in 1995. With the exception of Russia, all of the other Eastern European countries applied for EU membership. Negotiation rounds took place soon thereafter so that further Eastern enlargement was envisaged to be completed in the 2002-2005 year period. In 2004, eight Eastern countries became new member-states and further Eastern enlargement is already scheduled to take place within a ten-year period. Romania and Bulgaria plan to join the European Union by 2007. This Eastern EU enlargement has been perceived in Latin America as a negative factor because the new member-states will strongly compete in the manufacturing sector, reduce European FDI flows and development aid and, finally, slow down all ongoing bilateral and multilateral agreements (Maldonado and Durán, 2003). In the meantime, the European Union has developed assistance programs with all these countries known as PHARE and TACIS, respectively aimed for the East European countries and the Russian Federation.

The European Community's increased political, economic and monetary integration was pushed through the Maastricht Treaty (1992), the European Single Market (1993), the Amsterdam Treaty (1997), and the European Monetary Union (2000). The European Union became by the late 1990s a growing world economic power bloc provided with increased external relations and a strengthened inner integration. More recently, the proposed European Constitution, if backed by the member-states in 2005, will further integrate the European Union.

The EU's Latin American policy was also reinvigorated as trade relations and FDI flows bounced remarkably in the 1990s once the intensity of economic reforms in the American sub-continent generalized and created new trade and investment opportunities. EU trade exchange with Latin America doubled between 1990 and 2000. Trade links deepened with the prospect of creating strategic partnerships with Latin American countries. On a bilateral basis, a gradual free-trade agreement was reached with Mexico and Chile, and, on a regional level, a strategic association agreement with Mercosur scheduled for 2003 is being reconsidered in 2005, having in mind the original magnitude and reverberations of the Argentinean crisis, strongly curbed since 2004, and the new quest for social justice by the Brazilian government. However the EU Latin American trade involvement has been restrained from the outset by the European Common Agricultural Policy (CAP) and the Lomé Treaty that established Preferential Trade Agreements with former French and British overseas colonies in the Caribbean, African and Pacific areas, affecting basically sugar, cocoa, coffee and banana trade items, while the CAP restricted heavily agricultural imports from the Southern Cone. As a result, the trade exchange throughout the 1990s produced increasing Latin American deficits ($1.5 billion in 1995). Nonetheless, Latin America can greatly develop trade with the European Union as it only accounts for 5% of the EU's total foreign trade, while 18% of total Latin American exports are delivered to the European Union.

Table 4.2   Main FDI In/Outflows to Latin America, accumulated data for 1992-2001 in million Euro

Out/InflowS	Arg.	Brazil	MERC.	Andean Com.	Chile	Mex.	Colomb.	Venez	Total
EU-15	39.485	67.379	107.456	16.409	10.678	20.682	4.010	6.712	161.701
Spain	**26.281**	**26.292**	**53.488**	**8.232**	**7.816**	**9.197**	**2.667**	**1.607**	**80.479**
France	5.002	9.995	15.246	2.554	555	1.628	229	1.594	20.247
Netherl.	615	9.067	9.326	1.715	1.492	2.579	-424	1.064	15.932
UK	1.626	4,757	6.000	1.152	349	3.666	552	-126	13.175
Germany	2.116	3.625	5.851	1.673	418	1.751	502	1.275	9.966
Portugal	29	9.543	9.573	16	11	32	0	2	9.773
Italy	1.308	2.808	4.061	88	47	144	28	74	4.412
Other EU	2.508	1.293	3.913	979	-10	1.684	455	1.222	7.715
US	9.124	32.561	36.799	3.522	9.166	46.389	2.615	10.740	97.732

Source: W. Chislett (2003:40)

However, a step towards further EU economic involvement in Latin America came with the authorization in 1991 for the European Investment Bank to operate in Latin America. As the world's leading development financial institution in the 1990s, its contribution to the EU's investments in Latin America increased significantly after 1995, especially since Al-Invest was created in 1994 to promote European investments in Latin America. The European Development Fund also began dispersing funds for development-investment. Even if the average GDP growth rate for Latin America in the 1990-1998 period was a modest 2.8%, this figure was unevenly distributed by countries and time-periods (see Table 4.2).

Practically all Latin American countries began significant programs to liberalize their trade regimes between 1985 and 1995 following the Uruguay Round and the overall liberalization reform package of the Washington consensus. Average tariffs declined from 44.6% in 1985 to 13.1% in 1995, quantitative limits on imports were likewise gradually removed as well as restrictions on FDI flows, exchange rates became either effectively-valued or undervalued after the devaluation period of the debt crisis, enhancing rapid export growth, and reductions of direct government intervention through privatizations gave a new role to the private sector. As a result, the record of economic average annual growth for the period 1990-1997 improved significantly, although it varied distinctly from country to country (see Table 4.2).

Table 4.3   Average GDP growth rate for Latin America, 1990-1998

Country	1990-94	1995-99
Argentina	6.4	1.7
Brazil	1.3	1.9
Chile	7.0	5.3
Colombia	4.2	1.8
Mexico	4.0	2.7
Peru	3.1	4.1
Uruguay	4.2	2.3
Latin America	3.3	2.3

Source: IMF

Table 4.4   Average GDP growth rate for Latin America, 1990-2005

Country	1990-94	1995-99	2000-03	2004-2005
Argentina	6.4	1.7	-5.5	6.1
Brazil	1.3	1.9	2.2	4.0
Chile	7.0	5.3	3.3	4.9
Colombia	4.2	1.8	1.8	4.0
Mexico	4.0	2.7	2.4	3.8
Peru	3.1	4.1	2.6	4.6
Uruguay	4.2	2.3	-5.8	7.5
Latin America	3.3	2.3	1.1	4.5

Source: IMF and CEPAL's Economic Projections Center, 2004

Spanish MNEs designed a strategy between 1995 and 2000 for one of the most decisive Latin American privatization processes: clusters or constellations of banks and firms were formed to gather synergies in order to push away competitors, share the benefits of practical monopoly situation in specific large markets and specific economic strategic branches as infrastructure, energy, banking and telecommunications, diversify investments to control different stages of production, distribution and marketing, disseminate risk-ratios and pool the necessary capital assets. In 1995, "two main groups were created, one involving BBV, La Caixa, Argentaria, Iberdrola, Repsol, Gas Natural and Telefónica, the other one involving BCH, Endesa, Unión Fenosa, Retevisión, FCC and Dragados y Construcciones" (Toral, 2001: 154), plus Banco Santander, which soon merged with BCH. MNEs such as Telefónica, Endesa, Iberdrola, Repsol, Dragados, FCC and Gas Natural became the main non-banking actors in South America between 1996 and 1999, relying on huge financial resources supplied by the largest Spanish two banks that were simultaneously to different degrees stockholders of these MNEs. These two large Spanish banking corporations had in turn invested heavily, taking over small and medium private banks in Latin America since the early 1990s. Considerable additional capital assets were pooled by banks for further investment by means of pension and investment funds, which became a form of promoting popular capitalism in Spain by offering attractive profit opportunities or high interest rates. MNEs such as Telefónica, Argentaria, Repsol, Iberia, Cepsa, and Endesa were still in 1995 partially state-owned.

EU and Spain's foreign policy guidelines towards Latin America since September 11, 2001

Spanish foreign policy in Latin America created in the previous decades a favorable environment for Spanish interests and investment, supporting democratization and human rights, establishing friendly political and cultural relations on a bilateral and multilateral level, subscribing development aid and cooperation programs, promoting economic and informal diplomacy and involving the European Union in Latin America.

The world, and especially the United States, changed its outlook after the economic slowdown that began in mid-2000 and, especially, the terrorist attacks of September 11. The effect was especially negative for Latin America., making most macroeconomic indicators the worst since 1997. During a three-year period 2000-2003, Latin America had the most visible decline among all world regions.

This gloomy scenario switched drastically in mid-2003. The region's economic performance in 2004 was the best since the debt crisis in 1982. According to UNCTAD's 2004 Trade and Development Report, Latin America exhibited throughout 2004 a 4.7% GNP growth rate and the region was expected to deliver a still strong growth rate of 3.7% by 2006. In 2004, FDI levels were estimated to reach $35 billion after a four-year decline. Nevertheless the region was still fragile and vulnerable to higher interest rates and financial turmoil, specially having in mind that the economic upsurge of 2004 was basically caused by the spillover effects of the U.S. and China's economic expansion, the fall of imports and rise in exports and a more stable political, social and financial setting. UNCTAD underlined that "despite improved monetary conditions in several countries, fixed capital formation has fallen to its lowest level in decades. In order to achieve a substantial recovery of both investment and private consumption, it will be necessary to ease the public debt burden (especially in Argentina and Brazil), reform fiscal structures in some countries, and enhance the supply of domestic credit at lower interest rates than in the past, as well as achieve a more equitable distribution of income".

The policies of the European Union towards Latin America during the period 2001-2004 can generally be characterized as tilted towards retrenchment due to the global economic slowdown, the overall "flat" rates of growth in the European Union and the burden of strenuous financial commitments associated to the E.U.'s ambitious enlargement policy. In addition, the foreign policy of the Aznar's government – aligned with the Bush administration – strongly disengaged Spain in the region. Regardless of the priorities of the European Union during the economic slowdown, Spain's aloofness towards Latin America during these years reinforced the disentanglement of the European Union in Latin America, especially having in mind that Spain had acted in the past as the region's main bridge to Europe. As a result, both the EU-LAC Summits – the last one held in Guadalajara in 2004 – and the meeting of Ibero-American Chiefs of State have been beset by "low profile" policies, although some of the documents called for the future development of a "strategic alliance", social cohesion, stronger multilateralism, a reform of the architecture of UN and the Bretton Woods institutions and major participation of civil society. Nevertheless EU Commissioner Chris Patten, in his introductory address to the EU-LAC Summit held in Guadalajara in 2004, stressed that "the EU is Latin America's second most important trade partner, its largest source of FDI and the leading donor of development assistance". This statement became soon obsolete. In 2004, the United States was again the main source of FDI in Latin America as well as its foremost trade partner. EU and Spain's trade relations with Latin America as a whole experienced a noteworthy decline between 2000 and 2005. The European Union was the region's second main trade partner in 2000, but in 2003 it ranked third (the European Union accounted for 12% of Latin America's total exports and 14% of total imports). However, the EU remained as the first donor of development aid to the region (55% of total aid).[13] In the near future, the EU and Spain's foreign policy guidelines – intertwined as they are – may boost relations with Latin America. The Ibero-American Summit to be held in Salamanca in the Fall 2005 will certainly not solve all present uncertainties.

Notes

[1] For an historical approach to Spanish state-owned companies and the privatization process 1980-1995, see Fuentes, 1995. See also W. Chislett, 2002: 79-84.

[2] The volume of FDI yearly flows to Spain from 1989-1997 was only higher in the United States, the United Kingdom and France. See editorial of *ICE* (1997).

[3] For further reading, see Paul Isbell "La experiencia de España: lecciones y advertencias para América Latina" (9/13/2004), DT No. 20/2004, www.realinstitutelcano@org/document/139.asp.

[4] According to data released July 11, 2001, by Spain's Undersecretary of Trade, Juan Costa.

[5] See A.T. Kearney (2004), "The FDI Confidence Index", The Global Business Policy Council, Virginia, USA, October 2004, vol. 7, p. 24 in www.atkearney.com.

[6] Pampillón underlines that in 1990-1997 900 privatizations in Latin America amounted to $100 billion.

[7] A research project accomplished by Dirk Willem te Veldt on ODI's behalf entitled "FDI and Income Inequality in Latin America. Experience and Policy Implications" underlines on page 8 that inequality in Latin America remains persistently high and that FDI flows are likely to perpetuate inequalities as they induce skill-specific tecnological changes and wage bargains while allocated in skill- intensive sectors. See more in Overseas Development Institute, London, UK.

[8] Morán, who later became Foreign Minister in Felipe Gonzalez's socialist government, explores the origin of the term and how it became symbolically linked to king Juan Carlos as Spain's Head of State during the early years of democratic transition. For a more detailed and updated description of what the Ibero-American Commonwealth means see C. Arenal (1994), *La política exterior de España hacia Iberoamérica*, Ed. Complutense, Madrid, pp. 157-170.

[9] More details in Celestino del Arenal, "De la Cumbre Iberoamericana de San José de Costa Rica (2004) a la Cumbre Iberoamericana de Salamanca (2005)", 1/27/2005, DT no. 5/2005, www.realinstitutelcano@org/document/169.asp

[10] For an excellent account of the different interpretations given to the Spanish economy (1939-1959), see L. Gamir, "El periodo 1939-1959, la autarquía y la política de estabilización", pp. 13-30. J.M. Alvarez, "Política de financiación exterior", pp. 84-97, summarizes the impact of FDI in Spain since the 19th century.

[11] See special edition on Spanish cooperation policies in *ICE*, 778, May-June 1999.

[12] ODA funds amounted to $164 million in 1979 and $233 million in 1982, $147 million in 1984, $203 million in 1986, $248 million in 1988 and $959 million in 1990 (Mier, 1996).

[13] See more on Colombia's former President's address to the Forum held in Biarritz 28th October 2004 at Ernesto Samper Pizano, "Relanzamiento de la política América Latina-Europa", www.corporacionescenarios.org/docword/samperbiarritz.doc.

References

Alonso, J.A., and J.M. Cadarso (1982), "La inversión directa española en Iberoamérica", *ICE*, 590, November, pp. 105-121.

Alonso, J.A. (1993), "La cooperación oficial al desarrollo en España: balance de una década", *Anuario Internacional CIDOB 1992*, Barcelona, pp. 69-82.

Álvarez, J.M. (1975), "Política de financiación exterior" in L. Gamir (ed.), *Política económica de España*, pp. 84-97.

Arenal, C. (1994), *La política exterior de España hacia Iberoamérica*, Ed. Complutense, Madrid.

--- (2000), "La política exterior de España hacia Iberoamérica y las Cumbres Iberoamericanas", in Monografías del CESEDEN, *Iberoamérica, un reto para España y la Unión Europea en la próxima década*, pp. 59-85.

Barbé, E. (1999), *La política europea de España*, Ariel, Barcelona.

Barciela, F. (2002), "Empresas españolas en Latinoamérica, ¿un nuevo Eldorado?", *Economía Exterior*, 21, Summer, pp. 37-52.

BID (1998), *América Latina frente a la desigualdad. Progreso económico y social en América Latina. Informe 1998-1999*, Washington DC.

Carr, R. (1966), *Spain 1808-1939*, Oxford University Press, London.

Casilda, R., and D. Sotelsek (2001), "Del panamericanismo al ALCA. Implicaciones para la UE y España", *BICE*, 2710, Nov. 26-Dec. 2, pp. 19-32.

CEPAL (2001), *Panorama de la inserción internacional de América Latina y el Caribe 1999-2000*, Santiago de Chile.

--- (2003), *Foreign Direct Investment in Latin America and the Caribbean, 2003 Report*, Santiago de Chile.

Chislett, W. (2002), *The Internationalization of the Spanish Economy*, Real Instituto Elcano de Estudios Internacionales y Estratégicos, Madrid.

Chislett, W. (2003), *La inversión española directa en América Latina: retos y oportunidades*, Real Instituto Elcano de Estudios Internacionales y Estratégicos, Madrid.

Erice, F.S. (1978), "Las inversiones directas españolas en Iberoamérica", *ICE*, pp. 538-539.

Fernández, N. (1972), "La participación financiera de España en el desarrollo de Iberoamérica", *ICE*, 472, pp.149-156.

Ffrench-Davis, R. (1999), *Macroeconomía, comercio y finanzas para reformar las reformas en América Latina*, McGraw-Hill Interamericana, Santiago de Chile.

Filippi, A. (ed.) (1986), *Bolívar y Europa en las crónicas, el pensamiento político y la historiografía*, vol. 1, Ediciones de la Presidencia de la República, Caracas, pp. 99-148.

Fuentes, E. (1995), *El modelo de economía abierta y el modelo castizo en el desarrollo de la España de los años 90*, PUZ, Zaragoza.

Gamir, L. (1975a), "El periodo 1939-1959, la autarquía y la política de estabilización" in L. Gamir (ed.), *Política económica de España*, pp.13-30.

--- (ed.) (1975b), *Política económica de España*, Guadiana Pub., Madrid.

García, J.L. (1987), "La industrialización y el desarrollo económico de España durante el franquismo", in Nadal, Carreras and Sudrià (eds.), *La economía española en el siglo XX. Una perspectiva histórica*, Ariel, Barcelona.

García, J.L. (1999), *España, Economía: ante el siglo XXI*, Espasa Calpe, Madrid.

García, J.L. and J.C. Jiménez (1999), "El proceso de modernización económica: perspectiva histórica y comparada", in J.L. García (ed.), *España, Economía: ante el siglo XXI*, pp. 7-30.

Gil A. (1986), "Sección española. Introducción", in A. Filippi (ed.), *Bolívar y Europa en las crónicas, el pensamiento político y la historiografía*, pp. 99-148.

Gillespie, R., F. Rodrigo and J. Story, (eds.) (1995), *Las relaciones exteriores de la España democrática*, Alianza Universidad, Madrid.

González, M.J. (1999), "La economía española desde el final de la guerra civil hasta el Plan de Estabilización de 1959" in G. Anes (ed.), *Historia económica de España. Siglos XIX y XX*, Galaxia Gutemberg, Círculo de Lectores, Barcelona.

Grugel, J. (1995), *España y Latinoamérica*, in Gillespie, R. Rodrigo and F.-Story, (eds.), *Las relaciones exteriores de la España democrática*, Alianza Universidad, Madrid, pp. 191-205.

Gwynne, R.N. and C. Kay (1999), *Latin America Transformed. Globalization and Modernity*, Arnold, London.

ICE (1997), 765, Sept., p.7.

ICE (1999), 778, May-June.

Jones R. (2000), *Beyond the Spanish State. Central Government, Domestic Actors and the EU*, Palgrave, Hampshire.

Kearney, A.T. (2004), "The FDI Confidence Index", The Global Business Policy Council, Virginia, USA, October 2004, vol. 7, p. 24 in www.atkearney.com.

Maldonado, R. And J.J. Durán (2003), *La ampliación de la UE hacia los países de Europa Central y Oriental: una evaluación preliminar del impacto para América Latina y el Caribe,* CEPAL, Serie Comercio Internacional.

Marín, M. (2002), "América Latina en la nueva agenda internacional", *Política Exterior,* special issue, September, pp. 95-112.

Medina, G. (2002) "América Latina y la 'pax americana'", *Política Exterior,* 89, Sept./Oct, pp. 63-84.

Mier, F. (1996), "La cooperación de España al desarrollo: reflexiones y propuestas", *ICE,* 755, pp.13-37.

Morán, F. (1980), *Una política exterior para España,* Planeta, Barcelona.

Morata, F. (ed.) (2000), *Políticas públicas en la Unión Europea,* Ariel Ciencia Política, Barcelona.

Nadal, Carreras and Sudrià (eds.) (1987), *La economía española en el siglo XX. Una perspectiva histórica,* Ariel, Barcelona.

Pampillón, R. (1998), "Los procesos de privatización en América Latina: de la sustitución de importaciones a la eficiencia productiva", *ICE,* 772, Jul-Aug. pp. 73-87.

Pollack, B. (1987), *The Paradox of Spanish Foreign Policy. Spain's International Relations from Franco to Democracy,* Pinter Publishers, London.

Ruiz, A. (1978), "Las relaciones económicas y comerciales con Iberoamérica", *ICE,* 538-539, pp. 162-171.

Samper, Ernesto (2004), "Relanzamiento de la política América Latina-Europa", www.corporacionescenarios.org/docword/samperbiarritz.doc.

Sánchez-Robles, B. (1995), "Iberoamérica en la segunda mitad del siglo XX: tres enfoques alternativos de política económica", *ICE,* 741, May, pp. 111-129.

Silva, E. (1999), "Authoritarianism, Democracy and Development", in R.N. Gwynne, and C. Kay (eds.), *Latin America Transformed. Globalization and Modernity,* pp. 31-50.

Spanish Ministry of Defense (2000), *Monografías del CESEDEN. Iberoamérica, un reto para España y la Unión Europea en la próxima década,* Centro Superior de Estudios de la Defensa Nacional, Madrid.

Spanish Ministry of Foreign Affairs (2000), *Inversiones españolas e internacionalización de la empresa española en Iberoamérica,* 34, Madrid.

Tamames, R. (1968), "Las relaciones económicas entre España e Iberoamérica. Hacia un entendimiento global", *Economía Industrial,* 53, May.

Toral, P. (2001), *The Reconquest of the New World. Multinational Enterprises and Spain's Direct Investment in Latin America,* Ashgate, Aldershot.

UNCTAD (2004), *Trade and Development Report 2004,* New York.

World Bank Group (2002), *Regional Studies 2000/2001, Latin America and the Caribbean,* www.worldbank.org/prospects/gep2002 (observed October 11, 2002).

--- (2004), *Global Economic Prospects: Trade, Regionalism and Development,* Washington, DC.

Chapter 5

The Foreign Conquest of Latin American Banking: What's Happening and Why?

James R. Barth, Triphon Phumiwasana and Glenn Yago[1]

Introduction

Latin America's real GDP grew at a fairly rapid annual rate of 5.2% from 1950 to 1980. This growth was interrupted by a foreign debt crisis, however. It began in Mexico in the early 1980s and then spread throughout the region. Economic growth thus slowed to a sluggish 1.4 annual percentage rate during the 1980s. The slower growth and resulting greater unemployment helped bring about a change in political regimes. Authoritarian regimes were replaced with democracies. The decade of the 1980s began with 12 democracies out of 26 countries in Latin America. By the end of the decade, all but five countries were democratic. Today only Cuba is not.[2]

The new political environment of the 1990s was accompanied by the deregulation of national financial systems and the easing of controls on capital flows and foreign currency transactions in many Latin American countries. Government-owned firms were also privatized throughout much of the region. These actions made it easier and more attractive for foreign firms to enter those countries in which reforms were implemented. As economies became more open, Latin America's economic growth increased to an annual rate of 3.5% from 1990 to 1998. This more favorable economic environment boded well for the market-oriented reforms.

Severe financial crises in the latter half of the 1990s disrupted the progress being made in Latin America, especially in Argentina, Brazil and Venezuela. This situation continues to the present time and has generated growing criticism of the so-called "Washington Consensus," i.e., the American-backed free-market model that is frequently used to characterize the reform policies pursued by countries in the region. If the turmoil continues, it most likely will further stiffen and broaden local opposition to freer trade among countries, to still more privatization of government-owned businesses, and to even greater foreign ownership of domestic firms.

The purpose of this chapter is to examine an important aspect of the free-market model now common in Latin America. Specifically, we document and assess the recent and dramatic change that has occurred in the structure of banking markets in the region. The main focus is on the foreign "conquest" of Latin American banking. The striking penetration by foreign banks, particularly Spanish banks, into the domestic banking market, throughout the region is due to a variety of factors. Many of the more important factors in explaining this expansion will be examined and whenever possible evidence regarding their importance noted. Some of the broader effects of the increased foreign bank presence on several aspects of financial and economic activity will also be discussed.

The remainder of the chapter proceeds as follows: Firstly, an overview of some data and statistical measures that demonstrate the importance of a nation's financial system for economic growth and development. This overview includes a discussion of the overall size of a financial system as well as the major constituent components of such a system. Secondly, we present information on the wide disparity in the size of the banking sectors for different Latin American countries. Information on differences in output structure across countries is also presented and its implications for the allocation of credit within countries mentioned. Since six countries dominate the region in several important dimensions, a more detailed discussion of the changing structure of the banking industry of each of these countries is provided. This includes a discussion of differences in the structure, scope and independence of bank supervision in these countries. It also includes a discussion of what the term "bank" means in these countries. Third, we present data showing differences in the allocation of credit and the performance of foreign-owned and domestic-owned banks in the dominant six countries. Section V discusses several key questions raised by the recent changes in the structure of banking in Latin America. Next there follows more recent data and a few remarks about the two biggest Spanish banks that have expanded into the region. The last section contains the conclusions. Our main conclusion is that foreign participation in the banking system of the larger countries is quite high.

An overview of the importance of financial systems

There has recently been a tremendous resurgence in interest in the relationship between finance and economic growth. The figures presented in Table 5.1 underscore the reason for this interest. High-income countries account for 81% of the world's GDP but only 18% of the world's population. Low-income countries, in contrast, account less than 3% of the world's GDP but 34% of the world's population. High income countries also account for 94% of the world's total financial assets, whereas low-income countries account for less than 1%.[3] These figures clearly document the striking and alarming inequality in the distribution of world income and financial assets among countries. At the same time, they support those who believe efforts should be made to encourage and assist poor countries in doing more to develop their financial systems so as to promote economic growth and development.

Table 5.1 National financial systems promote economic growth, 1999

	Income				
	High	Upper middle	Lower middle	Low	L. America
Population	17.8	11.4	37.0	33.8	8.3
GDP	80.5	9.7	7.2	2.6	6.2
Bank assets	93.2	4.5	1.3	1.0	2.2
Equity market capitalization	93.4	4.0	2.0	0.7	1.6
Bond market capitalization	96.8	2.1	0.7	0.5	0.8
Total financial assets	94.3	3.6	1.4	0.7	1.1

Note: Economies are divided among income groups according to 1999 GNI per capita, calculated using the World Bank Atlas method. The groups are: low income, $755 or less; lower middle income, $756–2,995; upper middle income, $2,996–9,265; and high income, $9,266 or more.

Source: *Statistical Abstract of the United States: 1999*, U.S. Census Bureau; *World Development Indictors*, World Bank; World Bank and OCC Bank Supervision and Regulation Database; *Size of World Bond Market Capitalization*, Merrill Lynch.

Table 5.1 specifically shows that there is positive relationship between the income-category's share of GDP and its share of total financial assets as one moves successively from the lower to the higher income categories. It also shows that this relationship holds for each of the three separate financial components of the total. As one moves successively up the four income categories starting from the lower-income countries and ending with the high-income countries, the corresponding shares of world GDP, bank assets, equity-market capitalization, and bond-market capitalization accounted for by those categories all increase in tandem. It is clear from the table, moreover, that banks become increasingly less important than equity and bond markets as the level of income increases. Indeed, world equity-market capitalization tripled and world bond market capitalization almost doubled during the 1990s. World Bank assets remained relatively flat, however. In today's world, mature economies simply do not need the size of banking systems established in their earlier and more formative growth years. Even in such bank-centered countries as Germany and Japan the dominance of banks has declined relative to stock and bond markets over the past decade.

Some additional evidence to underscore the importance of finance for growth is presented in Table 5.2. This table contains the empirical results of several simple cross-country regressions. Although these results are only meant to be suggestive, they nonetheless emphasize that the size, composition, and ownership structure of a country's financial system may importantly affect its level of economic development (as measured by real GDP per capita). They also highlight how the tightness of restrictions a country places on permissible bank activities may importantly affect its level of economic development. The results in the table indicate the following:

Table 5.2   Simple regressions between real GDP per capita and selected measures of the size, composition and restrictions of a nation's financial system

Dependent variable: real GDP per capita

Independent Variable	Coefficient (t-stat)	R²	Number of Countries	Relationship
Bank Assets, Equities, Bonds / GDP	0.02 (2.94)***	0.22	33	Significantly Positive
Bank Assets / GDP	0.01 (4.11)***	0.19	74	Significantly Positive
Equity Market Capitalization / GDP	0.08 (5.61)***	0.29	78	Significantly Positive
Bond Market Capitalization / GDP	0.18 (4.76)***	0.39	38	Significantly Positive
Bank Assets / Equities and Bonds	-0.01 (-0.54)	0.01	33	None
Percent of Bank Assets Foreign Owned	-0.02 (-0.39)	0.00	81	None
Percent of Bank Assets Government Owned	-0.13 (-2.80)***	0.08	88	Significantly Negative
Overall Restrictions on Bank Activities	-8.35 (-5.11)***	0.22	97	Significantly Negative
Government Bonds / Bond Market Capitalization	-0.18 (-2.43)**	0.14	37	Significantly Negative

Note: ** and *** denote 5% and 1% level of significance, respectively.

- The size of a nation's financial system (i.e., bank assets, stocks, and bonds) is positively and significantly correlated with economic development. Levine (1997) provides an excellent review of the evidence linking finance and growth. Also, the importance of finance for growth is documented in the recent and comprehensive book by the World Bank (2001).
- All three of the individual components comprising a nation's financial system are positively and significantly correlated with economic development. Levine

and Zervos (1998) and Beck and Levine (2001) in rigorous studies find that both bank credit and stocks promote economic growth.

- The composition (i.e., bank assets relative to stocks and bonds) of a nation's financial system is not significantly correlated with economic development. This is consistent with the view that banks and capital markets should be viewed as complements, not as perfect substitutes for one another. Policy should therefore not favor the development of banks at the expense of capital markets, or vice versa. Demirgüç-Kunt and Levine's (2001) important book provides analyses that document the complimentary nature of banks and capital markets.

- The government-owned share of a nation's bank assets and economic development are negatively and significantly correlated. This is consistent with La Porta, Lopez-De-Silanes and Shleifer's (2002) finding that government ownership of banks is negatively associated with income per-capita. Barth, Caprio and Levine (2002), moreover, find that government ownership is negatively associated with bank development, which, in turn, has been shown in other studies to be positively associated with economic growth. This evidence supports the view that market-oriented privatization programs promote economic growth and development.

- The foreign-owned share of a nation's bank assets and economic development are not significantly correlated, either positively or negatively. This suggests, at the very least, that allowing foreign-ownership of domestic banks is not harmful. Importantly, Demirgüç-Kunt, Levine, and Min (1998) find that it is the foreign-owned share of the number of banks, not the share of total assets, which is positively and significantly related to economic growth. A greater presence of foreign banks, even without gaining greater asset share, can promote growth through competitive pressures and thus efficiency gains throughout the domestic banking sector. This is consistent with the view that market-oriented reforms that ease foreign-bank entry restrictions yield economic and social benefits.

- The government share of a nation's bond-market capitalization and economic development are negatively and significantly correlated. Although there is little evidence bearing directly on this relationship, Domowitz, Glen and Madhavan (2001) do find that macroeconomic stability is highly and positively correlated with the development of bond markets. Also, Herring and Chatusripitak (2000) state that "[a]s the Thai example shows, bond markets matter for financial development. Certainly an economy can grow rapidly without an active bond market. But the cost is an increased vulnerability to a financial crisis and a loss of information to guide savings and investment decisions."

- Tighter restrictions on the allowable activities of banks and economic development are negatively and significantly correlated. This is consistent with the view that broader powers for banks (e.g., universal banks) promote economic growth and development. Barth, Caprio and Levine (2001) find evidence that such restrictions retard bank development. And, based on the work of Beck, Loayza and Levine (2001), lower bank development adversely affects economic growth.

These types of correlations, of course, are only suggestive. They do not rigorously demonstrate that finance promotes economic growth and development. Nonetheless, it is widely agreed that financial systems do indeed mobilize savings, allocate savings and monitor firms, and augment liquidity and facilitate risk management. And it is in providing these services that one would expect finance to be an important driving force in promoting growth. Yet, some researchers express concerns about even rigorous empirical analyses demonstrating that such a relationship exits, and most importantly question whether there is a causal linkage running from finance to growth. The argument is that important factors affecting growth might be omitted, individual country-specific traits might be ignored, and/or endogeneity might not appropriately be taken into account in empirical studies of finance and growth. In response to these concerns, researchers have included in their analyses a variety of plausible conditioning or control variables, employed panel methods to allow for unobservable country specific heterogeneity, used plausible instrumental variables, employed firm-and industry-level data, used time-series data and methods, and performed individual country case studies. Some of the most rigorous and convincing recent studies finding a causal linkage between finance and growth include those by Beck, Loayza and Levine (2000), Demirgüç-Kunt and Maksimovic (1998) and Levine and Zervos (1998). The growing consensus based on the findings of these and other recent studies is that there is currently sufficient evidence to conclude that financial systems do indeed promote economic growth and development.

The structure of banking in Latin America

Some basic differences across countries

There are wide differences in population, GDP, and bank assets among Latin America countries. Table 5.3 documents that this is indeed the case for 26 countries. Brazil and Mexico clearly stand out from the others in terms of all three measures. They are the biggest by far in terms of these measures. Together they account for more than half of the region's total population, GDP and bank assets. Several countries do rank higher than these two countries on a GDP per capita basis. This is particularly the case for the Bahamas and Barbados. Some countries also rank higher than Brazil and Mexico when comparing bank assets as a share of GDP. This is particularly the case for the Bahamas and Panama. But on the basis of the absolute measures rather than ratios among the measures Brazil and Mexico are clearly dominant.

Table 5.3　An overview of Latin American countries: population, GDP and bank assets, 2001

Country	Population (000s)	GDP (US$ Millions)	GDP/ Capita (US$)	Bank Assets (US$ Millions)	Bank Assets / GDP (%)
Argentina	**37,385**	**268,697**	**7,187**	**99,717**	**37**
Bahamas	298	4,971	16,681	108,381	2,180
Barbados	275	2,484	9,033	2,392	96
Belize	256	786	3,070	557	71
Bolivia	8,300	8,002	964	4,794	60
Brazil	**174,469**	**504,030**	**2,889**	**303,806**	**60**
Chile	**15,328**	**66,450**	**4,335**	**47,355**	**71**
Colombia	**40,349**	**82,720**	**2,050**	**26,543**	**32**
Costa Rica	3,773	16,157	4,282	6,829	42
Dom. Rep.	8,581	21,395	2,493	9,131	43
Ecuador	13,184	17,896	1,357	7,296	41
El Salvador	6,238	13,739	2,202	N/A	N/A
Guatemala	12,974	18,716	1,443	5,595	30
Guyana	697	698	1,001	571	82
Haiti	6,965	3,685	529	1,056	29
Honduras	6,406	6,386	997	3,296	52
Jamaica	2,666	9,846	3,693	4,669	47
Mexico	**101,879**	**617,865**	**6,065**	**242,563**	**39**
Nicaragua	4,918	2,536	516	1,995	79
Panama	2,846	10,171	3,574	24,500	241
Paraguay	5,734	7,175	1,251	2,457	34
Peru	27,484	52,942	1,926	20,523	39
Suriname	434	749	1,726	357	48
Trinidad & Tobago	1,170	8,323	7,114	4,715	57
Uruguay	3,360	18,662	5,554	19,983	107
Venezuela	**23,917**	**126,158**	**5,275**	**23,831**	**19**
Total	509,886	1,891,239	3,709*	972,912	51*
Memo:					
Spain	40,038	583,656	14,578	908,857	156

Note:　　* denotes the average value.
Source:　Population, *Statistical Abstract of the United States*; GDP, *World Economic Outlook Database*, IMF; Bank Assets, *International Financial Statistics*, IMF.

The same basic information is presented for Spain for comparative purposes. Spain has less than one tenth of the total population of these 26 Latin American countries, but nearly one third of their collective GDP. Spain's banking system, moreover, is not much smaller than the combined systems of all these countries.

Latin America's Quest for Globalization

Table 5.4 Structure of output in Latin American countries, 2000

Country	Sector (% of GDP)			
	Agriculture	**Industry**	*Manufacturing**	**Services**
Argentina	5	28	*18*	68
Bahamas	N/A	N/A	*N/A*	N/A
Barbados	6	21	*9*	73
Belize	21	27	*17*	52
Bolivia	22	15	*13*	63
Brazil	7	29	*24*	64
Chile	11	34	*16*	56
Colombia	14	31	*14*	56
Costa Rica	9	31	*24*	59
Dominican Rep.	11	34	*17*	55
Ecuador	10	40	*17*	50
El Salvador	10	30	*23*	60
Guatemala	23	20	*13*	57
Guyana	N/A	N/A	*N/A*	N/A
Haiti	28	20	*7*	51
Honduras	18	32	*20*	51
Jamaica	6	31	*13*	62
Mexico	4	28	*21*	67
Nicaragua	32	23	*14*	45
Panama	7	17	*8*	76
Paraguay	21	27	*14*	52
Peru	8	27	*14*	65
Suriname	10	20	*8*	70
Trinidad & Tobago	2	43	*8*	55
Uruguay	6	27	*17*	67
Venezuela	5	36	*14*	59
Memo: Spain	4	31	*N/A*	66

Note: Agriculture includes forestry and fishing. Industry comprises mining, manufacturing, construction, electricity, water and gas. *denotes manufacturing is included in the industry total. Also, the correlation between real GDP per capita and the share of GDP accounted for by agriculture is negative and highly significant. Both bank assets/GDP and real GDP per capita are significantly, positively correlated with the share of GDP accounted for by services.

Source: *World Development Indicators*, World Bank.

The Latin American countries also differ with respect to the structure of output. Table 5.4 specifically shows that there are wide differences among these countries in terms of the contribution that agriculture, industry, manufacturing (which is a subcomponent of industry), and services make to GDP. The most significant differences involve agriculture, ranging from a low of 2% of GDP in

Trinidad and Tobago to a high of 28% in Haiti. Perhaps not surprisingly, the correlation between agriculture's GDP share and real GDP per capita for these countries is negative and highly significant. Furthermore, service's GDP share is significantly and positively correlated with both bank assets relative to GDP and real GDP per capita. As countries grow and develop their economies, they become increasingly service oriented and less agriculture dependent. This is also seen in the corresponding figures in the table for Spain.

The structure of a country's output has implications for the allocation of credit within it. To the extent that credit is needed to support the different sectors, one might expect the overall allocation of credit to each sector to reflect its relative contribution to GDP. One might not, however, expect the same to be the case for the proportion of bank credit allocated to each sector. The reason is that firms in the industrial sector, including its subcomponent manufacturing, may be better able to access funds by issuing stocks and bonds than firms in the other sectors. If this is the case, bank credit will be all the more important for those firms in the other sectors that are least able, if at all, to obtain funding from the capital markets. This would undoubtedly include SMEs. It is therefore important to assess the effect of the changing structure of banking markets on the allocation of bank credit. Some limited information on this issue will be presented later in the chapter.

Some basic differences among the dominant countries

Table 5.3 shows that six countries dominate Latin America in terms of population, GDP and bank assets. Table 5.5 reinforces this fact by showing that Argentina, Brazil, Chile, Colombia, Mexico and Venezuela collectively account for more than 75% of each measures total for all 26 Latin American countries. For this reason, the remainder of the chapter focuses on the changing structure of banking in these countries.

Table 5.5   Six countries dominate in terms of population, GDP and bank assets, 2001

	Share of Region Total (%)		
Country	**Population**	**GDP**	**Bank Assets**
Brazil	34.2	26.7	31.2
Mexico	20.0	32.7	24.9
Argentina	7.3	14.2	10.2
Chile	3.0	3.5	4.9
Colombia	7.9	4.4	2.7
Venezuela	4.7	6.7	2.5
Total Share of Top Six	77.1	88.1	76.5

Source: Population, *Statistical Abstract of the United States*; GDP, *World Economic Outlook Database*, IMF; Bank Assets, *International Financial Statistics*, IMF.

National financial systems. The size and composition of the national financial systems of the top six countries (scaled by their respective GDPs) are shown in Table 5.6. There are substantial differences across the countries in terms of total financial assets and their distribution among bank assets, stocks and bonds. Chile has the most developed financial system on the basis of all three components. Venezuela, on the other hand, has the least developed system. Chile, moreover, has the largest share of debt securities, both domestic and international, accounted for by the private sector. In Argentina, the heaviest debt burden is in terms of international public debt, whereas in Brazil it is domestic public debt. This means that Brazilians to a greater degree than Argentineans owe the public debt to themselves. The corresponding figures for Spain are also included for purposes of comparison. It ranks at the top in terms of all three components of a national financial system. Chile, however, is not far behind in terms of equity market capitalization and even slightly ahead in terms of private domestic debt securities.

Table 5.6   Size and composition of top six national financial systems, 2000

Country	Bank Assets	Equity Market Capitalization	Debt Securities / GDP (%)			
	/ GDP (%)		Domestic		International	
			Public	Private	Public	Private
Argentina	40.5	58.3	12.5	4.9	20.2	5.0
Brazil	50.6	38.0	41.8	8.1	4.5	5.0
Chile	71.9	85.6	28.1	18.1	0.7	6.5
Colombia	29.8	11.8	N/A	N/A	10.0	2.3
Mexico	36.8	21.8	10.2	2.3	5.8	5.6
Venezuela	19.1	6.7	N/A	N/A	4.8	4.3
Memo: Spain	151.8	90.3	50.0	14.0	6.2	21.7

Source: GDP, *World Economic Outlook Database*, IMF; Bank Assets, *International Financial Statistics*, IMF; Debt Securities, *Bank for International Settlements*.

Bank supervision. Attention is now focused more narrowly on the banking systems in these top six Latin American countries. Table 5.7 shows their structure, scope and independence of bank supervision. They have a single supervisor based upon official governmental sources. However, as documented more fully in Barth, Nolle, Phumiwasana, Yago (2002), governmental and private sources sometimes provide conflicting information as in the case of Argentina in which private sources indicate there are two supervisors. Furthermore, the Central Bank is a supervisor in only two, Argentina and Brazil, which have adopted the same practice as the United States. In contrast, the other four - Chile, Colombia, Mexico and Venezuela - have adopted the same practice as has been recently implemented in Germany and the United Kingdom. Barth, Nolle, Phumiwasana, and Yago

(2002) find that such differences are only weakly related, if at all, to bank profitability. More research is needed to determine whether these types of differences matter for other measures of bank performance and for bank stability.

Table 5.7 also shows that in four of these countries the supervisory authority has responsibility only for the banking industry, which is also the case in the U.S. In Colombia and Mexico, however, the supervisors' responsibility extends to the securities industry as well. The degree of supervisory independence is low in four of the countries, and only medium in the case of Venezuela. Without a high degree of independence, the supervisory authorities may not be able to exercise appropriate oversight of banks. This, in turn, may lead to imprudent bank behavior and thus to greater bank fragility than otherwise. The Central Bank of Spain, in comparison, is the sole bank supervisory authority, with responsibility only for the banking industry, and it has a high degree of independence.

Bank activity and ownership restrictions. Table 5.8 provides information that essentially tells one what the term "bank" means in these different countries. There are several points to be made in this regard. First, since there is an explicit deposit insurance scheme in every one of the six countries, a bank is an insured institution in these countries. This is also the case in Spain. Second, a bank may engage not only in commercial banking activities but also in securities and insurance activities in all of the countries (including Spain), except Mexico, where securities activities are restricted, and while insurance activities are prohibited. Third, in all the countries (including Spain) real estate activities are either restricted or prohibited, except in Argentina and Colombia, where there are no restrictions. Fourth, Chile and Venezuela restrict the mixing of banking and commerce (i.e., bank ownership of nonfinancial firms and vice versa), as does the U.S. The other four countries (and Spain) do not restrict nonfinancial firm ownership of banks. In the case of bank ownership of nonfinancial firms, Argentina and Mexico (and Spain) do not impose restrictions, whereas Brazil and Colombia do.

These types of differences in "banks" across countries should be recognized when comparing the banking industries in different countries. Differences in allowable bank activities, for example, may matter when attempting to explain differences in bank development, performance and stability across countries. Indeed, recent work by Barth, Caprio and Levine (2002) shows that this is the case. Also, Table 5.8 indicates that Spanish banks have experience in a wide range of activities and in broad ownership structures. This should make it easier for them to enter and adapt to banking markets with different types of banks.

Government vs. foreign participation in banking sector. Tables 5.9 and 5.10 show that the banking industries in the top six Latin American countries have undergone dramatic ownership change in recent years. In particular, Table 5.9 shows that the government-owned share of total bank assets declined in all six countries from 1996 to 1999. The relatively small decline in the case of Mexico is explained by the fact that it had already undertaken efforts earlier in the 1990s to re-privatize its banking industry, after its nationalization in the early 1980s.

Table 5.7   The structure, scope, and independence of bank supervision in the top six Latin American countries

Country	Bank Supervisory Authority	Structure		Scope of Supervisory Authority[2]	Degree of Supervisory Independence[3]
		Single Supervisor or Multiple Supervisors	Role of Central Bank[1]		
Argentina[4]	Central Bank of Argentina, Superintendency of Financial and Foreign Exchange Institutions	Multiple	CB	B	Low
Brazil	Central Bank of Brazil	Single	CB	B	Low
Chile	Superintendency of Banks	Single	NCB	B	Low
Colombia	Superintendency of Banking	Single	NCB	B&S	N/A
Mexico	National Banking and Securities Commission	Single	NCB	B&S	Low
Venezuela	Superintendent of Banks and Other Financial Institutions	Single	NCB	B	Medium
Memo:					
Spain	Bank of Spain	Single	CB	B	High

Notes: [1] "CB" indicates that the central bank is a banking supervisory authority; "NCB" indicates that the central bank in not a banking supervisory authority.

[2] "B" indicates that the supervisory authority(ies) has(have) responsibility only for the banking industry; "B&S" indicates that the supervisory authority(ies) has (have) responsibility for the securities industry as well as for the banking industry; "B&I" indicates that the supervisory authority(ies) has (have) responsibility for the insurance industry as well as for the banking industry; "BSI" indicates that the supervisory authority(ies) has (have) responsibility for the banking, securities, and insurance industries.

[3] See Barth, Nolle, Phumiwasana and Yago (2002) for an explanation of the categorization of the degree of supervisory independence.

[4] According to Courtis (1999), this country has a single bank supervisory authority.

Sources: Primary sources are Barth, Caprio, and Levine (2001 and 2002), and Office of the Comptroller of the Currency using information from national supervisory authorities; secondary source is Courtis (1999). Also, see Institute of International Bankers, various issues. Unless otherwise indicated, information is for 1999.

Table 5.8   Permissible activities, mixing banking and commerce, and deposit insurance in selected Latin American countries, 2001

	Securities	Insurance	Real estate	Bank Ownership of Nonfinancial Firms	Nonfinancial Firms Ownership of Banks	Explicit Deposit Insurance Scheme
Argentina	Permitted	Permitted	Permitted	Unrestricted	Unrestricted	Yes
Brazil	Permitted	Permitted	Restricted	Restricted	Unrestricted	Yes
Chile	Permitted	Permitted	Prohibited	Restricted	Restricted	Yes
Colombia	Permitted	Permitted	Permitted	Prohibited	Permitted	Yes
Mexico	Restricted	Prohibited	Restricted	Permitted	Permitted	Yes
Venezuela	Permitted	Permitted	Restricted	Restricted	Restricted	Yes
Memo: Spain	Unrestricted	Permitted	Restricted	Unrestricted	Permitted	Yes

Note: a. Securities Activities: the ability of banks to engage in the business of securities underwriting, brokering, dealing, and all aspects of the mutual fund industry.
b. Insurance Activities: the ability of banks to engage in insurance underwriting and selling.
c. Real Estate Activities: the ability of banks to engage in real estate investment, development, and management.
d. Banks Ownership of Nonfinancial Firms measures restrictions on the ability of banks to own and control nonfinancial firms.
e. Nonfinancial Firms Ownership of Banks measures restrictions on the ability of nonfinancial firms to own and control bank.

Source: World Bank's Banking Supervision and Regulation Database

Table 5.9   Government-owned bank share of total bank assets in top six countries

	1996	1997	1998	1999
Argentina	34%	31%	31%	27%
Brazil	52%	51%	47%	43%
Chile	15%	15%	14%	14%
Colombia	N/A	17%	23%	N/A
Mexico	41%	41%	40%	36%
Venezuela	30%	7%	6%	6%
Memo: Spain	1%	1%	1%	0%

Source: OCC Survey

Table 5.10   Foreign-owned bank share of total banks assets for top six countries

	1996	1997	1998	1999	2001
Argentina	27%	46%	48%	71%	64%
Brazil	10%	13%	21%	24%	31%
Chile	21%	21%	26%	47%	46%
Colombia	N/A	25%	15%	N/A	15%
Mexico	10%	4%	4%	8%	78%
Venezuela	38%	41%	46%	43%	41%
Memo: Spain	6%	5%	6%	5%	6%

Note: BankScope Release 147.1 does not include 2001 bank assets data for Banco Santiago, BS Chile and Banco Industrial De Venezuela. Both Banco Industrial de Venezuela and Banco Caracas are part of SCH as of December 2001. We included them as separate institutions. As of April 2002, Banco Industrial de Venezuela fully absorbed Banco Caracas. In Tables 5.10 to 5.15, information for these banks was obtained from http://www.santander.cl/, http://www.bancosantiago.cl and Solomon Smith Barney's *Venezuelan Bank Reference Guide*.

Source: OCC Survey and BankScope for 2001

Table 5.10 shows that accompanying the declining share in total bank assets accounted for by government-owned banks was an increase in the share accounted for by foreign-owned banks. The increases in foreign-bank shares have been quite large in countries experiencing severe banking crises during the past decade. This reflects the liberalization of foreign-bank entry and ownership restrictions to attract foreign banks with the capital necessary to help resolve the crises in a less-costly manner than would have otherwise been possible. In the case of Mexico, it also reflected the provisions provided by the North American Free Trade Agreement (NAFTA), which took effect in 1994. In Spain, both government and foreign ownership have been relatively small and stable over the past several years.

Domestic vs. foreign participation in banking sector. Table 5.11 provides more detailed information on foreign participation in the banking sectors of the top six countries. Foreign participation in all of these countries is quite high, in terms of both the share of the total number of banks and the share of the total assets of banks. The participation is greatest in Chile in terms of the share of banks (68%), while it is greatest in Mexico in terms of share of bank assets (78%). Colombia ranks lowest in terms of foreign-bank asset share (15%) and next to lowest in terms of foreign-bank number share (28%). Foreign banks have clearly reshaped the banking landscape in all these countries. Spain, in contrast, has relatively high foreign participation in terms of number share (35%), but very little participation in terms of asset share (6%).

Table 5.11 Top six national banking systems: domestic vs. foreign participation, 2001

		Number of Banks				Total Assets				
		Domestic		Foreign			Domestic		Foreign	
	All	Number	%	Number	%	All	Amount (US$ Bil.)	%	Amount (US$ Bil.)	%
Argentina	72	40	56	32	44	92.4	33.0	36	59.4	64
Brazil	102	58	57	44	43	445.2	307.8	69	137.4	31
Chile	22	7	32	15	68	55.8	29.9	54	25.9	46
Colombia	25	18	72	7	28	26.6	22.5	85	4.1	15
Mexico	30	12	40	16	60	164.8	35.8	22	128.9	78
Venezuela	42	28	67	14	33	29.8	17.5	59	12.3	41
Memo:										
Spain	85	55	65	30	35	811.1	766.4	94	44.7	6

Source: BankScope

Tables 5.12-5.15 show the degree of concentration of bank assets for the top six countries, broken down by all banks, foreign-owned banks and Spanish-owned banks. Table 5.12 shows that the top 5 banks in each of the countries account for a low of 45% of total bank assets in Colombia and to a high of 77% in Mexico. The top five banks across all six countries account for 32% of the collective bank assets of these countries. In Spain, the top five banks account for 84% of total bank assets. All these countries clearly have quite high concentration ratios.

Tables 5.13 and 5.14 show the relative importance of foreign-owned banks among the biggest banks in the top six countries. The two tables differ insofar as the former shows foreign presence in terms of number of banks, whereas the latter does so in terms of assets. There are 129 foreign-owned banks out of 293 banks

(Table 5.13) and they account for 45% of the collective bank assets (Table 5.14) in these countries. There are significant differences across the countries, however. Foreign-owned banks are very well represented in all the countries, with the possible exception of Colombia, in terms of both number of banks and share of total bank assets. Spain has quite a few foreign-owned banks but these banks account for a small percentage of total bank assets. Indeed, the foreign-bank share in Spain is smaller than for every one of the top six Latin American countries.

Table 5.12   Concentration of total bank assets for top six countries, 2001

	Total Bank Assets (US$ Millions)	Total Number of Banks	Top Bank	Top 3 banks	Top 5 Banks	Top 10 Banks	Top 20 Banks
Argentina	92,367	72	17%	39%	55%	75%	88%
Brazil	445,227	102	16%	38%	55%	74%	89%
Chile	55,807	22	17%	49%	75%	93%	100%
Colombia	26,645	25	13%	32%	45%	72%	97%
Mexico	164,758	30	28%	61%	77%	95%	99%
Venezuela	29,757	42	14%	41%	55%	79%	95%
Total of the six	814,561	293	9%	21%	32%	49%	63%
Memo: Spain	811,109	85	39%	77%	84%	90%	95%

Source: BankScope

Table 5.13   Foreign bank concentration among biggest banks in top six countries*, 2001

	Number of Banks		Top Bank	Top 3	Top 5	Top 10	Top 20
	Total	Foreign					
Argentina	32 (2)	72	0 (0)	2 (2)	4 (2)	7 (2)	15 (2)
Brazil	44 (5)	102	0 (0)	0 (0)	0 (0)	4 (1)	11 (3)
Chile	15 (2)	22	1 (1)	1 (1)	2 (2)	4 (2)	13 (2)
Colombia	7 (1)	25	0 (0)	0 (0)	0 (0)	2 (1)	6 (1)
Mexico	18 (4)	30	1 (1)	3 (2)	4 (3)	7 (3)	10 (4)
Venezuela	13 (3)	42	1 (1)	2 (2)	2 (2)	4 (3)	6 (3)
Total of the Six	129 (17)	293	0 (0)	0 (0)	1 (1)	4 (2)	10 (6)
Memo: Spain	30	85	0	0	0	3	4

Note: * in parenthesis is the number of Spanish Banks. Banco Santander Chile is a Spanish bank and is included in this table.

Source: BankScope

Table 5.14 Foreign bank concentration of total bank assets in top six countries, 2001

	Total Bank Assets (US$ Bil.)	Foreign Banks					
		Share	Top Bank	Top 3	Top 5	Top 10	Top 20
Argentina	92,367	64%	11%	30%	45%	56%	64%
Brazil	442,227	33%	5%	14%	18%	25%	29%
Chile	55,807	46%	17%	37%	42%	46%	46%
Colombia	26,645	15%	5%	11%	14%	15%	15%
Mexico	164,758	78%	28%	61%	74%	77%	78%
Venezuela	29,757	41%	14%	33%	40%	41%	41%
Total of the Six	814,561	45%	6%	13%	18%	24%	33%
Memo: Spain	811,109	5%	1%	3%	4%	5%	5%

Source: BankScope

Table 5.15 Spanish bank share of total bank assets in top six countries, 2001

	Total Bank Assets (US$ Bil.)	Spanish banks					
		Share	Top Bank	Top 3	Top 5	Top 10	Top 20
Argentina	92,367	22%	11%	22%	22%	22%	22%
Brazil	445,227	8%	5%	8%	8%	8%	8%
Chile	55,807	33%	17%	33%	33%	33%	33%
Colombia	26,645	5%	5%	5%	5%	5%	5%
Mexico	164,758	44%	28%	44%	44%	44%	44%
Venezuela	29,757	27%	14%	27%	27%	27%	27%
Total of the Six	814,561	19%	6%	10%	13%	18%	19%

Source: BankScope

These two tables also show that foreign-owned banks are among the biggest banks in all six countries. Indeed, in Chile, Mexico and Venezuela, the biggest bank is a foreign-owned bank. In these cases, moreover, it is a Spanish-owned bank. Furthermore, all three of the biggest banks in Mexico are foreign-owned banks, two of which are Spanish. More generally, four of the biggest ten banks across these six countries are foreign-owned banks and they account for 24% of the collective bank assets of these countries. The corresponding figures for Spain are three foreign-owned banks and 5% of total bank assets, respectively.

Table 5.15 shows the same total asset-share and concentration information for just Spanish-owned banks. These banks account for their largest shares of total bank assets in Mexico, Chile, Venezuela and Argentina. The shares in these countries are 44, 33, 27 and 22%, respectively. The corresponding shares for Brazil and Colombia are 8 and 5%, respectively. Overall, Spanish-owned banks account for 19% of the collective bank assets of these top six countries, or 40% of the total for all foreign owned banks in these same countries.

Differences in portfolios and performance of domestic- and foreign-owned banks

Table 5.16 presents information on the portfolios and performance of domestic-owned and foreign-owned banks in the top six Latin American countries. More detailed financial information than provided in these tables is very important for a more thorough examination of differences in the portfolios and performance of domestic-owned versus foreign-owned banks, and even government-owned banks. Nonetheless, the information presented in the table does enable one to draw the following broad but necessarily tentative conclusions:

- The allocation of assets to loans ranges from a low of 34% in Brazil to a high of 63% in Chile. In all the countries, moreover, the differences in allocation between domestic and foreign banks are relatively small, except for Chile. In this country, foreign banks allocate 20 percentage points fewer assets to loans than do domestic banks.
- The differences in the mortgage loans-to-total asset ratios between domestic and foreign banks are greatest in Colombia (20 percentage points) and Chile (6 percentage points). For the other two countries for which data are available, Argentina and Mexico, the differences are relatively minor.
- The allocation of assets to government securities is greater for foreign banks in every country, with the greatest difference being nearly 10 percentage points in the case of Venezuela. Although no data are available for Brazilian banks, it is widely reported that these banks hold significant amounts of public-sector bonds.
- In all the countries, equity investments are quite low as a percentage of total assets. This is the case for both domestic and foreign banks. Domestic banks in Mexico have a ratio of 3.2%, which is triple the ratio for foreign banks. The reverse holds in the case of Brazil.
- Mexico is the only country in which total deposits fund a larger proportion of the assets of foreign banks than domestic banks, but the difference is only 2.6 percentage points. Domestic banks account for larger ratios than foreign banks in the other countries, the biggest difference being 20 percentage points in the case of Chile.

Table 5.16   Domestic and foreign banks: selected balance sheet and income statement items, 2001

	Argentina Dom.	Argentina For.	Brazil Dom.	Brazil For.	Chile Dom.	Chile For.	Colombia Dom.	Colombia For.	Mexico Dom.	Mexico For.	Venezuela Dom.	Venezuela For.	Spain Dom.	Spain For.
Number of Banks	40	32	55	44	7	13	18	7	16	14	33	11	53	32
Balance Sheet														
Customer Loans to Total Assets	50.8	50.2	34.1*	33.6*	48.2	34.4	42.1	55.0	49.6	45.4	43.9*	48.3*	53.1*	56.2*
Mortgage Loans to Total Assets	9.8	8.1	N/A	N/A	14.2	8.3	20.0	0.3	6.1	7.2	N/A	N/A	N/A	N/A
Total Loans to Total Assets	60.6	58.3	34.1	33.7	63.3	43.5	62.7	55.6	59.3	54.6	47.6	50.9	53.9	56.4
Problem Loans to Total Loan	N/A	N/A	N/A	N/A	1.4	1.8	1.0	0.7	6.0	3.6	7.6	4.9	1.6	0.3
Loan Loss Reserves to Total Loans	6.4	7.2	6.3	5.2	2.3	3.5	6.9	4.2	6.7	5.2	7.2	4.7	2.8	0.3
Government Securities to Total Assets	5.2	6.2	N/A	N/A	3.3	6.5	5.4	13.3	8.6	8.7	5.7	15.1	17.5	6.4
Equity Investments to Total Assets	0.6	0.5	0.8	2.6	0.1	0.2	N/A	N/A	3.2	1.1	1.5	1.6	2.1	0.3
Demand Deposits To Total Assets	8.0	12.4	7.6	4.1	11.9	6.6	14.5	10.9	36.4	27.5	39.8	35.8	11.6	20.9
Total Deposits to Total Assets	69.8	62.9	40.9	29.8	70.4	59.8	76.4	70.2	81.9	84.7	82.2	80.8	71.1	85.6
Equity to Total Assets	11.2	10.6	8.3	10.7	7.1	14.0	12.5	10.7	11.0	8.6	13.9	15.0	7.3	6.4
Income Statement														
Return on Assets (Pre-Tax Profit to Total Assets)	1.2	0.2	2.0	-0.5	1.3	1.7	1.7	1.0	0.8	2.1	2.9	3.4	1.3	0.3
Net Interest Revenue to Total Assets	4.5	3.6	5.2	6.2	3.8	3.7	4.5	3.9	5.8	4.2	11.0	10.2	2.9	1.8
Return on Equity (Pre-tax Profit/Total Equity)	11.0	1.7	24.3	-4.6	18.3	11.8	13.7	9.8	7.7	24.5	20.6	22.3	17.2	5.3
Net Commission, Fee and Trading Income to Total Assets	3.4	3.4	1.0	0.5	1.0	1.8	4.6	7.0	2.6	2.8	N/A	N/A	1.4	1.3
Personnel and Administrative Expenses to Total Assets	3.4	3.5	5.8	5.6	1.7	1.8	2.7	2.7	5.1	4.2	9.2	8.4	2.2	2.4

Note: The figures are not averages of individual banks but instead unweighted totals. Also, customer loans include loans to municipalities and government, loans to group companies and associates, and other corporate loans and loans to bank.
   * denotes that these figures include mortgage loans.

Source: BankScope

- The profitability of domestic and foreign banks differs widely across the countries. In Argentina, Brazil and Colombia, foreign banks underperform domestic banks, whereas the reverse is the case in Chile, Mexico and Venezuela.
- Foreign banks generally neither uniformly generate more noninterest income nor operate less expensively than domestic banks in the top six countries.

  In the case of Spain, one of the biggest differences between domestic and foreign banks is that domestic banks allocate 11 percentage points more of their assets to government securities than do foreign banks. They also are more profitable and fund a much smaller percentage of their assets with deposits than do foreign banks. Much more detailed work remains to be done in examining the differences in the portfolios and performance of domestic and foreign banks. The conclusions just noted, once again, are quite tentative due to the nature of the data and the fact that even in this case the data only pertain to a single year.

Recent changes in bank structure raise important questions

The documented changes in the structure of Latin America's banking markets in recent years are quite profound. At the same time that governments have decreased their participation in these markets through direct ownership of banks, foreign banks have increased their participation through mergers and acquisitions of domestically-owned entities. These developments raise many important questions that merit further examination and discussion. A few of these questions will now be addressed.

1. What explains the recent penetration by foreign-banks into Latin America?
   There are several important factors that help explain this penetration. These include the following:
- Foreign banks may face less competition and have more market opportunities in Latin American than in their home countries. In this regard, Focarelli and Pozzolo (2000) find that foreign bank entry is greater in those countries with inefficient banking industries and expected high rates of economic growth.
- Entry restrictions and other financial regulations (including tax treatment) have been eased in recent years throughout Latin America, which makes foreign bank entry easier and more attractive. In many cases these actions coincided with banking crises and the privatization of government owned banks. The entry of foreign banks brought outside capital into the domestic banking sector.
- Spanish banks, in particular, face fewer linguistic and cultural barriers in Latin America as compared to other parts of the world. Furthermore, these banks can grow and expand more easily in this still financially less developed region

than in the more financially mature economies of the European Union (EU) or the U.S.

- Foreign banks have expanded into the region as their own domestic clients with international operations have done so in search of bigger markets. This does not necessarily imply that foreign banks will provide financial services to only or to even mainly the affiliates of their home-country clients. Foreign bank penetration in the region, moreover, may induce the entry of foreign nonbanking firms.

- Foreign banks with large home-market shares have incentives to seek risk diversification opportunities abroad. Also, economies of scale and scope may drive bank expansion into other countries. Facarelli and Pozzolo (2000), for example, find that bigger banks have greater degrees of internationalization.

2. Will the penetration by foreign-banks lead to safer and sounder banks and, more generally, to more developed and better functioning financial systems? Some points worth considering in this regard are as follows:

- Foreign banks can bring new technology, management skill, and capital to the domestic banking industry which should help promote safer and sounder institutions.

- Greater competition brought about by foreign banks should encourage domestic banks to search out the most profitable uses of their funds. In this regard, Levine (2000) finds that foreign banks tend to spur competition and contribute to a more efficient domestic banking industry. Claessens, Demirgüç-Kunt and Hizinga (2001) also find that foreign bank entry leads to greater efficiency in the domestic banking system.

- Rajan and Zingales (2001) find that international openness tends to limit the rent-seeking activities of domestic banks, and thereby promotes financial and economic development.

- Claessens and Glaessner (1998) point out that the "presence of foreign financial firms is more likely to reduce capital flight, as was observed in several recent episodes (e.g., in Argentina and Thailand foreign banks received large amounts of deposits from domestic banks when concerns arose about the quality of domestic banks)."

- Barth, Caprio and Levine (2002) find that restrictions on foreign entry are associated with greater banking-sector fragility.

- Peria, Powell and Hollar (2002) find that foreign banks are less susceptible to pro-cyclical shocks. Indeed, Dages, Goldberg, and Kinney's (2001) study of Argentina during the 1990s found that foreign banks had higher loan growth rates than domestic banks and foreign bank credit grew even during crisis periods.

- The presence of foreign banks may help to constrain any political efforts to use the banking system as an instrument of "crony capitalism."

3. How is the allocation of credit impacted by the presence of foreign banks and what is the reaction of domestic banks to the foreign-bank penetration?

- Dages, Goldberg, and Kinney (2000) examined the lending behavior of foreign and domestic banks in Argentina and Mexico during the mid-1990s. They found the portfolio compositions of both types of banks to be quite similar in Argentina, while this was also the case for banks with low levels of problem loans in Mexico.

- Clarke, Cull, Peria and Sanchez (2002) examined bank-level data for Argentina, Chile, Colombia, and Peru during the mid-1990s. They found that small foreign banks lent considerably less to small businesses than small domestic banks in all four countries. However, they found that large foreign banks lent more to small businesses (as a share of total lending) than large domestic banks in Chile and Colombia. In Argentina and Chile, they found that lending to small businesses by medium and large foreign banks grew faster than for domestic banks of similar size.

- Gelos and Roldos (2002) found that "at least 37 M&A transactions involving private sector financial institutions occurred in Brazil between end-1995 and end-2000. Several of these transactions were driven by the three largest domestic private banks' attempts to remain competitive in the main regions of the country, as well as the perception by many medium and small banks that they would not be able to sustain positive earnings in such a competitive environment, especially in the wake of few large foreign acquisitions."

    Much more detailed work needs to be done in assessing the effect of the changing structure of banking markets in Latin America on the allocation of credit, especially given how recent and dramatic these changes have been. However, Fernando de Paula (2001) provides an excellent assessment of the determinants and impacts of foreign bank presence in Brazil.

4. Will the penetration of foreign banks lead to greater integration of financial markets in the region?

- A few comments about financial integration both within and across national borders will be made on the basis of Table 5.17. It contains information on selected measures of the financial environment in the top six Lain American countries. The same information is presented for both Spain and the U.S. for comparative purposes. First, in every country, except Chile, a very low amount of bank credit is extended to the private sector (scaled relative to GDP). Indeed, despite being the second biggest economy in the region, the amount of private credit extended by Mexico's banks is only 10% of GDP. This indicates there is substantial opportunity for expansion in credit to the private sector by both domestic and foreign banks. Second, more progress can be made by these countries with respect to improving contract enforcement, curtailing corruption, reducing the costs of establishing a business, and providing greater access to capital by business firms. Third, the overall banking environment scores for the six countries emphasize the need for still more progress in improving the financial sector by all of them. Last, attention has to be paid to the extent to which the regulation and supervision of financial institutions and markets needs to be harmonized throughout the region, including whether a regional regulatory/supervisory authority should replace separate national authorities. Only through these efforts can one expect greater financial integration and convergence in Latin American countries.

Table 5.17   Selected measures of the financial environment in the top six Latin American countries, Spain and the United States

	Bank Private Credit/GDP (%) 2001[4]	Contract Enforcement 2001[2]	Cost of Business Entry (% of GNP Per Capita) 2001[2]	Corruption 2002[3]	Capital Access Index 2002[1]	Banking Environment Score 2002[1]
Argentina	20	5.39	10.38	2.8	4.02	5.89
Brazil	29	3.06	12.02	4.0	3.59	5.42
Colombia	19	4.11	14.13	3.6	3.35	5.97
Chile	65	4.56	13.44	7.5	4.53	N/A
Mexico	10	4.71	20.88	3.6	3.65	5.87
Venezuela	11	6.01	16.51	2.5	3.33	7.00
Spain	106	5.24	15.5	7.1	4.78	n/a
United States	50	2.61	0.69	7.7	5.5	3.24

Note: Banking Environment Index (BEI) ranks the banking environment with regard to legal systems, creditor and property rights, effectiveness of bank supervision, accounting practices, competition in the banking sector and financial environment.
Source: [1]Milken Institute (1 least access, 7 greatest access; 1 best environment, 10 worst environment).
[2]Worldbank (low value indicates greater contract enforcement).
[3]Transparency International (0 most corrupt, 10 least corrupt).
[4]International Financial Statistics.

Additional remarks about the two largest Spanish banks

The two largest banks in Spain are Banco Santander Central Hispano (BSCH) and Banco Bilbao Vizcaya Argentina (BBVA). As of June 30, 2002, BSCH had $387 billion in assets, and BBVA had $282 billion in assets. On the basis of total assets, these two banks ranked first and second in Spain. Together they account for nearly 70% of the country's total banking assets.

As of June 30, 2002, BBVA had 22% of its total assets in Mexico and 9% of its assets in other Latin American countries. Of its net profit of $1,163 million in the first half of 2002, 18% is from its operations in Mexico and 9% is from other Latin American countries. For the same time period, BSCH had 31% of its total assets in Latin America. Of its net profit of $1,194 million, 67% is from its operations in Latin America. These two banks account for about one-fourth of the total banking assets in Latin America.

Clearly, the fact that these two banks account for more than one third of Spain's banking assets means that their performance essentially drives the entire industry's performance. Their heavy exposure to Latin America, moreover, means that whatever happens in the region necessary affects the banking industry in Spain. To the extent that adverse shocks in Spain and in Latin America are negatively correlated, diversification benefits will be achieved.

Summary and conclusions

Many important developments occurred in Latin America over the past decade. Authoritarian regimes were replaced with democracies throughout the region. There has been a proliferation of multinational and bilateral free trade agreements in the region. The most important agreement is the Free Trade Agreement of the Americas (FTAA), which is due to be completed in 2005. The structure of Latin America's banking markets has also undergone a dramatic change. Government ownership of banks in most of the countries in the region has significantly declined, while foreign ownership has simultaneously increased. Indeed, the latter process has continued. For example, in 2002, HSBC acquired Mexico's Gupo Financiero Bital. This increased the foreign bank share of Mexico's total bank assets to 84%. Today, there is only one big domestic bank left to be acquired, Banorte. In Mexico and other parts of the region, Spanish banks have played an important role in this "conquest" of Latin American banking.

Recently, however, there has been turmoil in many of the countries in the region, especially Argentina, Brazil and Venezuela. This situation has promoted greater and more widespread uncertainty about the near-term prospects for further reform efforts toward freer trade, more privatization of government-owned enterprises, and increased ownership of domestic banking assets by foreign banks. There are reports, moreover, that some international banks are withdrawing from parts of Latin America or at least curtailing expansion plans given the current economic and political uncertainty. Esterl (2002), for example, states that "Canada's Bank of Nova Scotia, France's Crédit Agricole SA and Italy's Intesa BCI SpA all have announced plans this year to decamp from South America's second-largest economy after recession-racked Argentina defaulted on most of its public debt, scrapped dollar parity and imposed harsh capital controls."

Despite the current uncertainty about the economic, and even political, situation in many of the Latin America countries, and their implications for reform, one can nonetheless be optimistic about the longer-term prospects. Substantial progress in several important dimensions has already been made in the region and will not likely be totally reversed. Specifically, as regards financial systems, governments everywhere now recognize the importance of well functioning banking and capital markets for economic and social prosperity.

Notes

[1] The authors are grateful for the excellent assistance of Cindy Lee and for very helpful comments from Harry Makler.

[2] See Álvarez, Cheibub, Limongi, Przeworski (1999) for information on the categorization of political regimes of countries around the world.

[3] Latin America, in comparison, accounts for 8.3% of the world's population, 6.2% of the world's GDP, and 1.1% of world's total financial assets.

References

Álvarez, M., J.A. Cheibub, F. Limongi and A. Przeworski (1999), "ACLP Political and Economic Database Codebook," December.

Armijo, L.E., and W. L. Ness, Jr. (2002), "Modernizing Brazil's Capital Markets, 1985-2001: Pragmatism and Democratic Adjustment," Paper prepared for the *Annual Meeting of the International Studies Association, New Orleans*, March 25-28.

Barth, J.R., D.E. Nolle, T. Phumiwasana, and G. Yago (2002), "A Cross-Country Analysis of the Bank Supervisory Framework and Bank Performance," Economic and Policy Analysis Working Paper 2002-2, Office of the Comptroller of the Currency. http://www.occ.treas.gov/wp2002-2.htm.

Barth, J.R., G. Caprio, and R. Levine (2002), "Bank Regulation and Supervision: What Works Best?" World Bank Working Paper, no. 2725.

Barth, J.R., G. Caprio, and R. Levine (2001), "The Regulation and Supervision of Banks Around the World: A New Database," in R.E. Litan and R. Herring (eds), *Integrating Emerging Market Countries into the Global Financial System*.

Beck, T., N. Loayza, and R. Levine (2000), "Financial Intermediation and Growth: Causality and Causes," *Journal of Monetary Economics*, 46 (1), pp. 891-911.

Beck, T., and R. Levine (2004), "Stock Markets, Banks, and Growth," *Journal of Banking and Finance*, vol 28, March 2004, pp.423-442.

Claessens, S., and T. Glaessner (1998), "Internationalization of Financial Services in Asia," World Bank Working Paper, no. 1911.

Claessens, S. A. Demirgüç-Kunt, and H. Huizinga (2001), "How Does Foreign Entry Affect the Domestic Banking Markets?" *Journal of Banking and Finance*, 25 (5), pp. 891-911.

Clarke, G., R. Cull, M.S.M Peria, and S.M. Sánchez (2002), "Bank Lending to Small Businesses in Latin America: Does Bank Origin Matter?" World Bank Working Paper, no. 2760.

Courtis, N. (ed.) (1999), *How Countries Supervise their Banks, Insurers and Securities Markets*, Central Banking Publications, London.

Dages, G., L.B. Goldberg, and D. Kinney (2000), "Foreign and Domestic Bank Participation in Emerging Markets: Lessons from Mexico and Argentina," *Economic Policy Review*, Federal Reserve Bank of New York, September, 6 (3), pp.17-36.

Demirgüç-Kunt, A., and R. Levine (eds.) (2001), *Financial Structure and Economic Growth: A Cross Country Comparison of Banks, Markets, and Development*, MIT Press, Cambridge.

Demirgüç-Kunt, A., and V. Maksimovic (1998), "Law, Finance, and Firm Growth," *Journal of Finance*, December, 53 (6), pp. 2107-2137.

Demirgüç-Kunt, A., R. Levine, and H.G. Min (1998), "Opening to Foreign Banks: Issues of Stability, Efficiency, and Growth," in Seongtae, L. (ed.), *The Implications of Globalization of World Financial Markets*, Seoul, Korea: The Bank of Korea, pp. 83-115.

Domowitz, I., J. Glen, and A. Madhavan (2001), "International Evidence on Aggregate Corporate Financing Decisions," in A. Demirgüç-Kunt, and R. Levine (eds.), *Financial Structure and Economic Growth*, pp. 263-296.

Esterl, M. (2002), "Banks Pull Back From Latin America," *The Wall Street Journal*, October 30, pp. B5A.

Fernando de Paula, L. (2001), "The Recent Wave of European Banks in Brazil: Determinants and Impacts," Centre for Brazilian Studies, University of Oxford.

Focarelli, D. and A. Pozzolo (2000), "The Determinants of Cross-Border Shareholding: An Analysis with Bank-Level Data from OECD Countries," Paper presented at the *Federal Reserve Bank of Chicago Bank Structure Conference*, May 3-5.

Gelos, G.R., and J. Roldós (2002), "Consolidation and Market Structure in Emerging Markets Banking Systems," International Monetary Fund, Unpublished.

Herring, R. J., and N. Chatusripitak (2001), "The Case of the Missing Market: The Bond Market and Why it Matters for Financial Development," The Wharton School Financial Institutions Center, August.

La Porta, R., F. Lopez-De-Silanes, and A. Shleifer (2002), "Government Ownership of Banks," *The Journal of Finance*, 57 (1), pp. 265-301.

Levine, R. (1997), "Financial Development and Economic Growth: Views and Agenda," *Journal of Economic Literature*, 35 (2), pp. 688-726.

Levine, R. (2001), "International Financial Liberalization and Economic Growth," *Review of International Economics*, 9 (4), pp. 688-702.

Levine, R., and S. Zervos (1998), "Stock Market, Bank, and Economic Growth,*"* *American Economic Review*, 88, pp. 537-558.

Litan, R.E. and R. Herring (eds) (2001), *Integrating Emerging Market Countries into the Global Financial System*, Brookings-Wharton Papers on Financial Services, Brookings Institution Press.

Peria, M.S.M, A. Powell and I.V. Hollar (2002), "Banking on Foreigners: The Behavior of International Bank Lending to Latin America, 1985-2000" World Bank Working Paper no. 2893.

Rajan, R.G., and L. Zingales (2001), "The Great Reversals: The Politics of Financial Development in the 20th Century," NBER Working Paper w8178.

Seongtae, L. (ed.) (1998), *The Implications of Globalization of World Financial Markets*, The Bank of Korea, Seoul.

World Bank (2001), *Finance for Growth: Policy Choices in a Volatile World*, A World Bank Policy Research Report, Oxford University Press, New York.

Chapter 6

Big Spanish Banks in Brazil: Anything Different in their Asset and Credit Allocation?

Harry M. Makler and Walter L. Ness, Jr.

Introduction[1]

Credit allocation (lending) and the role of banks in this process has been the focus of social science for several decades yet the emphasis has been more on the supply rather than the demand side. If one is concerned with the growth and development of markets, be they nations or entire regions, the focus should be equally on both. Rather than only studying which intermediaries are supplying credit and how much they are allocating, there should be more emphasis on who receives credit, who is actually borrowing, what volume they are borrowing and what interest rate and other costs they are paying. Until such studies are performed we have to be content with supply side analyses, but even in this area, scholarship has not gone very far in differentiating among banks and comparing their lending with that of other financial intermediaries.

Among the reasons for this lag is a dilemma about the role of banks. In economics, one debate has to do with supply and demand. Some have characterized banks as demand following, or as passive, permissive intermediaries that, following market conditions, merely provide services or loans to creditworthy borrowers. Economists such as Goldsmith (1969), Gurley and Shaw (1967), and Patrick (1966) saw banks as supplying capital, encouraging efficient credit allocation, increasing accumulation and sometimes assisting in the founding of new enterprises or in promoting mergers but only upon the demands of their clients. Others viewed banks as supply leading. Among these was Schumpeter ([1934] 1961) who brought credit creation by banks to the forefront, identifying them as supply leading and growth inducing agents of development. In creating new sources of credit, banking systems were ranked slightly behind those of entrepreneurship and innovation as engines of growth. For Schumpeter, well-managed banks fuel technological innovation by identifying and funding entrepreneurs who are identified as most likely to successfully introduce and implement new products and production processes. But in his discussion of commercial banks, he simply mentioned the ability of banks to create money and thus purchasing power without analyzing their method of capital accumulation or their relations with the entrepreneurs to whom they allocated credit.

Political economy discussion focuses more on nation building, cross-national and cross-historical comparisons and institutional roles. Keynes (1960) saw banks as actors in development but essentially as financing development. It was Gerschenkron (1962) who introduced the importance of context and institutional form. In an often-cited explanation of the role of banks in development, he observed that the historical timing of a nation's industrialization determines which economic actors and social institutions will be involved. One of his principal hypotheses was that the more backward an economy relative to others in the same period the greater the likelihood that financial institutions will be created to supply capital in advance of demand. In the transformation of once backward countries through industrialization, he emphasized the role of the state, state-owned and specialized private (including foreign) banks in providing capital and entrepreneurial guidance to nascent industries. Because of the magnitude of bank lending to industry, Gerschenkron predicted that banks would acquire "...a formidable degree of ascendancy over industrial enterprises which extended beyond the sphere of financial control and into that of entrepreneurial and managerial decisions" (1962: 14). Yet he neither examined the extent to which this control was obtained nor did he identify the lenders, their clients, or the lending terms that were imposed. Nor have others extensively examined these topics. A good way to begin to get a handle on these topics is to study asset and credit allocation activities of the foreign banks whose role in many developing countries has recently and markedly increased. They are viewed as a principal source of capital to accelerate growth, and in several countries have replaced the state as banker.[2] Spanish banks in Brazil, as elsewhere in Latin America, have become formidable, if not, the hemisphere's principal foreign lenders (Barth et al. 2002).

Comparing the credit allocation and funding structure of the Spanish banks in Brazil with each other and with other banks will indicate to what extent they differ from one another and their foreign and local competitors. The questions to which we respond include (i) to what extent the Spanish banks adapted to the structure of the banks they acquired and to what extent they have transformed the banks according to their worldwide or regional strategies, (ii) to what extent the strategies of Spanish banks are similar, and (iii) to what extent the Spanish banks have investment and funding strategies similar to other foreign banks. Different or similar strategies are evidenced in our study by the similarity of investment allocation or funding, shown respectively in the assets and liabilities of a bank's balance sheet.

Objective

In this chapter, we propose to examine the asset and credit allocation activity of the Spanish banks in Brazil.[3] A principal characteristic of Brazilian private bank lending is its short-term nature which is of very little importance for financing investment. Most of our information is from financial statements and data provided by public financial authorities such as central banks and government statistical institutes. Learning who is receiving money is but a first step – and a modest one at that – toward illuminating credit allocation in its entirety. To best describe credit allocation, borrowers should be surveyed in order to learn how much money had been requested, for what purpose, how much had been received, from whom and on what terms.[4] One such study was conducted in the Brazilian Northeast when its industrialization began in the 1970s (Makler 1982).

Nevertheless, a supply side focus provides a good beginning and, as we will show, takes us quite a ways into where the money is going. By comparing credit and asset allocation by Banco Santander and Banco Bilbao e Vizcaya (BBVA)[5], the two world-class Spanish banks, with other financial intermediaries (domestic and other foreign-controlled banks) we are able to identify lending patterns, judge whether anything has changed, and assess the similarities or differences in credit allocation among banks in Brazil. Comparing current Spanish bank credit and asset allocation data with that from financial statements of domestic banks before they were acquired by Santander or BBVA, we will also examine whether credit allocation is shaped by the banking patterns inherited from the banks that they acquired or is the result of strategies peculiar to the Spanish banks. Basically we wish to test whether a domestic market is a more powerful determinant of credit and asset allocation than a bank's regional or global lending policy, or whether, in other words, homogenization of credit allocation is at play or not. If it is, then it could be argued that the Spanish banks are promoting harmonization of regional banking practices in Latin America. If not, they are basically responding to a market rather than imposing a particular model or style of banking.

The credit allocation activities of Spanish banks are thus hypothesized as influenced by:

a) the Brazilian banks that were acquired,
b) banking practices of foreign controlled Brazilian banks in general,
c) Spanish banking practice in general,
d) strategies of each Spanish bank which differ from one another, or
e) Brazilian banking practice in general which may reflect
    i   Brazilian banking strategies or
    ii   The market forces acting in Brazil.

Gorillas in our midst?

Foreign bank entry in emerging economies has as many advocates as it has opponents. Its "yea-sayers" (and there are many) claim that foreign banks a) increase access to international financing, b) provide greater liquidity in the financial system if it is "under banked", c) stimulate greater bank loan growth, d) provide greater stability in credit and investment in adverse economic cycles or are able to withstand macroeconomic shocks because of their geographic diversity, e) are more efficient, f) heighten competition in their sector, g) relieve overburdened regulation and supervision because they are primarily regulated by authorities of their home country, h) supply technical expertise in banking operations and the development of accounting and transparency standards, and i) encourage the creation of supporting agents such as rating agencies, independent auditors and credit bureaus (cf. Carvalho 2003; Claessens, Demirguç-Kunt, and Huizinga 1999; Mathieson and Roldos 2001; Dages, Goldberg, and Kinney 2000; Claessens and Glaessner 1998; Glaessner and Oks 1994; World Bank 2000).[6]

Associations with foreign capital, including banks, are also viewed as fostering local entrepreneurship and providing mobility opportunities for local businesses. In comparing Brazil, India and South Korea, Evans (1995) demonstrates that foreign capital and national governments can perform a nurturing or a midwifery role in the development of certain economies. In an earlier study of Brazil, Evans (1979) found that foreign capital formed alliances with prominent family-owned firms in order to access local markets. In exchange, these firms were promised technology and access to international markets. Some nations in their quest for rapid economic development have encouraged foreign direct investment and invited the participation of robust foreign banks not only because they were viewed as a means toward growth and development but to stabilize their economy and diminish balance of payments, savings, and fiscal deficits as well. The epoch of bank privatizations in the 1990s in Brazil and other Latin American markets demonstrated this policy.

"Nay-sayers" claim that foreign banks remit profits abroad without generating any foreign exchange earnings. They also accuse these banks of selective lending or "cherry picking" with respect to their alleged credit bias toward multinational and large domestic corporations. Mathieson and Roldes (2001) allege that "cherry picking" leaves small domestic borrowers without credit or forces remaining domestic banks to absorb greater credit risks. They may also have a greater propensity to invest in securities, especially of the government, than lend to the private sector. For 1999, Ness (2001) found that foreign banks allocated larger proportions of their assets than private domestic banks to government securities and a lower proportion of loans to the private sector. Similarly two years later the six largest foreign banks in Brazil reported a higher proportion of their loans in the lowest risk categories than the three largest private banks that made riskier loans (Carvalho, 2003).[7] Foreign banks could be cherry picking but Carvalho suggests that it is just as likely that the largest domestic banks, equally risk adverse and rigorous in their loan risk classification, were maintaining their control of the consumer loan market.[8]

Nay-sayers are also concerned that the welfare of the local subsidiaries of foreign banks is shaped by the financial health of the entire banking group whose monitoring remains beyond the reach of a central bank in an emerging market. And in terms of credit allocation and investment, the worry has been expressed that foreign control of a financial system may dislocate the credit decision-making for the economy out of domestic hands. As a result, local credit requirements can be neglected and ultimately national sovereignty compromised (Makler and Ness 2002).

Foreign banking in Brazil

Foreign banks dominated Brazilian banking in the 19th century and maintained an advantageous position until the 1930s. The first foreign banks in Brazil were the London and Brazilian Bank (1862) and the Brazilian & Portuguese Bank (1863), which became the English Bank of Rio de Janeiro (1866). These banks entered shortly after the founding of Banco do Brazil in 1853. Spanish banking was not important in Brazil during this period, although the Portuguese had a minor but persistent role.[9] In the 1930s, the Getulio Vargas government restricted foreign participation in Brazilian banks to one-third of voting shares and one-half of total capital. Exceptions were made through a "grandfather clause" permitting those foreign-controlled banks existing before enactment of the legislation to continue their operations and through reciprocity arrangements with countries that permitted the establishment of Brazilian banks in their territory. Existing foreign banks were severely restricted in opening new bank offices.[10] Their activities were concentrated in foreign trade finance, asset management for business groups and wealthy families, and booking corporate loans for the parent bank.

The 1988 Brazilian Constitution provides in its Article 192 for regulation of foreign banks through complementary legislation. In that such complementary legislation has never been passed by the Congress, the transitional dispositions of the constitution were interpreted to permit the Brazilian President to permit the entry of foreign banks on a case by case basis according to "national interests." The bank crises experienced by Argentina, Brazil, Mexico, and other Latin American nations were important in the Cardoso government's greater flexibility with respect to foreign banks. The first use of this authorization was for the purchase of the failing Bamerindus bank by the HSBC group by Legislative Intent no. 311 of August 1995 which specifies the following beneficial impacts expected from foreign banking: increase in domestic savings, improvement of operational efficiency, the supply of financial services with lower costs, and the introduction of new technologies. Other foreign banks were authorized until 1999. Restrictions on agency expansion and other activities by foreign banks were eased by a constitutional amendment requiring equal treatment of firms established in Brazil, regardless of their ownership or control.

The major foreign banks that compete today with Spanish-controlled banks in Brazil were present before the restrictions on foreign banking were imposed are: Citibank, BankBoston, Holandês Unido (now ABN Amro) and Sudameris (which has expressed its desire to sell its Brazilian operations). By acquiring Brazilian banks foreign competitors of the Spanish banks strengthened themselves. The Hong Kong Shanghai Banking Corporation (HSBC) purchased the failing Bamerindus bank, having originally entered through a minority participation. ABN-Amro purchased control of the Real bank group and later the state banks of

Pernambuco (Bandepe) and Paraiba (Paraiban). The Caixa Geral de Depósitos of Portugal purchased the Bandeirantes bank and later resold it to Unibanco, a large domestic Brazilian bank. The Italian-based Sudameris group bought the América do Sul bank. By the end of 2001, foreign-controlled banks were responsible for 22.5% of total bank assets as contrasted with only 7.2% at the end of 1994, 24.5% of loans, and 16.9% of deposits.

Credit and asset allocation: Spanish banks in comparative perspective

Background

The Banco Santander Central Hispano (BSCH) and Banco Bilbao Vizcaya Argentaria S.A. (BBVA) in less than a decade simultaneously became, respectively the first and third largest foreign commercial banks in Latin America (Paula 2002) and among the largest and most active in the European Union (Guillén 2001).[11] Until the 1990s Spanish banks had limited international presence. Yet within the next decade they had made heavy investments, mainly through the purchase of local banks in all the larger South American Spanish and Portuguese-speaking countries, to become among the largest foreign commercial banks in the Americas and one of the largest in the European market for financial services through alliances and minority equity share participations. These new *reconquistadores* had acquired "nearly 50 leading domestic institutions, compared to merely 13 by all other foreign banks combined, including Citibank, Deutsche Bank, Banque Nationale de Paris...." (Guillén 2001: 202). Spanish banks have been cast as the most aggressive multi-national enterprises in Latin America (Toral 2001: 139).

    Spanish bank expansion in the 1990s can be explained by a combination of factors that include the political economy of their home country, their own structure, and the European financial arena. Spanish banks, together with the church and the military, have been cast as powerful factions and as institutions that have long sustained a symbiotic relation with the government bureaucracy and various political regimes (Guillén 2001). To further its export-led development strategy the Spanish government enacted legislation in the early 1960s that enabled banks to expand their financial services and to take equity positions in non-financial enterprises. This universal banking model contributed to banks evolving into business groups, or more specifically, the emergence of financial-industrial groups with banks at the core of a variety of interconnected firms (cf. Johnson 2001). This domestic experience aided the Spanish banks when they turned abroad. In spite of 1992 Single Market Act, the persistence of national banking regulatory structures in Europe has impeded cross border acquisitions. The flagship Spanish banks thus have been protected from foreign competition. While foreign multinationals could dominate Spanish manufacturing, their takeover or even obtaining market share in the Spanish banking sector was not permitted. Nor did the proliferation of public financial intermediaries such as government savings banks and credit cooperatives strongly compete with private banking, perhaps because these public intermediaries were more regulated. Yet as a result of deregulation (liberalization) in the 1980s competition intensified. Both private and public banks also became active participants in the deregulated service sectors such as telecommunications and utilities, as well as in mass retailing, government procurement and broadcasting. Private banks improved their information technology, product differentiation, and services; but, most of all, the larger banks engaged in a series of mergers and acquisitions that consolidated the national banking sector. Thus BBVA and Santander became very powerful within Europe and by 1999 Santander had become the largest bank within the EU in terms of market capitalization (cf. Guillén 2001: 206).

Santander's and BBVA's styles and internationalization were shaped by their role in domestic and European markets. Santander is considered to be governed by a presidentialist style, while BBVA has a more collective governance structure, at least at the level of the Board of Directors. Through mergers and acquisitions Santander obtained important retail banks in Spain, focused more on banking and tended to divest from industrial activities (that were inherited when it acquired Banco Español de Crédito – Banesto). Santander's expansion into Latin America was initiated by the group's investment banking segment but its most recent expansion has been shaped by its commercial banking segment. Within a half dozen years Santander became a multinational retail bank. It is not heavily represented on the boards of key Spanish companies in telecommunications and energy and shies away from managerial control of non-financial firms in which they invest. Santander's president, Emilio Botín, has affirmed that his bank's investments in industrial corporations are purely financial (Toral, 2001: 154).

BBVA was different. The bank originated in the northern industrialized region of Spain, the result of a merger of the Banco de Bilbao with the Banco de Vizcaya. In contrast to Santander, the Bilbao bank was more grounded in industry. Among its top executives and major shareholders are "...a tight group of families that played a key role in Basque and Spanish industrialization at the turn of the century" (Guillén 2001: 209). Like its competitor BBVA grew by acquiring other domestic banks, yet the bank is viewed as more cautious and less acquisitive than Santander.[12] BBVA has been cast as assuming managerial control of all its acquisitions but this remains to be substantiated (cf. Toral 2001: 153-154).It has been more active in Mexico and other Latin American countries where it has a greater share of the banking market.[13] In 1997 its Latin American operations accounted for 23% of the group's consolidated assets and 17% of its net attributable profits (Guillén 2001: 209). In Brazil, BBVA purchased only one bank, Excel-Econômico. While that bank as a financial-industrial group included several non-financial enterprises, BBVA did not attempt to purchase any of them when they were auctioned.

Why did the Spanish banks spread into Latin America? It was not merely because of cultural and language affinities but factors such as increasing competition in their domestic market especially from savings banks, competition in European markets from other European banks, the skill they achieved in retail banking, the promise of greater profit opportunities of the Latin American markets as compared to the domestic and the European market, and what is also characteristic of Korean *chaebols*, a sheer zest for competing with and outdoing the bank next door. Paula (2003) attributes the expansion into Latin America to various motives:

a)   earnings diversification,
b)   increasing competition in Europe and a need to strengthen Spanish bank capitalization against future hostile takeover efforts,
c)   opportunities offered by privatization, deregulation, and restructuring of the banking sector in Latin America,
d)   the growth potential of a market that was underbanked,
e)   the high intermediation margins of Latin American markets compared with the rest of the world, and
f)   the potential gains from efficiency due to the high overhead costs existing in Latin American banking.

Other reasons for Spanish bank expansion were their decreasing profit margins in Spain, their maturation achieved through continuous adaptation to financial market liberalization at home, the permeability of the Latin American markets, and their governments' receptivity to foreign banks and to new kinds of financial services (Toral 2001: 139, 146). The priority given by these two banks to their Latin American investments is illustrated by their investment. By 1997, Santander had invested $3.5 billion, its assets amounted to $45 billion, and 57.6% of its global labor force worked in its Latin American subsidiaries. Its Latin American operations represented nearly 50% of the group's foreign assets and 48% of its net attributable profits (Guillén 2001: 208).

In the same year BBVA had $25.7 billion in assets invested in the Latin American banks it controlled (Toral 2002: 147). By June 2002, BBVA's Latin American assets grew to 31% of its worldwide assets and it had 52.5% of its 7685 offices in Latin America. It had banking activities in Argentina, Brazil, Chile, Colombia, Mexico, Panama, Paraguay, Peru, Puerto Rico, Uruguay, and Venezuela. Both banks rank in the second hundred of the world's largest businesses, according to Fortune magazine's ranking of the 2002 Global 500.The Santander Central Hispano group was ranked in 136th place according to revenues of $30.4 billion while Banco Bilbao Vizcaya Argentaria occupied 192nd place with revenues of $23.8 billion throughout the world.

The Spanish banks in Brazil

Differences in culture and language are not barriers to Spanish banks (cf. Toral 2001: 150). By the end of 2001, the Santander group had rapidly accommodated to Brazil's cultural and language difference (Portuguese is spoken in Brazil) to achieve third place by assets among Brazilian private banks. BBV held twelfth place. According to *Gazeta Mercantil* (2002), a Brazilian business daily, as of the end of 2001 (see Table 6.1) of 167 private banks, the Spanish-controlled banks represented 11.8% of total assets, 11.0% of total deposits, 8.3% of total loans, 11.5% of total net worth, and 12.5% of total receipts from financial intermediation.

Table 6.1 Spanish banks as percentage of total private Brazilian banks, 2001

Bank	Assets	Deposits	Loans	Net Worth	Fin. Int. Receipts
BBVA	1.9	2.7	2.3	1.1	2.2
Banespa	4.6	4.5	2.6	2.3	4.6
Santander Brasil	3.8	3.1	2.8	1.5	3.5
Santander	1.0	0.1	0.4	4.2	1.8
Santander-Meridional	0.5	0.7	0.3	1.0	0.5
TOTAL	11.8	11.0	8.3	11.5	12.5

Note: Due to cross holding of stocks by banks in the Santander group its participation in net worth and profits is overstated.

Source: *Gazeta Mercantil, Balanço Anual 2002*, pp. 393-395.

Santander's growth was based on the purchase of three non-failing private banks: Geral do Comércio and Noroeste de São Paulo in 1997 and Meridional/Bozano Simonsen in 2000, and the purchase of a restructured failed public bank: Banespa in 2000. Over US$700 million was paid for the acquisition of Comércio and Noroeste de São Paulo. Santander's growth strategy peaked with the purchase through privatization of Banespa (Bank of the State of São Paulo) in 2000 for over US$4 billion. Banespa, for all effects, had failed. Yet by substituting the huge debt of the State of São Paulo with federal securities, the federal government sustained the bank until it was sold to Santander. By 2001, classified by net worth, the Santander Banespa group had become the 17th largest business in Brazil. Of the Santander Group's registered consolidated earnings in Brazil in 2001, 84% was contributed by Banespa (*Financial Times*, March 5, 2002).

In 1998 BBVA purchased Banco Excel-Econômico with an investment of US$450 million used for a capital subscription. This bank, headquartered in Salvador in the Northeast state of Bahia, had failed twice as a private national bank, registering a negative net worth in June 1998. Because BBVA concentrated on Excel-Econômico's restructuring, involving various additional share subscriptions totaling around US$1 billion, it did not attempt to acquire other Brazilian banks. Yet this was consistent with its cautious style, at least in comparison to Santander. As illustrated in Table 6.2, Brazilian activities compose a substantial part of worldwide activities. BBVA was ranked as the 72nd largest business in Brazil in 2001 by the *Gazeta Mercantil* (2002). Its 441 offices, 39 electronic posts, and 38 bank posts represented the bank's largest network of offices outside of Spain. Its activities were divided into retail, commercial, business, and institutional divisions. It has stated that a medium-term objective was to be one of the six most important Brazilian banks in corporate business through its Global Wholesale Bank. The BBVA group has important worldwide investments and is an important stockholder in Iberdrola, the Spanish electricity company; Repsol, the petroleum company; and Telefónica de España (Toral 2001: 140). In Brazil, Iberdrola controls Coelba, the electricity distribution company for the state of Bahia, where BBVA's home office was located (*Estado de São Paulo*, November 21, 2000). Telefónica, the third largest company in Brazil according to the *Gazeta Mercantil* (2002), owns the fixed telephone company for the state of São Paulo and mobile telephone companies in the States of Rio de Janeiro and Espirito Santo and in the South of Brazil. Neither Spanish bank, so far as we know, had significant direct investments in other non-financial enterprises in Brazil.

Table 6.2   Spanish bank activity in Brazil compared to worldwide activity

Bank	% World Assets	%World Profits	Investment	% Core Capital
BBVA	<2%	2.4%	E1.2 bil.	25%
Santander	8%	18.3%	E2.7 bil.	10%

Source: Gazeta Mercantil, September 2002.

Spanish bank FDI in Latin America, and in Brazil specifically, produces opportunity and risks. Excluding the Spanish banks, private banks in Brazil earned a return on equity of 17.5% in 2001, comparing favorably with banking sectors in other countries. However, the concentration of Spanish bank FDI in countries with significant real current devaluations, lackadaisical or negative economic growth, and political risk, have led to questioning by rating agencies of their high exposure to the risks of Latin America. To fortify its worldwide capital position, SCH has recently indicated that it wished to sell part of its holding in the Spanish bank, Banesto. It also announced the sale of 24.9% of its Mexican Bank Serfin to the Bank of America for US$1.6 billion, and that it would close its retail banking in Colombia and Uruguay, to concentrate its efforts in the larger and more promising markets of Brazil, Chile, and Mexico (Medel, 2002).

Asset allocation

In this section and the following on funding and credit allocation, we attempt to determine which of the strategies listed in our "Objectives" section – such as Brazilian banking practices, banking practices characteristic of foreign controlled Brazilian banks in general, Spanish banking practices worldwide, or strategies of each Spanish bank which are different one from another – have been followed by Spanish banks in Brazil. Our analysis is based on year-end 2001 data.   It is important to observe the consistency of the allocations in future periods.

Foreign banks in general have different asset allocation and funding patterns than domestic banks. In a recent study Ness (2001) found that foreign-controlled banks in Brazil invested larger proportions of their total assets in predominantly federal government securities portfolios and in foreign exchange portfolios largely dedicated to financing international trade. Private domestic banks had larger proportions of their assets dedicated to loans, permanent investments, and fixed assets. We wondered whether the greater disposition of foreign banks to assume proportionally larger securities portfolios was a conscious policy of the foreign banks or resulted from prior restrictions on agency networks which limited their contacts with possible borrowers.

When the asset composition of the two Spanish banks is compared with the twenty-three other large foreign controlled banks and with the fifteen largest private domestic banks, the differences between the two Spanish banks were often larger than other foreign banks (See Table 6.3). This is consistent with Carvalho (2003), who indicated that the differences among foreign and domestic bank groups are larger than the difference between the group averages.

Table 6.3   Asset composition of Brazilian banks, end-of-year 2001 (as percentage of total assets)

Asset	Private Domestic	Other Foreign	Santander Banespa	BBVA
Cash	2.7	1.5	4.3	2.2
Interfinancial Applications	9.9	14.2	5.0	16.6
Securities	26.9	27.0	45.8	32.9
Interfinancial and Interdependency Relations	4.1	2.3	2.2	1.4
Loans & Leasing	34.4	31.5	20.5	33.9
Loan Loss Provisions	-2.2	-1.6	-1.8	-1.0
Other Credits	14.1	19.4	17.7	7.9
Other Securities and Assets	0.4	0.3	0.9	0.2
Assets for Leasing	3.3	2.2	1.6	1.6
Permanent Assets	6.4	3.0	3.7	4.3
TOTAL ASSETS	100.0	100.0	100.0	100.0

Notes: The private domestic and other foreign banks are those listed by the Central Bank as being among the largest 50 Brazilian banks at the end of 2001. The 50 largest banks represent 95.7% of total bank assets and 94.9% of total bank lending. Of the 50 banks, 10 are government-owned, 15 are private domestically controlled, and 25 are foreign-controlled. Government bonds are included in the "Securities" category. The data from the Central Bank does not differentiate them from other securities holdings.

Source: Central Bank of Brasil, www.bcb.gov.br.

How can we measure differences in asset allocation strategies, and later funding strategies? We do this in a descriptive manner, without testing for statistical significance, by first calculating the absolute value of the difference of the percentage of total assets invested in each category of assets in Table 6.3 for two banks or classes of banks shown in the table. Then these absolute differences are summed for all the asset classes. If banks had the same strategy, this sum would be little different from zero. If the asset allocation experience were different, the sum would have a high value. Figure 6.1 shows that the largest difference in 2001 was between Santander and BBVA and the smallest difference between the private domestic and other foreign bank groups. BBVA was hardly distinguishable from both the private domestic and foreign groups. However, Santander's asset composition differed far more from the domestic and foreign groups and also from BBVA. Figure 6.1 illustrates the extent to which the two Spanish banks differed in their asset allocation strategies.

Private Domestic vs. Other Foreign	19.6%
BBVA vs. Other Foreign	26.4%
BBVA vs. Private Domestic	26.8%
Santander vs. Other Foreign	45.7%
Santander vs. Private Domestic	49.3%
BBVA vs. Santander	52.7%

Figure 6.1 Sum of absolute differences in asset composition

Gruben and Welch (2001) showed that in the 1995-8 period banks, in general, increased the share of government debt in their asset portfolios, correspondingly reducing the share of loans. Securities, short-term investments, and cash account for over half of the Santander's group assets (55.1%). The Santander Banespa group had an atypically high percentage of its assets in its securities portfolio (45.8%). BBVA's percentage (32.9%) was also higher than the average for private and other foreign banks. This is partially the result of the privatization of Banespa. When it was being restructured for privatization in the Brazilian government's PROES program, Banespa's huge debt that originated from the State of Sao Paulo and its companies were exchanged for federal government securities. The federal government then renegotiated the conditions of the São Paulo state government debt. Banespa maintained this securities position until privatization and the Santander group continued to hold and expand the position after its purchase of Banespa. As a result, the group's net credit and leasing portfolio was only 18.8% of the assets of the group as compared with 48.5% of the assets of Santander on a consolidated worldwide basis. In contrast, net lending by BBVA was in percentage terms 76% more (equal to its securities portfolio at 32.9%) than Santander's lending. Net lending by BBVA was similar to the percentage of assets lent by other foreign and private domestic banks (30.0 and 32.2%, respectively). Santander, on the other hand, allocated the smallest portion of its assets to net lending in comparison with the largest Brazilian private banks.

The large investment of Spanish banks in government securities found in their asset portfolios may be explained by:

a) a high real interest rate earned on these securities,
b) speculation on exchange rate devaluation in that a substantial portion of them have their par value tied to the dollar,
c) the cleaning up of the balance sheets of newly acquired banks through tightening credit standards,
d) parking funds in a safe place until a better client base is developed,
e) a zero-weighted capital requirement on national government securities would help banks to conserve capital, and
f) portions of government securities portfolio inherited from acquired banks may be in illiquid, longer term securities.

It was recently disclosed that the SCH was the second largest contributor to the presidential campaign of Brazil's newly elected president, Luiz Ignácio Lula da Silva. To confirm their support of the campaign, Emilio Botin, co-chairman of Banco Santander Central Hispano, held a press conference with Lula da Silva a few days after his election. As a foreign bank Santander's open endorsement of a presidential candidate may seem inappropriate but illustrates the importance that this bank placed on maintaining a close relation with the Brazilian government toward its successful Brazilian operations, as indicated by its political support as well as its disproportionately large investment in Brazilian government securities.

Funding limitations on asset allocation

In Brazil, banks face severe limitations on how they can use certain of their sources of funding. Part of bank asset allocation is determined by Central Bank regulations; part is based on each bank's policies and priorities. For example, at the end of 2001, 45% of demand deposits in excess of R$2 million had to be deposited with the Central Bank and an additional 25% of all demand deposits had to be allocated to rural credit at below market interest rates. Likewise 15% of savings deposits had to be left with and remunerated by the Central Bank. An additional 60% of savings deposits had to be lent for real estate construction projects. Thus only 30% of demand deposits and 25% of their savings deposits could be freely lent or invested by banks.

Banks also act as agents for the National Economic and Social Development Bank (BNDES). They relend funds raised by that bank, in compliance with the BNDES's loan programs, to the private sector. In late 2001, excluding direct lending by the BNDES, 69.7% of total financial system lending and leasing to the private sector was from free resources and 30.3% compulsory directed lending programs. Therefore, credit allocation is partially determined by the composition of bank funding with respect to the use of demand deposits, savings deposits, and BNDES loans.

Table 6.4 shows the liability composition for the largest ten Brazilian private domestic banks and twenty-three foreign controlled banks in aggregate and for the two Spanish bank groups in Brazil.

Table 6.4   Liability composition of Brazilian banks, December 2001 (as a percentage of total liabilities)

Liability	Private Domestic	Other Foreign	Santander Banespa	BBVA
Demand Deposits	6.1	3.7	5.4	1.6
Savings Deposits	12.8	4.2	6.0	5.0
Time Deposits	17.0	10.4	16.1	38.0
Interfinancial and Other Dep.	0.6	2.4	0.1	0.3
Total Deposits	**36.4**	**20.6**	**27.6**	**44.8**
Open Market	18.6	16.4	13.4	13.8
Securities Issued	5.5	2.2	4.6	1.6
Interfinancial and Interdependency Relations	0.8	1.9	0.5	0.5
Loan and Relending Obligations	14.6	19.1	16.6	17.4
Other Obligations and Future Year Results	13.5	28.8	28.0	14.6
Net Worth	**10.7**	**10.1**	**9.4**	**7.2**
TOTAL	**100.0**	**100.0**	**100.0**	**100.0**

Source: Central Bank of Brazil, www.bcb.gov.br. See note for Table 6.3.

Table 6.4 shows that BBVA and Santander also had quite different funding structures. Santander's was most in line with other foreign banks while BBVA with its emphasis on time deposits as a source of funding is different than Santander and the groups of private domestic and other foreign banks. List 2 shows the sum of absolute differences of the percentage composition of bank funding. The banks have quite different structures as to the composition of their deposits.

Santander vs. other foreign	22.3%
Santander vs. private domestic	33.1%
BBVA vs. Santander	46.3%
Other foreign vs. private domestic	46.4%
BBVA vs. private domestic	50.0%
BBVA vs. other foreign	56.0%

Figure 6.2 Sum of absolute differences in liability composition

For their funding, both banks depended significantly on loan and relending obligations (principally foreign funding) – Santander Banespa 16.6% and BBVA 17.4 %. For both, funding for open market operations ranged between 13 and 14%. Each had relatively low (below 10%) capitalization. Yet, at the end of 2001, among other obligations, BBVA had a large capital advance for a future capital subscription. The banks had different funding structures with respect to the use of deposits. Retail deposits (demand and savings) furnished 11.4% of Santander's funding vs. only 6.6% for BBVA. While BBVA acquired a high 38.0% of its funding from the market through time deposits, Santander acquired less than half of their funding (16.1%) from this source. A large portion of Santander's funding came from the less clearly defined category of "other obligations" (28.0%), while this category was much less important for BBVA (14.6%) in spite of the 2001 inclusion of the large capital advance.

Credit allocation

The availability of sectoral and regional decompositions of bank credit data for Brazil is currently quite limited. The Brazilian Central Bank discriminates outstanding credit for only the following sectors: households, industry, services, commerce, rural, financial, and public administration. Some large domestic Brazilian banks such as Bradesco and Itaú voluntarily furnish more detailed sectoral credit allocation in their financial reports. For example, Banco Itau in its 2001 annual report divided industry into sixteen sub-sectors, commerce into three, services into nine, and treated the primary sector in three categories as it did in the financing of individuals. Banco Bradesco has the same number of industrial (manufacturing) subsectors, ten service subsectors aside from financial intermediation, and thirteen commerce subsectors, but combines primary sectors and individuals into one category each. The two Spanish banks only disclosed data according to the Central Bank classification.

Table 6.5 shows the allocation of credit at the end of 2001 for Brazilian banks according to their control. As might be expected, government commercial and multiple banks, for example, have their loan portfolio more concentrated in rural credit (22.6 vs. 5.4% for private banks) and in loans to the public sector (5.7 vs. 0.8% for private banks). Government banks lend substantially less to industry (20.4 vs. 31.3% for private banks), services (13.2 vs. 9.7 % for private banks), and commerce (10.4 vs. 13.7% for private banks). There are no substantial differences in government and private bank lending to individuals and financial institutions. The foreign exchange assets of private banks, which are not counted as loans, represent a much higher proportion (19.9%) of loans than they do for government banks (9.7%).[14]

Many Brazilian controlled private banks have minority foreign participations. In that the Brazilian controlling shareholders determine credit policy, we have lumped purely domestically controlled private banks together with domestically controlled private banks with foreign participation. Table 6.5 indicates that foreign lending is relatively over-weighted with respect to individuals (31.3 vs. 25.0% for domestic banks) and financial intermediation (2.0 vs. 0.8% for domestic banks). Foreign-controlled bank foreign exchange portfolios are also substantially larger in relation to bank lending (24.3 vs. 16.6% for domestic banks).[15] Foreign bank lending is underweighted with respect to lending to services (17.6 vs. 21.3% for domestic banks), commerce (12.9 vs. 14.3% for domestic banks), rural credit (5.0 vs. 5.8% for domestic banks), and to the public sector (0.2 vs. 1.3 % for domestic banks). The percentage of total lending dedicated to industrial loans is similar for the two groups. One might speculate whether domestically controlled banks substitute lending to individuals with loans to small service or commercial firms controlled by individuals. Greater rural lending is probably the result of higher percentages of demand deposits in domestically controlled private bank liabilities.

Differences among the various types of banks in foreign exchange assets is another noteworthy feature found in Table 6.5. The private banks as a whole have double the exchange assets as compared to the public banks (19.9 vs. 9.7%). Yet the foreign banks lead the pack as they lend more exchange assets than the private nationals (31.3 vs. 25%). This suggests that the foreign banks are more involved in international intermediation, especially in the financing of foreign trade.

Table 6.5   Bank lending to sectors in Brazil by type of bank, December 2001 (as a percentage of total loans)

Sector	Private Nat'l	Foreign	TOTAL PRIVATE	Federal	State	TOTAL PUBLIC	ALL BANKS
Industry	31.6	31.0	31.3	20.1	23.4	20.4	28.6
Services	21.3	17.6	19.7	13.0	15.4	13.2	18.1
Commerce	14.3	12.9	13.7	10.0	13.7	10.4	12.9
Rural	5.8	5.0	5.4	24.0	10.6	22.6	9.7
Financial	0.8	2.0	1.3	1.3	0.0	1.2	1.3
Public Admin.	1.3	0.2	0.8	6.1	1.7	5.7	2.0
Households	25.0	31.3	27.7	25.5	35.2	26.5	27.4
TOTAL	100.0	100.0	100.0	100.0	100.0	100.0	100.0
Foreign Exchange Assets as % of Loans	16.6	24.3	19.9	10.6	2.1	9.7	17.3

Source: Central Bank of Brazil, data furnished to authors.

In Table 6.6 the credit portfolio allocation of the Santander group banks and BBVA are compared with the allocation in general for foreign-controlled banks and all private banks. What is evident is that Santander and BBVA had substantially divergent credit compositions. Santander was heavily weighted toward individual, housing, and rural credit (43.9% of total loans outstanding) while BBVA was under-weighted in these items (20.7% of total loans). One would question whether it is a matter of demand or supply. BBVA was based in the State of Bahia, an area with rather low per capita income, while the Santander group's operations are concentrated in the richer São Paulo area.

Does Santander concentrate in individual credit because its clientele have higher incomes and thus presents lower risk? It would seem unlikely that this type of credit is more available from competitors in Bahia than São Paulo. However, the absence of credit data in the Brazilian Central Bank according to geographical area and type of borrower limits our comments in this respect. More likely is that Santander inherited an unusually large personal credit portfolio from Banespa. Santander also has a larger part of its credit portfolio allocated to the public sector (1.9 vs. 0.7% for BBVA), probably a residual of credit operations from the time that Banespa was a state government bank.

BBVA was more heavily weighted in its credit portfolio on industrial, commercial, and service loans compared to the Santander group. They constitute 77.8% of BBVA's credit portfolio as contrasted as to only 52.4% of Santander's portfolio. Santander also has relatively small foreign currency denominated assets, being equal to only 17.2% of the loan portfolio as compared with 24.3% for all foreign-controlled banks. The credit allocation data indicate substantial differences in bank strategies. The Santander Group appears to be building a consumer-oriented bank, while BBVA seemed to moving toward corporate banking. In its 1999 Annual Report, a little over a year after taking over Banco Excel Economico, BBVA indicated its intention "to procure a new profile of clients acting in the most dynamic sectors of the economy, that would share a relationship of greater partnership with the bank and which would have a better capacity for loan payments" (translation by authors). BBVA's bad loan provisions in relation to total loans were among the lowest for large Brazilian banks.

The differences in asset and credit allocation by Spanish banks in Brazil permit us to abandon the hypothesis that the Spanish banks had common strategies in Brazil. We also observe that they neither adhered closely to a common, or average, strategy for all foreign nor for all private domestic banks in Brazil. This leaves us with the hypotheses that either the Spanish banks follow individual strategies, different from one another and different from competitors, or that their asset and credit allocation policies reflected the inheritance of the policies of the Brazilian banks that they purchased. In the case of the former hypothesis, it remains to determine whether the asset and credit allocation policies are common to the Spanish bank operations in other Latin American nations and even in the home country, Spain.

**Table 6.6   Spanish bank lending in Brazil by sector, December 2001
(as a percentage of total gross loans)**

Sector	All Private Domestic	All Foreign	Santander Group	BBVA
Industry	31.6	31.0	22.9	36.8
Rural	5.8	5.0	9.2	1.4
Services	21.3	17.6	19.9	28.0
Commerce	14.3	12.9	9.6	13.3
Financial	1.3	2.0	1.8	0.5
Public Adm.	0.8	0.2	1.9	0.7
Households	25.6	31.3	28.7	14.0
Housing	n.a.	n.a.	6.0	5.4
TOTAL	100.0	100.0	100.0	100.0

Notes: The category "All Foreign" includes all foreign controlled banks. The category
            "All Private Domestic" includes banks with foreign minority participations. The
            loans of the four principal Santander group banks were summed. The four banks
            are Banco Santander S.A., Banco Santander Brasil S.A., Banco Santander
            Meridional S.A. and Banco Santander Banespa. n.a. =Not available.
Source: All Private Domestic and All Foreign loan data from data furnished to the authors
            by the Central Bank of Brazil; Santander and BBVA data from their Brazilian
            home pages.

Before turning to this question, we consider if the Spanish banks contributed to Brazil's development. Comparing sectoral credit allocation to GDP distribution is a rough measure. Table 6.7 offers some interesting comparisons with GDP. Are loans to a sector comparable to its contribution to GDP? Industry surpasses its GDP participation because it is organized in large firms that are easier for banks to monitor and negotiate. Comparing lending of the Spanish banks to GDP, Santander's lending to industry (32.1%) was consistent with its consumer lending strategy and was substantially lower than that sector's contribution to GDP. BBVA's share (42.7%) was greater reflecting its emphasis on corporate banking.

All banks would seem to underfund public administration through loans as compared to that sector's contribution to GDP. This is because public administration is principally funded by bank purchases of securities and not by loans. Santander's lending to this sector was slightly more because of its inheritance of Banespa. Likewise its overfinance of the "Rural" (agriculture) sector is explained by Banespa's continuing investments in rural areas of São Paulo state and the higher percentage of demand deposits in Santander's liability structure that must be partially allocated to rural credit.

Lending to the financial sector was also low compared to its contribution to GDP. A good deal of bank financing of other banks and financial institutions occurs through the purchase of certificates of bank deposits (CDBs that are included in Securities as shown in Table 6.3) and even more through the purchase of certificates of interfinancial deposits- CDIs (included in Interfinancial Applications also shown in Table 6.3). Brazil's Central Bank does yet disclose for the 50 largest banks the detailed composition of each of these accounts that preponderantly include government securities.

The remaining sectors in Table 6.7 are Commerce and Services. They are both overfinanced in relation to their GDP participation for all types of banks. Commerce is one of the easiest stages of the production/sales process to be financed by banks due to the existence of the final product. However, its value added, represented by its contribution to GDP, is small. Services include sectors such as telecommunications, transport, and utilities which are capital intensive in relation to their contribution to GDP.

Table 6.7   Sectoral composition by GDP and bank credit, 2001 (percentage distribution)

Sector	GDP	All Private Domestic	All Foreign	Santander	BBVA
Industry	33.7	42.1	45.1	32.1	42.7
Public Admin.	16.8	1.7	0.3	2.7	0.8
Other Services	16.4	28.4	25.6	27.9	32.5
Real Estate (rents)	11.6	n.a.	n.a.	8.4	6.3
Rural	7.5	7.7	7.3	9.2	1.4
Financial	7.3	1.0	2.9	2.5	0.6
Commerce	6.7	19.1	18.8	13.5	15.4
TOTAL	100.0	100.0	100.0	100.0	100.0

Notes: In the Brazilian national accounts, we attribute "rents" to be the value of the product of the real estate sector. The "All Private Domestic" category includes all banks controlled by private Brazilian capital as well as smaller banks that are not included in the 50 largest banks. The "All Foreign" category includes all foreign-controlled banks, including Santander and BBVA, as well as smaller foreign banks that are not included in the 50 largest banks.

Source: The Brazilian Institute of Geography and Statistics-IBGE and Table 6.6.

The Spanish banks' inheritance or conquest

In this section, we compare whether the Spanish banks in Brazil primarily adapted to the structures of the banks they bought or whether they applied their own policies. Little time has elapsed since the purchase of Brazilian private or state banks by the two Spanish banking giants. This is especially apparent in the case of Santander's purchase of Banespa, the State Bank of Sao Paulo. Because of Banespa's enormity, its complex structure, and the influence of a myriad of embedded political interests, its privatization lasted seven years and finally occurred in November 2000.[16] As a result, its new structure and objectives are only now being clarified. Nevertheless, we try to examine what has transpired. First, we examine how the structure of banking assets and liabilities changed by comparing the summed structure of the banks before their purchase by the Spanish banks with the asset structure of the Spanish banks in Brazil in 2001 in Table 6.8 and their funding structure in Table 6.8. Subsequently in Table 6.9 the composition of the loan portfolio for BBVA Bank in 2001 with the Excel-Economico Bank it purchased in April 1998 is compared. Unfortunately banks that Santander purchased did not detail the composition of their loan portfolios in their financial statements prior to their purchase so comparisons are not possible for this group.

Table 6.8   Comparison of asset composition of banks before purchase by Spanish banks and in 2001 (as a percentage of total assets)

Asset	Banks purchased by Santander	Santander Group pro forma 2001	Excel-Econômico, June, 1998	BBVA Consolidated, 2001
Cash	2.1	4.3	0.5	2.2
Interfinancial Applications	7.6	5.0	46.7	16.2
Securities	39.3	47.1	6.7	33.3
Interfinancial and Interdependency Relations	5.6	2.2	7.0	1.4
Net Loans & Leasing	19.7	19.6	30.4	34.6
Other Credits	19.4	18.1	5.8	8.5
Other Securities and Assets	0.4	1.0	0.9	0.2
Permanent Assets	5.9	2.8	1.9	3.7
TOTAL	100.0	100.0	100.0	100.0

Note: Financial statements of banks purchased by Santander were: Geral do Comércio unconsolidated- June 1997, Noroeste de São Paulo consolidated- Dec. 1997, Meridional unconsolidated- Dec. 1999, Bozano Simonsen unconsolidated- Dec. 1999, Banespa consolidated- Dec. 2000. Their accounts are summed, without adjustment, for the year before they were acquired.
Source: Annual reports of banks

Again if we calculate the sum of the absolute differences for the Santander and BBVA groups before acquisition and presently, we can see that Santander adhered to the asset structure of the banks it bought (sum of absolute differences = 21.1%), while BBVA greatly altered its structure (sum of absolute differences = 73.8%). The Santander Group maintained substantially the same allocation of resources as the sum of the banks it has purchased. Surprisingly it increased the percentage participation of its short-term investments from 49.0% for the combined purchased banks to 56.3% for the Santander Group in 2001, principally through increase in its government securities portfolio. It has been reported in press articles that Santander sold off a substantial part (roughly one-third) of this portfolio in the third quarter of 2002. The proportion represented by the group's loan and leasing portfolio remained virtually constant, comparing the group at the end of 2001 with the sum of the banks that were purchased. The reduction shown in Permanent Assets is due to the use of unconsolidated financial statements for some of the banks that were purchased by Santander showing subsidiaries as permanent investments rather than consolidating the asset categories.

BBVA changed significantly the composition of its short-term investment portfolio. Interfinancial applications, which are generally certificates of deposit issued by other financial institutions, that were major in Excel-Econõmico's short-term investments (46.7% of total assets) have been substituted by a predominantly government securities portfolio (increasing from 6.7% to 33.3% of total assets). Small increases were made in the relative participation of the loan portfolio and of foreign exchange assets in "other credits." This was largely achieved by the reduction in loan loss provisions as well as through small reductions in the total of short-term investments and in the compulsory deposits with the Central Bank included in "interfinancial relations."

Table 6.9 shows that both Spanish banks increased the use of foreign loans in their funding structures after purchasing Brazilian banks. For Santander, this source increased from 4.5 to 14.2% of total assets. For BBVA, the corresponding increase was from 10.6 to 14.4%. BBVA has also had to recapitalize the bank it bought which had a negative net worth of –7.8 as a percentage of total liabilities to the situation at the end of 2001 when bank net worth plus an advance for the capital increase realized in early 2002 amounted to 18.4% of total liabilities. BBVA significantly reduced its open market funding from 47.4% of total liabilities to 13.9% in 2001, while Santander increased this type of operation. BBVA substantially increased the use of time deposits as a source of funding, from 26.2% for Excel-Econõmico in June 1998 to 37.9% in 2001. Santander reduced moderately this source of financing. Savings deposits were increased as a percentage of liabilities in BBVA and reduced by a similar percentage in Santander.

Once again, using the sum of absolute differences in the categories in Table 6.9, we can see a much greater change in the funding structure of BBVA (sum equal to 87.4%) than in Santander (sum equal to 34.7%). Santander again followed more the structure of the banks it acquired while BBVA was substantially restructuring. BBVA's modifications may reflect the failing status of the bank it bought as compared to the more stable situation of the banks bought by Santander as well as the fact that it had less time to make changes as discussed in our study.

Table 6.10 shows the percentage composition of the loan portfolio and changes made from the existence of the Excel-Econõmico to the BBVA. Again there are no substantial changes in the sectors of the economy that receive loans from that bank. The great transformation was in the reduction of the provisions for loan losses which peaked at 24.6% of gross loans in December 1998 after the bank purchase by BBVA and which had been reduced to 2.8% of gross loans at the end of 2001. Loans to individuals, including real estate loans, fell from 32.7% of the loan portfolio at the end of 1998 to 21.7% at the end of 2001. Lending to the service sector had steadily increased from 1999 to 2001, while lending to commerce and industry had oscillated but stayed below half of all lending.

Table 6.9 Liability composition of Spanish banks before purchase of local banks and in 2001 (as a percentage of total liabilities)

Liability	Banks purchased by Santander	Santander Group pro forma, 2001	Excel-Econômico, June, 1998	BBVA Consolidated 2001
Demand deposits	5.6	5.4	1.2	1.5
Savings deposits	7.7	5.9	3.2	5.0
Term deposits	22.0	17.7	26.2	37.9
Interfinancial deposits	2.4	0.1	0.1	0.3
Total deposits	**37.8**	**29.2**	**30.8**	**44.7**
Open market funding	7.0	13.3	47.4	13.9
Securities issued	2.6	-	1.5	1.6
Interfinancial & interdependency relations	1.8	0.5	1.6	0.5
Borrowings	4.5	14.2	10.6	14.4
Relending	2.6	2.4	2.1	3.0
Other obligations and results for future years	30.1	28.2	11.2	3.4
Net worth	13.7	9.6	-7.8	18.4*
TOTAL	100.0	100.0	100.0	100.0

Notes: * Includes advance for capital increase, subtracted from "other obligations."
Source: Financial statements of the banks. See Note for Table 6.7.

Table 6.10 Evolution of the composition of the BBVA bank consolidated gross loan portfolio (as a percentage of total loans and leasing)

Sector	6/1997	6/1998	12/1998	12/1999	12/2000	12/ 2001
Households	20.4	15.1	32.1	25.1	19.8	15.7
Real Estate	n.a.	n.a.	0.7	1.3	4.0	6.0
Rural	1.9	1.1	1.4	1.8	1.7	1.6
Commerce & Industry	47.3	40.6	38.3	50.0	42.4	46.4
Leasing	10.5	19.7	n.a.	n.a.	n.a.	n.a
Other Services	11.2	16.4	19.8	19.2	25.0	28.9
Export-Import	1.5	2.0	1.3	0.7	n.a.	n.a.
Financial	4.2	3.3	4.4	1.1	0.2	0.6
Public	3.0	1.8	2.0	0.9	6.9	0.8
TOTAL	100.0	100.0	100.0	100.0	100.0	100.0

Source: Explanatory notes of the financial statements of the bank: Excel-Econômico for June 1997 and 1998, and BBVA Banco for the years 1998 through 2001.

Spanish bank credit allocation: a force for Latin American integration?

The question of whether an economic institution such as a bank, or a particular type of bank, contributes to a regional market's integration is intriguing. Banks, by the mere fact that money, their principal product, is highly liquid and easily flows across borders, ranks them potentially as among the top institutions in forging and blending of markets. A bank's stance in advocating a market would certainly be important and so would its origins, its structure and its investments. But more salient would be what it actually does, or principally does, and that is lending. Lending for banks is like voting with one's feet or putting one's money where one's mouth is.

First, voice and strategy. Even though there is substantial popular opposition in regional markets to the Free Trade Area of the Americas (FTAA), the Spanish banks appeared to favor the creation of this market because it would fortify their investments in the region. Spanish banks seem to favor Latin American interests over North American. Recently, for example, a Santander executive in Brazil supported FTAA negotiations but urged Brazil to take a tough position in negotiating its agricultural products (Jorge, 2002). Brazilian market analysts cast the Spanish banks as the initial agents in a drive to consolidate the FTAA with the European Union (*Estado de Sao Paulo*, November 26, 2000). A principal question is what would the Spanish banks try to achieve in terms of banking subsidiaries in the United States (and Canada). Both had substantial investments in Puerto Rico. They could try to become major players in the United States market or they could be niche players, primarily serving Spanish and Portuguese-speaking communities. There is some evidence of this strategy as America's Hispanic population is already being targeted by Puerto Rico's Banco Popular and Mexico's new Citibank-Banamex alliance. This was mirrored by Santander's sale of a portion of Bank Serfin to the Bank of America and suggests the debut of an alliance among these large banks. These alliances can also be interpreted as a way for the banks to counter the erosion of their worldwide capital base that has limit their capacity to make major new investments in North America.

Second, origins and structure. BBVA has industrial roots. In Brazil, it purchased Excel-Econômico, a financial-industrial group (FIG), in an emerging region of the country, and was becoming a corporate bank. In this respect, BBVA seems more similar to Itaú, a large domestic FIG, than Bradesco which is more like Santander. FIGs, owed to their very composition (multi financial and non-financial products), offer a greater potential for market consolidation via their financial hubs (banks) that can orchestrate, coordinate lending and compensate for market imperfections across intra and inter regional borders. To mention but one example, synergies are already occurring in telecommunications that span Brazilian states and are reaching into these sectors in other Latin American countries in which the banks hold equity (*Estado de Sao Paulo*, November 21, 2000).

The governance of the Spanish banks has yet to be systematically studied. Toward integration, the global headquarters of both banks remain homogeneous, at least as compared with global banks in other countries. A tightly linked group of wealthy Basque families that played a key role in that region's industrialization remain influential on BBVA's board, although in 2002 there have been some revisions (c.f. *Estado de Sao Paulo*, March 11, 2002; *Financial Times*, April 5, 2002; Guillén, 2001: 209).[17] Santander Group's board is controlled by the Botin family that owns about 3% of the voting shares of the bank and occupies a number of the key positions on the board (Guillén, 2001: 208). This would contribute to the integration of decisions across national borders at least in terms of bank policy. Yet the relation between a bank's global headquarters or decision-making center and its subsidiaries is, so far, unknown. Most (75%) of Santander Brazil's executive committee is composed of Brazilians. The rest are Spaniards with no apparent linkages to the Group's board. Populating their subsidiaries' management with locals is an objective of the bank to make it appear more of a domestic group with foreign capital rather than a purely foreign group (Toral, 2001: 150). Much still remains to be learned about the scope and extent of power of subsidiaries. Up to what amount, for example, can a local chief executive make a loan, spend to launch a new product, donate to a community project, or to acquire an enterprise such as a failed bank?

One more, albeit a passing, thought on structure. While they might differ in their governance, both banks are financial-industrial groups. They are inclined toward forging self-sufficiency and synergies among member companies. They could be conceptualized as encapsulated, or to use the current market integration terminology, self-sufficient sub-national units. Since the Spanish banks are currently among the principal investors in Latin America they might be creating through their credit allocation to other corporations and through new alliances, garrisons of business clusters throughout the Southern tier. The result, at least geographically, would be a series of sub-national units, internally integrated, self-sufficient, and able to endure fierce competition. Whether these units could be more easily combined to form a larger integrated, barrier free market remains to be seen. One wonders about the virtues of consolidating sub-regional units to achieve overall regional growth and development when there is evidence, even from regions within the United States, that when encapsulated some sub-national units have experienced remarkable economic growth in a relatively short period of time (Makler, 1999: 27).

Third, credit allocation is a possible way to measure bank relation to integration. Several times we have indicated that our analysis of lending is not as complete as we would like because we relied on data from the supply-side. The best method to study credit allocation is to focus on borrowers. From enterprises one can more reliably learn what amounts were borrowed, for what purpose, on what terms and from whom. For instance, it would be possible to more accurately differentiate what banks are lending and what they are selling their money for. In a study of Northeast Brazil during its industrialization in the 1970s, Makler (1982) showed a duality among banks. Foreign (at that time mainly Citibank and one or two Canadian banks) and public development banks, often in concert with one another, were providing long-term loans at very low interest rates to the newer, capital intensive sectors such as petrochemicals, electrical machinery and durable consumer goods industries that had intra and interregional linkages. In contrast local private banks and the Bank of Brazil were the principal lenders of short-term credit, usually at predatory rates, to the region's traditional labor intensive industries such as foodstuffs, tobacco, textiles, and wood and paper products. Based on the data we gathered, our analysis suggests that the duality continues as represented by the lending activities of the Spanish banks. While BBVA was moving to serve the corporate sectors that are likely to be interlocked, Santander was oriented more to lending to disparate households and small businesses. So far the asset allocation policy that most typifies Spanish banks in Brazil has been their acquisition and maintenance of larger than normal positions in short-term securities investments, concentrated in Brazilian government securities. This is especially the case with respect to Santander. It is especially overweighted in short term lending to the government. Garrido (2002) finds a similar pattern in Mexico where loans to government and government securities represented a large percentage of credit portfolios (72.2% of Serfin Santander's portfolio and 49.7% of BBVA Bancomer's). If this would be the trend for other Latin American nations, and even for Spain, it would indicate a strategic move by Santander to be a major financer of government wherever it is located. This mutual interdependence would lead Santander to contribute to the solvency of these countries and to influence their economic policies.

In this study we have concentrated on Brazil and have not offered systematic comparisons of Spanish bank performance and strategy in other Latin American nations. By expanding the study we would be able to determine the extent to which Spanish bank asset allocation and lending distribution were the result of common policies for each bank as a whole or were differentiated by national market conditions. In the former case, the harmonization of asset allocation and lending distributions would be a force to homogenize financial activities among the different Latin American nations. This could be interpreted as a force contributing to regional financial integration. The fact that both Spanish banks established banking operations in all major Latin American nations (11 by Santander and 10 by BBVA) indicates that initially both banks consider a region-wide presence more important than a concentrated one.

Conclusions

The Spanish bank investiture in Latin American markets has been rapid. Two major Spanish banks have consolidated a predominant position in the region as a whole and a significant position in the Brazilian market. From the analysis of their financial statements it appears that the two have taken different strategic paths, diverging from one another and from foreign banks as a group.

The BBVA group purchased but since has sold a twice-failed Brazilian private bank, concentrating on restructuring and growth from within. This process required several capital increases aside from the initial investment. From its base in the Northeast state of Bahia, the BBVA was being restructured to be a leading corporate bank, forsaking to some degree its regional and FIG origins. It became a market-oriented bank, raising most of its resources from the Brazilian market in the form of time deposits and specializing in lending operations oriented toward the corporate sector. BBVA adjusted its investment to its interpretation of where banking opportunities lie in Brazil, thereby substantially modifying the structure and operations of the bank. Yet regardless of improvements in the quality of its credit portfolio, the bank could not achieve sufficient scale and as a result its operating profits remained meager. In the end the bank evidently proved to be an unattractive stand-alone investment for the BBVA group and was sold to Bradesco which already had achieved economies of scale as Brazil's largest private bank. BBVA continues its presence in Brazil as the largest minority shareholder in Brazil's largest private bank.

The Santander Group has been more acquisitive in Brazil, taking over three middle-size successful banks and then through aggressive bidding purchasing Brazil's largest state government bank in a privatization auction. It has become Brazil's third largest private bank and fifth largest bank. Its current situation is largely a reflection of its inheritance of the structure of the Bank of the State of São Paulo (Banespa). It maintains a very large government securities portfolio created in the restructuring of that bank. It is also more concentrated in personal rather than corporate credit, a further reflection of the prior activities of the acquired state bank. Since that purchase was less than two years ago, the Santander group possibly has not had sufficient opportunity to adjust its activities in Brazil to general corporate strategy. It seems to have opted to obtain scale at the cost of operating with a more retail-oriented, government financing strategy than it might want to pursue in the long term. Thus in the short run, it is managing the assets it has acquired and is adapting its activities to the realities of the banks it has acquired.

Investment in Brazil is important to both of the Spanish banks. However each had a different strategy. The Santander Group took advantage of a non-recurring opportunity to obtain scale while BBVA has advanced in restructuring a primarily retail bank structure to attempt to be a major player in the Brazilian corporate finance market and to improve the quality of its assets. Both banks concentrated positions in short-term investments, principally in Brazilian government securities. This strategy may prove to be transitory and opportunistic if chances for valuation of these portfolios are limited by the new Brazilian government's capacity to stabilize the exchange rate and reduce interest rates paid on these securities.

Investment must be considered from another angle. To end this chapter, we return to the principal question with which we began: Are there any special characteristics to Spanish bank asset and credit allocation in Brazil? We have found that the Spanish banks have each followed their own course, conforming neither to practices of other foreign banks in Brazil nor to those of private domestic banks. Their courses have been different. BBVA pursued a strategy of organic growth yet it altered the nature of the bank it purchased to strengthen itself in the corporate market. Santander incorporated the traditions of the banks it had bought and emphasized retail banking. Both banks, but especially Santander, maintain large government securities portfolios, in effect financing the federal government. Not that this hasn't happened before. It occurred most recently and on a larger scale for Brazilian banks in the early 1990s. From a growth and development perspective, it is an odd state of affairs when banks lend, in effect, more to a government than to the private sector.

We have not evaluated the net benefits of the Spanish bank entry in Brazil with respect to either the Brazilian economy or with respect to the long-term success of the Spanish banks. However, we have shown that foreign banks are neither monolithic nor operate according to a fixed formula when they entered this emerging market. The Spanish banks may be as different from one another as from other foreign or other domestic banks. Based on the market we studied foreign bank strategy is not uniform. If foreign bank strategies are so diverse as in the case of Spanish banks in Brazil this could weaken their impact – whether favorable or not – on emerging economies. Increasing foreign participation in banking does not necessarily result in major changes to the local financial systems or development. Changes might occur if all Spanish or foreign banks utilized similar banking strategies.

Notes

[1] This paper was presented at the Conference on Spanish Investment in Latin America, Miami European Union Center and Latin American and Caribbean Center, Florida International University, Coral Gables, Florida, October 18-19, 2002. We are grateful to the Central Bank of Brazil, Banco Bradesco, Banco Bilbao Vizcaya Argentaria S.A.(BBVA), and Banco Santander Central Hispano (BSCH) for providing data for our analysis, and to James Barth, Celso Garrido, Luiz Fernando de Paula, Mauro Guillén, William Gruben, Pablo Toral and Adrian Tschoegl for their insightful suggestions. We also wish to acknowledge the support of the National Science Foundation (Grant #SES-8722581) that enabled Harry Makler to conduct research on the transformation of banking institutions in Brazil.

[2] Yet in several late developing nations the state remains as a formidable commercial and investment agent in spite of neo-liberalist recommendations and multilateral institution promotions of a market-based system.

[3] In this paper, asset allocation refers to all the assets of banks. Credit allocation refers only to loans.

[4] If one were studying medical prescriptions a systematic study of a sample of patients would be much more reliable than trying to obtain information from their doctors on what was dispensed.

[5] Banco Bilbao Vizcaya Argentaria S.A. is also known in Brazil as Banco Bilbao Vizcaya.

[6] Carvalho (2002:9) indicates that foreign banks may be more efficient than domestic banks in emerging economies "because they are used to operating in a more competitive environment, more propitious to innovation and more sensitive to operational efficiency, but also because the regulatory environment in developed countries is supposed to be more rigorous and supervision tighter."

[7] Carvalho reported that only one foreign bank had a lower percentage than one private national bank.

[8] Since 2000 Brazilian banks must classify their loans in nine categories according to their risk.

[9] Adrian Tschoegl provided us this detail.

[10] Adrian Tschoegl also suggested that we use the term bank offices or operations because in addition to making loans and trading in foreign exchange markets, they accept deposits while agencies do not.

[11] Three Spanish banks, Bilbao Vizcaya (BBVA), Central Hispano and Santander initially led this expansion. In 1999, Santander and Central Hispano merged to form the Santander Central Hispano group. Much of this overview is based on Mauro F. Guillén's chapter, "Developing Services: Banking as an Industry in Its Own Right," from his recent monograph (Guillén 2001) that includes research with his colleague, Adrian Tschoegl (Guillén, Tschoegl 2000).

[12] Similarly Sanchez Peinado (2002) chracterizes BBVA as conservative and prudent.

[13] BBVA's market share in Brazil is smaller than in other Latin American countries. In 2000, BBVA had 1.1% of the total market share of deposits in Brazil as compared to 26.1% in Mexico, 19.7% in Venezuela, 16.6% in Peru, 8.1% in Argentina and 6% in Paraguay (*Business Week*, March 27, 2000).

[14] Private banks' foreign exchange assets are not included as loans in the Central Bank of Brazil's classification. Yet to assess their magnitude we compare them with loans.

[15] The Central Bank of Brazil includes in the foreign exchange portfolio (carteira de câmbio) in bank assets the following: a) foreign currencies purchased and to be liquidated for exports, financial investments by the financial institution, or by investments in gold by the financial institution less advances received in foreign currencies; b) rights over the sale of foreign currencies for imports or financial investments less advances received in local currency; c) other amounts to be received in foreign currency; d) income to be received from advances conceded or imports financed; and e) expenses to be received from advances received.

[16] See, for example, *Quarterly Review of Economics and Finance*, vol. 40, 2000 for analyses of Banespa's transition.

[17] Early in 2002, mainly as a result of "international instabilities" and a drop of market share in Spain, BBVA's board was trimmed from 32 to 21 directors. This was viewed as a more manageable number than the previous board that was mostly populated with well-to-do Basque families who had little or no banking expertise (*Financial Times*, March 8, 2002).

References

Barth J R, Phumiwasana T., and Yago G. (2002), "The Foreign Conquest of Latin American Banking: What's Happening and Why?" Conference on Spanish Investment in Latin America, Miami European Union and Latin American and Caribbean Center, Florida International University, Coral Gables, Florida, October 18-19, 2002.

Brazilian Institute of Geography and Statistics (Instituto Brasileiro de Geografia e Estatística), GDP data, 2001.

Business Week, March 27, 2000.

Carvalho, F. J. C. De (2002), "The Recent Expansion of Foreign Banks in Brazil: First Results," *Latin American Business Review*, vol. 3, no. 4, pp. 93-119.

Central Bank of Brazil (Banco Central do Brasil) (2001), various statistical data.

Claessens, S. and Glaessner, T. (1998), "Internationalization of Financial Services in Asia," Conference on Investment Liberalization and Financial Reform in the Asia-Pacific Region, Sydney, Australia and Hong Kong. World Bank Working Paper #1911.

Claessens, S. and M. Jansen (eds.) (2000), *The Internationalization of Financial Services: Issues and Lessons for Developing Countries,* Kluwer Law International, The Hague.

Claessens S., Demirgüç-Kunt, A., and Huizinga, H. (1999), "How does foreign entry affect the domestic banking market." Background paper for Liberalization and Internationalization of Financial Services Conference, jointly sponsored by the World Bank and WTO Secretariat, Geneva. World Bank Working Paper #1918.

Dages, B., Goldberg, L., and Kinney, D. (2000), "Foreign and domestic bank participation in emerging markets: lessons from Mexico and Argentina," *Federal Reserve Bank of New York Economic Policy Review*, vol. 6, no. 3, pp. 17-36.

Estado de São Paulo, various numbers.

Evans, P. (1979), *Dependent Development: The Alliance of Multinational, State and Local Capital in Brazil*, Princeton University Press, Princeton.

--- (1995), *Embedded Autonomy: States and Industrial Transformation*, Princeton University Press, Princeton.

Financial Times, various numbers.

Fortune, July 22, 2002.

Garrido, C. (2002), "Economia, financiamiento y empresas en Mexico, evolucion desde de 1995, tendencias y desafios." Seminario internacional "Coyuntura microeconómica en América Latina", CEPAL (Santiago), August 29-30, 2002.

Gazeta Mercantil (2002), *Balanço Anual*.

Gazeta Mercantil, various numbers.

Gerschenkron, A. (1962), *Economic Backwardness in Historical Perspective*, Harvard University Press, Cambridge.

Goldsmith, R. (1969), *Financial Structure and Development*, Yale University Press, New Haven.

Glaessner, T., and D. Oks (1994), "NAFTA: Impact on financial sector efficiency and the case of capital in Mexico", draft.

Gruben, W. and Welch, J. (2001), "Banking and Currency Recovery: Brazil's Turnaround of 1999," *Federal Reserve Bank of Dallas Economic and Financial Review*, Fall Quarter.

Guillén, M. (2001), *The Limits of Convergence: Globalization and Organizational Change in Argentina, South Korea and Spain,* Princeton University Press, Princeton.

Guillén, M. and Tschoegl, A. (2000), The Internationalization of Retail Banking: The Case of the Spanish Banks in Latin America, *Transnational Corporations*, vol. 9, no.3, pp. 63-97.

Gurley J. and Shaw E. (1967), "Financial structure and economic development," *Economic Development and Cultural Change*. vol. 15, no. 3, April, pp. 257-68.

Honohan, P. (2000), "Consequences for Greece and Portugal of the opening-up of the European banking market," in S. Claessens and M. Jansen (eds.), *The Internationalization of Financial Services*, pp. 247-281.

Johnson, J. (2000), *A Fistful of Rubles: The Rise and Fall of the Russian Banking System*, Cornell University Press, Ithaca.

Jorge, M. (2002), "Um simples castelo de areia," *Gazeta Mercantil,* October 1, p. A-3.

Jornal do Brasil, February 26, 2002.

Keynes, J.M. (1960), *A Treatise on Money,* Macmillan, London.

Makler, H. (1982), "Financial institutions, credit allocation and marginalization in the Brazilian Northeast: the Bahian case," in H. Makler, A. Martinelli, and N. Smelser (eds.), *The New International Economy*, pp. 231-258.

--- (1999), "Regional integration and trends in financial services." in J. Haar and K. Dandapani (Eds.), *Banking in North America: NAFTA and Beyond.* Pergamon, Elsevier, Oxford, UK.

--- and W. L., Jr. Ness, (2002), "How financial intermediation challenges national sovereignty in emerging markets," *Quarterly Review of Economics and Finance*, vol. 42, no. 5, Winter, pp. 827-851.

--- A. Martinelli, and N. Smelser (eds.) (1982), *The New International Economy*, SAGE Studies in International Sociology, 26.

Mathieson, D. and Roldos, J. (2001). "The role of foreign banks in emerging nations," IMF-World Bank–Brookings Institution Conference on Financial Markets and Development.

Medel, A. (2002), "Luzón anunció que el SCH abandonará la banca minorista en Colombia y Uruguay," *ABC Economía*, November 21, www.abc.es (observed Nov. 21, 2002).

Ness, W. L., Jr. (2001), "Foreign Banks in Brazil: What Do They Do Differently?", Business Association of Latin American Studies – BALAS, Annual Conference Proceedings, CD-Rom.

Patrick, H. (1966), "Financial development and economic growth in underdeveloped countries," *Economic Development and Cultural Change,* vol. 14, no. 2, January, pp. 174-89.

Paula, L. F. R. de, (2002a), *The Recent Wave of European Banks in Brazil: Determinants and Impacts*, Banco Santos/Centre for Brazilian Studies, São Paulo/Oxford.

--- (2002b), "Expansion Strategies of European Banks in Brazil and Their Impacts on the Brazilian Banking Sector," *Latin American Business Review*, vol. 3, no. 4, pp. 59-91.

Sánchez, E. (2002), "Internationalisation Process of Spanish Banks: A New Stage After The Mergers," unpublished paper, University of Valencia.

Schumpeter, J. [1934] (1961), *Theory of Economic Development,* Oxford University Press, New York.

Toral, P. (2001), *The Reconquest of the New World: Multinational Enterprises and Spain's Investment in Latin America,* Ashgate Publishing Company, Aldershot.

World Bank (2000), *Entering the 21st Century.* World Development Report 1999/2000. Oxford University Press, NY.

Chapter 7

Spanish Banks in Latin America: Do They Need Each Other?

Álvaro Calderón[1]

Introduction

The deep changes that the economies of Latin America underwent in recent years (opening, liberalization, privatization of state-owned enterprises and deregulation) created a new business environment. One of the main aspects of this process was the large inflows of foreign direct investment (FDI). The amount of inward FDI in Latin America in the second half of the 1990s was unprecedented. Multinational enterprises (MNEs), mainly European ones, became market leaders in some of the main activities, mainly in services and infrastructure (see Figure 7.1).

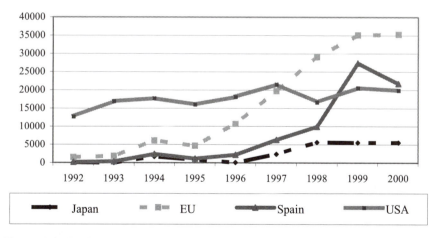

Figure 7.1 Latin America and the Caribbean: FDI flows, by home country, 1990-2000 (million US dollars)

Source: Compiled by the author with data from the European Union Statistical Office (Eurostat) and the Bureau of Economic Research, U.S. Department of Commerce (www.bea.doc.gov).

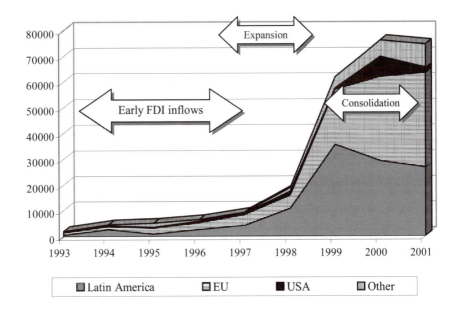

Figure 7.2   Evolution of FDI, by host region, 1993-2001 (in million euros)

Source: Compiled by the author with data from the Dirección General de Comercio e Inversiones, Secretaría de Estado de Economía y Comercio, Ministerio de Economía of Spain (www.mcx.es).

In this new context, Spanish firms became prominent actors. The establishment of the European Monetary Union (EMU) and the creation of a single currency in the European Union, the euro, increased competition in the union, including Spain. Taking advantage of the cultural proximity of Latin America, Spanish firms began an ambitious process of internationalization (based mainly in the acquisition of existing firms) as a defense mechanism against potential takeovers from competitors (Calderón, 1999a) (see Figure 7.2). Latin America became the main destination for the international operations of the largest Spanish firms and Spain became one of the main sources of foreign capital for the Latin American economies (see Figures 7.1 and 7.2).

The large Spanish investments in Latin America began in the early 1990s, when Telefónica and Iberia took part in the processes of privatization of state-owned enterprises in several countries. Repsol and Endesa came in the mid-1990s and since 1996 the main Spanish banks took the lead. In aggregate terms, the largest FDIs by Spanish firms occurred in the financial sector (mainly banking and insurance) until the late 1990s, when Spanish telecommunications and energy firms took the lead[2] (see Figure 7.3).

By early 2002, the main Spanish banks had invested over $25,400 in Latin America. Banco Bilbao Vizcaya Argentaria (BBVA) and Santander Central Hispano (SCH) believed that Latin America gave them an opportunity to grow, so that they could compete in the main international financial markets, by diversifying risk and yet, preserving their identity, in an increasingly volatile context. In several Latin American markets, the arrival of these banks was perceived as an opportunity to overcome the recurrent crises in their financial systems.

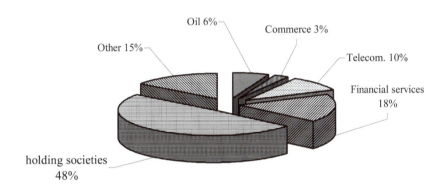

Figure 7.3 Spanish FDI by sector in the host country, 1993-2001 (percent)[3]

Source: Compiled by the author with data from the Dirección General de Comercio e Inversiones, Secretaría de Estado de Economía y Comercio, Ministerio de Economía of Spain (www.mcx.es).

Latin American financial markets: a metamorphosis led by the foreign banks

Since the early 1800s, foreign banks settled in Latin America by opening offices of representation to follow their customers (mainly MNEs) or by operating in niche markets, such as financing the large export companies in the host countries. They began to expand their operations in those countries whose legal systems allowed them to, through capital increases and by operating in the commercial banking sector, catering to specific clients only.

In the 1990s, Latin American governments eliminated institutional restrictions, such as the obstacles for the entry of foreign capital and legal requirements that discriminated against foreign firms. At the same time, the banking sector in the industrialized countries accumulated excess capital. Market growth stopped and intense competition reduced profit margins, putting pressure on firms to lower costs. As a result, firms began to expand outside of their home markets (Calderón and Casilda, 2000). In this context, they saw in their expansion in Latin America as a great opportunity.

Table 7.1 Latin America: participation of foreign banks in the assets of host markets, 1990-2001 (percent)

	1990	1994	1999	2000	2001
Argentina	10	18	49	49	61
Brazil	6	8	17	23	49
Chile	19	16	54	54	62
Colombia	8	6	18	26	34
Mexico	0	1	19	24	90
Peru	4	7	33	40	61
Venezuela	1	1	42	42	59

Source: CEPAL.

Moreover, Latin American markets had some characteristics that made them very appealing to the banks from the industrialized countries: the low percentage of citizens who used banking services, large mediation margins, great return potential, demographic factors (great growth potential), lack of domestic capital, the improvements of supervision mechanisms and regulation in the banking sector, and opportunities to diversify into new activities. Between 1990 and 2001, the share of total assets held by foreign banks grew rapidly from very insignificant (except for Chile) to a minimum of 34% in Colombia and 90% in Mexico (see Table 7.1) In the early 2000s, these figures grew as a result of the Mexican peso crisis and the Asian crisis. The reduction of short-term loans and the cancellation of external credit during the crisis weakened the home financial institutions, facilitating further investments by foreign banks (see Figure 7.4).

However, these investments occurred in a few international institutions, led by the Spanish banks SCH and BBVA. Recently, as a result of the acquisition of Mexican bank Banamex-Accival, US bank Citibank joined this select group. Behind these three are US bank Fleet Boston, British bank Hong Kong Shanghai Banking Corporation (HSBC), and Canadian bank Scotiabank (see Figure 7.5). In most cases, the strategy of these foreign banks was to provide universal financial services, by offering their traditional commercial banking services and products, as well as other services with more value added, such as pension fund management.

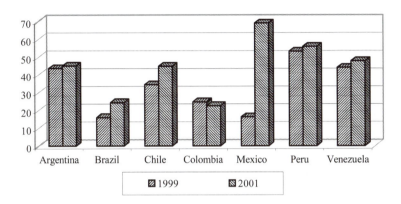

Figure 7.4 Effective control by foreign banks over credit in the financial system of some Latin American countries, 1999-2001 (percent)[4]

Source: Compiled by the author with data from Salomon Smith Barney, *Foreign Financial Institutions in Latin Americ*a, 2001, Equity Research, Latin America.

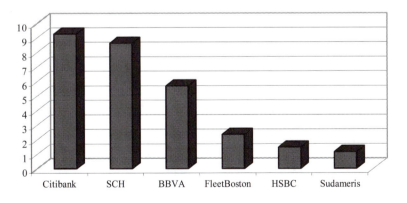

Figure 7.5 Largest banks in Latin America by share of credit (percent)

Source: Compiled by the author with data from Salomon Smith Barney, *Foreign Financial Institutions in Latin America*, 2001, Equity Research, Latin America.

The acquisition of shares was the most common mode of entry (in some cases with a domestic partner) in Latin America. Among the firms that followed the most aggressive strategies in order to gain control over management quickly were SCH, HSBC, Fleet Boston and Citibank. Other firms had a more conservative strategy, and expanded through alliances with local banks, although little by little they increased their share of assets in their subsidiaries. BBVA belongs in this group.

Foreign banks made their FDIs in middle-sized countries in an early stage (except for Argentina) of the Andean region and the Southern Cone. The quick liberalization and the relatively lower risk in these markets were key determinants (mainly the size and cost of the institutions that were taken over). The Spanish banks were the main players. The late entry of the international banks into the largest and most developed markets, such as Brazil and Mexico, varied in each country. In Mexico it was due to the fact that the government lifted the institutional impediments (explicit limits on the foreign ownership of banks) very late, only after the banking crisis of 1994, and that Mexican investors provided the capital the domestic banks needed during the banking crises. In Brazil, the strength of domestic banks and their degree of development and competitiveness slowed down the entry of foreign banks.

Transnational banks had important advantages in Latin America vis-à-vis domestic banks. First, they served the needs of the most demanding domestic sectors, mainly the large firms. Secondly, the Latin American subsidiaries of foreign banks implemented very flexible management techniques, incorporating the latest technological advances in information technology in sectors that were traditionally dominated by the domestic banks, like retail baking.

Foreign banks followed two strategies in Latin America. Some sought to operate over a larger geographic region, providing their services to more market segments. Others based their expansion on their specific knowledge of banking technologies and the use of sophisticated financial instruments in specific market niches. The largest investors can thus be grouped in the following categories:

- Institutions with a large presence in Latin America, based on universal banking. Spanish banks SCH and BBVA are the leaders in this group. They took advantage of the experience they developed in their local market. Citibank joined them in 2001, after taking over Banamex.[5] Until then, Citibank had operated mainly in corporate banking. These banks had expanded in several financial areas, mainly in pension fund management.
- Banks focused on the corporate sector across Latin America. The main banks in this group are FleetBoston and Scotiabank. Their focus is the provision of services for MNEs, as well as high income individuals.
- Banks that operate only in the main markets, mainly in corporate banking. HSBC and ABN AMRO are the main ones.

Transformation of the Spanish banking system

In the mid-1960s, the Spanish authorities began a process of liberalization and deregulation of financial activities. Since 1985, the transformation of the Spanish banking system gained momentum, when Spain joined the European Union (EU) and its firms adopted new technologies and products and consumers developed new habits. The changes in the structure and strategy of the financial institutions intensified as a result of the creation of the Economic and Monetary Union (EMU) (as a previous step for the adoption of a single currency in the EU).

Since the early 1980s, the Spanish banking system tried to satisfy the existing demand in Spain with little foreign competition. In the 1990s, the dramatic changes that occurred brought the Spanish banking market to the brink of saturation, forcing domestic banks to redefine their strategies. As a result, they began to listen more closely to consumers, in order to satisfy their needs (Calderón and Casilda, 2000).

In this context, their main goal was to keep up their rate of return on investment, and try to reduce operation costs. The number of offices and personnel feel (concentration grew due to mergers). In the late 1980s, competition in the Spanish banking market intensified, especially when Banco Santander launched a current account that paid high returns, called "Super Cuenta". Other banks soon developed similar services.[6]

The European Union eliminated barriers to the free movement of capital among the member countries of the European Union since the first of January, 1003. It also eliminated restrictions for the establishment of banking services. As a result, the banking system in Spain and in the European Union began a process of market concentration. On July 14th, 1995, a Spanish law internalized the European regulation. As a result, the banking system began to move from a scenario in which competition was based mainly on geographic proximity and the provision of services free of charge, to one dominated by price wars (Casilda, 1997). The single currency also forced banking institutions to develop economies of scale (size) or a competitive advantage in a specific market segment (specialization).

Since the late 1980s, private banks followed a strategy of growth, based on mergers and acquisitions, with two main purposes: to strengthen their presence in the national (and eventually in the international) market, and to increase their competitiveness.[7] In 1998, Banco de Bilbao and Banco de Vizcaya merged, creating Banco Bilbao Vizcaya (BBV). In 1991, Banco Central and Banco Hispano merged to create Banco Central Hispano (BCH). In 1994, Bancon Santander took over Banco Español de Crédito (Banesto) and in 1998, Banco Exterior de España (BEX), Caja Postal and Banco Hipotecario merged with Argentaria. In early 1999, Banco Santander and BCH merged, creating one of Europe's largest banks and, in October, BBV and Argentaria merged, establishing the second largest Spanish bank, Banco Bilbao Vizcaya Argentaria (BBVA).

The result was that the Spanish market became one of the most concentrated banking markets in Europe. The market share of the five largest banks grew from 33% in 1987 to 50% in 1996. The market share for the five largest banks in 1990 was 41% in France, 35% in Italy, 28% in the United Kingdom, and 25% in Germany (Casilda, Lamothe and Monjas, 1997). In mid-2002, the two largest Spanish banks, SCH and BBVA, controlled close to 70% of credits and deposits. This process of concentration came with important gains in efficiency and competition (as a result of the fall in mediation margins), contributing to modernization and innovation of processes and technology, and improvements in service quality.

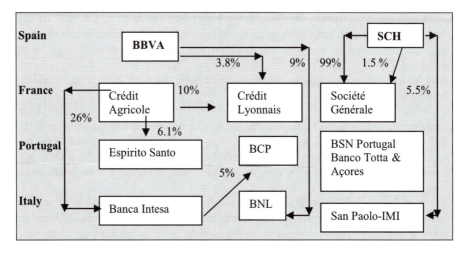

Figure 7.6   Cross investments in Spanish, French, Portuguese and Italian banking institutions, December 2001

Source: Compiled by the author with data from the annual reports of the firms and by Spanish Comisión del Mercado de Valores and the Madrid Stock Exchange.

This process of mergers and acquisitions allowed the largest banks to reach the appropriate size to begin a strategy of internationalization. The Spanish banks focused on Portugal, France, Italy, Morocco and Latin America mainly.[8] The number of alliances among banks from different EU countries also grew. With these alliances, banks seek to increase their competitiveness vis-à-vis the larger banks that grow to become real pan-EU institutions. In this sense, BBV acquired 10% of Banca Nazionale del Lavoro (BNL) in Italy, 3.8% of Credit Lyonnais in Frnace and Midas in Portugal. Banco Santander took over 5% of Italian bank San Paolo-IMI and 10% of Royal Bank of Scotland. BCH had small stakes in Commerzbank (3%) and Société Général (1.2%) and created an alliance with Banco Comercial Portugués (BCP). Argentaria established an alliance with French-Belgian group Dexia. SCH increased its stakes in the European banks through investments worth more than €5.5 billion (SCH, 2001). In Portugal, SCH took over banks Totta & Açores and Crédito Predial, becoming the third largest financial institution in the country with a market share of 10.1% (SCH, 2002). SCH also strengthened its network of alliances with Royal Bank of Scotland, Société Général, San Paolo-IMI and Commerzbank[9] (see Figure 7.6). In early 2000, there was speculation that BBVA would develop a strategic alliance with Italy's third largest bank, Unibanco Italiano[10] (this would have become the largest international alliance in the European Union).

Many analysts thought that this was just the beginning of a process that would lead to the creation of large European banks, with presence in the main European markets. However, this process has not taken place as fast as they had predicted. Foreign banks in Spain have been unable to take away a significant share of the market from the Spanish banks. The network of offices of the Spanish banks is an important barrier that the new entrants cannot overcome, forcing them to make substantial investments to reach out to their potential customers. In fact, no single bank from a member country holds a leading position outside of their home market. Therefore, for the Spanish banks, as well as for most European entities in their home markets, the physical proximity to their customers is still a main competitive advantage. This is precisely the basis for concerns about potential takeovers by other European banks.

The creation of the euro accelerated some changes and reduced timeframes, modifying the expansion strategies of the main European banks. As a first step, analysts think that in the 2000s mergers will mainly take place among banks from the same country, because transborder mergers are difficult due to linguistic and cultural differences and to tax and regulatory frameworks. As a result, the leading European banks will try to strengthen their position in a single market (by growing domestically), and only later will they try to expand in the European Union. Several large mergers and acquisitions already took place in different European countries (Spain, France, Italy and Germany). If successful, each of the new companies would create large national banks that would be very well positioned for further competition in Europe.

Internationalization of Spanish banking: the Latin American option

To maintain a competitive position and to defend themselves from potential takeovers, the large Spanish banks decided to look for new markets. In the early stage they sought alliances and cooperation agreements with other institutions, mainly from the European Union. In the second stage, they undertook a quick and aggressive strategy of expansion in the main Latin American markets. Their internationalization process relied on four main factors:

- Search for size and competitiveness.
- Entry into markets with growth potential.
- Global use of resources, organizational and technological capabilities.
- Appropriate diversification of risk.

Latin American countries offered a unique opportunity for the Spanish banks, because the European markets were too mature and acquisitions were very expensive. In general, the financial systems of the main Latin American countries were open and in the process of deregulation. Banks and governments regarded the entry of foreign partners as a good way to solve some of the critical problems of their markets, like the modernization of the local financial systems. Moreover, the Spanish banks regarded their expansion in Latin America as a mechanism to diversify risk.[11] All of the above occurred in a context of common language, culture and history, which facilitated not only transfers of capital, but technology and management know-how. Thus, the Spanish banks managed to spread quickly in the main economies, leading the growing penetration of foreign banks in the Latin American financial systems (see Figure 7.5 and Table 7.1).

The Spanish banks first went to Latin America with the non-financial Spanish firms (providing funding and financial services for them) but tried to become prominent players in retail banking, their main activity. They developed an active plan of diversification and development of new businesses, including investment banking, insurance and especially the management of pension funds. Moreover, they acquired minority participation in non-financial firms (as they did in Spain), mainly in sectors in which other Spanish firms were very active, such as telecommunications and energy.

SCH: A leader

In late 2001, SCH was the largest financial group in Spain, with a market share of almost 29%, and the sixteenth in the world and the seventh in the European Union by market capitalization (*The Banker*, 2002: 172). SCH had 9,817 offices in forty countries and 39 million customers (www.gruposantander.com). Santander was the Spanish bank that first developed a strategy of international expansion, based on its capacity to innovate, its flexibility and its policy of gaining control over its foreign operations (Calderón and Casilda, 2000). The international experience and leadership of the bank's chairman, Emilio Botín, made its managers prefer a strategy of not-relying on local partners.

SCH has been in Latin America since the 1950s, growing slowly in the Southern Cone, mainly in Chile. In 1996 it began an active strategy of expansion by taking over many banking firms in the region. Between 1996 and 2001, the weight of Latin America in its net profits grew from 8% to 68%. This strategy allowed SCH to reach a market share of more than 10% in Latin America, both in terms of assets and liabilities, reaching 23 million customers (SCH, 2002). In 2002, SCH owned 15 banks in Latin America (some of them were market leaders in their countries, such as Brazil, Chile, Mexico, Puerto Rico and Venezuela), six pension management firms, 13 mutual fund firms, 10 insurance companies, 9 firms for leasing and factoring, and 10 brokerage firms.

Table 7.2   SCH in Latin America, 2001 (million dollars)

	Bank	%	Rank	Market value	% Market share		Year of investment
					Loans	Deposits	
Argentina	Banco Río de la Plata	98	4	9 330	10.72	9.04	1997
	Banco de Galicia y Buenos Aires	10	3	10 798	11.76	7.44	1998
Bolivia	Banco Santa Cruz	90	2	634	13.13	15.76	1998
Brazil	Banco do Estado de São Paulo (Banespa)	98		12 859			2000
	Banco Santander Brasil (former Banco Geral do Comercio)	100	5	24 753	4.12	4.26	1997
	Banco Noroeste [a]	76	18	4 509	-1.41	0.83	1998
Chile	Banco Santander Chile	90	2	10 467	11.37	13.27	1996
	Banco Santiago [b]	79	3	10 430	15.90	13.70	1991
Colombia	Banco Santander Colombia	60	12	1 265	2.63	2.68	1997
Mexico	Grupo Financiero Serfin	100	3	14 870	9.37	8.45	2000
	Grupo Financiero Bital (includes Banco Internacional de México)	8	4	14 670	7.74	10.22	1993
	Banco Santander Mexicano	100	5	12 421	7.63	8.24	1996
Paraguay	Banco Asunción	39	9	106	4.63	4.27	1996
Peru	Banco Santander Perú	100	6	1 312	7.08	5.75	1995
Uruguay	Banco Santander Uruguay	100	10	819	4.60	4.00	…
Venezuela	Banco de Venezuela	98	3	3 700	12.94	12.31	1997

Source: SCH, *Informe Anual 2001,* "Los 100 mayores bancos", *Revista Latin Trade,* september 2002 and "Latin Banking Guide & Directory 2002", *LatinFinance,* August 2002.

a   In 1998 SCH merged its Brazilian subsidiaries.

b   BCH consolidated its FDIs in Argentina, Chile, Paraguay and Peru through O'Higgins Central Hispano (OHCH), in conjunction with Chile's Luksic group. In late 1998 OHCH's assets were worth $12,800 million, with 276 offices and 7,511 employees. On 12 February 1999, BCH decided to terminate this joint-venture and buy Luksic's share. SCH stipulated that OHCH was worth $1,200 million, $600 million from each partner. This estimate caused controversy, because when BCH merged with BS it estimated that its share was worth $400 million. However, Luksic group accepted the offer.

In 1997 SCH expanded in Argentina, Brazil, Colombia and Venezuela (see Table 7.2). This first phase of expansion rested on the acquisition of six banks in five countries in less than a year, paying $3,500 million. These acquisitions were partly influenced by the quick expansion of BBVA in Latin America. SCH was trying to prevent BBVA from taking over the most attractive banks, pushing up prices and limiting opportunities for further expansion (Calderón and Casilda, 2000). With these acquisitions, SCH sought to position itself in the medium-sized economies, with the exception of Argentina, before beginning another phase of expansion in Brazil and Mexico. In 1998, SCH used part of the profits from the sale of its 8.8% share of First Union Corp to buy Banco del Noroeste in Brazil. In 2000 SCH bought 33% of Banco do Estado de São Paulo (Banespa) by paying $3,550, gaining control over 60% of the voting rights. SCH's aggressive strategy led its managers to offer three times more money for Banespa than the second bidder and five times more than the fifth (CEPAL, 2001). Between December 2000 and April 2001, SCH tried to buy the remaining shares, increasing its ownership to 97.8% (see Table 7.2). SCH also took advantage of the liberalization of the Mexican banking sector that followed the peso crisis of December 1994. In May 2000, it took over 100% of Serfin after paying $1,560 million.[12]

SCH invested $15 billion in Latin America, mainly in Argentina, Brazil, Chile and Mexico (see Table 7.3). Its strategy was always to gain majority control in its subsidiaries. In Latin America it kept an average percent of ownership of 78% (Grupo Santander, 1999a). Its subsidiaries had an average return on investment of 20%. However, its managers expected this figure to fall over time, in part due to the growing competition and in part because of the instability of the economies. To compensate, SCH expected to increase its revenue (by raising efficiency).

Table 7.3 SCH's FDIs in Latin America, 1996-2001 (million dollars)

Country	Investments
Brazil	7,157
Mexico	2,661
Argentina	2,154
Chile	1,537
Peru	438
Colombia	421
Bolivia	235
Puerto Rico	198
Uruguay	67
Paraguay	63
Panama	25

Source: *Latin Finance*, December 2001

Moreover, SCH tried to be present in most countries by first entering the Southern Cone (Argentina and Chile), then the Andean economies (Bolivia,

Colombia, Peru and Venezuela) and finally the largest markets (Brazil and Mexico). To promote its corporate image, SCH introduced the services that had been more successful in Spain, like Súper Cuenta, Súper Depósito, Súper Hipoteca and Súper Crédito. Its high profile forced other banks (domestic as well as foreign) to redefine their strategies. SCH (and its main competitors BBVA and Citibank) did not focus exclusively on banking and pension fund management. In this latter category SCH was market leader in Spain, with 15.6% of the market, and in Latin America it managed $6 billion worth of assets through its pension fund business in Argentina, Chile, Mexico, Peru and Uruguay. It had 4.3 million customers (Grupo Santander, 1999b). This strategy was criticized by some stakeholders who believed that this heavy exposure to the Latin American markets increased the bank's exposure to risk and made management more complex.

BBVA: Is Latin America a path towards a leading position in the Euro zone?

In late 2001 BBVA was the second financial institution in Spain, with a market share of 25% in terms of assets. Like SCH, BBVA managed to develop large international ventures, becoming the eighteenth largest bank in the world and the eights in the European Union by market capitalization (*The Banker*, 2002: 172). In early 1995, BBVA decided to reorient its international strategy by increasing the size of its operations overseas. In 2002 60% of its assets were in the Euro zone (mainly in Spain) and 36% in Latin America (in fourteen countries, where it has 23 million customers) (BBVA, 2002). The process of internationalization was quick. In 2001, 21% of the bank's assets were in Latin America, 52% of its offices and 66% of its employees. Its market share in that region was 11.7% (BBVA, 2002).

BBVA's strategy was to gain control over its foreign subsidiaries progressively, but without necessarily having majority ownership. Its managers also emphasized consensus and joint management with local partners (Burns and Weeks, 1998). A central aspect of its strategy was to become a leader in each business segment in which it operated (BBVA, 1999a). To achieve this, it followed a policy of organic growth (by increasing the operations of existing firms) and a policy of acquisitions to expand in those markets that BBVA wanted to prioritize. In 1995 it took over banks in Mexico and Peru, in Colombia, Argentina and Venezuela in 1996, in Brazil and Chile in 1998 and in Mexico again in 2000 (see Table 7.4). BBVA developed a unified model of management in its subsidiaries, adapting it to the peculiarities of each financial system and to the particularities of each country. In the late 1990s, BBVA had a strong presence in Latin America and its managers considered that the bank's early phase of positioning in middle sized countries was over (like that of SCH). In general, BBVA invested in leading banks that could guarantee returns on investment of at least 20% (Uriarte, 1997), with market shares of more than 6% in each country, and with good financial health (BBVA, 1999a).

According to the bank's managers, BBVA had not yet reached a satisfactory market share in Brazil and Chile because these were the last countries in which they made FDIs and because of the peculiarities of these markets, the large size of

Brazil and the high competition in the case of Chile. The Mexican market was one of BBVA's priorities and in 2000 it took over Bancomer. BBVA offered $1,400 million for one third of the bank's stocks and an additional $450 million through bonds. Prior to the takeover Bancomer had promised to buy Banco Pomex from IPAB for $209 million, adding this bank's assets to the merger (CEPAL, 2001). The resulting institution, Grupo Financiero BBVA Bancomer, became the market leader, with one quarter of the market's assets. BBVA gained control over management, although it only held 35% of the ownership.

Table 7.4 BBVA in Latin America in 2001 (percent and million dollars)

Country	Bank	%	Rank	Assets	% Market share		Year of investment
					Loans	Deposits	
Argentina	BBVA Banco Francés	67	5	8 444	8.46	9.09	1996
	Corp Banca Argentina	100	...	...			1999
Brazil	Banco Excel-Económico (actualmente BBVA Brasil)	100	16	5 419	1.65	1.52	1998
Chile	Banco Hipotecario de Fomento (BHIF), actualmente BBVA Banco BHIF	56	10	4 492	6.08	5.44	1998
Colombia	BBVA Ganadero	99	3	2 557	7.44	9.46	1996
Mexico	BBVA México (ex Probursa)	68	...	...	...	...	1995
	BBVA Bancomer	35	1	45 185	30.90	29.52	2000
Peru	BBVA Continental	50	3	2 999	13.83	19.41	1995
Puerto Rico	BBVA Puerto Rico	100	3	...			...
Uruguay	BBVA Banco Francés	100	5	1 071	0.26	5.17	1995
Venezuela	Banco Provincial	53	1	4 255	16.61	16.03	1997

Source: BBVA, *Informe Anual 2001,* "Los 100 mayores bancos", *Revista Latin Trade*, September 2002 and *Latin Banking Guide & Directory 2002*, section *LatinFinance*, August 2002.

BBVA managers promised to increase Bancomer's return on investment by rationalizing the use of its assets and by expanding in the areas of e-commerce and pension fund management. Moreover, BBVA's managers were developing an aggressive strategy to expand in the Hispanic markets of the United States, hoping to gain a share of 15% (CEPAL, 2001). In late 2001, BBVA had invested $9 billion in Latin America. One of the bank's main goals has been to increase BBVA's value in the stock exchange. The appreciation of the value of the bank's stocks has been above the sector's average, vis-à-vis other Spanish and European banks. This was reflected in the positive evaluation of the main international risk agencies. In spite of the economic crises in some Latin American countries, BBVA's profits did not fall. The main reason was the bank's conservative approach to credit and the growth of the pension fund segment.

BBVA was a leader in Spain in the management of pension funds. In Latin America, BBVA was the second firm in this sector in 1998, with a market share of 25% in the countries in which it operated. It was the market leader in Argentina, Bolivia, Colombia, El Salvador, Mexico and Peru. In 1999 BBVA strengthened its position by taking over Chile's leader, Provida.[13] Through this acquisition, BBVA tripled its assets in Latin America, reaching a value of $15,400 million and 8 million customers, becoming the market leader, with a market share of 30% in terms of assets. In 2001 BBVA consolidated its operations, by lowering costs and by increasing its revenue (BBVA, 2002).[14] The highlight was the integration of the bank's assets in Mexico (BBVA Probursa, Promex and Bancomer) to constitute the new Grupo Financiero BBVA Bancomer, which held 30.9% of the market share for loans and 20.5% for deposits (see Table 7.4). In the pension fund segment, Grupo Financiero BBVA Bancomer had a market share of 22% (BBVA 2002). The worsening of the economic situation in Argentina forced BBVA to increase its provisions for losses, leaving the book value of its Argentinean subsidiary Banco Francés at zero dollars.

New problems in the twenty-first century

In the late 1990s, the Spanish economy was growing at a rate of 4% and interest rates were the lowest in decades. However, the worsening of the international economic crisis, as result of the crises in Russia and East Asia, affected Latin America. In this context, the market value of the Spanish banks deteriorated. Nevertheless, the high profitability of their Latin American operations made their FDIs in the region pay off soon, thus the managers reiterated their commitment to stay. This was the beginning of a second stage of their strategy in Latin America, based on increasing efficiency and competitiveness. The first big setback for the Spanish banks came as a result of the Russian crisis in 1998 and the contagion of Brazil. BBVA's and SCH's stocks fell almost by 50% between July and September 1998 (see Figure 7.7). The Bank of Spain also regarded their Latin American exposure as a risky choice and recommended the managers of the two banks to reconsider the acquisition of further assets, favoring quality over short-term profit.

However, the Spanish banks were ready (Calderón and Casilda, 2000). The default ratios of their Latin American subsidiaries were below the average of the domestic banks. The implementation of strict programs to lower costs and reduce non-performing loans allowed them to overcome the crisis, raising their stock value.

SCH

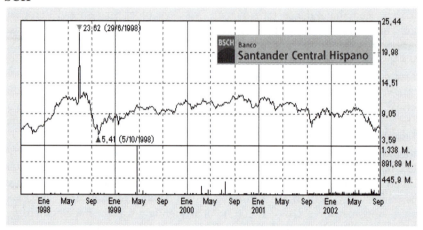

BBVA

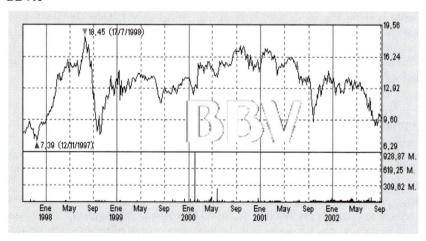

Figure 7.7 SCH and BBVA in the stock exchange, 1998-2002 (Euros)

Source: Madrid Stock Exchange

The timing of the introduction of the euro put additional pressure on the Spanish banks. The possibility of a merger between Spanish banks or between

Spanish and other European banks grew. In early 1999 BS and BCH merged to create SCH and BBV and Argentaria created BBVA.[15] These mergers helped to raise their market value (see Figure 7.7). Their repercussions in Latin America were important too, especially in the case of BCH and BS, because as a result of the merger SCH had dominant positions in Argentina, Bolivia, Chile, Mexico and Venezuela and BBVA in Mexico and Venezuela (see Tables 7.2 and 7.4). It is interesting that both gained a larger market share outside their own home market (Calderón and Casilda, 2000). The most important concerns as a result of the creation of SCH were raised in Chile, where Banco Santiago and Banco Santander Chile were first and second in the market, with a combined share of one third. The Bank of Spain also showed concerns that it had to supervise a bank that took up 30% of the banking risk of another country, because a crisis might have important repercussions on the Spanish bank itself and on the Spanish banking system in general. This was the case in Argentina during the crisis that erupted in 2001.[16]

From the perspective of the Latin American economies (apart from the problems of market concentration), the arrival of Spanish banks had important consequences:

- It strengthened the domestic financial systems, given the larger capacity of foreign banks to raise funds at a lower cost in international markets.
- It contributed to lower mediation margins as a result of growing competition. Foreign banks are used to working with lower mediation margins (3% in the United States and the United Kingdom, as opposed to 6.4% in Brazil). In the new framework, those who borrow money can profit from lower financial costs. However, the reduction of mediation margins was relative, because those of foreign banks were still higher than in their markets of origin and even though operating costs fell considerably the costs of credit did not fall accordingly.
- Growing competition and falling operating costs forced domestic banks to increase efficiency.
- Growing financial mediation as a result of new and sophisticated products.

The main result was the strengthening of domestic markets, which went through two great crises in 1994 and 1997, but the impact was lower than previous ones, especially the debt crisis of the 1980s. However, the worsening economic conditions after 2000, the financial crisis in Argentina and the contagion effect in Uruguay, Brazil and Chile, were a good test for foreign banks. The most serious problems affected Argentina. Some banks left the country and some others decided not to come to the rescue of their subsidiaries.

Conclusions

After ten years of liberalization and financial deregulation, the financial, insurance and pension funds markets of Latin America have changed radically due to the entry of foreign global firms. The large Spanish banks have been the main players, becoming leaders in most countries and segments. In the early 1990s the Spanish banks went to Latin America following their clients. In 2005 they were following their own interests. The financial crisis that affected Latin America in the late 1990s did not affect their strategies. In general, the first stage was over by the turn of the century. In retail banking BBVA and SCH have similar positions. Until mid-2001 they were market leaders in the most attractive segments. However, the acquisition of Banamex by Citibank introduced a new big player. Brazil has been the most difficult of the large markets for the Spanish banks due to the strength of the domestic banks. SCH managed to achieve a more solid position than BBVA. In Mexico both institutions had similar shares in the market. Since the late 19990s they began a process of diversification, combining their investments in baking with those in insurance, pension funds and public health, more recently. The strong impact of their Latin American exposure on market value forced them to adjust their internationalization strategies, focusing on a reduction of their coverage ratio and on improving the competitiveness of their subsidiaries, and on expanding in Europe.

The FDIs of Spanish banks have not yet reached the point of maturity. Their first years have been affected by financial crises; their commercial policies are still expansive (they continue to open new offices); in the first years they made investments in infrastructure and in the adoption of new software systems that will likely fall; and both banks are trying to pay off goodwill in consolidation quickly. The elimination of these expenses are crucial for the development of their strategies in the long run. From the Latin American perspective, the arrival of foreign banks, especially the Spanish, has had a positive effect on the modernization of the domestic financial systems. In general terms, the foreign banks introduced new instruments and technologies, they increased the degree of competition (thus making access to credit easier) and they gave the domestic systems more strength and stability. Nevertheless, there are some difficulties, such as the concentration and the slow transfer to the clients of the efficiency gains in the form of cheaper services.

Notes

[1]   Oficial de Asuntos Económicos, Unidad de Inversiones y Estrategias Empresariales, División de Desarrollo Productivo y Empresarial, Economic Commission for Latin America and the Caribbean (ECLAC-CEPAL), United Nations. Article prepared for the conference on "Spanish Investment in Latin America", organized by the Miami European Union Center, Miami, October 18-19, 2002.

2   The participation of Telefónica de España in the process of privatization of the
       Telebras system in 1998 and the acquisition of majority control over its Latin American
       subsidiaries in 2000 (Operación Verónica) was especially important, as well as the
       takeover of the largest Argentinean and Chilean energy firms (Yacimientos Petrolíferos
       Fiscales –YPF- and Enersis) by Repsol and Endesa, respectively, in early 1999.

3   Holding societies are mainly transportation, telecommunication, energy and financial
       service firms that use this mechanism for tax purposes.

4   By "effective control" I mean more than 40% of a firm's capital.

5   Although Citibank became the largest bank by credit in Latin America by taking over
       Banamex, its strategy is still selective. Citibank may be waiting for new opportunities
       for the acquisition of new institutions in retail banking, mainly in Brazil.

6   "Super Cuenta" was the first current account that paid interests. After it was launched,
       Banco Santander's market share grew by 50%. Bancon Santander launched similar
       services thereafter, like "Super Depósitos" and "Super Hipotecas", triggering the
       reaction of other banks. The result was a higher degree of competition, both in products
       as well as in market share.

7   This trend also affected the public banks, which were grouped by the Spanish
       government under the umbrella of Corporación Bancaria de España (Argentaria).

8   There are many large European banks that did not choose a strategy of
       internationalization, concentrating on their domestic markets.

9   SCH became the main stockholder in Britain's second largest bank, Royal Bank of
       Scotland, with 9.6% of its stocks. It also increased its share in Société Général to 1.5%,
       in Commerzbank to 4.7%, and in San Paolo-IMI to 5.5% (SCH, 2002).

10   In September 1999, both banks developed a plan in which BBV would buy 10% of the
       stocks of Unicredito and Unicredito would buy 5% of the Spanish bank. Moreover,
       Unicredito would merge with BNL, reaching a size similar to that of BBV. This was
       the basis for an alliance, which could lead to a merger. However, the merger of BBV
       and Argentaria broke the balance of power between the two banks and the negotiations
       ended.

11   The deepening of the process of European integration made the Spanish economy
       integrate itself with those of the other European countries. Latin America was an
       attractive region because of the correlation of the economic cycles of Europe and Latin
       America.

12   The Mexican Instituto de Protección del Ahorro Bancario (IPAB) took control of
       Grupo Serfin in June 1999 to protect the savings of its customers, when the bank was
       going through a critical crisis, and auctioned its assets (CEPAL, 2001).

13   AFP Provida had 2.4 million customers, its assets were worth $10,200 million and it
       had five foreign subsidiaries (Colombia, Ecuador, El Salvador, Mexico and Peru). In
       Chile, Provida had 40% of the customers.

14   Between 1999 and 2001, BBVA's revenue in Latin America grew from €1,039 to
       €2,918 million and its profits grew from €342 to €752. The default ratio fell and the
       coverage ratio grew (BBVA, 2002).

15   The Latin American assets of BS and BCH were complementary. In the case of BBVA,
       Argentaria had small subsidiaries, mainly in the pension fund management industry.

16   In early 2002 the anti-trust authorities approved SCH's policy of keeping its
       subsidiaries as independent entities and revised a previous agreement with SCH that
       required the bank to reduce its share of the market gradually. In this new scenario, SCH
       decided to merge its Chilean subsidiaries.

References

BBV (1999a), *Informe Anual 1998,* Bilbao.

BBV (1999b), Relación con Inversores (http://www.bbv.es), Bilbao.

BBVA (2002), *Informe Anual 2000,* Bilbao.

Burns, R. and S. Weeks (1998), "The man of the year: Emilio Botín", *LatinFinance,* 95, March.

Calderón, A. (1999a), "Las renovadas estrategias de los inversionistas extranjeros en América Latina y el Caribe: La participición de la empresa española", *Síntesis,* 29/30, Madrid.

Calderón, A. (1999b), "Las inversiones de la empresa española en América Latina: ¿Una estrategia agresiva o defensiva?", *Economía Exterior,* 9, Grupo Estudios de Política Exterior, Madrid.

Calderón, A. and R. Casilda (1999), "Grupos financieros españoles en América Latina: Una estrategia audaz en un difícil y cambiente entorno europeo", *Serie Desarrollo Productivo,* 59 (LC/L. 1244-P), Comisión Económica para América Latina y el Caribe, Santiago de Chile, September.

Calderón, A. and R. Casilda (2000), "La estrategia de los bancos españoles en América Latina", *Revista de la CEPAL,* 70 (LC/G.2095-P), Comisión Económica para América Latina y el Caribe, Santiago de Chile, April.

Casilda, R. (1997), *La banca española. Análisis y evolución,* Ediciones Pirámide, Madrid.

Casilda, R., P. Lamothe and M. Monjas (1997), *La banca y los mercados finacieros,* Alianza Universidad Textos 166, Editorial Alianza, Madrid.

CEPAL (1998), *La inversión extranjera en América Latina y el Caribe, Informe 1998* (LC/G.2042-P), Santiago de Chile. Publicación de las Naciones Unidas, no. de venta: S.98.II.G.14, December.

CEPAL (2000), *La inversión extranjera en América Latina y el Caribe, Informe 1999,* Santiago de Chile, January.

CEPAL (2001), *La inversión extranjera en América Latina y el Caribe, Informe 2000,* Santiago de Chile, April.

Durán, J.J. (1999), *Multinacionales españolas en Iberoamérica. Valor estratégico,* Centro Internacional Carlos V, Universidad Autónoma de Madrid, Ediciones Pirámide, Madrid.

Falcão, Aluizio (1997), "Cambio de marcha. Banco Santander no quiere comprar más. ¿Se lo permitirá el mercado?", *América economía,* Santiago de Chile, December.

Freres, C. (1991), "Spain Rediscovers the Americas", *Spain Rediscovers the Americas,* Suplemento Especial, LatinFinance, August.

Grupo Santander (1999a), *Informe Anual 1998,* Madrid.

Grupo Santander (1999b), *Resultados de 1998 del Grupo Santander,* (http://www.bancosantander.es), Madrid.

Hernández, U. (1999), "Banca extranjera nuevos conquistadores", *Expansión,* 773, vol XXX, Ciudad de México, September 1.

Moore, L. (1999),"Santander Investment: radiografía de un repliegue", *América economía,* Santiago de Chile, 17 June.

Rodríguez, M. (1998), "La expansión de las empresas españolas en Iberoamerica: el caso de la banca", *Economía exterior,* 7, 1998/99, Madrid.

Salomon Smith & Barney (1998), *Foreign Financial Institutions in Latin America,* Latin America Equity Research, New York.

Salomon Barney (1999), *Update on Foreign Financial Institutions in Latin America,* Latin America Equity Research, New York, March.

SCH (2001), *Informe anual 2000*, Santander.

SCH (2002), *Informe anual 2001*, Santander.

Sullivan, T. (1998), "Voy de compras, ¿me acompañas?", *América economía*, Santiago, Chile, 4 June.

The Banker (2002), *The 1000 World Banks*, London, July.

Uriarte, P. (1997), *La estrategia de expansión del BBV en América Latina*, Banco Bilbao Vizcaya, Bilbao, March.

Chapter 8

Spanish Telecoms in Latin America: Telefónica

Fernando Gallardo

Introduction

The telecommunications sector (TMT) has played a leading role in the last few years both in the rise and fall of different stock market prices. The internationalization of telecommunications firms and Internet-related enterprises have been an important part of the general process of internationalization. In this context, Spanish enterprises – and more specifically the Telefónica Group companies – have undertaken an internationalization project focused on Latin American.

This chapter addresses the internationalization strategy of the sector's enterprises and analyzes the case of Telefónica in Latin America. The following section examines, from an historical perspective, the causes, phases and strategies that operators in the telecommunications sector have used in their internationalization strategies. The case of Telefónica and Terra is then discussed. The study ends with an analysis of the financial crisis that is affecting the TMT sector.

Internationalization strategy in the telecommunications and internet sectors

Telecommunications operators began to internationalize in the late 1980s, and the process accelerated until it was curbed by the general crisis that the TMT sector has been experiencing since late 1999. This section will analyze the process up to the beginning of this crisis, which in turn will be examined along with its implications in section five. Three aspects will be examined: (i) what were the causes that allowed the internationalization process to begin and evolve towards globalization?, (ii) what strategic patterns have been identified in the internationalization processes of leading telecommunications operators?, and (iii) how have alliances with other operators been addressed from a strategic point of view?

Causes of internationalization and globalization

The internationalization and globalization of firms that operate telecommunications services can be linked to technological progress, which made experts question the situation of natural monopoly that characterized the sector. The collapse of the natural monopoly concept has led to implementation of liberalization and privatization[1] policies in the sector. Thanks to these two policies, operators have been able to develop offensive internationalization and globalization strategies.

Technological progress can be broken down into five major areas: digitization of switching and transmission networks, breakthroughs in the area of mobile networks and communications, progress in the field of satellite communications, extension of fiber optics as a transmission medium, and the spectacular emergence of the world of Internet. Technological innovation has drastically changed the process of operating telecommunications services, the product offerings to customers, and the business cost structure. It more specifically has the following implications:

- Technological enhancements have increased equipment capacity and at the same time lowered prices.
- Technological progress makes it possible to offer a wider range of services to customers. In addition, services can be tailored to the customer's specific needs.
- The new business and value chain structure creates incentives for new startup firms to successfully compete at different links of the business value chain without any detriment to sector efficiency.

In short, the most beneficial attribute for the sector is to have not only one firm that provides the services, but rather to have several competitors that can improve the unit cost of service provision for society.[2] Governments should deregulate the sector and remove various existing barriers so that the advantages of the new situation can be exploited. The most important measure is liberalization; the entry of new competitors must be allowed. Another of the initiatives being put into practice is privatization of public telecommunications operators that were acting as monopolies. Both liberalization and privatization are seen as key instruments for implementing the internationalization strategy. They act as entry signals for multinational operators or operators seeking to become multinational.

Evolution of expansion and internationalization

In the national monopoly stage, there was a very limited amount of internationalization, although revenues were high, that focused on the area of service exportation (see Figure 8.1). The first possibility was to provide international call services to customers. The monopolist operator that provided this service required the network of another foreign operator to be able to place the call.

Therefore, an amount had to be paid for using the foreign network. The maze of operators resulted in a multitude of payments. These activities are called correspondent operations and imply the export and import of services. There were also cases of technology transfers, especially in the field of advanced communications.

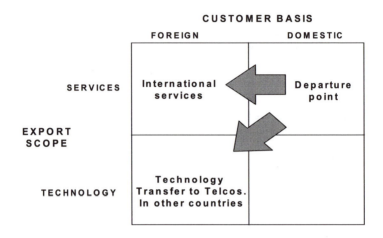

Figure 8.1 International activities before FDI

There are two general approaches (see Figure 8.2) when operators initiate an internationalization strategy through FDI (Durán and Gallardo, 1994). Some operators make an FDI by acquiring an existing operator or by creating a new one to operate services in another country, in many cases starting from a monopoly situation. This strategy, which can be called multidomestic, was the one used by Telefónica, France Télécom and Deutsche Telekom when they began internationalizing, to name just a few examples. The second includes a group of operators that focus their internationalization on the supply of advanced enterprise services to their national customers for their international and global communication needs. This strategy could be called multinational and is the case of BT and AT&T.

The two strategic approaches have their own financial and technological implications. In regards to necessary funding, an operation carried out as part of a multidomestic strategy requires more financial funds than a multinational strategy. As for technological issues, a multidomestic operation allows for a high level of transfer of technology already owned by the parent company, whereas there are fewer possibilities for accumulating new technological capabilities. The opposite is true for a multinational operation. Regardless of whether operators initiate their internationalization based on a multidomestic or multinational focus, they both tend to evolve towards a global strategy.

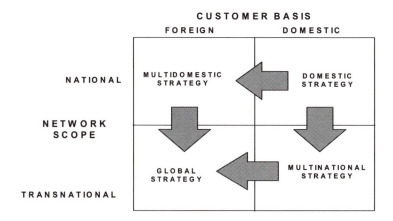

Figure 8.2 FDI strategic approaches

Unlike other businesses and contrary to the dictates of the general theory of internationalization, operators have internationalized very rapidly. By 1994, the world's major operators, except for the Japanese operator NTT, had a very important international presence. In oligopolistic industries in which there are few enterprises and a high degree of strategic interdependence, the enterprises tend to imitate each other. In addition, the existence of economies of scale favors speed of action. On the other hand, the nature of the business also favors the first to make a move, as they acquire market power that they can later use to establish standards and negotiate interconnections.

Patterns of evolution of international alliances

A phase began in the 1980s and early 1990s in which telecommunications firms became involved in international alliances as part of their internationalization strategy. From that time to the present, a series of changes have been observed in the patterns of international alliances between operators. Four phases are distinguished, some of which overlap for some operators. In the beginning, agreements were reached between different operators to design and subsequently implement, if research was successful and the operators reached a commercial agreement, services targeted at large enterprises or specific collectives (e.g., the financial sector) that demanded transnational services. A feature of these agreements was their non-exclusive nature, so that almost all operators were present in almost all projects. Competition was incipient in some countries and practically non-existent in others. The operators were not overly confident but, as the alliances required few financial resources and some of them were promising, they took part.[3]

The following stage involved alliances in which more resources were required to develop networks that were going to be commercially operated. It was thus a matter of undertaking shared-risk projects. These networks were deployed to provide global telecommunications services to large multinational firms that demanded global services. The figure used to form these alliances was normally the joint venture. Main alliances reached by mid 1990s were dismantled a few years later.[4] One reason given to explain these failures is the lack of predisposition to make a common pool of customers when operating the services. Customers are essential assets and operators were reluctant to share them with their partners.

A third phase consisted of cross shareholdings between operators. On many occasions, seats on the boards of directors were also exchanged. This operation was not usually undertaken on an isolated basis, but rather was a way to provide stability to a global alliance that had already been formed beforehand (an example is the case of France Télécom and Deutsche Telekom). The exchange of shareholdings could also be considered, in some cases, as a preliminary period that served to see if progress could be made towards a merger.

The last stage, i.e. mergers, is in an incipient stage. There have been operations that failed when negotiations were very advanced (Deutsche Telekom and Telecom Italia; Telefónica and KPN), and there have been negotiations that failed in the initial phases (Telefónica and BT) or that culminated some initiatives (Sonera, Vodafone, Verizon). This last phase has been curbed by the crisis that began in late 1999.

As the four phases described above progress (from agreements to mergers), the alliance's level of definition, level of partner commitment, assets provided and risks assumed increase. All of this is consistent with the goal of capturing the greatest possible market share in a business of high expectations such as the telecommunications business. Based on the cases of failed and successful mergers recorded to date, a series of patterns can be determined:

- Many mergers have been completed in which the leading roles were played by the RBOCs (Bell Atlantic and GTE merged in 2000, giving rise to Verizon; SBC and Ameritech also merged that year; Cingular is a joint venture between SBC and BellSouth for mobile communications created in 2001) and by Worldcom (acquisition of MCI and Sprint). The RBOCs are companies that, in these turbulent times in the sector, enjoy good financial health and good prospects for the future[5], i.e. the opposite of what is happening to Worldcom. An analysis of the evolution of telecommunications operators in the United States is interesting. In 1984, the great AT&T was dismantled and seven regional companies (RBOCs) were created. They had a monopoly on local communications in a geographic area. Long-distance communications were liberalized that same year. Subsequently, market initiatives have been the force behind mergers between the RBOCs and the long-distance firms.
- Mergers of European telecommunications operators linked to former monopolies (Deutsche Telekom and Telecom Italia, Telefónica and KPN) have failed. The presence of public capital and the existence of golden shares

have acted as impediments.

- The merger by absorption that Vodafone[6] carried out in 2000 on the German firm Mannesman was the largest operation ever undertaken in the TMT sector. The promising future of mobile communications thanks to the implementation of the UMTS technology in many countries was a driving force behind this merger. It gave rise to the largest mobile communications operator in the world, which aimed to take advantage of economies of scale. Vodafone posted the largest losses in its history due to the crisis of confidence in UMTS, which has forced the company to make provisions for the loss of value of its goodwill.

- The second largest merger in the TMT sector was between AOL and Time Warner. AOL was the world's leading company in the Internet business and Time Warner a leader in content. A very important feature of this operation is that it is a case of vertical integration at a time when the opposite has been true, i.e. vertical disintegration. The explanation for this operation can be found in the fact that Internet businesses are in an early stage of development and, to leverage them, it is advisable for the best positioned firm in the market to control contents, which are what make Internet networks so attractive. The TMT sector crisis has also affected AOL-Time Warner, and they posted heavy losses because the goodwill dropped in value.

Telefónica and the internationalization strategy

This section begins with a brief historical synopsis of Telefónica. The different stages of its internationalization activities are then analyzed. The financial internationalization phase is reviewed first, and then its FDIs.

Historical synopsis

From December 1877, when the first telephone communication took place in Spain, to 1924, the country's telephone service was operated by different private companies and municipalities that were licensed by the state. This diversity led to a problem of interconnection between the different networks and therefore, in 1924, the state granted a sole license for operating the service throughout the country to Compañía Telefónica Nacional de España, which was constituted on April 19 of that year. The company was controlled by the North American multinational ITT.

Telefónica was nationalized in 1945, with the state as principal shareholder and in charge of management. Telefónica's contract with the state was signed one year later. This contract, which served to define the company's activity, remained in effect until December 1991, when a new contract was signed in order to adapt Telefónica's activity to the new situation.

The liberalization of the communications sector began in 1991. The first relevant measure was liberalization of the terminals market that same year. Subsequently, different services were gradually opened up to competition: radio tracking, data transmission, closed-cluster radiotelephony, mobile telephony (by granting of GSM licenses), public-use telecommunications, resale of leased circuit capacity and VSAT services. All services were being liberalized except for basic telephony. But in 1997 a second license was granted and a third the following year. The sector was completely opened up to competition in late 1998. This measure was not an isolated case, but rather a transposition to Spanish legislation of the European Union's directives on this matter. Throughout the 1990s, the state sold off its shareholdings and, in early 1997, Telefónica was completely privatized. However, the Spanish state retained a golden share until 2007, which allowed it to veto certain company decisions, including a merger.

Financial internationalization

Before beginning its FDIs, Telefónica carried out a financial internationalization process during the second half of the 1980s, which helped it gain experience that it has subsequently been able to exploit. This experience included an understanding of international financing mechanisms and a network of contacts established by financial agents, many of whom would subsequently take part in the FDI by providing consulting and appraisal services and, naturally, financing. During this period, Telefónica confronted the need to develop and modernize its national network to upgrade it to the same levels attained by neighboring countries. This raised the need to resort to external funding to finance the large volumes of investments. The tight domestic financial markets and the fact that more financial instruments were available on foreign markets, together with the Spanish operator's good credit rating, drove Telefónica to obtain financing on international financial markets, from both European markets and the U.S. capital market. In addition, Telefónica undertook a plan to internationalize its shareholders. Telefónica began to be traded in 1985 at the London, Frankfurt, Paris and Tokyo stock exchanges. Even more important was quotation of Telefónica's ADR (American Depositary Receipt) at the New York stock exchange. This policy has made it possible to diversify the shareholding base with a view to acquiring shareholder equity. International institutional investors have shown a great interest in Telefónica's shares.

First phase of Telefónica's internationalization in Latin America

Telefónica's first phase of internationalization in Latin America took place from 1989 to 1998. The analysis addresses two questions: what are the grounds for undertaking an internationalization process in the region, and what benefits and advantages have been achieved. The determining factors of a telecommunications operator's FDI can be put into context with Dunning's (1988) eclectic approach. In accordance with this paradigm, FDIs are explained by the exploitation of three types of advantages that companies can obtain: proprietary competitive advantages, internalization advantages and localization advantages.

A telecommunications operator can initiate an internationalization process through FDIs if it owns proprietary competitive advantages that are embodied in intangible assets and translate into a certain leadership in product costs and/or differentiation. Cantwell (1991) distinguishes between two types of proprietary competitive advantages that a company can achieve and that are perfectly applicable to the case of a telecommunications operator. In the first place, there are advantages that can be exploited by the company in an FDI or sold for use by another company. This is the case of technology. On the one hand, there is another type of advantage that can be exploited by the company that owns it. This is the case of an operator's organizational capabilities in matters of network development and modernization, with the existence of highly qualified human resources, company prestige and a network of contacts of all sorts (politicians, manufacturers, other operators, etc.) established by the operator over time. On the other hand, the operator could achieve a third advantage that results from a combination of the previous two, which is the ability to generate new technologies and capabilities.

Telefónica has an essential competitive advantage: its experience in Spain in telecommunications network development and modernization in a short period of time. In the late 1980s, Telefónica had a long waiting list in Spain. More than a half a million people wanted a telephone line, and the waiting time was very long in some cases. Service quality was at very low levels. The company decided that the situation had to be rapidly changed. An investment plan was devised to develop and modernize the network in a short period of time, and the goal was achieved in a couple of years. Telefónica demonstrated that it had the management capabilities to achieve these objectives. The Latin American governments that began to decisively privatize their telecommunications in the early 1990s were looking for multinational operators that had capabilities that would allow them to undertake plans similar to the ones that Telefónica implemented in Spain. Therefore, Telefónica's proprietary competitive advantage lies in its ability to develop and modernize basic telecommunications networks in a short period of time.

The second component in Dunning's focus is formed by internalization advantages. Proprietary competitive advantages can be exploited by internalizing them in the corporate group through direct investments or by selling them to another firm to exploit. The selection of one option or the other will be contingent on the costs of the associated transaction and the potential for incrementing the proprietary competitive advantages or creating new ones that derive from each of the options. However, in accordance with the preceding paragraph, some of the advantages can only be exploited by internalizing them. Telefónica's proprietary competitive advantage could be exploited to the utmost on an internal basis, i.e. within the corporate group.

The third component of the eclectic paradigm is composed of localization factors. The company must duly assess the possible targets of investments so that the proprietary competitive advantages can be successfully exploited. Telefónica's localization factors are marked by cultural and linguistic similarities in the Latin American region. As this area is the natural target for many other Spanish firms' FDIs, Telefónica could follow its business customers to offer them global services when they embarked on their international expansion strategies.

The entry signals in the Latin American market were very clear. The most important one was the beginning of a privatization process, and subsequently market liberalization. Telefónica has made most of its FDI in Latin America after privatizations. But it has also entered some countries (e.g., El Salvador) as a second operator as a result of a privatization process. In addition to these two entry signals, Telefónica at the same time has always been attuned to another entry signal, which has to do with market expectations. Telefónica invested in markets with a high growth potential. Latin American markets meet this requirement. We must not forget that these high expectations also have considerable country risks and exchange rate risks associated with them.

From a historical perspective, we can make several points concerning Telefónica's experience with its investments in Latin America. The first refers to aspects concerning the profitability and financial flows obtained. It can be safely said that these investments have been profitable for Telefónica, even though some markets have suffered problems at certain moments. Financial profitability comes from three sources: profits earned by the companies, cash flows by way of management fees and royalties, and synergies generated, one of which refers to the savings obtained by the Telefónica Group by coordinating purchases made by group companies.

The second element to be analyzed refers to the development of intangible assets by Telefónica as a result of its Latin American investments. There are two sources of intangible asset generation. On one hand is development of management capabilities from three sources:

- Learning in markets other than the Spain.
- Learning in competitive markets. Telefónica began to manage companies in competition in Latin America before it did in Spain. This experience was very useful when it had to operate competitively in Spain.
- Learning in markets as a second operator, since Telefónica has achieved some licenses to operate in this way.

The second source refers to generation of strategic assets that increase the group's value. The strategic asset is the value of its position in the region, which makes Telefónica one of the most appealing and valued firms in the sector. Although the sector is currently going through hard times, Telefónica is one of the most highly appraised companies in terms of a possible future merger thanks to its position in Latin America. This is Telefónica's great competitive advantage at this time.

Second phase of internationalization

This second phase of internationalization in the region started in 1999. The most important privatizations had already been completed (Brazil was the last in 1998), and Telefónica was fully aware of its new competitive advantage and implemented major strategic changes to exploit it. The first change was in

Telefónica Group's organizational structure. It was transformed from a geographical structure, in which the subsidiaries operated all services in one geographical zone, to a structure based on the branch of business. Thus, the Telefónica Móviles subsidiary took control of all mobile communications businesses distributed around the world, Terra did the same with the Internet business for the private and SME segments, Admira absorbed the content business, etc.

Along with this organizational change, consolidation in Latin America allowed Telefónica to offer integrated, homogeneous networks and services to the multinational firms present in several countries (Alierta, 2002). This major undertaking was the responsibility of the subsidiary named Telefónica Data. Telefónica has developed a ring-shaped (backbone) transmission network in Latin America to satisfy its customers' international communications needs. This network is managed by another subsidiary, Emergia. A very interesting recent initiative that illustrates the new strategic focus is creation of the Telefónica Soluciones subsidiary. The idea is to concentrate in one single enterprise the services that Telefónica had previously been offering in a widely dispersed manner from different areas and subsidiaries, in order to gain a maximum return on the Group's assets and take advantage of synergies.

The investment rate in the region dropped in this new phase, since the major privatizations were completed and a crisis hit the sector. The most important operation was the takeover of several mobile enterprises in Mexico, a country where Telefónica did not have a major presence. After this operation, Telefónica became the second largest mobile communications operator in a country with a high growth potential in this market.

A significant financial operation in this period was the so-called Operation Verónica, in which Telefónica launched a series of public share offerings on some of its Latin American subsidiaries to take over 100% of their shares. The operation was announced in January 2000 and should have been concluded in four months. Payment was not made in cash, but rather with shares from a Telefónica S.A.[7] share issue. The operation was delayed for several months because of repeated requests for information from the SEC. The explicit purpose of the operation was to increase control over these companies and thus to maximize synergies generated by the group. In fact, absolute control over a subsidiary facilitates management and helps achieve this goal. But most synergies are obtained with a share of less than 100%. The implicit reason for Operation Verónica was that Telefónica posted a considerable increase in its stock market capitalization. With a view to a potential merger, Telefónica would be in a much better position to negotiate the distribution of power and internal relationships. The multidomestic and multinational approach followed by Telefónica is made evident in the fact that almost half of EBITDA in 2001 was reached out of Spain (Telefónica 2002).

Terra's investments in Latin America

Terra's history

Terra is one of Telefónica's subsidiaries with FDIs in Latin America. Terra became well known after its merger with Lycos and because it is one of the enterprises that has been affected by the dot.com financial crisis. Terra has had a short life. It was founded in November 1998 under the name of Telefónica Interactiva. It was meant to focus on the Internet business for the private and SME segments. However, other Telefóncia subsidiaries also take part in the Internet business, such as Telefónica Data and TPI (Telefónica Publicidad e Información). Telefónica Data serves the large enterprise market segment and TPI focuses on electronic commerce, which means that TPI competes with Terra. Telefónica Interactiva was renamed Terra Networks following the summer of 1999. In November 1999, Telefónica issued 13.8% of Terra's shares for market trading through a public share issue. Terra began to be traded on Spain's continuous stock market and on NASDAQ. Since April 2000, it was traded on Spain's New Stock Market.

Since it was created as Telefónica Interactiva, its content was purchased at arms' length in the market from other firms or it was acquired by taking over other enterprises in the Internet business both in Spain and Latin America. These initial acquisitions include the purchase of the portal Olé.[8] The idea of going public with the company emerged in March 1999, and the operation was carried out in November of that year. Telefónica issued 38 million shares (13% of the total). On the first day of the public offering (November 2), the demand for shares exceeded supply by 83%. The shares began to be traded on the stock market on November 17. The issue price was €13 per share for the institutional and international segment and €11.81 for the retail segment. The closing price on the first day of trading was €37. Terra's worth, at the closing price of the retail segment, amounted to some 550,000 million pesetas. At the end of the first day of trading, the company was worth more than 1.7 billion pesetas. Telefónica earned 82,000 million pesetas by going public, thus more or less recovering the outlays it had previously made to provide the company with content. Terra's market price rose spectacularly after that. Terra's stock market capitalization climbed to more than 6 billion pesetas. For a time it was the third highest company in the stock market capitalization ranking of companies traded on the Spanish stock exchange. It reached a price of €154 per share, before falling to around €4 in 2002. Telefónica Group completed a strategic alliance with BBVA in 2000, whereby the bank acquired share in Terra and Terra acquired a share in the capital of uno-e, BBVA's Internet bank.

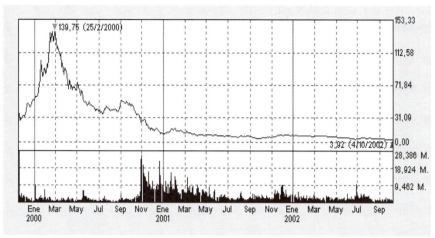

Figure 8.3   Evolution of Terra's stock market price
Source: Madrid stock exchange

The merger of Terra and Lycos

The most important operation to date by Terra was the merger with Lycos. In mid-May 2000, Terra surprised the markets by launching a merger operation by absorption with Lycos. The agreement appraised each Lycos share at $97.55. The surcharge was 68% with respect to Lycos' quoted price on Nasdaq just before the operation was officially announced. If Lycos' quoted price before the market discounted the early rumors of the operation is used as a reference, the surcharge goes up to more than 100%. Telefónica did not pay in cash but rather with Terra shares from a capital increase. The announced operation had a negative impact on Terra's price due to the offered surcharge. After the merger with Lycos, Telefónica had a 37.63% share in Terra-Lycos.

Nevertheless, it was a very attractive operation for Terra, as the company was purchasing highly valuable intangible assets. Lycos was a company serving the world's principal Internet market (the United States) and that was earning profits when most companies were posting losses. With the operation, Terra accessed a management team with proven expertise and capabilities in the market. The drawback of the operation was, as already indicated, the high price that was paid.

Terra-Lycos: Recent financial evolution and position in Latin America

Terra-Lycos' presence in America is notable, both in the U.S. market thanks to the merger and in Latin America as a result of the acquisitions made and the transfer of assets from the parent company to Terra. The results from 2000 and 2001 did not show a profit (see Table 8.1). As a positive element, it is worth mentioning the improvement posted in the EBITDA. Terra-Lycos' primary goal was to find its way as soon as possible to profitability and profits.

Table 8.1 Terra's consolidated income statement (million euros)

	2000	*2001*
Operating revenues	304.0	690.0
EBITDA	-359.3	-232.0
Operating profit	-442.9	-417.4
Income before taxes	-804.2	-931.3
Net income	-555.2	-566.3

Source: Telefónica's quarterly results

Throughout 2001, Terra-Lycos adopted a new strategic model called OPB (Open, Basic, Premium). This focus was intended to generate revenue, based on the payment of subscriptions. The ADSL service launch has been a major source of business. Terra marketed the service to the private segment and Telefónica acted as wholesaler. However, Telefónica also began to offer the service as retailer, in competition with Terra-Lycos. This is not the case for the subsidiaries of the major European operators. There is also another drawback that puts Terra at a disadvantage with respect to some of the large European portals, which has to do with the directory business. For example, Wanadoo has integrated this business, whereas in the Telefónica Group the business is conducted by TPI. Terra-Lycos also focused its strategy on offering different channels to its customers. In late 2001, Terra had 1.7 million paying subscribers.

Some issues of interest can be identified on examining the first quarter earnings of 2002. Turnover in this period amounted to €322.2 million, which is less than the same period of the preceding year (€357.5 million). If we look at the second quarter of the year, turnover can be broken down as follows:[9]:

- 56%: Spain and Latin America
- 44%: USA

In terms of lines of business, Terra's turnover can be broken down as follows:

- Media (advertising, marketing solutions, electronic commerce, subscriptions to portal content and services): 60%
- Communications services and access business: 40%

At the end of June 2002, Terra had 2.3 million paying subscribers. Terra's financial state of affairs does not differ much from that of the other leading European portals (T-Online, Wanadoo, Tiscali and Seat PG).[10] None of them turned a profit in the first quarter of 2002. In line with enterprises that are suffering from the TMT sector crisis, Terra proceeded to sell assets considered as non-strategic (Lycos Korea and Lycos Canada).

The TMT sector crisis

This section analyzes the crisis experienced by the TMT sector since early 2000 and how Telefónica was affected by it.

The crisis of internet enterprises

The TMT sector crisis began around February 2000, when the trading prices of enterprises associated with the world of Internet reached their highest levels, falling sharply thereafter. The Internet bubble had burst. Some enterprises went bankrupt and others, especially those with stronger financial backing, managed to survive at very low market value. Electronic commerce, both in terms of replacing commerce through traditional channels and of new products and services for Internet, did not take off as quickly as expected. As a result, real income from commissions was well below the forecast figures.

At the time, investors provided the money required for starting up Internet-related businesses. There were expectations for long-term. The problem arose when actual data were compared with the forecasts. The losses were much heavier than expected, and the new short-term forecasts were not very promising; expected revenue from advertising had to be drastically reduced because of the slow takeoff of electronic commerce, and because Internet access (one of the most important initial sources of revenue) was free for a normal connection that was not high-speed and the user was reluctant to pay for content. Internet enterprises begged investors to increase capital to finance upcoming expenses. Now the investors were reluctant and did not provide funds as readily as before. They wanted more specific business plans that outlined a credible scenario of a quick road to profits. This was not possible and many enterprises went bankrupt. Others, especially those with solvent reference shareholders in the telecommunications sector, continued forward but implemented strategies to strictly control expenditures and seek revenue-generating business lines.

The application of real options to appraise Internet enterprises should be analyzed from a historical perspective. It was said that the traditional methods based on cash flow discounts were not applicable, as there was no historical basis to establish a cash flow growth scenario for the future. There were some who resorted to appraising these enterprises solely on the basis of their real options, especially growth options. This was true in part. These enterprises undoubtedly had (and continue to have in spite of the burst financial bubble) real growth options. But these options were not of a proprietary nature.[11] They were options that could be exercised by different enterprises. For this reason (although other issues not related to real options also played a part), there were no grounds for the joint stock market capitalization achieved by the innumerable companies on the market.

Generalization of the TMT sector crisis

Many other firms linked to the TMT sector have been affected by a serious financial crisis. Next to suffer the crisis were the mobile communications firms, which paid exorbitant amounts for third-generation UMTS licenses. These payments were made just when mobile telephone users were recording high growth rates and were widely accepting the mobile telephone. It was also a time of high Internet business expectations. The UMTS technology is capable of providing more bandwidth for accessing Internet services at a higher speed than possible with non-enhanced narrow networks. Therefore, the mobile-Internet combination was magic. Operators contracted debts to be able to pay the licenses. When the Internet bubble burst, business expectations dropped abruptly but the cost of UMTS licenses did not. Debts lost in quality and became a burden. Moreover, deployment of UMTS networks required heavy material investments, which had to be put off due to lowered expectations and the problems to obtain additional financing.

Firms in the world of television and content also had serious financial problems. The most outstanding case was Vivendi, which had to implement a strict restructuring and disinvestments plan. The German Group Kirch also experienced these problems. Large operators with subsidiaries in Internet and mobile businesses were affected by these business crises, and stock market prices dropped sharply. Entrant operators also suffered from the crisis. Many of these companies emerged with the liberalization processes. Most of them did not see their business expectations fulfilled. Internet traffic did not grow as much as expected, and heavy investments were made in fiber optics. There was therefore surplus capacity. Many of them were on the verge of bankruptcy, as they were unable to pay back the credits and interest on bonds they used to finance their projects. NTL, Global Crossing, UPC (a Dutch company and the largest cable company in Europe with a presence in 17 countries and in which Microsoft held a share), KPNQwest (the Dutch-North American company with the largest fiber optics network in Europe)[12] and ITV were all on the verge of collapsing.

Finally, the crisis affected equipment manufacturers. Their customers were going bankrupt, they had serious financial problems or they had to face cutbacks in investments. The sector's leading manufacturers (Alcatel, Ericsson, Lucent, Siemens, etc.) also suffered from the crisis and, along with significant losses, they had to address the need to downsize. The economic crisis also had a negative impact because it did not generate a suitable atmosphere for expansion plans. An example of the apathy generated by this crisis was the drop in the number of mergers and acquisitions. According to UNCTAD (2002), the value of transnational acquisitions and mergers completed in 2001 was cut in half, down to $594,000 million divided among 6,000 operations, compared to the 7,800 operations carried out in 2000. In addition to these problems, some firms in this sector were involved in questionable accounting practices (Worldcom, Global

Crossing) or were affected by the fall of their visionaries (Worldcom) or prestigious CEOs (Vivendi), as well as by resignations (Deutsche Telekom and France Télécom)

The crisis and P&L accounts of the sector's enterprises

The TMT sector crisis had a major impact on the P&L accounts of the affected enterprises. Changes in American accounting rules (Financial Accounting Standards Board) forced many companies in the country, as well as foreign companies that traded on U.S. stock exchanges, to make major provisions against the P&L account to reflect trading fund losses stemming from acquisitions made in more optimistic times. This is what happened to AOL after its merger with Time Warner, to AT&T after devaluation of TV assets, France Télécom after the purchase of Orange, Vivendi after Seagram, Vodafone after Mannesman and J-Phone, Deutsche Telekom after VoiceStream, etc.

Telefónica did not escape these accounting adjustments. In fiscal year 2001, Telefónica admitted to losses of €7,182 million on applying USA accounting rules (€2,106.8 million in profit according to Spanish accounting rules). The main charges were to the Trading Fund of Lycos, Medyaways and Endemol. The takeover of the Latin American subsidiaries in Argentina, Brazil, Chile and Mexico also had a strong impact on accounts. Other losses were posted in the first six months of 2002. The Board of Directors approved a provision of €4,837 million to cover its investment in the purchase of UMTS licenses. It also announced that these businesses were being frozen in Europe. The Argentine crisis and depreciation of the region's currencies caused a 25% drop in operating revenue during the first half of the year in relation to the same period the previous year. On the other hand, debt was cut by €2,895 million during the last 3 months. It should be noted that Telefónica's debt, in comparison to other operators in its environment, had a relatively lower debt burden (see Table 8.2).

Table 8.2 Debt ratio in telecom operators

	2001		January-June 2002	
	Debt (mill. €)	Debt / EBITDA	Debt (mill. €)	Debt / EBITDA
Telecom Italia Mobile	1,532	0.3	614	0.1
Telecom Italia	21,942	1.6	21,100	1.5
Telefónica Móviles	9,032	2.7	5,602	1.5
Portugal Telecom	5,456	2.6	4,762	2.1
Telefónica	28,942	2.3	25,789	2.1
KPN	15,746	4.4	15,000	3.7
Deutsche Telekom	62,111	4.1	64,148	4.1
France Telecom	63,423	5.1	69,696	5.7

Source: *El País* (September 2002)

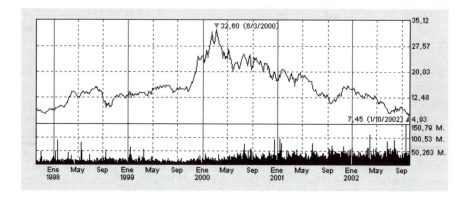

Figure 8.4 Evolution of Terra's stock market price
Source: Madrid stock exchange

Conclusions on the crisis

Several conclusions regarding the TMT sector crisis are summarized below:

- In spite of the severe crisis that Internet enterprises experienced, the Internet is the present and its future is ensured. It is going to be consolidated as an authentic revolution in the social and economic arenas. Economic history reminds us that enterprises in sectors that have proven to be authentic revolutions, such as the railroad and automobiles, have suffered the same as the dot.coms.
- Which companies will best survive the crisis? The North American RBOCs and the European companies that operated as monopolies before markets were opened up to competition are the ones in the best position at this time. They have access to the customer (local loop)[13] and it is easier for them to put obstacles in the way of their competitors. In times of crisis, they fall back on new businesses and concentrate on mature markets that, in addition to generating cash flows, allow them to innovate with solutions that are technologically unperfected but that are low cost and very much in demand, e.g. the extension of ADSL networks.
- Entrants have proved to be very aggressive. Incumbent operators have also been aggressive, but they had financial reserves and customers in mature businesses to hold their ground. Many entrants have found themselves with networks with an immense capacity but no demand. The solution, among other measures, will be in mergers of survival, not in aggressive mergers.
- The future of the UMTS mobile business in Europe will be in launching new services other than voice and simple Internet access. It is essential that attractive, cheap services based on user positioning be offered. In addition, a mobile-based

payment system could be an application to drive UMTS. In short, there is no single killer application, but rather the solution will most likely be found in an abundant, varied series of new services that add value to the user.

Notes

[1] There are no privatizations in the United States because the enterprises were private already.

[2] That does not mean entry barriers do not exist. Economies of scale and scope are present. It is necessary to bear in mind that economies of scale are a sufficient condition for a natural monopoly. Necessary condition is subadditivity.

[3] Some examples are FNA (Financial Network Association) and JNI (Joint Network Initiatives). Telefónica and France Télécom took part in both alliances, which can not be called strategic. None of them reached relevant results.

[4] This is the case of Unisource, where Telefónica was present. Telefónica left Unisource to create an alliance with BT. This alliance was not stable and, after breaking up, Worldcom became Telefónica's ally. This link was also broken. To give another example, the alliance between France Télécom, Deutsche Telekom and Sprint was also a failure.

[5] In exchange, the competitive and financial position of CLEC (Competitive Local Exchange Carriers) was not good.

[6] Vodafone had acquired already the US company Airtouch, the most robust mobile communications enterprise in USA.

[7] Telefónica S.A. is the holding firm in the upper position.

[8] Before this acquisition Telefónica was working in developing its own portal.

[9] Source: Telefónica's Second Quarter Results.

[10] T-Online was the subsidiary of Deutsche Telekom, Wanadoo was France Télécom's and Seat PG, Telecom Italia's.

[11] Trigeorgis (2000) identifies eight types of real options when combining three criteria that take into account strategic aspects. The first criterion refers to the exclusivity of the option and to the effect on competition. According to it there are proprietary real options, which can be used only by one firm; and shared real options, that are available to several competitors

[12] This company had a debt of €1,800 million because of the funding for the deployment of a network of more than 25,000 km of fiber optic, which linked the main European cities. It did that just in the moment when Internet services prices began to fall.

[13] Rifkin (2000) underlines the importance of access.

References

Alierta Izuel, C. (2002), "Telefónica: de un operador local a un operador multinacional y multidoméstico". *ICE*, 79.

Cantwell, J. (1991), "A survey of theories of international production", in N. Pitelis and R. Sugden (eds.), *The Nature of the Transnational Firm*, Routledge, London.

Dunning, J.H. (1988), "The Eclectic Paradigm of International Production: A Restatement and some Possible Extension", *Journal of International Business Studies*, Spring.

Durán, J.J. and Gallardo, F. (1994). "La estrategia de internacionalización de las operadoras de telecomunicaciones", *ICE*, 735.

Gallardo, F. (2002), "XDSL services: an strategic approach". Paper presented at the ITS Regional Conference. September. Madrid.

Rifkin, J. (2000), *La era del acceso: la revolución de la nueva economía.*

Telefónica (2002 and 2001). *Annual Reports and Quarterly Results.* (www.telefonica.es)

Trigeorgis, L. (2000), "Real Options: a Primer", in J. Alleman and E. Noam (eds.), *The New Investment Theory of Real Options and its Implications for Telecommunications Economics*, Kluwer Academic Publishers, Boston.

UNCTAD (2002), *World Investment Report 2002. Transnational Corporations and Export Competitiveness*, New York.

Chapter 9

Stakeholder Impact of Telefónica's Latin American Investments

Michael Periu, Jr.

Introduction

Spain has played a critical role in the development of the Latin American telecommunications sector. The importance of Spain in this sector corresponds to its traditionally central role in the overall development of Latin America. Through financial investment and knowledge transfer, Spanish companies brought much-needed service level improvements and tariff reductions throughout the region. As a key business infrastructure, improvements in telecommunications served as a catalyst for overall economic growth. By fostering the development of telecommunications, Spanish firms provided a key pillar for further investment and development in derivative and complementary sectors.

The company most responsible for this investment and innovation is Telefónica. Since the early 1990s and continuing today, Telefónica has executed an aggressive investment and expansion plan throughout Latin America. The region now represents the principal market for Telefónica in terms of customers, lines in service ("LIS") and revenues.[1] This study analyzes the impact of Telefónica's investments in Latin America on two key stakeholder groups: consumers and investors. By using industry standard metrics, the study assesses the impact of Telefónica's investment on Latin American consumers and businesses. The study also analyzes the impact that this Latin American investment strategy has on Telefónica's equity investors. The analysis arrives at two key conclusions: (1) Consumers were clear winners. The evidence clearly indicates that, for consumers, Telefónica's investments provided overwhelmingly positive benefits. They transformed the lives of millions of people and provided opportunities for local and regional businesses. They served as a catalyst for economic growth throughout the region. (2) Investors were not losers. For investors, the period between 1998 and 2003 was challenging given the correction in the equity markets and the subsequent implosion of the telecommunications sector. Telefónica's investment strategy pursued riskier opportunities in Latin America instead of more stable markets in Europe or domestically. The returns for equity investors prior to the market collapse were above Telefónica's peer group returns. Subsequent to the meltdown, the returns have been in line or above peer group returns. This indicates that Telefónica investors were rewarded for a successful investment strategy in Latin America before the collapse and subsequent to the collapse.

Since the inception of Telefónica's aggressive Latin American investment strategy, numerous studies have been conducted analyzing the company's transition from domestic monopoly to multinational enterprise, expansion strategy, execution plan, financing structure, implementation of technology, human resources practices, relations with local governments and tariff setting policies. This study builds on previous analyses by reviewing the whole of Telefónica's Latin American expansion.

Setting the stage: foreign direct investment in Latin America

Latin America has traditionally been a major recipient of foreign capital, primarily from Europe and the United States. Throughout the 1990s, in sequence with aggressive privatization plans in Latin America, foreign capital flows increased to record levels.[2] By the end of the 1990s and through the first years of this decade, capital flows declined due to regional economic conditions, global economic conditions and increase political uncertainty. Despite these adverse circumstances, the region still remains a large recipient of foreign capital.[3]

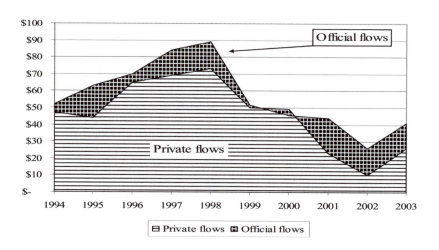

**Figure 9.1	Net capital flows to Latin America from abroad, 1994-2003(amounts in billions of US dollars)**

Source: IMF

The principal component of these capital inflows has been foreign direct investment (FDI). During the 1990s, Latin America received approximately $440 billion in FDI.[4] From 2000 through 2003, FDI totaled an estimated $235 billion.[5] While in 2003 FDI was approximately half of the figure in 1999, it still remained an impressive $65 billion.[6] Between 1995 and 2000, the region received an average of 40% of all FDI to developing countries around the world.[7]

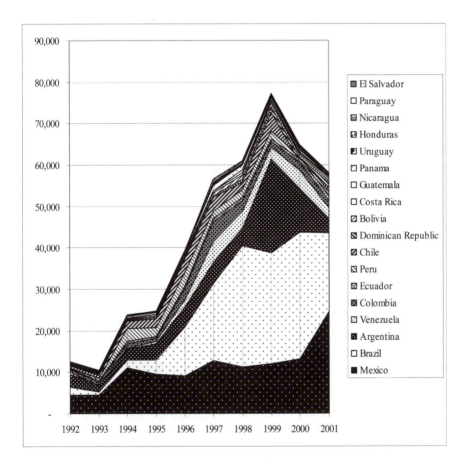

Figure 9.2   Net foreign direct investment in Latin America (amounts in billions of US dollars)[8]

Source: CEPAL, Centro de Información de la Unidad de Inversiónes y Estrategias Empresariales de la División de Desarrollo Productivo y Empresarial

This flow of investment provided the necessary resources to stimulate the regional economies and achieve the GDP growth experienced throughout the 1990s. Despite heightened economic uncertainty and political turmoil in many parts of the region over the time period addressed in this study, GDP growth continued for the majority of countries. Additionally, the negative trend in foreign investment is showing strong signs of reversal and economic growth is returning to some of the most recently troubled markets.

During the 1990s, a fundamental shift occurred in the nature and distribution of FDI in Latin America. Initially, Latin America served as an export platform for wealthier countries.[9] MNEs were attracted by the region's low wages and built manufacturing and processing facilities for the exclusive or main purpose of exporting the goods produced to their domestic markets.[10] Most FDI concentrated in Mexico, due to the North American Free Trade Agreement (NAFTA).[11]

As the region began to experience economic growth throughout the 1990s, two important shifts occurred. First, there was a geographic diversification of FDI.[12] Foreign investors recognized the opportunity that existed in the large domestic markets of Latin America. Argentina, Brazil and Mexico were largely underserved markets with pent up demand for goods and services. The concentration of FDI began to shift from Mexico and the Caribbean to target large markets in South America.[13] Secondly, there was a sector shift. Instead of focusing on manufactured goods for export, investors began to focus on the non-tradable services sectors such as telecommunications, energy, transport and banking. This reflected the growing confidence in Latin America as a viable market for international investors.

Table 9.1 Annual GDP growth rates in Latin America (percentages)

	1990	1991	1992	1993	1994	1995	1996	1997	1998	1999	2000	2001	2002	2003
Argentina	-1.3	10.5	10.3	6.3	5.8	-2.8	5.5	8.1	3.8	-3.4	-0.8	-4.4	-10.9	8.7
Bolivia	4.6	5.3	1.6	4.3	4.7	4.7	4.4	5.0	5.0	0.4	2.3	1.5	2.8	2.6
Brazil	-4.2	1.0	-0.5	4.9	5.9	4.2	2.7	3.3	0.1	0.8	4.4	1.3	1.9	-0.2
Chile	3.7	8.0	12.3	7.0	5.7	10.8	7.4	6.6	3.2	-0.8	4.2	3.7	2.2	3.3
Colombia	4.3	2.4	4.4	5.7	5.1	5.2	2.1	3.4	0.6	-4.2	2.9	1.4	1.8	3.6
Costa Rica	3.9	2.6	9.2	7.4	4.7	3.9	0.9	5.6	8.4	8.2	1.8	1.1	2.9	5.6
Dominican Rep.	-5.5	1.0	8.0	2.9	4.3	4.7	7.2	8.3	7.3	8.0	7.3	3.2	4.7	-1.3
Ecuador	3.0	5.1	3.6	2.0	4.7	1.7	2.4	4.1	2.1	-6.3	2.8	5.1	3.3	2.6
El Salvador	4.9	-2.0	3.2	3.3	5.4	6.4	1.7	4.2	3.7	3.4	2.2	1.7	2.1	2.2
Guatemala	3.1	3.7	4.8	3.9	4.0	4.9	3.0	4.4	5.0	3.8	3.6	2.3	2.2	2.1
Honduras	0.1	3.3	5.6	6.2	-1.3	4.1	3.6	5.0	2.9	-1.9	5.7	2.6	2.7	3.0
Mexico	5.1	4.2	3.6	2.0	4.4	-6.2	5.2	6.8	5.0	3.6	6.6	-0.2	0.7	1.3
Nicaragua	-0.1	-0.2	0.4	-0.2	3.3	4.3	4.8	5.1	4.1	7.0	4.2	3.0	1.0	2.3
Panama	8.1	9.4	8.2	5.5	2.8	1.8	7.4	6.4	7.4	4.0	2.7	0.6	2.2	4.1
Paraguay	3.1	2.5	1.8	4.1	3.1	4.7	1.3	2.6	-0.4	0.5	-0.4	2.7	-2.3	2.3
Peru	-3.8	2.9	-0.5	4.8	12.8	8.6	2.5	6.8	-0.6	0.9	2.8	0.3	4.9	4.0
Uruguay	0.3	3.5	7.9	2.9	7.3	-1.4	5.6	5.0	4.5	-2.8	-1.4	-3.4	-11.0	2.5
Venezuela	6.5	9.7	6.1	0.3	-2.3	4.0	-0.2	6.4	0.2	-6.1	3.2	2.8	-8.9	-9.2

Source: IMF, World Economic Outlook Database, April 2004

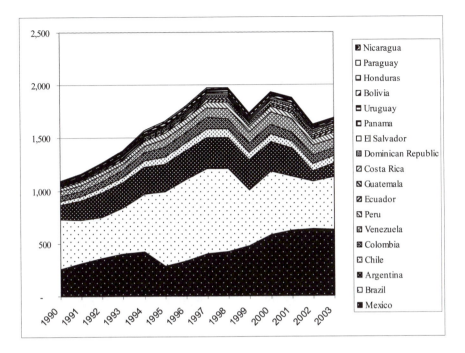

Figure 9.3   Aggregate GDP in Latin America (billion US dollars)

Source: IMF, World Economic Outlook Database, April 2004

Telefónica: An overview of the company and its role in Latin America

Among European countries, Spain has been the key player in FDI to Latin America. In 1995, 6% of all European FDI to the region came from Spanish firms.[14] This amount totaled approximately $1 billion. By 1999, at its peak, Spain's FDI to Latin America skyrocketed to $27 billion, representing 65% of all European FDI to the region.[15] The importance of the relationship was reciprocal, as Latin America received 77% of Spain's total FDI.[16] In key markets, Spain's dominance was apparent. Spanish firms were the number one foreign investor in Argentina, representing over 50% of that nation's FDI receipts.[17] Spain was the second largest foreign investor in Brazil, jumping from 3% to 24% of total FDI to Brazil by the end of the 1990s.[18] The key recipient sector in Latin Americas was telecommunications, headed by Telefónica.

Telefónica, S.A. (Telefónica) is a global, diversified telecommunications and media company with over 100 million customers around the world.[19] Originally Spain's lethargic, state-owned telephone monopoly, Telefónica was transformed into a competitive, multinational corporation through privatization, which yielded efficient management, a risk-taking culture and a growth-oriented strategy. The company has also expanded beyond standard wire-line services to become a major global player in wireless telephony, data services, Internet services, media and content.[20]

Telefónica achieved consolidated, global revenues of $28.4 billion 2003.[21] This figure has remained stable over the past 4 years, except for a jump to over $27.6 billion in 2001.[22] Given the significant turmoil in the global telecommunications sector during this period, this may be considered positive. Net Income has returned positive in 2003 after a large loss in 2002 due primarily to extraordinary charges from asset write-downs and restructuring.[23]

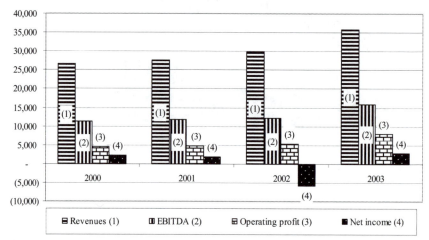

Figure 9.4 Key financial performance indicators for Telefónica (billion US dollars)

Source: Telefónica Annual Report for 2003, converted into US dollars from Euros

After completing an extensive restructuring and asset streamlining in 2003, Telefónica was organized around three core areas: (1) fixed-line operations, (2) wireless operations and (3) other value-added services. Telefónica's fixed-line operations are located in Spain and Latin America. The management of the lines is organized under three key sub groups: Telefónica de España, Telefónica de Latinoamerica and Telefónica Empresas. As of December 2003, Telefónica de España (TdE) had 19.3 million fixed lines in service, generating 138.2 billion minutes of traffic during 2003.[24] TdE represents 44% of Telefónica total lines in service. Telefónica de Latinoamerica (TdL) had 24.8 million lines in service as of December 2003. Telefónica Empresas provides complete telecommunications services for approximately 21,000 businesses. 90% of these clients are outside of Spain.[25]

Telefónica Móviles, the global wireless arm of Telefónica, is a market leader in Spain and Latin America. Including the recent acquisition of BellSouth's wireless assets in Latin America, Telefónica has over 62.5 million wireless customers. Telefónica's third group is composed of companies offering publishing, content, media and other value added services. It includes the remaining assets of Internet company TerraLycos. Telefónica bought all outstanding shares from third party investors and folded TerraLycos back into Telefónica's operations. In 2004, Telefónica sold the Lycos portion of the business to Daum Communications, owners and operators of the Daum Internet portal in South Korea.[26]

Table 9.2 Telefónica corporate structure as of March 2004

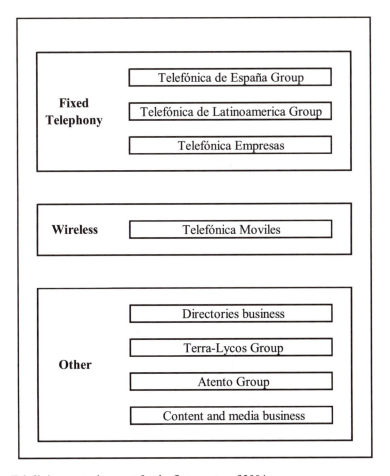

Source: Telefónica quarterly report for the first quarter of 2004

Telefónica in Latin America

Telefónica stands as one of the largest and most successful telecommunications companies in the world. It is the third largest fixed line operator in Europe by customers and the number one in Spain, Brazil, Argentina, Chile and Peru.[27] It is also one of the largest wireless operators in the world. Since privatization, Telefónica has expanded aggressively beyond its home market of Spain. With a strong emphasis on Latin America, Telefónica has a significant presence in fifteen countries and operations in a total of forty around the world.[28] This position was recently strengthened with the announcement in early 2004 that Telefónica was acquiring all of BellSouth's wireless assets in Latin America. This acquisition added 10.5 million wireless customers in ten countries to Telefónica's portfolio. Telefónica paid a total of $5.7 billion or $540 per subscriber.[29] Since the early 1990s, Telefónica has invested heavily in Latin American telecommunications and related sectors. These investments made Latin America the most important market for Telefónica not just on a customer basis, but also on the basis of revenue, EBITDA and operating profit. Currently, 65% of Telefónica's customers are located outside of Spain. Virtually all of these customers are in Latin America[30]. In 2003, the Latin American division of Telefónica accounted for 31.20% of the overall company's EBITDA and was one of the most profitable divisions.[31]

Table 9.3   Latin American customer breakdown for Telefónica, as of March 2004 (amounts in thousands of clients)[32]

	Wireless	Fixed	Total
Brazil	20,656	12,781	33,437
Argentina	3,311	4,238	7,549
Chile	3,571	2,542	6,113
Venezuela	3,307	2,679	5,986
Peru	2,149	2,260	4,409
Mexico	3,454	-	3,454
Colombia	1,915	-	1,915
Ecuador	816	-	816
Guatemala	409	25	434
Panama	420	-	420
El Salvador	248	-	248
Nicaragua	229	-	229
Puerto Rico	175	-	175
Uruguay	146	-	146
Total	40,806	24,525	65,331

Source: Telefónica Investor Relations Presentation, March 2004

Table 9.4 Telefónica's EBITDA margin by operating group (US dollar billion)

	Revenues	EBITDA	EBITDA margin
Telefónica de España Group	12,871	5,712	44.4%
Telefónica Latinoamericana Group	8,033	3,861	**48.1%**
Telefónica Empresas	2,245	383	17.1%
Telefónica Móviles Group	13,137	5,772	43.9%
Directories Business	742	232	31.2%
Terra-Lycos Grupo	687	(50)	-7.2%
Atento Group	621	84	13.5%
Content and Media Business	1,736	265	15.3%
Other companies	512	(262)	-51.2%
Eliminations	(4,809)	(122)	2.5%
Total	35,775	15,875	44.4%

Source: Telefónica 2003 Annual Report, converted into US dollars from Euros

Table 9.5 Lines in service as of December 2003 (millions of lines in service)[33]

Fixed	
Telefónica in Latin America	**24.5**
Telmex	15.7
Brasil Telecom	10.7
Portugal Telecom	5.9

Wireless	
Telefónica Moviles in Latin America	40.1
America Movil	43.7
Portugal Telecom	20.7
TIM	19.8

Sources: Presentation by César Alierta, São Paulo, March 17, 2004; 2003 annual reports for competitors

Telefónica's impact on Latin America touches every sector of the economy. The firm is the largest operator in the Latin American telecommunications sector with more lines in service than any other company in the region.[34] Between 1990 and 2003, total fixed LIS increased almost 10-fold from 2.5 million to 24.5 million. Telefónica expanded their customer base in the region during the same period from less than 100,000 to over 65 million today. Since 1990, the company has invested over $68 billion in acquisitions and capital expenditures in the region, making it the largest sources of FDI.

Table 9.6 Telefónica's types of investments in Latin America ($ million)

	1990 -1997	1998	1999	2000	2001 -2002	2003	Total
Acquisition	2,902	5,134	1,477	20,209	4,294	5,850	**39,866**
Infrastructure	9,802	4,402	3,863	5,023	5,436	N/A	**28,526**
Total	12,704	9,536	5,340	25,232	9,730	5,850	**68,392**

Source: Investor presentation, March 2004

Telefónica's dominant role in Latin American telecommunications continues relative to other multinational telecommunications companies with a presence in the region. Leading firms from Europe and the United States trail in all major metrics. Only one company, Mexico-based America Móvil, competes at the same level with Telefónica, and this is in only one category: wireless customers. With the recent acquisition of BellSouth's wireless assets in the region, Telefónica's dominant position for the medium-term is virtually assured.

Telefónica's impact on key stakeholders – metrics

Given the company's pervasive presence, large investment and multi-sector reach, Telefónica has had a major impact among key stakeholders including consumers and investors. Both groups have been materially impacted by Telefónica management's decision to invest heavily in the region. In order to quantify and evaluate the impact on stakeholders by Telefónica's decision to invest heavily in Latin America, key metrics were selected.

For the evaluation of Telefónica's impact on consumers in Latin America, six principal metrics were selected. Total fixed lines in service and fixed line penetration rates evaluate the growing access to standard telephone services for consumers. Total wireless lines in service and wireless penetration rates evaluate both the absolute penetration and relative growth in mobile telecommunication services for consumers in the region. Internet access penetration quantifies access for consumers to value added and data services. Tariff reductions quantify in economic terms the savings experienced by consumers. Reduction of wait times for installation offers a qualitative measure of the improved service provided by

Telefónica. This also captures the indirect economic costs of living without phone service during long installation times. Availability of value added services is a general measure, including time saving and enriching communications tools such as call waiting, call forwarding, voice mail, three way calling and related services.

For the evaluation of the investor stakeholder group, two principal metrics were selected. First, total return on common stock. Common stock holders represent the broadest base of investors, including U.S. institutional investors, European institutional investors, other institutional investors, U.S. retail investors, European retail investors and other retail investors. Total return measures the real gain or loss experienced by holders of common stock. It includes the return from both dividends and capital gain. It assumes that all dividends are reinvested into Telefónica common stock. Total return provides a clear and objective measure for evaluating the impact on shareholders. Secondly, relative return of Telefónica common stock is used. Simply evaluating total return is insufficient as this return must be placed in the context of competing investments. In this case, a peer group of large, European, U.S. and Asian multinational telecommunications companies was used as the peer group. The group includes companies such as Vodafone, Verizon, NTTDocomo, SBC Communications, Deutsche Telekom, France Télécom, China Mobile, Bell South, TEM, TIM, Telecom Italia, Telstra and AT&T Wireless. Both wire line and wireless companies are used, given Telefónica's presence in both. Analyses were adjusted to reflect the spin-off into separate publicly traded companies of certain wireless divisions of large multinational conglomerates in the peer group.

Telefónica's impact on key stakeholders – consumers in Latin America

Consumers in Latin America have been the most prominent beneficiaries of Telefónica's investment in the region. By most metrics, the quality of service and value provided has improved drastically in the markets where Telefónica operates. Both the quantitative and qualitative evidence suggests that consumers are much better off as a result of Telefónica's investments in the region. Given the previously weak state of the telecommunications industry, including outdated infrastructure, non-competitive market places, non-market driven innovation and overall management inefficiency, it was imperative that the region be transformed with the assistance of global telecommunications leaders. Telefónica played an important role in this development. During the period of Telefónica's investments in the region, all key penetration metrics increased substantially in Latin America.

Table 9.7 Subscribers per 100 inhabitants in Latin America

	1996	1998	2000	2002	2004
Fixed	10.01	11.96	14.81	17.26	20.22
Wireless	1.35	4.21	12.06	16.68	23.14
Total	11.36	16.17	26.87	33.93	43.36

Source: ITU Statistical database

While both fixed and wireless penetration increased dramatically throughout the region, wireless penetration exploded, virtually equaling fixed penetration in 2002 and surpassing it by 2004. Telefónica's Móviles division was an integral component in the expansion of wireless. The total number of phone lines in Latin America is expected to grow for the foreseeable future, with the prevalence of wireless over wire line also continuing.

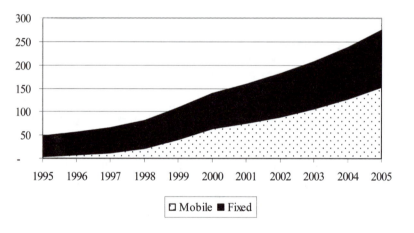

Figure 9.5   Total lines-in-service in Latin America (millions of lines)

Source: ITU Statistical abstract

While the region overall benefited from Telefónica's investments, certain markets benefited more than others. Argentina, Brazil and Peru are key examples of the positive economic and quality-of-life benefits that large-scale infrastructure investments can have in a developing economy.

Telefónica's impact on key stakeholders – Argentina

Consumers in Argentina experienced dramatic benefits from Telefónica's investments. Between 1994 and 2005, Telefónica invested over $10.7 billion to install 4.8 million lines, in addition to the 4.5 million of lines already in service. A 100% digitalization rate was also achieved during this period. Most dramatically, the waiting time for the installation of a new phone line was reduced from 49 months to 2 weeks. The telephony penetration rate also doubled to 24%.

Table 9.8 Key telecommunications metrics for Argentina

Argentina	1995	1996	1997	1998	1999	2000	2001
Internet users, thousands	30.0	50.0	100.0	200.0	500.0	2,500.0	3,000.0
Internet users per 100 population	0.1	0.1	0.3	0.6	1.4	6.8	8.0
Fixed and wireless lines, millions	6.0	6.8	8.4	9.9	11.8	13.9	15.1
Fixed and wireless lines per 100 pop.	17.2	19.3	23.7	27.3	32.2	37.7	40.2

Source: Comisión Nacional de Comunicaciones y Centro Argentino de Ingenieros

Telefónica's impact on key stakeholders – Brazil

Consumers in Brazil also experienced dramatic improvements in service since Telefónica became involved in the market after the privatization of Telebras. Since 1998, Telefónica has invested over $27 billion in Brazil's telecommunications sector, with $25 billion dedicated to fixed line investments and $2 billion in wireless. Since Telefónica entered the market in the third quarter of 1998, the wait list for phone service was reduced to zero. Lead times that were once measured in months are now down to 2 weeks. In São Paulo, where Telefónica operates, penetration reached 34 lines per 100 inhabitants, representing an 80% reach.

Table 9.9 Key metrics for Brazil

Brazil	1998	1999	2000	2001
Internet users, thousands	2,500.0	3,500.0	5,000.0	8,000.0
Internet users per 100 population	1.5	2.1	2.9	4.6
Fixed and wireless lines, millions	14.5	17.6	21.6	27.4
Fixed and wireless lines per 100 pop.	16.5	23.8	31.8	38.4

Source: ITU Statistical abstract

Telefónica's impact on key stakeholders - Peru

Since Telefónica's launch in Peru in May 1994, the industry has transformed. The improvements touch consumers, business-owners, telecommunications employees and the government. Consumers have benefited from a reduction in wait times from almost 10 years to less than two weeks for the installation of a telephone. Connection fees were also reduced dramatically, by 90% making phones far more affordable than before. Telecommunications services are now prevalent among all stratifications of Peruvian society. Even for those individuals that cannot afford a fixed-line or wireless phone installation, almost 90,000 public telephones were installed, making their presence pervasive. While Telefónica made phone service more efficient and pervasive, over 20,000 net jobs were created as well.

Table 9.10 Peru's statistics before and after Telefónica's investments

	1993	2001
Fixed lines installed, millions	0.7	2.0
Average waiting time, months	118.0	0.5
Fixed line telephone companies	2	8
Connection fee	$1,500	$156
Public telephones	8,000	94,600
Digitalization	33%	96%
Fiber optic cable, Km	200	8,971
Cities with celular service	7	120
Employment	13,000	34,000

Source: Osiptel

Table 9.11 Key metrics for Peru

Peru	1995	1996	1997	1998	1999	2000	2001
Internet users, thousands	8.0	60.0	100.0	900.0	1,500.0	2,500.0	3,000.0
Internet users per 100 population	0.0	0.3	0.4	3.6	6.0	9.7	11.5
Fixed and wireless lines, millions	1.2	1.6	2.1	2.3	2.7	3.0	3.6
Fixed and wireless lines per 100 pop.	5.0	6.8	8.5	9.3	10.7	11.7	13.7

Source: Osiptel, Documento de trabajo numero 57

Telefónica's impact on key stakeholders – investors

The last several years have been quite challenging for institutional and private investors in the telecommunications sector. Overcapacity, overvaluation and a lack of trust in performance figures for the industry have lead to the collapse of equity prices, a dramatic, industry-wide downgrading of credit ratings and the inevitable bankruptcy of household names in the sector. As typically happens in these post-bubble explosions, investors overreact and do not discriminate as carefully as they should. Thus, firms that are in a sound financial position are grouped with those that are in a precarious situation with little or no attempts at distinguishing them. This has been the case with Telefónica, which despite its relatively sound financial position has suffered along with the laggards of the industry. As seen below, Telefónica stock has lost most of the gain achieved during the period in question.

Telefónica's stock price at the end of the period did not necessarily imply that investors have fundamentally changed their views on the underlying performance of the company. Despite the overall malaise of the telecommunications industry, there are still many opportunities in the sector and it remains a growth industry when measured over decades instead of quarters. Telefónica is among the best-positioned companies to capitalize on the long-term opportunities of the industry. The fall in the stock price is primarily due to a fundamental change in how much risk investors are willing to take in the telecommunications sector, which is reflected in the amount they are willing to pay for future earnings. It also reflects a shift in investor perspective, realizing that global telecommunications firms offer a service that is similar to electricity, water and other basic household services. Companies that provide these services offer less-risky and lower returns. As investors arrived at the consensus that telecommunications companies are really just another utility, they began to value them as such. In the case of Telefónica, however, the growth opportunities that its Latin American presence presented continued to generate superior returns to utilities.

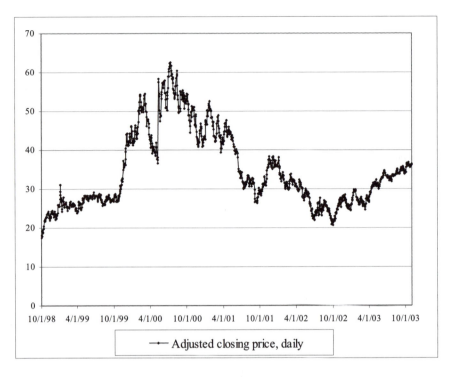

**Figure 9.6   Performance of Telefónica common stock from October 1998
through October 2003 (US dollars)**

Source: Compiled from Yahoo! Finance data

During the turn of the century, investors valued telecommunications companies
like Telefónica not as large utilities, but rather as growth-oriented, technology
companies. Investors erroneously assumed that large multinationals that invested
in media and high-technology properties could consistently generate the high-
levels of earnings and performance associated with smaller, nimbler growth
companies. As Figure 9.8 shows, the risk-return profiles of large vs. small firms
became skewed. Telefónica stock was valued in line with the technology index,
despite the fact that the nature, scale and focus of the company did not fit the
profile of a technology company. As investors came to this realization, the stock
changed.

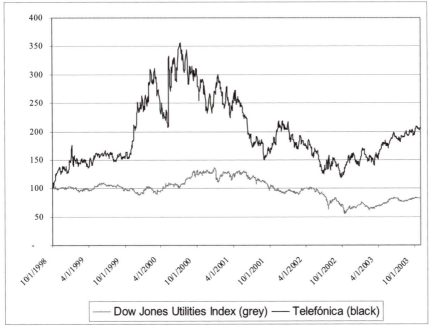

Figure 9.7   Performance of Telefónica common stock vs. the Dow Jones Utility Average from October 1998 to October 2003. Indexed to 100 on October 1, 1998

Source: Compiled from Yahoo! Finance data

Telefónica's decision to diversify and invest heavily in Latin America does not appear to have had an adverse impact on the stock for equity investors. Among its peer group, large European telecommunications companies, Telefónica is the most diversified. No other peer has invested as heavily in Latin America or has such a large percentage of revenues originating from foreign markets. Therefore if there were a material difference in the performance of Telefónica stock relative to their peers, it may be attributable to its Latin American investment decisions. As Figure 9.9 demonstrates, however, this does not appear to be the case. Telefónica investors valued the stock in line with its peer group. The stock did not underperform its peers during the period, but rather performed in line or better throughout the period. Therefore the impact to equity investors was not negative relative to its peer group.

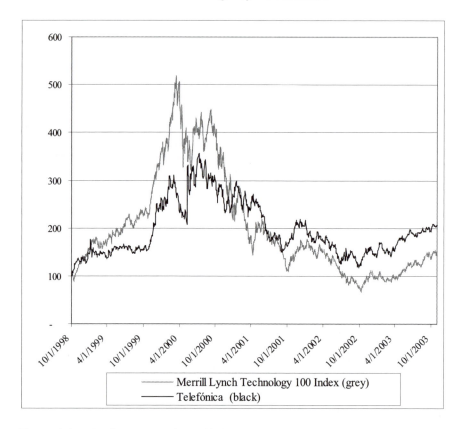

**Figure 9.8   Performance of Telefónica common stock vs. the Merrill Lynch
              Technology 100 Index from October 1998 to October 2003.
              Indexed to 100 on October 1, 1998**

Source: Compiled from Yahoo! Finance data

Taking a look at Telefónica's stock price vs. a broader index, the Nasdaq
Telecommunications Index, the trend continues to corroborate the premise that
Telefónica's decision to invest in Latin America did not adversely impact the stock
price. Telefónica did not fall below the broader index during this period, but rather
during a majority of the time period outperformed the index.

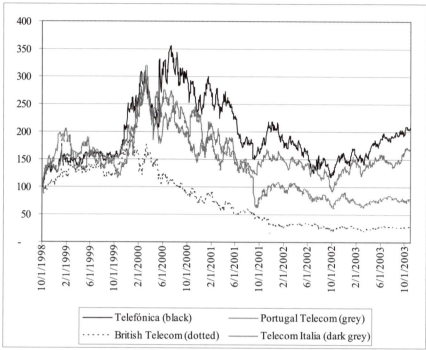

Figure 9.9   Performance of Telefónica stock price vs. peer group consisting of Telecom Italia, Portugal Telecom and British Telecom from October 1998 through October 2003

Source: Compiled from Yahoo! Finance data

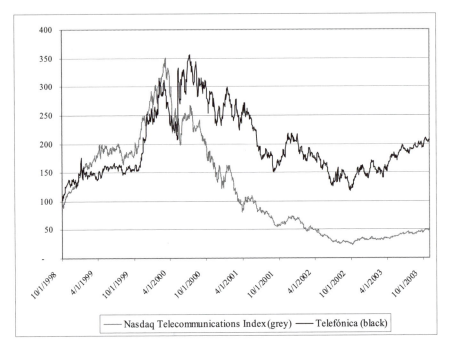

**Figure 9.10   Performance of Telefónica stock vs. Nasdaq Telecommunications
Index from October 1998 through October 2003 – index to 100
on October 1, 1998**

Source: Compiled from Yahoo! Finance data

Conclusions

Telefónica investments in Latin America provided positive benefits for both of the
key stakeholder groups analyzed in this study. Consumers in Latin America
benefited through lower tariffs, access to value added services, reduced wait times
for installation, improved call completion percentages and improved call quality.
Both retail consumers and businesses in Latin America benefited. Since
telecommunications is a backbone infrastructure, Telefónica's investments
generated tremendous derivative benefits for this stakeholder group. Reliable
telecommunications services facilitate business transactions, entrepreneurship and
trade. The benefits can be quantified through improvements in all key metrics:
increased fixed lines-in-service; increased wireless telephony; increased value-
added services; reduced tariffs; and reduced or eliminated waiting lists for access
to phone service.

   The second key stakeholder group in this study, equity investors in Telefónica,
also benefited from the company's decision to investment aggressively in Latin

America. They were not adversely impacted by Telefónica management's decisions to focus its operations and investments in this region. This is demonstrated by the key metrics used to evaluate the impact on this group: Telefónica common stock performance did not underperform the telecommunications index composed of the company's peers; Telefónica common stock performance did not underperform other large European telecommunications companies that did not invest so heavily outside their domestic markets; and Telefónica stock performed in line with its true peer group, large utilities.

As political and economic uncertainty continue to impact Latin America, future investments in telecommunications infrastructure in the region will be scrutinized very carefully by managers and investors. Given Telefónica's experience and track record in Latin America, continued investments in the region should benefit consumers and investors for the foreseeable future.

Notes

[1] 2003 Telefónica Annual Report.

[2] Stephen Everhart and Mariusz Sumlinski, "Trends in Private Investment in Developing Countries", International Finance Corporation Discussion Paper Number 44, pp.37-42.

[3] United Nations Conference on Trade and Development (UNCTAD), World Investment Report 2001, New York, Chapter 1 and Statistical Annex.

[4] Economic Commission for Latin America and the Caribbean, *La inversion extranjera en Latinoamerica y el Caribe*, United Nations Publications, Geneva, 2002, p. 13.

[5] Ibid.

[6] Ibid.

[7] Ibid.

[8] Figure 9.2 is in accordance with the fifth edition of the IMF Balance of Payments Manual. All transactions between non-financial direct-investment enterprises and their parent companies and affiliates are included in direct investment. Net FDI refers to direct investment in the reporting economy minus direct investment abroad by residents. For some countries this information is not available. It also includes reinvested earnings.

[9] Characteristics of FDI in Latin America, ECLAC, Santiago, 1999, pp.2-6.

[10] Ibid., pp.2-6.

[11] Ibid., pp.6-9.

[12] Ibid., pp. 6-9.

[13] Ibid., pp.9-17

[14] Ziga Vodusek (ed.) (2001), *Foreign Direct Investment in Latin America: The Role of European Investors*, IDB.

[15] ECLAC, *Foreign Investment in Latin America and the Caribbean, 2000*, Santiago de Chile.

[16] Ziga Vodusek (ed.) (2001), *Foreign Direct Investment in Latin America: The Role of European Investors*, IDB.

[17] Matías Kulfas, Fernando Porta, Adrián Ramos, "Inversión extranjera y empresas transnacionales en la economía argentina", Oficina de la CEPAL en Buenos Aires, 2002, pp.11-12.

[18] ECLAC, *Foreign Investment in Latin America and the Caribbean, 2000*, Santiago de Chile.

[19] Telefónica, www.telefonica.com (observed August 15, 2004).

[20] Ibid.

[21] Telefónica, 2003 annual report. US dollar amounts derived from Euros were converted using the exchange rate on the last weekday of the year from which the amount was presented: $0.938808: €1 (2000); $0.890099: €1 (2001); $1.0485: €1 (2002); $1.2597: €1 (2003); $1.3538: €1 (2004).

[22] Telefónica, 2003 annual report, converted from Euros.

[23] Ibid.

[24] Ibid.

[25] Ibid.

[26] Yahoo News, news.yahoo.com (observed June 5, 2004).

[27] César Alierta, CEO of Telefónica Group, European TMT Conference presentation, Barcelona, September 18, 2002.

[28] Santiago Fernández Valbuena, CFO of Telefónica Group, London, March 11, 2004.

[29] Telegeography, www.telegeography.com (observed January 5, 2005). Values converted from Euros.

[30] Telefónica corporate news release, "Telefónica Móviles posts strong client growth in first quarter of 2004, as net profit rises 17.9% to 423 million Euros", May 5, 2004.

[31] Telefónica, 2003 annual report.

[32] In Table 9.3, the amounts for Brazil refer to the joint venture with Portugal Telecom.

[33] In Table 9.5, both TEM and PT include 100% of Brasilcel customers. Tem includes clients from BellSouth acquisition and from Mediterranean but excludes CANTV clients.

[34] César Alierta, São Paulo, March 17, 2004; 2003 Annual reports for competitors.

References

Baskerville Communications (2002), *LatinCom Yearbook*, Baskerville Communications, New York.

Brown, Christopher L. and C. Kauffman (2003), *Latin America in Transition, Lesson 6, February 2003 update*, Southern Center for International Studies, Miami.

Bulmer-Thomas, V. and D. Kincaid (2000), *Central America 2020: Towards a New Regional Development Model*, Institut für Iberoamerika-Kunde, Hamburg.

Calcagno, A., S. Manuelito and R. Gunilla (20001), *Proyecciones latinoamericanas 2001-2002*, ECLAC, Santiago de Chile.

Camron, H. (1999), *Characteristics of Foreign Direct Investment (FDI) in Latin America*, ECLAC, Santiago.

CEPAL (2003), *La inversión extranjera en América Latina y el Caribe*, Santiago de Chile.

CEPAL (2001a), *Inversión y volatilidad financiera: América Latina en los inicios del nuevo milenio*, División de Desarrollo Económico, Santiago de Chile.

CEPAL (2001b), *Estudios estadísticos y prospectivos*, División de Estadística y Proyecciones Económicas, Santiago de Chile.

CEPAL (2002), *Anuario Estadístico de América Latina y el Caribe*, Santiago de Chile.

Comisión Federal de Telecomunicaciones de México (1999), *La Cofetel da a conocer las nuevas tarifas de Telmex y su fórmula de ajuste*, CFTM, Mexico City.

Everhart, S. and M. A. Sumlinski (2001), *Trends in Private Investment in Developing Countries Statistics for 1970-2000 and the Impact on Private Investment of Corruption and the Quality of Public Investment*, International Finance Corporation, Santiago de Chile.

Hosono, A. (2000), *Investment Opportunities in Latin America and the Pacific*, United Nations Economic and Social Commission for Asia and the Pacific, Bangkok.

Ma, N. and Kehlenbeck, A. (2001), *Foreign Direct Investment in Latin America: Building a new paradigm*, Phillips Academy, Andover.

Machinea, J.L. (2003), *Balance Preliminar de Las Economías de América Latina y El Caribe, 2003*, CEPAL, Santiago de Chile.

Miotti, L., D. Plihon and C. Quenan (2001), *The Euro and Financial Relations between Latin America and Europe: Medium and Long-term implications*, ECLAC, Santiago de Chile.

Novaes, A. (2003), *The Privatization of the Brazilian Telecommunications Sector*, Pictet Modal Asset Management, Rio do Janeiro.

Ovum (2002), *Future of Telecoms*, London.

UNCTAD (2003a), *UNCTAD WID Country Profile: Argentina*, New York.

UNCTAD (2003b), *World Investment Report: FDI Policies for Development: National and International Perspectives*, New York.

Wohlers, M. and A. Bourdeau de Fontenay (2003), *Brazil's Unfinished Telecom's Revolution: State Control to Competition*, BNAmericas, Santiago de Chile.

Chapter 10

The Prospects of Spanish Investment in the Latin American Energy Sector: Will the Reconquest Unravel?

Gustavo de las Casas

Introduction

It is hard to come up with a better poster child for economic liberalization in Latin America than Repsol-YPF. The company, which envisions itself as "an integrated oil and gas company" (Repsol-YPF, 2003: 5), has a history that itself reflects current liberalization trends. Repsol was created in 1987 as the successor of a group of monopolistic enterprises that the Spanish government owned and managed under its *Instituto Nacional de Hidrocarburos* (INH) (Toral, 2003: 363-364). Under pressure from the European Union, Spain began privatizing Repsol in 1989, but by then numerous challenges became apparent. Facing an increasingly competitive domestic market and scarce oil reserves, Repsol focused its attention on Latin America. The region, reeling economically from the "lost decade" of the 1980s, found hope in the liberal prescriptions of the Washington Consensus. Many Latin American states during the 1990s saw themselves opening their markets, eliminating state monopolies, and promoting private investment (Campodónico, 1999: 138). The energy sector was not exempt to these newfound solutions, and Repsol rode the wave of opening markets hailed by economic liberals. With a strategy that mimicked the pseudo-monopoly it once had in Spain, the firm took over Argentina's *Yacimientos Petrolíferos Fiscales* (YPF) in 1999 and changed its name to Repsol-YPF (Repsol, 1999: 2, 6, 8). Repsol-YPF became the leading seller of oil derivatives in Argentina, Chile, Peru, Bolivia, and Ecuador; the leading distributor of natural gas in Mexico, and the largest private producer of oil in Brazil. By 1999, the company was already in seventh place among the world's largest oil companies (Toral, 2003: 81, 437).

The company appears unstoppable, even in two countries where one would least expect it. In Venezuela, a country known for the firebrand leadership of its nationalistic president Hugo Chávez, Repsol became the leading private producer of oil and gas (Repsol-YPF, 2004). And in communist Cuba, the firm allied with state-owned Cubapetróleo to search for oil in Cuban waters (Romero, 2004). In short, economic liberals can point to Repsol's involvement in Latin America as the quintessential success story of international capitalism. Latin American governments finally got rid of the nationalist antics of people like Argentina's Enrique Mosconi, the early head of YPF in the 1920s, who saw multinational oil companies "as agents of neocolonial exploitation seeking to despoil the Latin American countries" (Solberg, 1979: 177). YPF's ironic purchase by a company from, of all countries, a former colonial ruler seemingly signals that Latin America is growing out of its pubescent, nationalist phase and helping fulfill that nirvana of economic liberals: "a truly global economy…in which distinct national economies and, therefore, domestic strategies of national economic management are increasingly irrelevant" (Hirst and Thompson, 1999: 1).

But should we accept this at face value? While "foreign oil companies are finding their appetites for exploration whetted by increasingly liberal terms" in the Latin American oil and gas cafeteria (Fuad, 1993: 162), who is to say that the restaurant owners will not demand higher prices in the future, a stricter dress code, or kick out their patrons altogether? In other words, are we seeing a secular, indefinite trend of economic liberalism in the region's energy sector, or rather a cyclical trend to meet its demise once certain conditions appear? More fundamentally, what determines a state's openness to foreign energy firms?

Besides their intellectual value, these questions are of instrumental importance to all parties involved. Their answers can make the difference between sizable profits and losses to the multinational oil companies in the region, and to the investors whose money undergirds them. Likewise, policymakers would be wise to contemplate the implications of answering these questions wrongly. Leaders who assume that liberalization will advance undaunted could find themselves in the unsavory position of Bolivia's ex-president Sánchez de Lozada, "whose downfall came after he proposed building a gas pipeline through Chile, Bolivia's historic enemy, in order to export gas to the United States" (Forero, 2004a).

This chapter seeks to explain patterns of liberalization in the Latin American energy sector by using a model grounded on realist theory. The chapter begins by identifying key weaknesses in one standard argument that economic liberals offer for these patterns. According to this argument, the ideology of resource nationalism was the greatest culprit of barriers to liberalization, but now the region experiences a continuous trend of states discarding ideology for the clear benefits of liberalization. As will be shown, that explanation exaggerates the progress achieved, is not able to account for recurring fluctuations in liberalization during the 20th century, and is often contradicted by historical events. At the same time, however, ideology cannot be dismissed altogether. Certain events suggest that ideology can influence a state's energy policies under particular circumstances. Using a deductive approach, this chapter builds an alternative explanation incorporating key realist premises, with one premise – that of rational-egoist states- qualified to account for societal preferences. A model is then produced to show the relationship between two variables – a state's power status and its degree of resource nationalism – and a state's sensitivity to foreign investment in its energy sector.

Once this is done, the model is compared against Argentinean oil policies during the 20th century. With two exceptions, there is a negative correlation between Argentina's power status fluctuations in its oil sector and its openness to foreign investment. When Argentina's power status was low, it cooperated with foreign firms out of necessity. When its status was high, it curtailed this cooperation. The two exceptions to this correlation suggest that the role of resource nationalism is more limited and nuanced than previously thought. In these two instances, Argentina's power status showed only marginal declines, and nationalistic pressures were able to prompt the state to curtail its relationship with foreign firms. However, both cases were later followed by repeated declines and a drastically lower power status, which prompted the state to reverse its position and liberalize the energy sector. As a whole, the model explains the cycles of state-firm cooperation that emerged as Argentina repeatedly cooperated with firms and then attempted branching off on its own, only to find that its managed enterprises failed to sustain its power status.

Besides this historical case, Repsol's reserves in Latin American states also reflect the dynamic between power status and foreign investment. The more powerful and wealthier states cooperated the least with Repsol, while the weaker cooperated the most, presumably out of necessity. Also, current events in Latin America, pertaining to both states' projected power statuses and societal preferences, suggest pessimistic prospects for Repsol and the liberalization of the energy sector in general. At best, Repsol will maintain its position in the region; at worst, it will find itself exiting increasingly difficult relationships with states. Finally, the chapter offers prescriptions for both states and firms to benefit the most from current and future circumstances. These prescriptions cover both the role of power status and resource nationalism.

The fallacies of relying exclusively on ideology

As mentioned above, one standard answer for the previous protectionist stance of Latin American states, and their current liberalization forays, is the influence of ideology on policymakers. Solberg credits Enrique Mosconi, head of YPF in the 1920s, as "the first Argentine or Latin American to publicize an integrated set of assumptions, theories, and goals regarding state ownership and control of petroleum resources. As a result, his ideas had (and continue to have) a powerful impact on government oil policy, both in his homeland and in much of the rest of Latin America" (Solberg, 1979: 132).

To Solberg, the "popular appeal of YPF" and "mass political mobilization" provided added strength to the appeal of Mosconi's ideas (Solberg, 1979: 179). Across Latin America, this ideology spread virus-like. In 1929, Mosconi met Edmundo Castillo, Uruguay's Minister of Industry, and passed his ideas onto him. Shortly afterwards, "these ideas became the seeds of ANCAP (Administración Nacional de Combustibles, Alcohol y Portland), the state energy corporation that Uruguay's Congress created in 1931". By 1939, ANCAP became a virtual monopoly that supplied 90% of Uruguay's gasoline. Similarly, Solberg credits Mosconi for influencing Bolivian, Brazilian, and even Mexican petroleum policy. In 1938, Mexican President Lázaro Cárdenas, who ten years earlier heard Mosconi speak during the latter's visit to México City, embraced "an ideology of petroleum nationalism similar to [Mosconi's]" and nationalized the oil industry under the state monopoly PEMEX (Solberg, 1979: 179-182).

Today, resource nationalism is likewise credited with being "the driving force" behind state-owned energy companies (Fuad, 1993: 154). By the 1980s, however, financial crises forced many states to reevaluate both their ideological dreams and the prospects of their oil and gas companies. Eventually, two reactions emerged from the ideologically-driven states. The larger companies, like PDVSA (Petróleos de Venezuela, S.A.), Mexico's PEMEX, and Brazil's PETROBRAS, could afford to hold onto their ideological foundations, so they "retrenched and waited for better days to continue expansion plans." Smaller companies, conversely, could not afford humoring their ideologies anymore and sought reform (Fuad, 1993: 155). In Argentina, for instance, "it became clear that a debt-ridden and inefficient state-owned YPF was unable to maintain the nation's oil sufficiency, let alone produce an exportable surplus" so reforms began to deregulate and privatize the sector (Fuad, 1993: 159). Overall, despite this varied degree of openness to foreign participation, Fuad asserts that "once state oil companies…follow a more commercially oriented course, increasing opportunities for the private sector should emerge" (Fuad, 1993: 156).

Others also observe the liberalization that started between the 1980s and 1990s in the Latin American energy sector. However, they do not question whether it will continue or not, just how fast it will spread across the region. Campodónico observes that, despite varying degrees of reform, the majority of Latin American states he analyzed – Argentina, Bolivia, Colombia, and Chile – did introduce "important" liberal legislative reforms regarding the exploration and exploitation of hydrocarbons. He recognizes that Mexico did not reform its legislation covering petroleum per se, but introduced "important modifications" to norms governing the transportation, storage, and distribution of natural gas. As a whole, he attributes these changes as occurring within a framework of economic globalization (Campodónico, 1999: 135). In analyzing the liberalization of the gas sector in Argentina, Colombia, and Mexico for the Inter-American Development Bank, Beato and Fuente also see that "gas producing countries have progressively opened their markets in order to attract private capital and achieve greater efficiency and competitiveness" (Beato and Fuente, 2000: 1). Even in the case of México's maintenance of PEMEX's monopoly in the natural gas industry, they do not see the glass as half-empty. Instead, they perceive the separation of policy-making, regulation, and service provision functions among the government, the regulatory commission, and the companies as "an initial step in the right direction" (Beato and Fuente, 2000: 47). In fact, of all the gas-producing countries, Beato and Fuente only consider Venezuela to be the exception in an overwhelming pattern of states implementing "reforms aimed at introducing competition and obtaining the funds needed for the expansion of the natural gas infrastructure" (Beato and Fuente, 2000:

2). In sum, these views do not discuss if the liberalization trend will continue – it is assumed to – , but rather at what pace it will continue.

The conclusion that the Latin American energy sector is on a teleological – but often bumpy – path of greater liberalization seems ill-founded if it relies only on the explanation that ideology is responsible for the energy policies in the region. As an analytical piece of real estate, that explanation is an edifice that is simply not tall enough to claim victory and exhibits serious structural weaknesses. First, the sporadic liberalization of the energy sector worldwide does not offer enough proof to conclude that the sector's liberalization will continue. Of 115 developing countries in 1998, just a minority have taken the liberal route: only 24% have privatized their energy industries while 40% allowed private investment in the sector (Lewis, 2004: 1). Latin America is no exception. While on the one hand he sees as likely a "gradually increasing foreign participation" in several Latin American countries, Fuad also recognizes that "ownership and development of Latin America's oil and gas should remain largely in the hands of state companies" and that YPF's privatization "is likely to prove the exception" (Fuad, 1993: 153-154, 163). This hardly seems to constitute a turnaround by Latin American governments in the energy sector. Similarly, Mexico's breakup of functions in its gas industry, and other Latin American countries' actions for that matter, can be seen as a step in the right direction by Beato and Fuente (2000: 47), but they do not necessarily indicate that further steps forward will be taken. In fact, steps back are also possible.

This analytical edifice also offers logical gaps in its treatment of ideology as the principal influence behind Latin American energy policies. If Enrique Mosconi and Hipólito Yrigoyen "established the institutions and ideologies that have shaped Argentine petroleum affairs during the remainder of the century" (Solberg, 1979: ix), how do we explain the several drastic policy reversals that confronted Argentina during the greater part of the 20th century? In fact, Argentina reversed its policy towards oil companies no less than seven times from 1907 to 1999. How could these many changes be attributed to a constant variable that, by definition, should yield constant results? Of course, it can be argued that ideological influences ebbed and flowed among different policymakers throughout Argentina's history. The downside to this explanation is that it makes for an extremely messy story that is hard to follow and much harder to prove. If we go beyond the level of individuals or small groups, and focus on collective attitudes about foreign investment, there is a dearth of standard polls allowing for an accurate measurement of public attitudes for almost one hundred years of Argentinean history. In short, ideology seems to be the ineffectual enemy of economic liberalism. It is always there but somehow cannot prevent policy reversals, some of them positive towards oil companies. On the other hand, if the strength of ideology somehow varied across many decades, how can it be rigorously proven in the case of Argentina, much less the rest of Latin America?

More examination only reveals further weaknesses. If ideology breeds distrust towards oil companies, we would expect countries known for their resource nationalism to curtail their cooperation with oil companies. In fact, the opposite happened in several instances. In Argentina, after General Uriburu deposed Yrigoyen in 1930 and assumed control of the government, he had Enrique Mosconi "fired from his post as Director-General of YPF" and "order[ed] into exile in Europe". Meanwhile, Uriburu "created a favorable climate for the foreign oil companies, which expanded their operations dramatically and nearly doubled their output of crude oil during the two years following the 1930 coup" (Solberg, 1979: 157). How could Mosconi and his ideas be literally cast aside in Argentina, the cradle of oil nationalism, at a time when that ideology should have been in full bloom? The next presidency was not any kinder to Mosconi; upon his return from Europe, President Agustín P. Justo "sentenced him to the obscure and powerless post of Director of the Army Fencing and Shooting Academy" (Soberg, 1979: 157). This is not the only instance in which ideology is shoved aside when least expected. In 1955, a hitherto nationalistic Perón became pragmatic and signed an agreement with a subsidiary of Standard Oil of California (SOCAL) (Gadano 1998:10). Contemporary examples also exist. For all his rhetoric, Venezuela's Hugo Chávez treats us to the paradoxical spectacle of "[railing] against the Bush administration, accusing it of coveting Venezuela's resources, and… [threatening] to withhold oil if [it] tried an invasion. Yet, days after the threat, he warmly greeted ChevronTexaco executives at a ceremony at the presidential palace to celebrate the granting of a gas exploration license" (Forero, 2004b). The apparent ease with which resource nationalism is neglected by its seemingly staunchest believers casts considerable doubt on an explanation that relies exclusively on ideology as a determinant.

These criticisms are not meant to dismiss the role of ideology as a whole. Instead of adopting an either-or attitude, it is entirely plausible that ideological preferences have a nuanced effect on policymaking. In fact, there are instances in which resource nationalism arguably influenced state energy policy. Popular protests in 2003 forced the resignation of Bolivian President Sánchez de Lozada, and derailed his plans of cooperating with Chile to build a gas pipeline (Forero, 2004a). Similarly, public indignation influenced the suspension of Perón's aforementioned SOCAL agreement in its first year (Gadano, 1998: 9). But what determines when ideology can and cannot affect policy? What negates and what adds to its effect? If anything, it is premature to forget about ideology because it can possibly belong in a model that delineates its role alongside other variables. The objective of the next section is to conceptualize such a model.

A realist model of sensitivity to foreign investment in the energy sector

In light of more contemporary theories of international relations, building a model grounded on realist theory might seem to some as a thinly-disguised attempt to plod on with a creaky tradition. Quite to the contrary, realism offers an excellent starting point to deduce testable hypotheses because it offers a systemic view of the international arena. This view stems from the following core premises: states are the major actors in world affairs; they are unitary rational-egoists in an international environment that penalizes lack of self-protection; a system of international anarchy is the principal force in shaping state motives and actions; states are preoccupied with their survival in issues of conflict and cooperation; and international institutions are of limited or marginal effectiveness in fomenting cooperation (Grieco, 1988: 488). This clear depiction of the environment where states exist offers a broad framework in which to situate our model. At a unit level, however, the assumption of states as rational-egoists can be refined to yield a more comprehensive model of behavior. This assumption is a compound one. First, the egoism component establishes that "actors, including states, care only about their own utility. They have no *intrinsic* interest in the welfare of others" (Keohane, 1993: 274). Second, the rationality component presupposes that actors "seek to maximize value across a set of consistently ordered objectives" (Snyder and Diesing, 1977: 81). In short, states are preoccupied with their own survival, which they will pursue rationally. But this premise does not preclude states from being biased; that is, from consistently preferring particular means to achieve security.

The realist tradition sheds some light on the biases of states by recognizing the role of societal preferences in decision-making. As Morgenthau points out, "the rational requirements of good foreign policy [to seek security] cannot from the outset count upon the support of a public opinion whose preferences are emotional rather than rational". As a result, states cannot allow themselves to coolly pursue security in a vacuum of societal preferences. The policymaker, the brains behind unitary states, "must perform that highest feat of statesmanship: trimming his sails to the winds of popular passion while using them to carry the ship of state to the port of good foreign policy, on however roundabout and zigzag a course" (Morgenthau, 1973: 545-546). In sum, states must not only contend with an environment of precarious anarchy, but with their internal constitutions as well, which intertwine societal preferences with security concerns.

Needless to say, injecting societal preferences into the conceptual picture can make things very murky. The behavior of states might not be so easy to deduce if they must balance concerns other than survival. But this addition need not make things significantly more complex in the sought model. Delineating societal preferences can be made simple by understanding their nature, their general direction in foreign affairs, and their resulting tendency in international economic matters. Regarding their nature, it is reasonable to assume that the popular mind, as opposed to the policymaker's mind, is "unaware of the fine distinctions of the statesman's thinking, reasons more often than not in the simple moralistic and legalistic terms of absolute good and absolute evil" and "wants quick results; it will sacrifice tomorrow's real benefit for today's apparent advantage" (Morgenthau, 1973: 147). This simplistic nature of the popular mind is coupled to a particular attitude about foreign affairs, whatever differences of opinion might exist about purely domestic matters. Because the state can "exert moral compulsion upon its members", and this loyalty "requires the individual to disregard universal moral rules of conduct", nationalism wins over internationalism in the popular mind. Moreover, as the popular mind "experiences in [its] own conscience [a conflict between] the feebleness of [desirable] universal standards and the preponderance of national morality", it adopts a nationalistic universalism. That is, the popular mind "identifies the morality of a particular nation with the commands of supranational ethics" so that "each nation comes to know again a universal morality – that is, its own national morality – which is taken to be the one that all the other nations ought to accept as their own" (Morgenthau, 1973: 251-252). This self-attribution of moral superiority presupposes that foreign nations are inherently less moral than one's own and, consequently, that their intentions are always suspect to some degree. In the economic realm, this can foster a pronounced distrust of "intruding" foreign entities and a keen desire for the state to exert an active role in protecting economic interests. In sectors like energy, such predisposition can turn into a heavy bias against foreign investment and towards state-owned enterprises.

The difference between this popular stance – polarized by the emotional biases of nationalistic universalism – and the policymaker's is one of intensity and not direction. What the policymaker is concerned about, the public downright fears. What she dislikes, the public hates. Effectively, accepting the influence of societal preferences does not unduly complicate the conceptual picture of states living in anarchy. Popular preferences regarding international economic affairs, like a state's openness to foreign investment, are far from volatile. They are invariably one-way – favoring the public's own state and very distrustful of others. At most, the result of this assumptive qualification is that states where economic nationalism is strong are even more sensitive to foreign economic involvement than they would be without the added pressure of nationalism, and even more risk-averse in contemplating economic bargains. In fact, they are more likely to "work to maintain a measure of independence and...even strive for autarky" (Waltz, 1979: 104, 106-107). As such, states remain selfish utility-maximizers concerned with their survival. But they are *biased materialists*, concerned about their material welfare but also biased in how to pursue it.

Having established the environment and internal predispositions facing states, let us discuss the resulting behavior of bargaining states. In anarchy, a state contemplates cooperation with others with concern or even fear – depending on its bias – that today's partner will be tomorrow's adversary. This is not only the case in the security realm, or issue-area, but also in the economic one. States must consider the possibility that wealthier bargaining partners will convert their greater wealth into force to be employed against them. Of course, they can assume that nonmilitary instruments, like economic wealth, in themselves "are rarely powerful enough to threaten the vital interests of a major state" (Jervis, 1978: 403). But energy does not lend itself to such offhanded dismissals. It helps win wars. This is particularly the case with oil, as "most mechanized weapons and vehicles are driven by oil, and, consequently, countries that possess considerable deposits of oil have acquired an influence in international affairs which in some cases can be attributed primarily, if not exclusively, to that possession" (Morgenthau, 1973: 117). Of course, a state bargaining with a foreign energy firm typically needs not worry about the firm's military power for the latter has none. Yet, the state must consider how the bargain benefits the firm's parent state and other host states. For instance, Bolivia might worry that building a gas pipeline to Chile, a former enemy, will enrich the latter and enhance its military power. Moreover, Bolivia will retain this worry irrespective of its relationship with the energy firms involved in the project.

Even if a bargain does not pose immediate security risks, states also worry "that others might achieve disproportionate gains *and thereby become more domineering friends*" (Grieco, 1993: 303, emphasis added). In the energy sector, a Latin American state would gauge its relationship with Spain when negotiating with Repsol. Because Repsol privatized recently, the state could suspect that Spain coordinated the firm's expansion with its own foreign policy. In the long run, the host's cooperation with Repsol may enrich Spain more than the host itself. Consequently, a stronger Spain could extract concessions from the host by threatening, for instance, to limit Repsol's activities in the host's territory. In sum, a state worries how a bargain will benefit other parties, including tangential stakeholders, more than it; that is, the state worries about incurring relative losses.

To further understand this concept, it is useful to refer to Grieco's relative gains utility function:

$$U = V - k \, (W - V)$$

In this function, a state derives its utility U from a bargain by gauging its payoff, V, against its partner's payoff, W. The greater a partner's gain vis-à-vis its own, the less utility a state derives as it worries that its partner will use those relative gains against it. In bargains with energy firms, of course, the state's notion of the "partner" necessarily enlarges to encompass the firm's other partner states. The relative gains (W-V) are in turn multiplied times a coefficient of sensitivity, k (Grieco, 1988: 497-498). This coefficient is a function of at least six things:

1) "Experience with and the character of the partner": a longstanding ally will reduce k, while a longtime adversary is likely to enlarge it.

2) "The presence or not of external challengers": a common enemy could reduce k, while the lack of a mutual threat increases the sensitivity to relative losses.

3) "The domain in which cooperation occurs": k is lower in economic bargains than in military-security ones.

4) "The convertibility of gaps into influence and the fungibility of this influence across domains": the easier relative gains can be used against another state, and the easier they can be converted from one issue-area to another, the higher k will be.

5) "A state's power trajectory": Grieco states that "k will be lower for a state in ascendancy than for one in decline" presumably because a declining state is more concerned than one in ascendancy about others taking advantage of its positional weakness.

6)   "The current power status of the state": to Grieco, extremely powerful and powerless states have a lower k than states of medium power; powerful states are less concerned about others, while extremely powerless states in a dire situation might settle for whatever gains are offered (Grieco, 1988: 497-498; 1990: 43-44, 46; 1993: 323-4).

Of the variables above, the model in this chapter utilizes the sixth variable, a state's power status. This variable holds certain advantages over all the others in building an explanatory model. It is much easier to measure than the first variable, the previous experiences with and character of the partner. Measuring the latter variable involves a greater deal of interpretation about how states assimilate specific historical events. Measuring the power status in the issue-area in question is simpler – one can quantify a state's ranking among its neighbors in such terms as energy reserves or gross domestic product. The power status variable also exhibits more fluctuations for the states examined than the presence of a common threat, the domain of cooperation, and the fungibility of influence across domains. The latter first has not changed frequently in the region throughout the 20th century (there have not been recurring instances of common threats), while the last two are largely fixed (the deals are economic but energy retains a potential security value). The higher frequency of power status fluctuations holds greater promise of spotting correlations with varying energy policies.

The fifth variable, a state's power trajectory, is closely tied to a state's power status (it is the change in power status over time). But a state's power status likely has a stronger effect on its sensitivity than its power trajectory. For instance, an ascendant state might be power-hungry and sensitive about others interfering with its rise. However, if it has not yet attained a high power status, said state will moderate its sensitivity as it negotiates with needed partners and even forgoes relative gains to build its power base. Once it actually reaches a high power status, the state holds all the cards. It no longer needs its partners like before. The state can patiently pick and choose deals, and thus will be much more sensitive about relative losses than when it needed to swallow them during its power rise.

The model adopted in this chapter assumes a positive correlation between a state's power status and its sensitivity to any relative losses associated with foreign investment. This relationship can be observed in Figure 10.1, where a state's sensitivity is depicted as an S-shaped curve. A weak state – one with a low power status – is less sensitive to foreign investment as it has no choice but to bargain with energy firms in the hopes of becoming more powerful. However, as it gains power, that state will be more sensitive about foreign firms extracting the same concessions it yielded at a time of weakness. In turn, it will make business more difficult for the firms involved (through higher taxes, more regulations, etc.). Finally, a very powerful state will be highly sensitive about sharing control over its developed energy sector with foreign firms. As it has little need for the firms, it might end its relationship with them altogether. Its higher-sensitivity actions can range from not renewing contracts with the firms to nationalizing the industry.

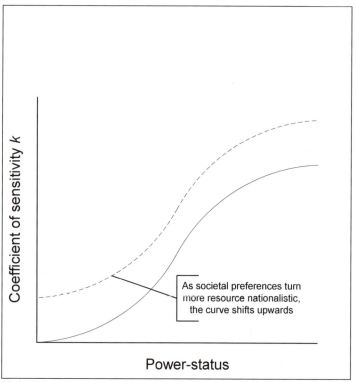

Figure 10.1   **The effects of power-status and resource nationalism on the coefficient of sensitivity *k***

It should be noted that Grieco argues a different correlation for this variable. He assigns a higher sensitivity to medium-power states than powerful or powerless ones, presumably because powerless states are desperate for gains while powerful ones are more relaxed about relative losses (Grieco, 1988: 497-498; 1990: 43-44; 1993: 323-4). But let us assume that states seek a degree of independence and even autarky, as Waltz suggests (Waltz, 1979: 104, 106-107). Then, it makes more sense that powerful states, having secured their independence, will be more sensitive to bargains that jeopardize this independence than weaker states that lack independence and are hard-pressed into accepting relative losses to acquire power.

What effect do resource nationalistic preferences have on this relationship? Since these preferences intensify a state's concerns about foreign investment, as resource nationalism grows stronger, the S-shape curve will shift upwards (see Figure 10.1). In certain cases, this upward shift can mean the difference between the policies that a state adopts. In others, especially towards either extreme, shifts might not matter much. For example, an extremely powerful state that decides to end its relationship with a firm would do so because of its higher power status. Nationalist fervor thus would be overkill when the state-firm relationship would have ended anyway. A similar case applies to severely weakened states – their lack of power might make them so insensitive to foreign involvement that any nationalist sentiment would do little to prevent bargains. Figure 10.2 offers a simple 2x2 matrix with a state's resulting sensitivity from different combinations of power status and resource nationalism.

	State's power-status	
	Low	High
Resource nationalism	Coefficient of sensitivity k	
High	Medium	Highest
Low	Low	High

Figure 10.2   A two-variable model of sensitivity to energy liberalization

From this simple matrix we can deduce the following general conditions:

1. If a state has a low power status and a low degree of resource nationalism, it will be highly insensitive to foreign involvement in its energy sector. This will translate to very liberal policies like privatization of state-owned enterprises, deregulation, and accommodative agreements with oil companies.
2. If a state has a low power status but a high degree of resource nationalism, it will still cooperate with oil companies out of necessity. However, the relationship will be a strained one. The state will temper its relationship with the companies and begin demanding more – higher concessions fees, taxes, shorter contract terms, etc.
3. If a state has a high power status and a low degree of resource nationalism, it will seek to terminate its relationship with the oil firms as soon as possible. However, it will tend to do so gradually and without harsh measures. The state will not renew its agreements with the companies, or might push strongly to buy out the companies' local subsidiaries.
4. If a state has a high power status and a high degree of resource nationalism, it will not hesitate to forcibly terminate its relationship with the oil firms. It could nationalize the industry at a fast pace and even appropriate the firms' assets.

As can be seen from the conditions above, a state's power status and its societal preferences can combine into a coherent set of reactions to foreign involvement. This model does not contradict realist premises. States are still behaving rationally in an anarchical setting that prompts them to adopt a risk-averse attitude. They are concerned about their material welfare but have varying degrees of bias about the risks of cooperating with foreign firms. This bias ranges from the panic of strong resource nationalism to the moderate concern from having little nationalism. Furthermore, while resource nationalism intensifies a state's prevalent concerns about cooperation, its material power status remains a greater determinant of its attitude towards foreign involvement. If powerful, a state rejects cooperation with energy firms no matter its degree of resource nationalism. If weak, the opposite will result. This is in accordance with the realist tenet that the system of international anarchy, and each state's place in the distribution of power, is the principal force behind a state's actions.

The next section of this chapter tests this model against the history of foreign investment in the energy sector of Argentina. Subsequently, the model is also tested against two contemporary snapshots of Repsol's presence in energy-owning states in Latin America. These tests help determine whether the model holds against analysis across time and various present-day states.

Resource rationalism and nationalism in Latin America: the case of Argentina

Argentina presents a hard case of the proposed model. This is because Argentina represents the largest degree of liberalization of the energy sector in Latin America. It has fully privatized its energy enterprise, YPF, and allowed it to come under the direct management of a foreign company whose home state is Argentina's former colonial ruler. If Argentina is shown to be prone to defecting on energy firms when it no longer deems their help necessary, stronger states with a more protectionist stance may not be likely to liberalize substantially in the future. Argentina is also a good case study because it offers several policy reversals and significant fluctuations in the power status of its energy sector, which will be measured in terms of production and imports of petroleum. If the model is correct, liberalizations by the Argentinean government occurred whenever the state's power status was at a low level. Once its energy sector has gained (or regained) strength, Argentina would limit its relationship with foreign firms through measures of increasing severity.

Figure 10.3 offers a graph depicting Argentinean petroleum production and imports from 1907 to 1999. From the accidental discovery of petroleum at Comodoro Rivadavia in 1907 to the mid-1930s, the Argentinean state lacked the infrastructure to exploit this newfound resource. Production remained low during this initial phase, and Argentina's power status in the energy sector was rather weak. At the same time, the period featured private enterprises, largely subsidiaries of the international oil trusts, playing an important role in Argentinean petroleum production through a liberal scheme of mining concessions. This happened despite resource nationalistic pressures. Hipólito Yrigoyen, president from 1916 to 1930, and his *Partido Radical*, supported the full-scale nationalization of oil production. Nevertheless, even during most of Yrigoyen's presidency, the Argentinean government allowed private entities to produce 49% of Argentinean petroleum between 1920 and 1937. In addition, the firms had an active participation in the refining, importing, and commercialization of fuels (Gadano, 1998: 9). As expected in the model, a positive relationship between Argentina's power status and its sensitivity to foreign involvement is evident in this period. Being weak, Argentina had to cooperate with foreign oil firms, nationalistic misgivings notwithstanding.

By the late 1930s, however, the attitude of Argentina's government towards its oil partners began to change. The state decided not to give any more new concessions and established export and price controls over derivatives. By the end of the 1940s, the Peronist constitutional reform succeeded in nationalizing the industry and giving YPF a monopoly over exploitation in the sector (Gadano, 1998: 9). This marked the first significant policy reversal towards the oil companies. Why did this happen then and not before? An important development during this period was that Argentinean petroleum production finally took off, raising the state's power status. By the time the industry is nationalized in the late 1940s, as seen in Figure 10.3, Argentinean yearly petroleum production was steadily increasing and surpassed the 3,500-thousand-cubic-meter mark by 1942. Compared to earlier years, this growth was spectacular. In 1920, yearly production was 262-thousand-cubic meters; 1942's production represented an increase of over 1300% (Gadano, 1998: 73). Facing this sizable power status gain, in accordance with the model, Argentina saw it fit to end its relationship with foreign companies it did not deem necessary anymore.

The 1950s were less generous to Argentina. Without the necessary know-how and financial resources, domestic petroleum production stagnated and fuel imports reached 23% of total imports by 1953. Facing this severe underperformance by YPF, Perón turned pragmatic. In a second policy reversal for Argentina, in 1955 he signed an agreement with Standard Oil of California (SOCAL) to develop and exploit Argentinean petroleum fields (Gadano, 1998: 10). The model offers a clear explanation for this reversal. Argentina faced a surprising decline in its power status, and the negative prospect of rising imports that would extend its dependency on other states. Faced with two undesirable choices – allow the oil firms back in or become more dependent of other states –, Argentina opted for the lesser evil and allowed an oil firm back in.

A tumultuous domestic political situation confronted Argentina. The overthrow of Perón in September 1955 suspended the SOCAL agreement (Gadano, 1998: 10). This third reversal contradicts the power status component of the model. Instead of maintaining a liberal attitude – that is, a low sensitivity to foreign involvement in the oil sector – at a time of weakening power, Argentina did away with an existing agreement. On the other hand, the resource nationalism component of the model explains this action. At the time, Argentina had a high level of resource nationalism. In fact, Perón's decision sparked heavy criticism by several influential sectors of Argentinean society, including members of his own party, the opposition Radical Party, and the military (Solberg, 1979: 165-166). After Perón's overthrow, it is plausible that this flaring nationalistic bias led to the state's suspension of the SOCAL agreement. This period arguably was one where Argentina's decreasing power status was not yet sufficient to prompt more liberalization, and the existing resource nationalism was strong enough to intensify the state's sensitivity to the SOCAL agreement.

A firm believer in the exclusive power of ideology may, at this point, speculate that the suspension of the SOCAL agreement marked the beginning of a long period of nationalistic policy by the Argentinean government. But this did not happen. Arturo Frondizi assumed power in 1958 and, despite being a previous critic of energy liberalization, implemented a fourth policy reversal: an "aggressive" program of private involvement in the petroleum sector (Gadano, 1998: 10). Figure 10.3 reveals that the period confronting Frondizi was, as it was for Perón, characterized by a deceleration in national production and a rise in imports. However, this time the repeated decline in power status overcame the pressures of resource nationalism. In the five years from 1951 to 1955, Perón saw annual imports rise 35%. When Frondizi took over in 1958, he saw annual imports rise at over twice that rate, 74%, in the last five years (Gadano, 1998: 73). There was no uncertainty about a deterioration of the Argentinean power status, so the state arguably opted for cooperation when faced with the concrete prospect of further weakness.

By December 1962, the tables turned for Argentina. It achieved the "desired objective of self-sufficiency" as annual production increased 30% and reserves increased by 50% between 1958 and 1962. As the model would indicate, Argentina once again sought to end its previous agreements. After a 1962 military coup removed Frondizi, in a fifth policy reversal, a new president in 1963 annulled Frondizi's agreements with the oil firms. Despite the fact that three years later a new government allowed oil firms back in, Argentina's higher power status meant that its relationship with the firms would be limited. By 1967, the new Ley de Hidrocarburos (Hydrocarbons Law) permitted both contracts and concessions with the private sector while maintaining YPF's control over exploitation. However, there were only few contracts between YPF and private firms (Gadano, 1998: 10-11).

The years between 1966 and 1973 continued to be marked by limited state-firm cooperation. Between 1972 and 1975, petroleum production fell by 9% and imports rose. Nevertheless, this decline was not immediately accompanied by a more liberal attitude by the Argentinean state in the energy sector. Rather, in a sixth policy reversal, the period between 1973 and 1976 saw Argentina nationalizing its commercialization of fuels under YPF (Gadano, 1998: 11). This period presents another anomaly when considering only the effect of power status changes. Again, if we take into account the role of resource nationalism in Argentinean policy decisions, it is plausible the former contributed to the state's rush to nationalize when a more prudent course of action would have been to wait longer.

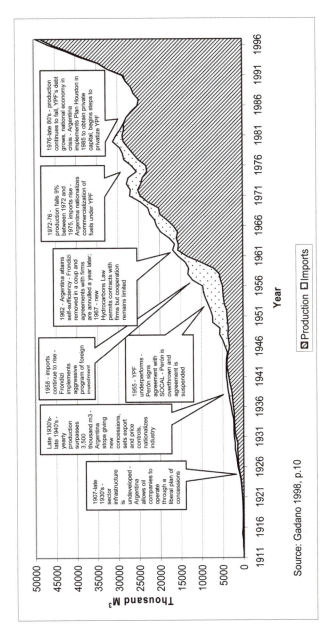

Figure 10.3 Cycles of state-firm cooperation in the Argentinean petroleum sector/petroleum production and imports, 1907-1999

Source: Gadano (1998: 10).

By 1976, the effect of a patently lower power status manifested itself. With production still about 8% lower than in 1972, Argentina began, in a seventh policy reversal, to encourage private investment in the oil sector (Gadano 1998: 11, 73). However, the situation continued to worsen. YPF's debt grew more than sevenfold, from $640 million in 1976 to $4,646 million in 1982. At the same time, the whole Argentinean economy was suffering a severe financial crisis. With annual production almost 7% lower between 1980 and 1985, the Alfonsín Administration implemented Plan Houston in 1985 to obtain more private capital for exploration. The program did not have a major impact (Gadano 1998: 12). Given its undeniably decreasing power status during this period, Argentina did not pursue more policy reversals. Instead, it became more accommodating towards foreign private involvement.

The position of Argentina's YPF by the end of the 1980s was of weakness. Unlike stronger state-owned companies in Mexico and Venezuela, YPF required constant financial assistance from the Treasury (Gadano 1998: 12). By 1990, the Menem Administration began plans to privatize YPF. By 1993, YPF underwent an initial public offering in which the private sector acquired 59% of the company (Gadano 1998: 25-26). Six years later Repsol took over YPF. In retrospect, the substantial power status decline of the Argentinean energy sector during the 1980s, and the general weakness of the economy, help explain this final trend of liberalization. With no increase in yearly production from 1980 to 1990 (Gadano, 1998: 73), and much turmoil in between, the rational course of action for Argentina was to turn even more economically liberal in hopes of resuming its power status growth. Defection would have to wait for another day.

A look at Figure 10.3 reveals that power status fluctuations can explain most of the Argentinean oil policy reversals of the 20th century. Whenever it gained strength in the oil sector, Argentina became more sensitive to its dealings with oil companies and curtailed its relationship with them, and vice versa. However, of seven reversals, there were two anomalies. Perón's agreement with SOCAL was suspended after his overthrow despite lagging production and rising imports, and the period between 1973 and 1976 saw Argentina nationalizing the commercialization of fuels amidst comparable conditions. However, as the model incorporates resource nationalism, these periods arguably were ones when nationalism prompted a policy reversal amidst declines in power status that were only marginal. But both reversals proved short-lived because the declines in power status continued. Frondizi in 1958 saw that the rise in imports was accelerating, while there was no denying the severe production stagnation facing Argentina in 1976. This smoking-gun evidence of weakness proved too much for resource nationalism, and the state became less sensitive to foreign investment. This conclusion is in keeping with the realist assumption of international anarchy being the primary influence on states' motives and actions. When faced with undeniable weakness, states are more concerned about their survival than about nationalistic biases, and will reluctantly cooperate with foreign firms. One could also argue that were not for the further declines in power status, these two policy reversals would have remained in place. That is, an Argentina with a stable or rising power status may have continued curtailing its relationship with foreign firms. Nevertheless, while ideology can be said to matter, more often than not, a state's position in the international distribution of power matters more. Overall, the combined model encompassing both variables of power status and resource nationalism seems to account for all the Argentinean oil policy reversals of the 20th century.

An appraisal of the future of Spanish investment in the Latin American energy sector

Besides offering an explanation for previous energy policies, the model also allows us to understand present patterns in the Latin American energy sector, and to make an educated guess about the future. The strong influence of power status on states' sensitivity to foreign investment in the energy sector can be seen by examining Repsol's ownership of reserves per country in Latin America. Table 10.1 ranks Latin American countries in descending order of their share of total oil and gas reserves in the region. For those countries owning at least a tenth of the total reserves, Repsol's average percentage ownership of a country's reserves is 0.16%. On the other hand, for the bottom tier of countries owning less than 10% each, Repsol's average ownership per country rises to 6.98%, with Argentina, Bolivia, and Trinidad and Tobago being the primary contributors to this rise. Corroborating the relationship between power status and sensitivity to foreign investment, Repsol's penetration is higher in those states of relative weakness. For the largest owners, which also have historically nationalistic policies, Repsol's ownership is minuscule.

A look from another vantage point further corroborates the role of power status. Table 10.2 shows the gross domestic product (GDP) of each country with substantial reserves of oil and gas in Latin America, and their respective share of the total group's GDP. Once again, for the richest countries, with at least 10% of the total group's GDP, Repsol's involvement as a percentage ownership of reserves is limited to 0.23%. It is only when looking at those countries with a GDP ownership below 10% of the total that Repsol's involvement increases, to 6.97%. Argentina, where Repsol has the highest percentage of ownership per country reserves (44.03%), does come third-place in the GDP ranking, so it would seem that its higher power status and high level of ownership by Repsol contradicts the model. However, Argentina's ranking is not a close third place. In fact, there is a chasm between it and the top two states, with Argentina's GDP less than a quarter that of second-place Brazil. For those states with a higher power status, whether in terms of total reserves or GDP, Repsol's involvement remains limited.

We can extrapolate this contemporary picture into the future. As time advances, the stronger states are unlikely to substantially increase their cooperation with foreign firms. Brazil, for instance, given "PETROBRAS's success in developing offshore oil reserves using its own technology" (Fuad, 1993: 160), is unlikely to consider compromising its high power status in the region. As seen from Tables 10.1 and 10.2, in 2002, Brazil was the third largest owner of reserves and the second wealthiest of the energy-owners in the region. If any cooperation will ensue, Brazil will likely limit it to activities not likely to compromise its power status – like the sale of non-strategic assets and specific projects with short time horizons.

Table 10.1   Total oil and gas reserves and Repsol's reserves in Latin America per country, 2002

Country	Total oil and gas reserves (billions boe)	Country reserves as % of Latin America's	Repsol reserves in country (billions boe)	Repsol reserves as % of country's
Venezuela	79.70	57.24%	0.26	0.32%
Mexico	19.87	14.27%	0.00	0.00%
Brazil	11.30	8.12%	0.05	0.47%
Argentina	6.99	5.02%	3.08	44.03%
Bolivia	5.93	4.26%	1.29	21.81%
Ecuador	4.68	3.36%	0.07	1.47%
Trinidad & Tobago	4.61	3.31%	0.24	5.12%
Perú	2.50	1.79%	0.00	0.00%
Colombia	2.38	1.71%	0.01	0.28%
Cuba	0.61	0.44%	0.00	0.00%
Other	0.43	0.31%	0.00	0.00%
Chile	0.23	0.16%	0.00	0.00%
Total	139.24	100.00%	4.99	3.59%

Average Repsol reserves as % of country's for countries owning each at least 10% of Latin American reserves: 0.16%

Average Repsol reserves as % of country's for countries owning each below 10% of Latin American reserves: 6.98%

Sources: Energy Information Administration (2004); Repsol-YPF (2002b)

Table 10.2   Gross domestic product and Repsol's reserves in Latin America per country, 2002

Country	GDP (billions current US$)	GDP as % of total GDP of Latin American oil-and-gas owning countries	Repsol reserves in country (billions boe)	Repsol reserves as % of country's
Mexico	637.20	41.67%	0.00	0.00%
Brazil	452.39	29.58%	0.05	0.47%
Argentina	102.04	6.67%	3.08	44.03%
Venezuela	94.34	6.17%	0.26	0.32%
Colombia	80.93	5.29%	0.01	0.28%
Chile	64.15	4.19%	0.00	0.00%
Perú	56.52	3.70%	0.00	0.00%
Ecuador	24.31	1.59%	0.07	1.47%
Trinidad & Tobago	9.63	0.63%	0.24	5.12%
Bolivia	7.80	0.51%	1.29	21.81%
Cuba	0.00	0.00%	0.00	0.00%
Other	0.00	0.00%	0.00	0.00%
Total	1529.31	100.00%	4.99	3.59%

Average Repsol reserves as % of country's for countries with at least 10% of total group's GDP: 0.23%

Average Repsol reserves as % of country's for countries with less than 10% of total group's GDP: 6.97%

Sources: Repsol-YPF (2002b); World Bank(2004)

Ironically, in those states where Repsol is contributing to the energy infrastructure, the firm's success can be a curse in disguise. Since those positive contributions will enhance those states' power statuses, the states might curtail their relationship with Repsol once things improve. In Argentina, as can be seen in Figure 10.3, the liberal reforms of the 1980s and 1990s have been largely positive. Several indicators, including reserves, production, costs, refining, and exports significantly improved in both petroleum and natural gas (Gadano, 1998: 5). According to the model, we could reasonably expect Argentina to begin curtailing its relationship with Repsol. Although the recent economic woes that confronted Argentina might have postponed stronger measures, Argentina already started to impose more taxes on Repsol. In August 2004, the Kirchner Administration announced a new system of progressive taxes on oil exports, by which the applicable rate increases with the price of oil. This rate begins at 25% when the barrel of oil is below $32, and reaches 45% if the barrel price surpasses $45. On top of this tax system, in May of the same year, Argentina raised its export tax rate from 20% to 25% (Casado, 2004). Assuming its power status is higher in the future, Argentina is likely to demand more from its relationship with Repsol.

Another state where Repsol has a significant presence is Bolivia, and here too the effects of a higher power status make themselves evident. Bolivia started the 1990s with a marginal power status in the energy sector. It was able to "cover only part of [its] oil needs" and consequently liberalized its sector to become an exploration "hot spot" (Fuad, 1993: 157, 161). It even privatized its former energy concern Yacimientos Petrolíferos Fiscales Bolivianos (YPFB) in 1997 (AFP, 2004). Subsequently, these actions contributed to an increase in Bolivia's power status. Explorations by foreign firms found that Bolivia was the second-largest owner of gas deposits in Latin America (Forero, 2004a). As expected from the model, with its newfound riches, Bolivia now seeks to curtail its relationship with the energy firms. In a referendum conducted on July 2004, the Mesa Administration obtained popular approval for five measures: 1) to take back ownership of gas at the wellhead, 2) repeal the current hydrocarbons law granting companies leeway in exploiting gas, 3) re-nationalize YPFB, 4) boost royalties from 18% to 50%, and 5) use gas as a "strategic resource" to obtain a sea outlet from former enemy Chile. Nevertheless, as Bolivia's power status is not high enough to prompt stronger measures against the firms, President Mesa has stated "that he would honor prior contracts with the foreign gas companies" and his referendum plan "did not include taking facilities away from private companies" (AFP, 2004; Forero, 2004a; Monforte, 2004). As in Argentina, however, these developments do not bode well for Repsol as Bolivia will likely curtail its relationship with foreign energy firms.

Overall, these findings suggest that the state will remain the predominant figure in the Latin American energy sector. This prediction converges with Fuad's conclusion that state companies will largely own and develop Latin America's oil and gas. While Fuad attributes this role mainly to "the proven ability of [the states companies of Mexico, Venezuela, and Brazil] – and, to a lesser degree, of a few others – to develop successfully their countries' oil and natural gas", he does not translate this proven ability by state companies into the high power status that states seek in a system of international anarchy. On the other hand, he rightfully attributes a secondary role to resource nationalism in "provid[ing] a prop for some of the region's less efficient state companies" (Fuad, 1993: 153-154). In fact, a present look at popular sentiment in Latin America suggests that resource nationalism is likely to resurge and contribute to increasing restrictions on foreign investment.

Latin America emerged from the 1990s in a condition of popular dissatisfaction. By 2003, poverty had reached 43.9% of the region's population and extreme poverty touched a sizable 19.4%. In addition, the 2002 unemployment rate was 9.4%, the highest in two decades. These economic ailments do not afflict everyone equally. The richest 10% of the population earns 30 times as much as the bottom 10%. Using the Gini coefficient, which measures the degree of inequality in income distribution, Latin America is the most unequal region in the world. Additionally, the region's population has yet to enjoy widespread rewards from following the liberal economic reforms associated with the Washington Consensus. As a result, the idea of an intervening state is gaining ground: in a 2002 poll, 70.3% of respondents supported state intervention in the economy and only 26.4% preferred a market-oriented economy (United Nations Development Programme, 2004: 25, 49, 80, 81). Needless to say, this is hardly a harbinger of further liberalization in the region.

The democratic reforms that took place in Latin America will arguably magnify the effects of this public dissatisfaction as politicians must become more responsive to public opinion. By 2002, the Index of Electoral Democracy for Latin America reached an unprecedented high of .93. This index aggregates four variables: voting rights, clean elections, free elections, and elections as the means of access to public posts (United Nations Development Programme, 2004: 33-34). With the fall of four Argentinean presidents in two weeks during the 2001 economic implosion, and the resignation of Bolivian President Sánchez de Lozada in 2003 amidst popular protests, history has served Latin American politicians fresh reminders of the price of going against the winds of the populace. In sum, strong societal preferences for a prominent state role in the economy, coupled with a political environment favoring responsiveness to said preferences, suggest that Latin American economic liberalization will remain stable at best, and recede at worst. In the energy sector, these preferences will likely manifest themselves as variants of resource nationalism. Fuad, again, is on the right track when he asserts that "resource nationalism in Latin America may be down, but it is not out" (Fuad, 1993: 156). In fact, given the manifest societal preferences in the region, resource nationalism might well be making a comeback.

Looking at the present trends of the two variables in the model, the future does not seem to hold an indefinite, secular extension of liberalization in the energy sector. If the case of Argentina is any indication, states engage in cyclical cooperation with energy firms, cooperating when their power status is low and curtailing this cooperation once they attain a higher status. For Argentina, these actions constantly backfired and gave rise to the recurrent cycles of cooperation evident in its history. Other states, like Brazil, seemed able to successfully branch off and maintain viable state-owned companies. As states find ways to increase the power status of their energy sectors, and pressured by dissatisfied populations to assert themselves in their economies, firms like Repsol will likely find themselves cooperating mostly with the laggards and weaklings that, albeit reluctantly, will put aside their concerns and nationalism for the time being.

Conclusions

This chapter sought to explain the dynamics behind liberalization in the Latin American energy sector to determine whether the latest trend will be of indefinite duration, or secular, or of definite duration followed by an eventual decline, or cyclical. It used a model incorporating both the effects of power status and resource nationalism on a state's sensitivity to foreign investment in its energy sector. A higher power status would raise this sensitivity and prompt states to curtail their less-needed relationship with foreign companies, while a lower power status lowered this sensitivity and encouraged energy liberalization. At the same time, resource nationalism would have a supplementary, but lesser, effect on the states' sensitivity. In the case of Argentina during the 20th century, power status fluctuations in that state's energy sector accounted for most of its energy policy reversals. As expected, resource nationalism had a secondary effect. It seemed to prompt two of the seven policy reversals that occurred in Argentina. But in line with realist premises, when nationalistic pressures contended with an evidently low power status, Argentina overcame these pressures and yielded to foreign companies.

A look at Repsol in Latin America today revealed that its ownership of reserves also reflects the model: it owns more, as a percentage, in the smaller and poorer energy-owning states, and less in the bigger and richer ones. When examining recent evidence regarding both the power status trends of Latin American states and their nationalistic pressures, the prospects for the firm in the region, and the liberalization of the energy sector, are pessimistic. The latest liberalization of the region's energy sector is more likely to be cyclical than secular.

This study has practical implications, but the pessimistic prospects for the liberalization of the Latin American energy sector should not be taken with alarm. Massive expropriations and the financial ruin of energy firms comprise as far-fetched a prospect as the full-scale liberalization of the region. In fact, the curtailment of state-firm relationships is likely to be a gradual process from which both states and firms can derive some benefit if they understand the effect and history of power status changes and resource nationalism in the region.

States should be mindful of acquiring self-reliance in their energy sector, to be sure, for that raises their prospects of survival in war and prosperity in peace. However, a lesson from Argentina's policy reversals is that policymakers ought to be conservative in timing the curtailment of ties with foreign energy firms. It is better to err on the conservative side and delay strict measures until a state is confident it can perform on its own. Rushing to kick out foreign firms can involve risky delays in a state's power status rise, and also foster a bad reputation as a reneger of deals.

States should also actively manage the resource nationalism incipient in the region. At times, the winds of popular passion might run so strong as to prohibit a deal that is beneficial on purely economic grounds. In these cases, clever negotiation and even compromise might be necessary. For instance, the Mesa Administration's 2004 referendum about the future of Bolivia's gas used popular passions against Chile in obtaining approval to use the gas as leverage in negotiations with that country for a sea outlet (AFP, 2004; Forero, 2004a; Monforte, 2004). Other states can carefully ride the winds of popular passion to similar results.

If history is any guide, firms should understand that their successful stay in weak Latin American states is prone to be a short-term affair or an increasingly difficult one. However, some actions can delay the inevitable. Firms should be aware of the regional political landscape and avoid playing blind matchmaker, lest they link feuding states. Firms should develop their host states' energy infrastructure to reap enough profit and prevent competition from firms offering better deals. On the other hand, they should not develop it so quickly or thoroughly as to drastically elevate the host states' power status. Doing so would invite an earlier curtailment of the state-firm relationship. Another option is to prevent host states from acquiring all the components necessary for the continuous growth of their energy sectors. Repsol seems to be doing this by centralizing all its research-and-development in Madrid (Repsol-YPF, 2002a: 31). By keeping tight reins on their knowledge, foreign firms can make their hosts hesitant about risking a premature break-up. Nevertheless, the state-firm relationship is bound to end as states leave their low power status, and strategic concerns and resource nationalism work in unison to promote a separation. Consequently, firms should diversify their operations. Repsol's recent focus on the emerging states of Trinidad and Tobago, and Libya suggest that it is aware of this strategy (Repsol-YPF, 2003: 11). Whether they like it or not, multinational energy firms must strategize with the understanding that they are not only involved in the economy of their host states, but in their *political* economy as well. Unlike many other commodities, energy resources like oil represent "geopolitics with a vengeance" (Solberg, 1976: 11). Firms would be wise to remember that.

References

Agence France-Presse (2004, Jul 19), Bolivians approve gas industry nationalization, more exports",
    http://www.keepmedia.com/ShowItemDetails.do?itemID=509651&extID=10030&oliI D=226 (observed July 25, 2004).
Beato, P., and C. Fuente (2000), "Liberalization of the gas sector in Latin America: the experience of three countries", *Sustainable Development Dept. Best practices series.* Washington, D.C.: Inter-American Development Bank.
Campodónico, H. (1999), "La industria del gas natural y su regulación en América Latina", *Revista de la CEPAL*, 68, pp. 135-154.
Casado, R. (2004), Argentina y Bolivia presionan con más impuestos a Repsol-YPF", *Expansión*, August, 5, p. 3.
Energy Information Administration (2004), "International energy annual 2002", http://www.eia.doe.gov/emeu/iea/contents.html (observed August 1, 2004).
Forero, J. (2004a), "Bolivians support gas plan and give president a lift", *The New York Times*, July 19, p. A6.
Forero, J. (2004b), "Oil, Venezuela's lifeblood, is now its social currency, too", *The New York Times*, July 24, p. C.1.
Fuad, K. (1993), "Oil and Natural Gas Privatization", in P. Boeker (ed.), *Latin America's Turnaround: Privatization, Foreign Investment, and Growth*, International Center for Economic Growth, San Francisco, pp. 153-163.

Gadano, N. (1998), "Determinantes de la inversión en el sector petróleo y gas de la Argentina". Serie reformas económicas, 7, CEPAL, Santiago de Chile.

Grieco, J.M. (1988), "Anarchy and the Limits of Cooperation: A Realist Critique of the Newest Liberal Institutionalism" *International Organization*, 42 (August), pp. 485-507.

Grieco, J.M. (1990), *Cooperation Among Nations: Europe, America, and Non-Tariff Barriers to Trade*, Cornell, University Press, Ithaca.

Grieco, J.M. (1993), "Understanding the Problem of International Cooperation: the Limits of Neoliberal Institutionalism and the Future of Realist Theory", in D.A. Baldwin (ed.), *Neorealism and Neoliberalism: the Contemporary Debate*, Columbia University Press, New York, pp. 301-338.

Hirst, P.Q., and G. Thompson (1999), *Globalization in Question: The International Economy and the Possibilities of Governance* (2nd ed.), Polity Press, Malden.

Jervis, R. (1978), "Cooperation Under the Security Dilemma", in R.K. Betts (ed.), *Conflict after the Cold War* (2nd ed., 2002), Longman, New York, pp. 400-415.

Keohane, R.O. (1993), Institutional Theory and the Realist Challenge After the Cold War", in D.A. Baldwin (ed.), *Neorealism and Neoliberalism: the Contemporary Debate*, Columbia University Press, pp. 269-300.

Lewis, S.W. (2004), "Critical issues in Brazil's energy sector", James A. Baker III Institute for Public Policy, Rice University, Houston.

Monforte, C. (2004), "Bolivia dice "sí" a la política de reservas de gas propuesta por el gobierno, *Cinco Días*, July 20, p. 3.

Morgenthau, H.J. (1973), *Politics among Nations; the Struggle for Power and Peace* (5th ed.), Knopf, New York.

Repsol-YPF (1999), *Informe anual 1999*, Madrid.

Repsol-YPF (2002a), *Informe anual 2002*, Madrid.

Repsol-YPF (2002b), *Áreas de negocio 2002 – Exploración y Producción*, http://www.repsolypf.com/comunes/archivos/AreasDeNegocio2002_esp_definitivo__4 3377.pdf (observed August 1, 2004).

Repsol-YPF (2003), *Annual Report 2003*, Madrid.

Repsol-YPF (2004), "The President of Venezuela inaugurates Repsol-YPF project in Barrancas", (press release), http://www.repsolypf.com/eng/todosobrerepsolypf/saladeprensa/noticias/ultimasnoticia s/noticias.asp?PaginaID=61088, (observed August 1, 2004).

Romero, S. (2004), "Spanish seek oil off Cuba; potential shift in Gulf output", *The New York Times*, July 6, p. C.1.

Snyder, G.H., and Diesing, P. (1977), *Conflict among Nations: Bargaining, Decision Making and System Structure in International Crises*, Princeton University Press, Princeton.

Solberg, C. (1976), *Oil Power*, Mason/Charter, New York.

Solberg, C. E. (1979), *Oil and Nationalism in Argentina: A History*, Stanford University Press, Stanford.

Toral, P. (2003), *The Advantage of Spanish Multinational Enterprises in Latin America*, Doctoral dissertation, Florida International University.

United Nations Development Programme (2004), *La democracia en América Latina: hacia una democracia de ciudadanas y ciudadanos*, Aguilar, Altea, Taurus, Alfaguara S.A., Buenos Aires, and Programa de las Naciones Unidas para el Desarrollo, printed by Panamericana Formas e Impresos S.A.

Waltz, K.N. (1979), *Theory of International Politics*, Addison-Wesley, Reading.

World Bank (2004), *World Development Indicators*, http://devdata.worldbank.org/dataonline/, (observed August 1, 2004).

Chapter 11

Challenges for Spanish Investments in the Latin American Energy Industry

Carlos Seiglie

Introduction

In Latin America and the Caribbean, the beginning of the 1990s showed a fairly small increase in foreign direct investment (FDI), yet by 1993 the annual growth rate of FDI was approximately 30% (see Baer and Miles, 2001 for details). There were several factors that account for this new trend. First, the economic policies of the host countries, as well as that of the home countries, impacted on both the size of the flows, and the targeted economic sectors. In particular, the decade of the 1990s ushered in the political and economic maturation of the region in terms of the policies adopted by Latin American countries. These included changes in macroeconomic policies, as well as structural and legal reforms emphasizing the benefits of the market (see Stein and Daude, 2001). Finally, the privatization of state-run enterprises provided a vehicle for the transfer of capital across the globe.

Despite the euphoria of the 1990s, the start of the new millennium has shocked the pattern established previously. While the 1980s was the "lost decade" for Latin America, the first decade of this millennium could prove to be equally costly for Spain, the former "mother country." In this chapter, I explore why the risks of FDI increased in general and proportionately more for Spain, in particular in the energy sector. The next section provides an overview of the major Spanish firms operating in Latin America. It is followed by a discussion of the inherent risks of FDI to the shareholders of the parent companies. Evidence on the economic impact of recent privatizations in Latin America is presented and I discuss how these changes may affect the long-term outlook for Spanish investments in the energy sector. The final section provides concluding remarks.

Spanish FDI in the energy sector of Latin America

Spanish direct investment in Latin America during the 1990s was especially significant in the energy and public utility sectors. Spain began its investment participation tentatively during the privatization process that occurred during this decade. Initially, other competitors outbid Spain for the assets of several privatized companies. Later on in the process, however, it appears that Spain bid substantially more than any of its rivals to acquire certain assets. Since the return to an investment depends upon the price paid for the assets, the outcome of these "auctions" is extremely important for shareholder wealth. Therefore, if the Spanish acquisition of assets in the region can be characterized by an initial phase of underbidding and, subsequently, of overbidding, then those assets that were acquired during this latter phase could yield a lower rate of return than the other alternatives available and passed up.

The main Spanish firms in the energy sector in Latin America and the Caribbean are Repsol-YPF, Endesa, Gas Natural, Union Fenosa, and Iberdrola. Over the years, these firms have acquired either direct or indirect control of firms in different segments of the energy sector in Latin America and the Caribbean. Similarly, their degree of involvement has varied across the region's countries. For example, Repsol acquired the Argentine company of Yacimientos Petrolíferos Fiscales (YPF) in 1999. In the process, Repsol-YPF became Spain's largest company in terms of revenue, the largest private energy company in Latin America in terms of total assets, and one of the world's ten largest oil companies. In Latin America it is involved in the exploration and production of crude oil and natural gas in various countries as well as in other energy-related businesses. Repsol-YPF's oil and gas reserves in Latin America are located in Argentina, Bolivia, Brazil, Colombia, Ecuador, Trinidad and Tobago, and Venezuela. It operates refineries in Argentina and Peru and is involved in the liquefaction of natural gas in Trinidad and Tobago, as well as the distribution of natural gas in Argentina, Brazil, Colombia, and Mexico. Finally, in the electricity sector it is engaged in the generation of power in Argentina.

In the area of public utilities, Endesa acquired shares in numerous companies throughout the region along with a controlling share (61%) of the electricity group Enersis of Chile (with approximately 10 million customers) with purchases in 1997 of 29% and another 32% stake in March 1999. It is present in electricity generation in Chile, Argentina, Colombia, Peru, Brazil, and the Dominican Republic. Endesa engages in electricity generation and its transportation, distribution, and retailing activities in Chile, Argentina, Brazil, Colombia, and Peru. It has a share in several electricity companies in these countries, directly or through the Enersis group. Although it is primarily involved in the energy sector, Endesa has also become involved in the telecommunication sector in Chile where it is sole owner of the Chilean wireless telephone company, Smartcom.

The other large Spanish firms include Gas Natural, an energy services multinational focusing its activity on the supply and distribution of natural gas in which Repsol-YPF owns a 31% stake. It is the main distributor of natural gas in South America, where almost half of its worldwide customers are located. It has a presence in five countries: Argentina, through the distributor, Gas Natural BAN; Colombia, with the company Gas Natural ESP; Brazil, through CEG, CEG Rio and Gas Natural SPS; Mexico, where it operates with Gas Natural México; and Puerto Rico, where it manages the company Ecoeléctrica. Unión Fenosa, whose main business is the supply of energy, has a large presence in Mexico where it has gas power plants and generates electricity in the country and is one of the main independent electricity firms. It is also present in electricity generation and distribution in Guatemala, Nicaragua, Panama, Colombia, Costa Rica, and the Dominican Republic. In these other countries it has controlling stakes in several distribution companies, such as Deocsa and Deorsa in Guatemala (85% stake), and Disnorte and Dissur in Nicaragua (79.5% holding). Finally, the Spanish company, Iberdrola, is the leading private electricity producer in Mexico. It is also the leading electricity distribution company in Guatemala through its interest in EEGSA, as well as in the northeast of Brazil, where it services 6.8 million customers. Through this nexus of direct or indirect control of the energy sector of much of Latin America, the shareholders of these firms expose themselves to economic and political shocks in the region. It is instructive to see how this affects the financial performance of these companies and to a great extent the well-being of the Spanish economy.

The performance of Spanish FDI in the energy industry

International diversification of securities held in a portfolio is an important strategy undertaken to reduce risk. This strategy can be partially implemented by holding the securities of a domestic firm that has international operations, i.e., by holding the stocks of multinational firms. These multinationals must themselves be diversified in their international operations. While FDI by US firms is diversified across different regions of the world, in the case of Spain they are disproportionately concentrated in one region, Latin America. Making matters worse, it is estimated that 30% of the revenues of the top twenty-six Spanish firms come from Latin America (see Casanova, 2002). These firms constitute more than 55% of the stocks traded on the Bolsa de Madrid (IBEX). In terms of country risk, 10% of the profits of Endesa are estimated to come from Argentina, while for Repsol, 40% of its profits come from this country, where the economy has been severely battered. This heavy exposure to a region and in the case of Repsol-YPF, a specific country, can have a disastrous impact not only on the firm's shareholders, but on Spain itself. To make matters worse, other Spanish firms are large shareholders of some of these energy firms. For example, Santander Central Hispano Group owns a 23.8 % stake in Unión Fenosa, while Caja de Ahorros y Pensiones de Barcelona controls over 30% of Gas Natural.

Figures 11.1-3 show the returns for shares of American Depository Receipts (ADRs) of Repsol, Endesa, and Enersis as compared to the returns of companies in their respective industries as represented by the relevant industry index. As we can see, it appears that the Argentine crisis has had a profound effect on the value of the shares of Repsol-YPF and, to a lesser extent, on those of Endesa. For example, as Figure 11.1 shows, Repsol had been outperforming the AMEX Oil Index throughout the greater part of the five-year period shown. It continued to do so after Repsol acquired YPF in 1999. Yet we can see that the situation began to change in the middle of 2001 with the Argentine economic crisis. To put the timing in perspective, in March of that year, Domingo Cavallo replaced Ricardo López Murphy as Economy Minister. This had no effect on the crisis and the downward plunge continued after President Fernando de la Rúa's resignation in December 2001. The negative differential in returns accelerated with the news of the devaluation of the peso in January 2002 and began to stabilize by the end of the year.

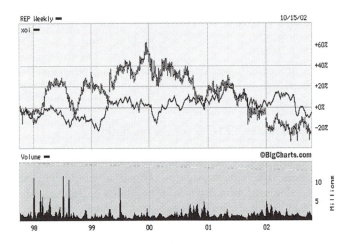

Figure 11.1   Repsol-YPF vs. AMEX Oil Index

Source: www.BigCharts.com

In the case of Endesa, we can see that as compared to the Dow Jones Utility Index the company tracked the index quite well up until it gained majority control of Enersis in March 1999. At this time, we see that it dipped below the index for several months but rebounded during the early months of 2000, and then again began to drop below the index up until the present. In other words, as compared to other possible investments, Endesa has tended to underperform as the new millennium began. Figure 11.3 shows the performance of shares of Enersis against the DJ Utility. As can be seen from this graph, it does not appear that Endesa's controlling stake in the firm had any notable impact on improving the firm's performance versus other utility companies in the index since its returns continued to be lower than those of other firms.

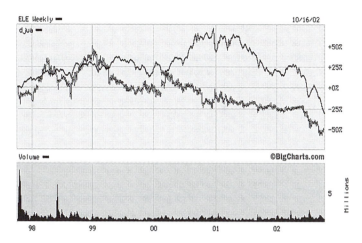

Figure 11.2 Endesa vs. DJ Utility Index

Source: www.BigCharts.com

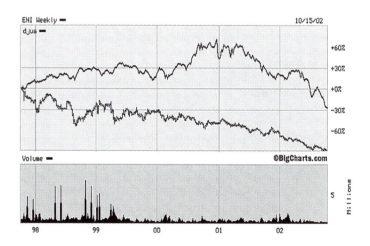

Figure 11.3 Enersis vs. DJ Utility Index

Source: www.BigCharts.com

It is important to realize that with globalization, Spanish firms are competing in the same capital market as U.S. firms, i.e., the capital markets are international. Consequently, they are held to the same standards as those of investments emanating from companies based in other parts of the world. Finally, we can look at the performance of Unión Fenosa, Gas Natural and Iberdrola securities in the Bolsa de Madrid. As Figures 11.4-6 show, the security prices of all three companies suffered as a result of the Argentine crisis even though for Unión Fenosa and Iberdrola their exposure in Argentina was minimal as compared to Repsol-YPF. This shows the ripple effect on shareholder value from country-specific shocks in the region. Therefore, it is important that we explore the issue of risk more closely.

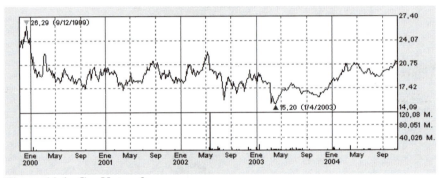

Figure 11.4   Gas Natural

Source: Madrid Stock Exchange

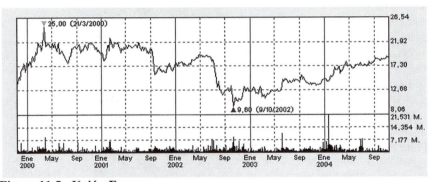

Figure 11.5   Unión Fenosa

Source: Madrid Stock Exchange

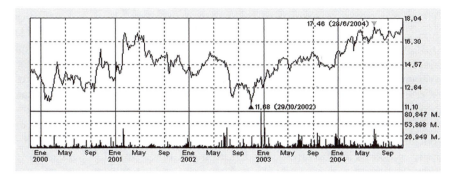

Figure 11.6   Iberdrola

Source: Madrid Stock Exchange

Risks of Spanish FDI in the Latin American energy industry

There are several risks for FDI by Spanish firms in general and for energy firms and some of the largest Spanish firms, in particular. All investments, whether domestic or foreign carry some degree of risk. In the case of FDI, they are compounded by country and exchange rate risk. In the case of country risk, I include such factors as the macroeconomic environment of the host country, the country's regulatory environment, institutions including the bureaucracy and the quality of the legal system. Other factors include political instability and the degree of corruption in the host country that can act as a tax on corporate earnings.

In addition, given any of these characteristics, FDI will be affected by foreign exchange risk generated not only by the monetary and exchange rate policies adopted in the host country, but also by those in the country of origin and in the case of Spain, by the European Central Bank. General shocks to the world economy also contribute to risk. For example, in the case of Spanish firms in the energy sector they have to be concerned not only with the macroeconomic policies of the host countries that can lead to devaluations of the host country's currency, but also by monetary policy of the European Central Bank that can affect the euro and their earnings and the value of profits remitted from their investments in the region.

The case of Repsol-YPF in Argentina during the economic crises provides an interesting example of how host governments react towards foreign firms following some adverse economic shock. On January 9, 2002, the government of Argentina passed Law no. 25.561 entitled "Law of Public Emergency and Reform of Currency Exchange Regulations," derogating the currency conversion regime of one Argentine peso to one US dollar, and decreed a change in price regulations (Law no. 24.076) by converting tariffs previously charged in dollars directly into pesos, and forbidding their adjustment based on the US Producer Price Index. In addition, on February 3, 2002, Decree Law no. 214/2002 was promulgated, establishing that the Argentine economy be totally "pesified." Lastly, on February 12, 2002, Decree Law 310/2002 governing exports was passed, developing article 6 of Law 25.561, that imposed a 20% tax on crude oil exports and a 5% tax on refined oil products. In June 2002, there were agreements signed between the government and the oil sector that led to reductions of some of the original taxes and regulations, such as the law permitting the availability of only 70% of foreign currency from exports.

Yet other regulations, such as the one limiting crude oil exports to 36% of production were imposed with a promise to lift this restriction as soon as "short-supply" problems had been resolved. The economic objective of this policy was to reduce the domestic price of oil paid by Argentines, and thereby gain their political support. This policy amounted to a transfer of income from the shareholders of Repsol to the citizens of Argentina. All these policies taken by the Argentinean government reduced the profitability of Repsol-YPF and therefore their shareholders' wealth. They provide an example of some of the obstacles and inherent risks faced by firms investing in developing countries with a tendency toward enacting populist policies whenever an economic crisis ensues. Latin America historically has seen its share of these types of regimes.

More generally, there are other long-term risks involved for Spanish investments in energy in Latin America. A study by Ugaz and Waddams Price (2002) for the World Institute for Development Economics Research (WIDER) examined how consumers in Latin America were impacted by the privatization of public utilities. This study concentrated on the experiences of four countries: Chile, Argentina, Bolivia, and Peru. These countries' experiences with privatization were compared with those of Spain and the United Kingdom. The distributional impact of reforms in these countries depended upon two main factors. The first was on how access to services changed after privatization. More specifically, privatized firms generally increased investments in order to expand services and networks to customers after the privatization, i.e., better geographic coverage was provided. This obviously has a positive effect on the wellbeing of those consumers who were previously excluded from access to the services of the utility firm. The second factor is based on how prices for these services changed as a result of privatization. For example, after privatization the price structure facing rural and urban customers, or residential and industrial, changed. If prices increased to a specific group, *ceteris paribus*, then they were made worse off.

The results of the study showed that access has improved in all countries after privatization. In particular, for Bolivia there is evidence that the connection rate for the poor increased faster than for other groups across all utilities. A similar pattern emerges in Peru. In Chile, service coverage increased for most income groups, increasing most for electricity coverage among the lower income deciles. Yet for pre-existing customers, the evidence showed consumer welfare losses associated with the increase in fixed charges in all of the countries studied, with heavier losses incurred by the poor from price changes. Combining the two effects, we find a mixed picture of who gained from privatization based on the different income groups. For example, the poor benefited from access but were adversely affected by price, while for other income groups, benefit and cost varied across the services. These findings are extremely important for firms investing in energy and utilities since it highlights the political risks generated by the current incentives towards increases in government regulation or even the nationalization of Spanish firms in these industries. Given the strong pressures for governments to cross-subsidize more powerful political groups by limiting the ability of firms to charge the appropriate price, e.g., by the use of price controls, shareholders must be wary of their firm's investments in these politically volatile countries.

Conclusions

This chapter has presented an overview of Spanish foreign direct investments in Latin America, and in the energy sector in particular. By emphasizing how the capital markets have reacted to these investments, it appears that they have not been completely successful. As the Argentine crisis has shown, there are inherent risks to these investments when deteriorating economic conditions lead host governments to enact policies that are not market-friendly. These policies reduce the profitability of these firms and therefore, their shareholder's value. Recent research has shown that the distributional impact of privatization is mixed, with some income groups benefiting and others made worse-off. Since many Spanish investments came about due to the privatization of state-owned enterprises, one must be vigilant to a swing in attitudes towards greater regulation of these firms by Latin American governments aiming to quell political dissatisfaction.

References

Baer, W. and W. Miles (eds.) (2001), *Foreign Direct Investment in Latin America: Its Changing Nature at the Turn of the Century*, Haworth Press, New York.

Casanova, L. (2002), "Lazos de Familia: la Inversión Española en América Latina," *Foreign Affairs en Español*, Summer.

Endesa, S.A. *Annual Reports*, Madrid (various years).

Gas Natural SDG, S.A., *Annual Reports*, Madrid (various years).

Iberdrola, S.A., *Annual Reports*, Madrid (various years).

Investment Corporation (2001), Santiago de Chile.

Repsol-YPF, *Annual Reports*, Madrid (various years).

Stein, E. and C. Daude (2001), "Institutions, Integration and the Location of Foreign Direct Investment." Paper presented at the Annual Meeting of the Board of Governors, Inter-American Development Bank, Mexico City, November 26-27.

Ugaz, C. and C. Waddams (2003), *Utility Privatization and Regulation: A Fair Deal for Consumers?*, Edward Elgar Publishing, Ltd., Cheltenham.

Unión Fenosa, S.A., *Annual Reports*, Madrid (various years).

Chapter 12

The Socio-Political Dimension of Spanish Direct Investment in Latin America

Félix E. Martín

Introduction

The rapid increase of Spanish direct investments in Latin America since 1990 captures the attention of the general public, entrepreneurs, and students of the international political economy alike. Some explain Spain's aggressive investment drive in Latin America stemming from purely opportunistic and pecuniary factors. Others argue that the experience of Spanish enterprises in a corporatist economic environment in Spain in the 1960s and 1970s gave these companies an edge or a competitive advantage in the Latin American market, which presented similar conditions to those prevailing in Spain just prior to, during, and subsequent to the political transition in 1975. Yet, still others, including this author, while sympathetic to the basic economic rationale argument, and to the "competitive edge" of some Spanish enterprises thesis, question whether or not the Spanish direct investment drive in Latin America may have been motivated partly by larger societal and political factors in Spain, and in the external environment.

In the midst of the accelerated process of economic globalization, where the corporate quest for efficiency, productivity, and profitability seem to transcend international boundary lines — and nationalism — it is a significant factor that many experts still find it empirically and theoretically necessary to classify foreign direct investments in terms of their national origin. Further, it is even more puzzling to find that in a period where economic globalization seems to be prevailing over nationalism, the state-centric interpretation of multinational enterprises is still an important perspective to classify and analyze differences in corporate strategy and the investment philosophy of the top managerial and administrative body of these companies (Gilpin, 2001: 298). Commenting on this point, Peter J. Katzenstein remarked several years ago that "the nation-state has reaffirmed its power to shape strategies of foreign economic policy." (Katzenstein, 1978: 4) Thus, it is fitting to analyze to what extent, if at all, have socio-political factors in Spain and in the external environment played a determining role in the process of Spanish direct investments in Latin America?

This chapter argues that the national origin of Spanish multinational firms and the concomitant socio-political milieu of the home and host countries are crucial causal variables for the analysis of the international behavior of these companies. In addition, prevailing conditions in the international environment are considered important factors in this analysis. I pay close attention to the socio-political and economic dimensions of the trilateral dynamics, involving Spain (as the investment initiator), Latin America (as the recipient of investments), and the U.S.A. (as the potential competitor).

In an attempt to gauge whether or not socio-political motivations, in addition to purely pecuniary objectives, have played a part in Spain's aggressive investment drive in Latin American economies since 1990, this chapter focuses on home-based societal factors and on the socio-political and economic dimensions of the trilateral relations, linking Spain, the U.S., and Latin America. In the first part of this chapter, I present the theoretical argument and the causal model. In the second part, I discuss the methodology and the reasons for selecting the type of data that I gathered for this study. In the third part, I present the data and discuss their limitations and possibilities. Finally, I discuss my findings and conclusions on the possible socio-political determinants of Spanish direct investments in Latin America.

Assumptions, causal model, and hypothesis

The theoretical framework of this study rests on two basic assumptions. First, I assume that the international business activity of multinational enterprises is, in fact, an integral part of the home country's foreign economic policy process. This reasoning is in contraposition to that of neoclassical economists who believe that the behavior of a corporation is determined strictly by market forces and, thus, the national origin of a firm is an unimportant and irrelevant explanatory variable.[1] Instead, I base my argument on the thesis advanced by Paul Doremus *et al.*, in their book, *The Myth of the Global Corporation*. In this work, the authors develop a state-centric interpretation of the origin and the international operations of multinational corporations. They argue that these enterprises are products of their home base and are inclined to project the social, economic, and political values of their national origin (Doremus, Keller, Pauly, and Reich, 1998; and Sally, 1994). They reach this conclusion specifically by examining significant differences between companies in the United States, Germany, and Japan. They find that domestic factors, such as the socio-political experience of the country, different economic ideologies, the structure of the economy, and the internal mechanism of corporate governance, are important determinants of the business activity of multinational enterprises. Accordingly, despite the emphasis on economic globalization and borderless economies in recent years, I still concur with Robert Gilpin that multinational firms "have not shorn themselves of national coloration" and are actually deeply "embedded in and very much a product of the history, culture, and economic systems of their home societies" (Gilpin, 2001: 289).

Table 12.1 Unemployment rates in five-year intervals among leading economies in the world, 1980-2000

Country	1980	1985	1990	1995	2000	Average
Belgium	9	11	7	9	7	8.6
Denmark	7	8	8	7	5	7
France	6	10	9	12	10	9.4
Germany	N/A	N/A	N/A	8	8	8
Greece	2	8	7	9	11	7.4
Ireland	N/A	17	13	12	4	11.5
Italy	8	10	11	11	11	10
Japan	2	3	2	3	5	3
Luxembourg	1	3	2	3	2	2.2
Netherlands	5	13	7	7	3	7
Portugal	7	9	5	7	4	6.4
Spain	11	21	16	23	14	17
United Kingdom	7	11	7	9	6	8
United States	7	7	6	6	4	6

Source: World Development Indicators Database at
http://devdata.worldbank.org.ezproxy.fiu.edu/dataonline

Table 12.2 Gross national income per capita in 2003 international U.S.$ in five-year intervals among leading economies in the world, 1980-2000

Country	1980	1985	1990	1995	2000	Average
Belgium	9,910	13,400	18,140	21,870	26,990	18,062
Denmark	11,190	15,160	18,270	22,950	28,720	19,258
France	9,680	13,280	17,820	20,890	25,530	17,440
Germany	9,560	13,190	17,960	21,920	25,950	17,716
Greece	7,300	9,210	11,260	13,190	16,860	11,564
Ireland	5,420	7,620	11,400	15,820	25,970	13,246
Italy	9,180	12,850	17,360	20,780	24,730	16,980
Japan	8,830	13,010	18,930	22,770	26,300	17,968
Luxembourg	11,690	17,000	27,490	35,250	50,940	28,474
Netherlands	9,850	13,230	17,670	21,530	27,340	17,924
Portugal	5,150	6,790	10,630	13,060	16,930	10,512
Spain	6,560	8,850	12,810	15,510	19750	12,696
United Kingdom	8,450	11,990	16,330	19,970	24,840	27,664
United States	12,230	17,600	23,120	27,800	34,690	23,106

Source: World Development Indicators Database at
http://devdata.worldbank.org.ezproxy.fiu.edu/dataonline

The second assumption presupposes that in a strong, open, and democratic society neither governmental, nor entrepreneurial decision-makers can afford to be sheltered from and remain indifferent to the social mood and public opinion of the population at large, particularly in regard to important socio-economic and political decisions that are likely to affect the national interest and wellbeing of the people.

On two different counts I consider the process of Spanish FDI flow into Latin America in the last twenty years as a politically important economic decision. First, Spanish direct investments in Latin America have taken place at a time when the unemployment rate in Spain has remained steadily high and per capita gross national income (GNI) low. This is particularly evident, as shown in Tables 12.1 and 12.2, when Spain's levels are compared to those prevailing in the U.S., Japan, and twelve other Western European countries. Over a twenty-year period, from 1980 to 2000, Spain's average unemployment rate ranks fourteenth at 17%, and its U.S.$ 12,696 GNI per capita is number twelve, only slightly better than Greece and Portugal. Given these rather weak economic indicators in Spain and the high investment risk in Latin America, I extrapolate that the general public could have misconstrued the large outflow of capital to Latin America as a political decision. Arguably, they could have interpreted these capital flows as an irresponsible decision, indicating a lack of governmental and entrepreneurial support for the labor force, and a marked neglect for the national economic well-being.

Second, since I consider foreign direct investment (FDI) is one of several key tools of statecraft available to any government for the pursuit of its foreign economic policy goals (Baldwin, 1985: 40-50), I maintain that the decision to invest abroad is partly political in nature. Underscoring this point, Robert Gilpin, in his analysis of the domestic political aspects of U.S. foreign investment strategy, affirmed that "market forces do not operate in a political vacuum; on the contrary, the domestic political order and public policies seek to channel economic forces in one direction or another." (Gilpin, 1975: 50-60) Similarly, I presuppose that FDI, particularly a major investment drive in a highly risky socio-economic and political environment (Seiglie, 2005),[2] is necessarily a political national decision. As such, it needs to be in harmony with the general popular will. Also, it requires, at a minimum, the tacit political acquiescence and support of the general public. Based on these stipulations, I argue that, society-state relations and the resulting societal context from which multinational companies emerge and remain operating have a profound impact on their political and economic objectives.

The causal nexus running from societal factors to state actions takes two different forms, according to Peter Katzenstein, and both reflect societal pressures on the formulation and implementation of foreign economic policy. First, he identifies the democratic model that suggests a direct causal link from the mass preferences of all society's members — translated through elections — into governmental policies. Second, he discusses the interest group model in which the interests of groups are more influential than political parties and elections on governmental action in the area of foreign economic policy. Conceivably, the causal direction of the society-state argument may run the opposite way too (Migdal 1988, 2001). But the problem with this alternative causal direction is that it emphasizes the state's influence on society and downplays the potential effects from mass preferences, political parties, and elections on a state's policies (Katzenstein, 1978: 17-18). This is particularly problematic for explaining the evolution of the foreign economic policies of a democratic country. Since 1980, Spain is one of those cases where a decentralized and open state has coexisted with a strong, vibrant, and influential civil society. This renders the democratic interpretation model a more fruitful approach for illuminating the domestic political relations to the Spanish investment drive in Latin America.

The Spanish state is undeniably strong. It has endured a full democratic transition, administrative decentralization, sustained terrorism from separatist groups, and a drive for increasing political autonomy in several regions. Yet I argue that Spanish society is considerably stronger than the state. On a continuum of state power, ranging from the weak-state-and-strong-society pole to the opposite strong-state-and-weak-society end, Spain is closer to the weak-state-and-strong-society parameter of the spectrum.

Stephen Krasner offers three defining questions to gauge the domestic strength of the state in relation to its own society. One is about the state's capacity to formulate policy independent of particular groups. The second touches on the power of the state to change the behavior of groups. The third asks if the state can directly change the structure of the society in which it operates (Krasner, 1978: 60). The answers to these three questions are largely a resounding negative. First, splinter political parties and small nationalist political organizations have played pivotal roles in preventing the state from formulating policies independently from small groups. This is particularly evident in the important role of small, nationalist parties in legislative coalitions in the last two decades. Second, the Spanish state has faced very strong societal opposition whenever it has tried to change the behavior of small groups such as those opposed to joining the North Atlantic Treaty Organization (NATO) in the mid-1980s, or those opposed to the war in Iraq in 2003, or even those smaller groups interested in pursuing greater political autonomy for their regions. Finally, while Francisco Franco was able to change significant elements of the structure of Spanish society, the transition to democracy precludes that possibility. For instance, barring a return to an autocratic state, it would be unthinkable that the Spanish state could unilaterally outlaw the official policy guaranteeing cultural and linguistic diversity in Spain. These conditions illustrate the relative weakness of the Spanish state *vis-à-vis* its own society.

The causal argument presented here originates with the people's demand from the national government to protect their welfare. In turn, the governmental authorities utilize a variety of tools of statecraft including the promotion of portfolio and direct investments abroad, to create wealth and advance the national interest (Baldwin, 1985: 40-50). For this purpose, the state both regulates and assists simultaneously national enterprises engaged in international business operations.[3] In strong, open societies, such is the case in Spain, popular preferences and the will of the people influence state policies. Concomitantly, the government influences business firms and investment processes. Thus, one can deduce from this causal relation that multinational corporations are indirectly influenced by societal factors and the politics of the home country. Consistent with this reasoning, FDIs are ultimately considered in this study an integral element of the foreign economic policies of the nation-state.[4]

Based on the assumptions and causal sequence discussed above, I hypothesize that domestic-level variables — such as social perception and popular preferences, as revealed by public opinion and national mood — may have, among other possible alternative explanations, a direct causal effect on foreign policy choices and on international outcomes such as the decision to pursue and support a foreign direct investment strategy in Latin America. Second, I maintain in this study, too, that the character of the external environment may either constrain or facilitate the nature of an international investment decision. On the one hand, if the systemic leaders are imbued with a mercantilist or economic nationalist ideology, then international closure and beggar-thy-neighbor policies will prevail, stymieing in this manner all economic exchanges of goods and services. On the other hand, if the international system is managed by a liberal international leader,[5] then the predominant economic ideology will promote capital flows and free trade across boundaries. As part of its liberal economic ideology, the hegemon will promote and support unfettered access to markets. This reasoning is predicated on the notion of hegemonic stability theory and the provision of a public good such as an international liberal economic order.[6] In this sense, the Spanish decision to invest in Latin America required Spain to take into account the public reception by Latin Americans and the potential reaction of the United States as the major competitor and economic hegemonic power in the region.

Decision on data selection and methodology

In terms of data-collection for this study, the original intention was to interview both Spanish and U.S. middle-level managers whose enterprises were directly involved and were actively investing in Latin America. The rationale was to uncover how each group viewed each other's investment strategy in Latin America: what were their respective perceptions as potential competitors for the same market, and how did they see their respective roles benefiting their corporate and national interests. Moreover, I intended to learn if there was any type of business animosity or harmony among the old and the new investors in Latin America. Particularly, my objective was to understand why Spanish multinational enterprises were pursuing an aggressive investment drive in the region during the 1990s while U.S. firms were either reducing their financial exposure there or keeping their stakes unchanged. The result of that original effort was discouraging. Most U.S. employees who responded to my preliminary survey asserted that the Spanish investment drive had to be partly motivated by "other" objectives. They could not understand why Spanish firms were "paying such outrageous sums of money for badly functioning and insolvent Latin American companies."[7] They generally concluded that there had to be some sort of ulterior socio-political motive behind Spain's decision to invest in this region. On the other hand, Spanish corporate respondents largely maintained that their enterprises viewed the Latin American market as an emergent economic opportunity and a great chance to improve the economic and political environments of a region for which they felt a strong cultural and historical bond and affinity.

I concluded that this type of survey analysis was leading my study nowhere. Since Spanish and U.S. investors had opposing economic interests in Latin America and both seemed to have a keen interest in projecting a positive public image at home and abroad, it was difficult to glean from their respective responses and public statements whether or not Spanish investors had pursued a set of ulterior socio-political objectives in Latin America. Also, it was impossible to establish reliable evidence of economic and political collusion between the government and the investment sector in Spain through context analysis of the public record, interviews of key decision-makers, and process-tracing of the investment drive since 1990.

To circumvent these shortcomings and obtain a more balanced explanation of the domestic and international political nature of Spanish direct investment in Latin America, I executed an internet-based, tri-continental survey of the public perceptions and opinions of the people of Spain, Latin America, and the U.S.A. I prepared three versions of the same survey for the three audiences: one version was to gauge the perception of the Spanish population regarding their national enterprises' investment drive in Latin America; a second version targeted the U.S. public to assess their attitude toward Spanish investment strategy and how they view that process; and a third version focused on the perception of the Latin American countries and how they perceive FDI in general for their economic development and their perception of both Spanish and U.S. FDI in their respective countries.

In addition, for the Spanish case I controlled the sample by measuring the public opinion of the people through a telephone survey of 600 subjects in three mid-size cities in different regions. This methodological approach is consistent with the basic premise of this study. I believe that neither governmental nor entrepreneurial decision-makers can be sheltered from and indifferent to the mood and opinion of the population at large regarding important national decisions such as a major investment drive in a highly risky socio-economic and political environment. Accordingly, I contend here that if one is able to assess reasonably closely how the people of Spain, Latin America, and the U.S. view the Spanish investment process in Latin America, it is possible to impute a discrete causation regarding the socio-political motives surrounding the national decision to invest heavily in Latin America.

Data presentation

The data gathered for this study was derived from two separate sources. First, I conducted a tri-continental, internet-based survey over a two-year period from October 2002 to October 2004. This was a purposive, open-sample survey to gauge discretely general trends in the opinion and perception of the public in Spain, the U.S., and Latin America regarding the nature and international impact of Spanish direct investment in Latin America since 1990. Each version of this survey included fourteen different questions constituting five different categories. First, I established the level of public awareness about the existence and magnitude of Spanish FDIs in Latin America. Second, I assessed how the public viewed the nature and effects of Spanish direct investment on Latin American countries. Third, I asked the public to compare and evaluate the nature of Spanish and U.S. investment processes. Fourth, I asked the public to define what they thought to be the motivations behind Spanish foreign investments. The last set of questions explored whether or not the three different population samples viewed or perceived any sort of collusion and collaboration between the public and private sectors in Spain regarding the investment drive in Latin America. This attempt produced a total of 1753 responses: 648 from Spanish nationals; 353 from U.S. nationals; and 752 from various Latin American countries.

This first survey (for summary of the results, see Appendix 1) was intended to be only a preliminary and unscientific effort to evaluate randomly general opinion patterns in several countries concerning the nature, motivations, incentives, objectives, and impact of Spanish investment in Latin America. Hence, its methodology prevented me from gauging precisely the statistical significance and confidence level of the results for the causal relations of the model discussed earlier in this chapter. The data, nevertheless, revealed some interesting results that corroborated strongly the causal argument of this study. The information obtained clearly warranted a further scientific polling of the Spanish population. Therefore I executed a second survey of the Spanish public from October 15 to November 15, 2004 (for summary of the results, see Appendix 2). This attempt aimed at surveying a representative sample of the Spanish population on the same themes evaluated previously.

Utilizing a standard simple random method for the second and shorter survey of Spanish nationals, I identified three small cities from the 2001 Spanish National Census. These cities were situated in different regions of Spain and their combined population total was over 50,000 people. Then, I tried to reach randomly 600 telephone numbers listed in the electronic version of the Spanish telephone directory at http:www.paginasblancas.es/. I obtained 387 respondents scattered in the following manner: 113 from Cangas del Narcea, Asturias; 144 from Navalmoral de la Mata, Cáceres; and 130 from Hondarribia, Guipúzcoa. The number of respondents to the telephone survey provides my study with a better than 95% confidence level about the causal relations stipulated in the model. Evidently the empirical results obtained in the second survey are significant in their own right and quite useful to either confirm or falsify some of the unscientific findings revealed in the first and less rigorous polling method of the Spanish public. The primary objective of the second opinion poll was to ascertain whether or not the findings of the first survey could be used to infer causality about the nature and motivations of Spain's foreign economic policy towards Latin America.

Data analysis: Findings and conclusions

The data compiled in the first survey for this study reveal that an average 75% of the Spanish and Latin American respondents are aware that Spain and the U.S. are the two largest state-investors in Latin America. In Spain, this finding is corroborated in the second, simple random sample analysis of the population of three small, representative cities. According to the second polling, with a better than 95% confidence level, 59% of Spaniards are cognizant of this foreign economic development. Thus, given the levels of awareness in these three regions, the results are important for several reasons. First, these findings demonstrate that further questioning of the Spanish and Latin American publics about the impact, nature, socio-political motivations, and public perception of Spain's investment drive in Latin America will test a fairly knowledgeable population. Second, the significant level of public awareness in Spain and Latin America—and the relative ignorance of the U.S. public about this matter—disclose the socio-political importance that each people attach to something as arcane and remote as international capital flows and Spanish direct investment in Latin America. Finally, the distinct levels of public knowledge about this economic development help explain the divergent public perceptions, beliefs, and attitudes in Spain, the U.S., and Latin America regarding the social and political impacts of international investment in developing countries.

On the socio-political impact of Spanish direct investment in Latin America, questions 2, 3, and 4 in the first survey reveal some interesting attitudinal patterns. First, the purposive, open-sample survey demonstrates that the Spanish and U.S. publics coincide in their assessments of the socio-political impact of foreign investment in general and Spanish investment in particular on Latin American societies. While an average 69% of the total respondents in Spain and the U.S. see FDI generally and Spanish FDI in particular as beneficial, a combined 94% of the Latin American public perceive FDI as either inconsequential (22%) or harmful (53%) for the economic growth and development of Latin America. A similar trend is registered when respondents evaluate the impact of FDI generally and Spanish in particular on the political and economic sovereignty of Latin America. A combined average of 85% of Spaniards and U.S. nationals do not see any harm deriving from FDI on the political and economic independence of Latin American polities. On the other hand, 85% of Latin American respondents agree that general FDI affects negatively the political and economic sovereignty of their respective countries.

Regarding the nature of Spanish investment in Latin America, questions 5, 6, and 7 in the first survey expose several interesting public opinion patterns. First, an average 44% of Spanish and Latin American nationals believe that Spanish FDI in Latin America is motivated by political and economic rivalry with the U.S. This is an important disclosure about how much of the general public in two different continents believe that there is a political dimension to Spain's economic behavior in Latin America. It is interesting to underscore that important segments of the public in Spain and Latin America see a real and palpable factor in the Spanish and U.S. rivalry over influence and economic resources in Latin America. This finding contrasts sharply with an overwhelming 85% of the U.S. respondents who believe that the Spanish investment process was purely motivated by economic and lucrative objectives. Third, the cultural affinity and altruistic motivations arguments are weakly supported by only 20% of Spanish nationals. This rationale received only a meekly average 7% support among U.S. and Latin American respondents. Fourth, on the comparison of Spanish and U.S. direct investments in Latin America, 84% of U.S. nationals take a very un-nationalistic stance and respond that Spanish and U.S. direct investments are equally interventionist. The Spaniards, on the other hand, respond in more nationalistic terms. 60% of the Spanish nationals consider Spain's investment less interventionist than those from the U.S. Finally, on the potential threat of a Spanish-American union to U.S. economic interests in Latin America, an average 81% of the U.S. and Latin American nationals, trailed closely by 61% of Spaniards, think that this is a real possibility. In all, these findings strongly buttress the notion that any economic activity is influenced and contextualized by the people's socio-political beliefs. Ultimately these attitudes influence the foreign economic policy decision process in the respective countries.

The last major themes of the surveys — the causes, socio-political motivations, and public attitudes in Spain about its investment program — are addressed in the remainder of the surveys. First, on the question of whether Spanish investment in Latin America is the result of planned state investment policy and/or collusion between the public and the private sectors, 54% of U.S. nationals do not see this as a possibility. On the other hand, 78% in Spain, and 70% of the respondents in Latin America see this as a strong reality (question 8). Again, specifically for the case of Spain, this finding is corroborated by the second survey, when 65% of the respondents strongly believe (question 5) in the possibility of close coordination and collusion between the state and the private investment sector. When the respondents appraise the same relation about U.S. investment in the region (question 9), only 38% of U.S. respondents consider it possible. In contrast, 82% of Spaniards and 72% of Latin Americans believe in a planned state policy and/or collusion between the private and public sectors in the U.S.

The opinion pattern exposed in questions 8 and 9 are corroborated by the answers to other questions in the rest of the first survey. For example, when Spanish nationals respond to question 12 about possible "collaboration" instead of the more sinister concept of "collusion" between the private and public sectors in Spain, 84% consider this a strong possibility. Also, in question 14, all respondents are either free to reject the assertion of collusion between the private and public sectors, or to accept it. If the respondents agree with the contention of this question, then they must classify the socio-political motives for Spanish FDIs in Latin America, rather than in other potentially more profitable regions of the world. It is impressive to observe, however, that while 49% of U.S. nationals reject this premise, only an average of 16% of Spaniards and Latin Americans disagree with the statement. Further, an average of 61% of Spanish and Latin Americans argue that Spain chose to invest heavily in Latin America either to challenge U.S.

economic and political leadership — a claim, by the way, supported only by 3% of U.S. nationals — or to capitalize from the similarities of economic practices and business ethics between Spain and Latin America.

The issue of Spain's challenge to U.S. interests in Latin America is present, also, in question 10 of the first survey. Responding to this question as whether or not the respondents consider Spain's main motivation for investment in Latin America as its desire to regain its lost Great Power status and political influence in the region, an average of 55% of Spanish and Latin American nationals, and only 17% of U.S. respondents, consider this a strong possibility. Finally, question 11 of the first survey demonstrates a very proud Spanish public of the direct investment drive in Latin America. 87% of the Spaniards feel either satisfied (24.53%) or proud (61.88%) of Spain's economic role in the region. This finding is confirmed by the results of the second and shorter survey in question 2, where 86% of Spanish respondents are either satisfied (27.64%) or proud (58.67%) of Spain's investment in Latin America since 1990. On the other hand, while 87% of U.S. respondents feel indifferent to Spanish economic involvement in the region, 77% of Latin American nationals feel either indifferent (22%) or dissatisfied (55%) with the new Spanish economic involvement in Latin America.

Finally, on the more direct query (question 13) on either the political or the economic motivations of Spanish direct investment in Latin America, almost 70% of the Spanish respondents think that "politics more than economics motivated Spanish direct investment in Latin America." This is strongly substantiated in question 3 of the second, telephone survey, where 58% of the respondents in Spain believe that politics more than economics motivated Spanish investment in Latin America in the 1990s. Also, 68% of Spanish nationals indicate in question 4 of the telephone survey that they consider Spanish direct investments in Latin America as part of Spain's foreign economic policies. On the other hand, 51% of Latin American respondents believe that politics more than economics motivated the Spanish investment drive into Latin America. Only U.S. nationals think (67% of respondents) that economics is the motivating factor for the Spanish investment drive in Latin America since the 1990s.

Conclusions

The findings discussed above present a fairly strong corroboration of the causal argument of this chapter. First, the results from the two surveys demonstrate decidedly that the Spanish investment drive in Latin America is part of Spain's foreign economic policy objectives. This point is confirmed in various forms in questions 8, 12, and 14 of the first survey and in question 4 of the second, telephone polling. Second, Spaniards are clearly "proud" and "satisfied" with the investment program in Latin America (see responses to question 3). This level of satisfaction and awareness lends political support and political capital to the governmental and entrepreneurial authorities to pursue their investment program in a highly risky economic region. Third, there is ample confirmation from Spanish nationals that politics, rather than economic considerations, has been the major force of the investment drive in Latin America (see question 3 of the second survey). Fourth, the general public in Spain considers the Spanish investment drive in Latin America since the 1990s has been an integral part of Spain's foreign economic policy objectives (see responses to question 4). Finally, there is a strong corroboration that most Spaniards believe in a "close coordination and collusion" between the public and the private sectors (see responses to question 5).

On another level, this study demonstrates that the external environment was not unforgiving, at least from the vantage point of the U.S. It is interesting to confirm that most respondents in the U.S. do not see or believe in the socio-political overtones of Spanish FDI. In fact, most of the U.S. nationals either have a very scant knowledge of Spain's economic role in Latin America or believe that it is part of the economic dynamic of the world market system. In short, those polled in the U.S. do not see a threat coming from Spain. But the external environment is more problematic when examined from the Latin American angle. Most Latin American respondents fear equally Spanish and U.S. investments. Most respondents in the host countries believe that foreign capital flows are detrimental to their economic independence, growth, and political sovereignty. This reaction from Latin Americans renders the cultural affinity argument doubtful.

This chapter does not provide a "smoking gun" or concrete data establishing a robust support of the causal link between the Spanish political authorities and the entrepreneurs who have invested heavily in Latin America since 1990. Nevertheless, the study demonstrates rather convincingly, first, that people in Spain viewed these capital flows as politically motivated and as a sign of pride for the new Spain in the post-democratic transition. Also, this chapter reveals that the external environment was led by an international economic leader who seemed to welcome — as measured by the public responses in the U.S. — this type of economic activity, despite the public and loud discontent that was registered in most the host countries in Latin America against FDI in general. In all, if one accepts the basic premise of the model expounded above that societal factors, such as public opinion and perception, do influence the socio-political milieu where elected officials and entrepreneurs have to make important economic decisions, then one can surmise that Spanish direct investments in Latin America entailed a socio-political dimension in addition to the obvious pecuniary objectives of the program. To neglect this important aspect of the Spanish investment drive amounts to serious limitation of the general understanding of the multiplicity of factors that may influence the foreign economic policies of a nation-state.

Appendix 1

Summary of the Surveys of Spanish, U.S., and Latin American Nationals' Public Opinion on Spanish Direct Investment in Latin America

Organizer:
Félix E. Martín, Ph.D., Assistant Professor in the Department of International Relations at Florida International University, Miami, Florida, e-mail address: martinf@fiu.edu

Level of Analysis:
International.

Population Sample or Universe:
Spanish, U.S., and Latin American nationals 18 and older.

Sample Size:
1753 individuals responded to the questionnaire via electronic mail. This sample was obtained randomly.

Distribution of the Population:
648 Spanish Nationals
(Andalucía 37; Asturias 23; Cantabria 27; Castilla-León 58; Castilla-La Mancha 53; Cataluña 78; País Vasco 89; Galicia 83; Islas Canarias 48; Comunidad de Valencia 21; Comunidad de Madrid 114; others 17.)
353 U.S. Nationals
U.S. respondents were not classified by region or state.
752 Latin American Nationals
(Argentina 167; Brazil 109; Colombia 81; Chile 78; Mexico 114; Peru 76; Venezuela 103; and other countries 24.)

Procedure:
This is a purposive, open-sample survey to gauge the public opinion and perception of Spanish, U.S., and Latin American nationals regarding the nature, incentives, objectives, and impact of Spanish direct investments in Latin America since 1990. I mailed three national versions of the same survey to electronic addresses in Spain, the U.S.A., and Latin America. To create a multiplying effect, I requested from the first wave of recipients to forward the same to their personal and professional contacts in their respective regions and countries. I repeated this procedure twice, producing a total of 1753 individual responses.

Dates:
September 2002 to September 2004. The initial survey was mailed out July 2002. Since, I electronically mailed out three waves of the same survey, the first attempt produced 704 respondents. The two subsequent appeals produced 1049 additional respondents for an overall total of 1753 respondents as of September 6, 2004.

1. Are you aware that Spain and the U.S.A. are the two largest investors in Latin America?

Spanish Nationals

	%	Number
Yes	64.70	419
No	35.30	229
TOTAL	100.00	648

U.S. Nationals

	%	Number
Yes	23.50	83
No	76.50	270
TOTAL	100.00	353

Latin American Nationals

	%	Number
Yes	89.50	673
No	10.50	79
TOTAL	100.00	752

2. In general, how would you define the impact of foreign direct investment in Latin America for regional economic growth and development?

Spanish Nationals

	%	Number
Inconsequential	21.75	141
Beneficial	67.00	434
Harmful	11.25	73
TOTAL	100.	648

U.S. Nationals

	%	Number
Inconsequential	27.80	98
Beneficial	70.50	249
Harmful	1.70	6
TOTAL	100.00	353

Latin American Nationals

	%	Number
Inconsequential	22.20	167
Beneficial	25.70	193
Harmful	52.10	392
TOTAL	100.00	752

3. Do you consider that foreign direct investment in Latin American countries undermines the sovereignty and economic independence of these countries?

Spanish Nationals

	%	Number
Yes	16.36	106
No	83.64	542
TOTAL	100.00	648

U.S. Nationals

	%	Number
Yes	13.00	46
No	87.00	307
TOTAL	100.00	353

Latin American Nationals

	%	Number
Yes	79.52	598
No	20.48	154
TOTAL	100.00	752

4. In particular, how would you define the impact of Spanish direct investment in Latin America for regional economic growth and development?

Spanish Nationals

	%	Number
Inconsequential	18.80	122
Beneficial	77.60	503
Harmful	3.60	23
TOTAL	100.00	648

U.S. Nationals

	%	Number
Inconsequential	27.20	96
Beneficial	71.70	253
Harmful	1.10	4
TOTAL	100.00	353

Latin American Nationals

	%	Number
Inconsequential	25.70	193
Beneficial	30.30	228
Harmful	44.00	331
TOTAL	100.00	752

5. How would you define the nature of Spanish direct investment in Latin America?

Spanish Nationals

	%	Number
Purely motivated by economic and lucrative objectives	35.33	229
Motivated by political and economic rivalry against the U.S.	41.82	271
Spanish neocolonialism and a desire to re-conquest Latin America	2.63	17
Partly motivated by altruism and cultural affinity	20.22	131
TOTAL	100.00	648

U.S. Nationals

	%	Number
Purely motivated by economic and lucrative objectives	85.50	302
Motivated by political and economic rivalry against the U.S.	9.70	34
Spanish neocolonialism and a desire to re-conquest Latin America	1.10	4
Partly motivated by altruism and cultural affinity	3.70	13
TOTAL	100.00	353

Latin American Nationals

	%	Number
Purely motivated by economic and lucrative objectives	38.20	288
Motivated by political and economic rivalry against the U.S.	47.50	357
Spanish neocolonialism and a desire to re-conquest Latin America	3.90	29
Partly motivated by altruism and cultural affinity	10.40	78
TOTAL	100.00	752

6. In comparison with U.S. direct investment in Latin America, how would you rate the nature of Spanish direct investment in the region?

Spanish Nationals

	%	Number
As interventionist as that from the U.S.	35.80	232
Less interventionist than that from the U.S.	60.60	393
More interventionist than that from the U.S.	3.60	23
TOTAL	100.00	648

U.S. Nationals

	%	Number
As interventionist as that from the U.S.	84.10	297
Less interventionist than that from the U.S.	13.60	48
More interventionist than that from the U.S.	2.30	8
TOTAL	100.00	353

Latin American Nationals

	%	Number
As interventionist as that from the U.S.	41.10	309
Less interventionist than that from the U.S.	31.50	237
More interventionist than that from the U.S.	27.40	206
TOTAL	100.00	752

7. Do you think that a Spanish-American economic union would undermine U.S. economic interests in Latin America?

Spanish Nationals

	%	Number
Yes	61.30	397
No	38.70	251
TOTAL	100.00	648

U.S. Nationals

	%	Number
Yes	81.90	289
No	18.10	64
TOTAL	100.00	353

Latin American Nationals

	%	Number
Yes	80.20	603
No	19.80	149
TOTAL	100.00	752

8. Do you think that the large increase in Spanish investments in Latin America in the last fifteen years is the result of a planned state investment policy and/or collusion between the public and private sectors in Spain?

Spanish Nationals

	%	Number
Yes	78.50	509
No	21.50	139
TOTAL	100.00	648

U.S. Nationals

	%	Number
Yes	45.30	160
No	54.70	193
TOTAL	100.00	353

Latin American Nationals

	%	Number
Yes	70.10	527
No	29.90	225
TOTAL	100.00	752

9. Do you think that U.S. direct investments in Latin America are the result of a planned state investment policy and/or collusion between the public and private sectors in the U.S.A.?

Spanish Nationals

	%	Number
Yes	82.90	537
No	17.10	111
TOTAL	100.00	648

U.S. Nationals

	%	Number
Yes	38.50	136
No	61.50	217
TOTAL	100.00	353

Latin American Nationals

	%	Number
Yes	72.20	543
No	27.80	209
TOTAL	100.00	752

10. Do you consider that Spanish direct investments in Latin America are motivated mainly by Spain's political desire to regain its lost Great Power status and political influence in Latin America *vis-à-vis* the U.S.A.?

Spanish Nationals

	%	Number
Yes	56.10	364
No	43.90	284
TOTAL	100.00	648

U.S. Nationals

	%	Number
Yes	17.00	60
No	83.00	293
TOTAL	100.00	353

Latin American Nationals

	%	Number
Yes	53.00	399
No	47.00	353
TOTAL	100.00	752

11. How do you feel about the dramatic increase of Spanish direct investment in Latin America since 1990?

Spanish Nationals

	%	Number
Indifferent	4.47	29
Satisfied	24.53	159
Dissatisfied	9.12	59
Proud	61.88	401
TOTAL	100.00	648

U.S. Nationals

	%	Number
Indifferent	87.53	309
Satisfied	10.48	37
Dissatisfied	1.99	7
Proud	0	0
TOTAL	100.00	353

Latin American Nationals

	%	Number
Indifferent	21.67	163
Satisfied	16.88	127
Dissatisfied	55.18	415
Proud	6.27	47
TOTAL	100.00	752

12. Do you think that there has been a close collaboration between the Spanish public and private sectors to increase the volume of direct investment in Latin America since 1990?

Spanish Nationals

	%	Number
Yes	83.60	542
No	16.40	106
TOTAL	100.00	648

U.S. Nationals

	%	Number
Yes	53.50	189
No	46.40	164
TOTAL	100.00	353

Latin American Nationals

	%	Number
Yes	79.40	597
No	20.60	155
TOTAL	100.00	752

13. Would you say that Spanish direct investment in Latin America since 1990 have been motivated by … ?

Spanish Nationals

	%	Number
Politics more than economics	69.90	453
Economics more than politics	30.10	195
TOTAL	100.00	648

U.S. Nationals

	%	Number
Politics more than economics	32.90	116
Economics more than politics	67.10	237
TOTAL	100.00	353

Latin American Nationals

	%	Number
Politics more than economics	50.70	381
Economics more than politics	49.30	371
TOTAL	100.00	752

14. If you believe that there is collusion between the public and private sectors in Spain, would you argue that these opted to invest in Latin America, rather than in other potentially more profitable world regions:

Spanish Nationals

	%	Number
I do not agree with the premise of the question	17.40	113
Because of altruistic investment motivations	12.00	78
Because of the similarity in economic practices and business ethics	32.00	207
To challenge U.S. economic and political leadership	32.60	211
Because it was facilitated by cultural and linguistic affinity	6.00	39
TOTAL	100.00	648

U.S. Nationals

	%	Number
I do not agree with the premise of the question	49.60	175
Because of altruistic investment motivations	5.90	21
Because of the similarity in economic practices and business ethics	34.60	122
To challenge U.S. economic and political leadership	3.10	11
Because it was facilitated by cultural and linguistic affinity	6.80	24
TOTAL	100.00	353

Latin American Nationals

	%	Number
I do not agree with the premise of the question	15.15	114
Because of altruistic investment motivations	11.85	89
Because of the similarity in economic practices and business ethics	30.85	232
To challenge U.S. economic and political leadership	29.65	223
Because it was facilitated by cultural and linguistic affinity	12.50	94
TOTAL	100.00	752

Appendix 2

Summary of Representative, Random Sample Survey of the Public Opinion of Spanish Nationals on Spanish Direct Investment in Latin America.

Organizer:
Félix E. Martín, Ph.D., Assistant Professor in the Department of International Relations at Florida International University, Miami, Florida, e-mail address: martinf@fiu.edu.

Level of Analysis:
National.

Population Sample:
Three small cities in Spain: Cangas del Narcea, Asturias, total population 16, 340; Navalmoral de la Mata, Cáceres, total population 16, 382; and Hondarribia, Guipúzcoa, total population 15, 493.

Sample Size:
387 individuals responded to the questionnaire over the telephone. This sample was selected randomly by calling 600 local telephone numbers accessed at http://www.paginasblancas.es/.

Distribution of the Population:
387 Spanish Nationals: (113 from Cangas del Narcea, Asturias; 144 from Navalmoral de la Mata, Cáceres; and 130 from Hondarribia, Guipúzcoa.). Total population in Spain is 40,847371 as reported in the 2003 Spanish National Census, http://www.ine.es/censo/es/listatablas.jsp?table=tablas/nacional/NP3.html.

Procedure:
This is a representative, random sample survey to gauge the public opinion and perception of Spanish nationals regarding the nature, incentives, and foreign policy objectives of Spanish direct investments in Latin America since 1990. It was conducted in Spanish and translated here by the author.

Dates:
October 15 to November 15, 2004. The survey was conducted over the telephone, selecting numbers randomly from the white pages of Spain's National Telephone Directory.

1. Are you aware that Spain and the U.S.A. are the two largest foreign investors in Latin America?

	%	Number
Yes	59.18	229
No	40.82	158
TOTAL	100.00	387

2. How do you feel about Spanish investment in Latin America since 1990?

	%	Number
Satisfied	27.64	107
Dissatisfied	13.69	53
Proud	58.67	227
TOTAL	100.00	387

3. Would you say that Spanish direct investment in Latin America since 1990 have been motivated by. . .?

	%	Number
Politics more than economics	58.14	225
Economics more than politics	41.86	162
TOTAL	100.00	387

4. Do you think that Spanish investments in Latin America are part of Spain's foreign economic policy objectives since the 1990s?

	%	Number
Yes	67.96	263
No	32.04	124
TOTAL	100.00	387

5. Do you believe that there has been a close coordination and collusion in Spain between the public and the private investment sectors?

	%	Number
Yes	64.35	249
No	35.65	138
TOTAL	100.	387

Notes

1   Evidence of this position can be found in Grossman (1994: pp. 8-10) and Ohmae (1990).

2   In chapter 11, Seiglie discusses the risks involved, and demonstrates the poor returns on investments in the energy sector in Latin America.

3   On how the Spanish government is helping multinational enterprises do business in Latin America, see R. Muñoz (2004).

4   Foreign economic policy is defined in terms of governmental action to affect the international economic environment for the protection and advancement of its national interest; see B.J. Cohen (1968: 10).

5   On the management of the international system, see K.N. Waltz (1979), especially chapter 9.

6   For background literature on the origin and evolution of hegemonic stability theory, see Kindleberger (1974); Gilpin (1975); Krasner (1976); Keohane (1980); and Nye (1990).

7   This is part of my private correspondence with several middle-level international investment managers in Citibank and Chase. They agreed to discuss their views, but requested to maintain their identity anonymous.

References

Baldwin, D.A. (1985), *Economic Statecraft*, Princeton University Press, Princeton.

--- (1998), *Economic Statecraft*, Princeton University Press, Princeton.

Cohen, B.J. (ed.) (1968), *American Foreign Economic Policy: Essays and Comments*, Harper and Row, New York.

Doremus, P.N., W.W. Keller, L.W. Pauly, and S. Reich (1998), *The Myth of the Global Corporation*, Princeton University Press, Princeton.

Gilpin, R. (1975), *U.S. Power and the Multinational Corporation: The Political Economy of Foreign Direct Investment*, Basic Books, Inc. Publishers, New York.

--- (2001), *Global Political Economy: Understanding the International Economic Order*, Princeton University Press, Princeton.

Grossman G.M. (ed.) (1994), *Imperfect Competition and International Trade*, MIT Press, Cambridge.

Holsti, O.R., R.M. Siverson, and A.L. George (eds.) (1980), *Change in the International System*, Westview Press, Boulder.

Katzenstein, P.J. (ed.) (1978), *Between Power and Plenty: Foreign Economic Policies of Advanced Industrial States*, University of Wisconsin Press, Madison.

Keohane, R.O. (1980), "The Theory of Hegemonic Stability and Changes in International Economic Regimes, 1967-1977," in O.R. Holsti, R.M. Siverson, and A.L. George (eds.), *Change in the International System*, Westview Press, Boulder, pp. 131-162.

Kindleberger, C.P. (1974), *The World in Depression, 1929—1939*, University of California Press, Berkeley.

Krasner, S.D. (1976), "State Power and the Structure of International Trade," *World Politics*, vol. 28, no. 3, April, pp. 317—347.

--- (1978), "United States Commercial and Monetary Policy: Unraveling the Paradox of External Strength and Internal Weakness," in P.J. Katzenstein, pp. 51-87.

Migdal, J.S. (1988), *Strong Societies and Weak States: State-Society Relations in the Third World*, Princeton University Press, Princeton.

--- (2001), *State in Society: Studying How States and Societies Transform and Constitute One Another*, Cambridge University Press, Cambridge.

Muñoz, R. (2004), "El Gobierno crea un foro empresarial para defender intereses en Latinoamérica," *El PAÍS*, Economía, November 9, p. 51.

Nye, J.S. (1990), *Bound to Lead: The Changing Nature of American Power*, Basic Books, New York.

Ohmae, K. (1990), *The Borderless World: Power and Strategy in the Interlinked Economy*, Harper Business, New York.

Sally, R. (1994), "Multinational Enterprises, Political Economy and Institutional Theory: Embeddedness in the Context of Internationalization," *Review of International Political Economy*, vol. 1, no. 1, Spring, pp. 161-192.

Seiglie, C. (2005), "Challenges for Spanish Investments in the Latin American Energy Industry", in F. Martín and P. Toral (eds.), *Latin America's Quest for Globalization*, Aldershot, Ashgate, pp. 253-261.

Waltz, K.N. (1979), *Theory of International Politics*, Addison-Wesley, Reading.

Chapter 13

The Latin American Image of Spain in the Aftermath of Recent Investments

Joaquín Roy

Introductory considerations: mutual perceptions

With the turn of the century, in the context of political upheavals, a climate of economic crisis, most especially in sectors recently privatized where foreign investment is heavy, the image of Spain in Latin America (more specifically in Argentina) has become a matter of concern for Spanish government officials, businesspeople, media, and public at large. While the general image of Spain as whole can be termed as positive (about 60% of Latin Americans consider it good), the role of Spanish investment received a mixed reaction: about a third think its has benefited Latin American economies, more than a third labeled negatively, and about 25% has no opinion.[1] However, the high visibility of Spanish investment in sectors of greater social impact, have caused a notable deterioration in the public perception of the European country that is closer to the human fabric of Latin America. Although the injuries are not terminal or fatal, the future, permanent consequences still remain unknown (Ceccine and Zicolillo, 2002; Petroselli, 2001; *Diario 16*, 2001). On the other side of the equation, the perception of Latin America (specifically, Argentina) in Spain (and in Europe, in general) has deteriorated, confirming a negative trend of a chronic outlook in the last quarter of the preceding century, softened only by brief periods of hope (Abellán, 2001; A.M.A./C.R.G., 2001; Patten, Lamy and Solbes, 2002; Rebosio, 2002; Yárnoz, 2002). This cloudy perception of Latin America will not help alleviate the difficulties associated with Spain's economic and political activities.

The first part of this double diagnosis is, ironically, a collateral consequence of Spanish investments in Latin America, a leading force in the recovery of the continent's economies.[2] On paper, it would appear that this business-oriented move from Spain was an explicit European endorsement of the IMF-prescribed liberalizing measures implemented by the Latin American governments and the perennial demands of the United States. The investments also expressed a vote of confidence on the consolidation of democracy and a reassurance that Spanish companies felt at ease in a climate of legally protected economic transactions.

However, the deterioration of the image of the Latin American political atmosphere in the eyes of Europeans, especially Spaniards, simply represents the settling of a long trend in negative European attitudes, losing hope after the return of democratic rule to most of the subcontinent. The "third wave of democratization," according to Huntington's label, had lost its strength and appeal. This negative perception was comparatively reinforced by the rebirth and consolidation of the Iberian democratic regimes after the end of the Franco regime and the post-Salazar governments. On the economic side, caution was dictated by the frustration of the EU caused by the absence of Mercosur's economies in meeting the expectations of effective regional integration. In essence, compared to the self-perceived political success in Iberia and the progress towards an "ever closer Union" (as stated in the Maastricht Treaty), the Latin American experience lacks clear results and future prospects remain uncertain.

An intriguing angle of the combination of these two intuitively perceptive and arbitrary lines of thought points to the fact that this situation has actually developed in a unique stage of Spain's international activities. In contrast with Spain's historical political isolation and its limited economic possibilities, Spanish companies opted for a heavy, spectacular (in terms of volume and visibility) investment policy in Latin America in the 1990s. This was an apparent crowning touch of the democratic Spanish government in its political backing of the difficult transition process of most of the Latin American countries in the 1980s.

The topic of a negative backlash against Spain in the wake of investment and politico-economic failures in some Latin American countries (notably, Argentina) in the first years of the new century has attracted the attention of numerous media observers, has been the constant subject of rushed opinions, and has alarmed casual readers of the international pages of leading Spanish newspapers and magazines. Difficulties associated with Spanish investments have ceased to be a simple business problem normally tucked away in the economic sections of newspapers, but have become a political problem. This situation has also caught the eyes of government officials and perceptive think-tank researchers. It has not yet become a sub-genre in the field of Spain-Latin American relations, but it may well be in the future, as is the case of the U.S. image in Latin America. Based on its importance for the Spanish economy, it is expected that in years to procede, the political and economic consequences and perceptions of Spain's investments in Latin America will become the object of rigorous studies.

The present commentary only intends to target some basic considerations and to open some avenues for further analysis. It does not intend to provide a scientific, data-oriented explanation or inquiry into the consequences of the recent Spanish investment in Latin America in terms of the image of Spain, but simply to provide some ground for interpretation, based on intuitive observation and a review of some relevant dimensions of the history of Spain's relations with Latin America. It is also limited to the filtering of these perceptions as expressed in the Spanish media (although some of the commentaries were actually crafted by Latin American authors and politicians), mostly newspapers and magazines, and secondarily in Latin American books of an investigative, journalistic, and impressionistic nature, however well documented (*Cambio 16*, 2002; Cecchine and Zicolillo, 2002). The fact that this pattern reveals a self-imposed punishment, makes the image of Spain a target for foreign competitors to worsen it and exploit it in their benefit, in line for the ancient way the enemies of imperial Spain used the "black legend." This ever present attitude in the Americas, still surviving in the United Kingdom, has been reinforced by a sudden loose campaign of "bashing Europe," in the wake of the disagreement between the United States and Europeans regarding the way to deal with the post-September 11 problems, a trend that worsened with the war in Iraq. A "blaming Spain" strategy for old or new problems has been collecting steam in the context of economic and political problems in Latin America, by virtue of an odd, ad hoc coalition formed by U.S. interests and Latin American activists and media (Roy 2002a, 2002b).

In all, this essay is a reading of a provisional Spanish perception of the current image of Spain in Latin America, especially in Argentina, in the context of Spanish investment. It has to be placed in the context of Spain's relations with Latin America in the aftermath of the extraordinary effort of closer linkages as a result of the commemoration of 1992, with mutually beneficial projects such as the Ibero-American summits and the creation of an Ibero-American Space and community of interests (Roy, 1997).

The image of Spain: A change for the worse

In essence, the negative change in the perception of Spain is a drastic contrast with the extremely positive perception enjoyed by Spain's many cultural and political dimensions, as well as the warm, intimate personal relationship between millions of Latin American families and those in the *madre patria*. In the eyes of Latin American political observers, Spain's political transition is still considered by some as a role model worthy of adopting, making the Spanish process synonymous with a successful regime change and a must-read for experts in what in some Latin American circles is called *transitología*.[3] Moreover, the material and moral help in terms of development assistance and political support of the incipient resurgent democracies in Latin America provided by the new democratic regime of Spain is still considered as valuable capital that was well invested and still renders substantial returns.

In contrast, in recent years Spain's activities seem to be the object of criticism and accusations of economic imperialism and blunt arrogance, charged with causing some of the current socioeconomic ills in Latin America. Economic deterioration and rising unemployment in some key Latin American countries has resulted in a depletion of savings. Banking, one of the central sectors of Spain's investment, has been singled out of the culprit not only of bad economic policies, but also of negative political consequences. The discovery of corruption practices in the acquisition of certain privatized companies and the illegal or improper channeling of funds to the campaigns of political figures in polemic-plagued countries has been the focus of media attention and the irritation of the poor majority in Latin American societies.

This intriguing combined trend has been generated simultaneously by the novel way in which Spain's judicial power became involved in seeking punishment for the human rights violations committed during the Latin American dictatorships of the 1970s and 1980s (especially in Chile). While internal arrangements such as "punto final" laws, or extreme military pressure had muted the prosecution of abuses, Spanish judge Baltasar Garzón undertook the task of unearthing the recent Latin American past, pursuing the extradition of General Pinochet from London, attracting the wrath of the conservative establishment. The negative result of Garzón's activities was that the positive image of Spain's transition now appeared to reveal a unique double standard: Spain elected to forgive and forget the past, but opted to punish Latin American human rights abuses. The collateral consequence was that while in the past, the left (a sector that applauded Garzón's actions with gratitude) had the monopoly on anti-imperialist critical views, in recent years the displaced establishment has joined in denouncing foreign intervention in Latin America.

The Latin American setting: From political confrontation to social clash

This complex panorama has been generated in the context of an even more perturbing and novel trend in the socioeconomic atmosphere of some important Latin American countries. It is a fact that the economic evolution has produced an increase in poverty and income gap.[4] However, the general situation no longer threatens only one sector of society, such as the economic and social oppression of the lower classes, or the need of the upper classes to protect themselves against high crimes. Economic uncertainty and fear of kidnappings now affect all strata. This is an important aspect that is not only perceived by the expert elite and scholars, but is also detected by the masses on the lower end of the economic scale, in going about their everyday activities.

The fact is that Latin American societies have experienced an unstoppable drastic shift from political violence to confrontation and criminal activity of an economic and social nature. The perceptions of civil society and casual outside observers backed by solid research in the best tradition of social sciences is that the apparent or alleged benefits of liberalization, privatization, and economic integration not only have produced an alarming increase in income distribution inequality, but have engrossed the ranks of individuals and families with chronic poverty levels.

To use a fitting image used by a European observer (Ramonet, 2002), in the past when anger propelled activists, seekers of justice and wouldbe revolutionaries, they would grab a gun and would go to the mountains to organize guerrilla movements or rush directly downtown and storm the presidential palace. Today, they walk to the bank with weapons in hand and extract what in their internal logic is considered by modern-day political activists as "revolutionary taxes." Worse, they engage in an alarmingly growing and profitable industry of kidnappings seeking ransom. The novel angle of this old-fashioned criminal activity is that it not only affects the rich and famous as was the case in the past, but today the victims are from the lower middle classes. While extortion used to have seven-digit expectations, today authors of "express kidnappings" in middle-class Buenos Aires expect a weekly salary in exchange for survival.

The combined result of these trends is that for the first time in the history of Latin America three distinct sectors are united by fear. The top is as scared as it was perennially in the past. However, now it feels that it is dependent on economic interests based not only in New York, but also in Europe. These interests are now perceived to be impersonal. In the past, the economic establishment in a Latin American capital was composed of a good old-boys club, transactions were made in Spanish, and foreign influence was administered by straw men as delegates from the U.S. capital. Power to be used in an emergency was kept off-shore in the form of U.S. navy vessels loaded with marines. This is not the case any more. Now all seems, in the eyes of observers with sometime comparative terms, to be run by officers of a special kind of international organization, with no clear national anchoring. In the midst of these new scenarios, concrete Spanish investments became the norm. What was impersonal in the past later became very personal. And this time it spoke Spanish, again. But it was a different kind of Spanish, strong in interdentals, sounding like sermons from the pulpit, with strange reminiscences of grandfather's accent. In some Latin American cities, it seemed as if now some people spoke louder than the natives.

The middle class, in contrast to the expectations of scholars and political idealists, began to shrink or to vanish. Instead of providing social mobility, liberalization and privatization are now generating the destruction of the feeble middle class. Economic pressure and crime have propelled the middle sectors of Bogotá and Buenos Aires, among other Latin American cities, to flee to the United States, especially to Miami, joining their predecessors, the landowners and bankers of the past. In essence, they are replicating the path of the *mojados* and illegal immigrants who were supposed to be exclusively Caribbean, Central American, and mostly Mexican. Across the Atlantic, the arrival of the Latin American middle class has become a daily routine in Madrid and Barcelona. Argentines are, by far, in the lead (Socolovsky, 2002).

In Spain, more acutely than in other European countries, citizens of the Southern cone have met similar resistance or ambivalent welcome (it depends on individual circumstances) experienced by their predecessors escaping the dictatorships of Argentina, Uruguay, and Chile in the 1970s. Then, while Spain was undergoing the excruciating transformation caused by the political transition, Latin Americans had to deal with the harsh reality of economic and social downgrading. Doctors, architects, sociologists, and lawyers were forced to compete for menial jobs in a society besieged by political and economic pains. That was when the word "sudaca" was coined, the label bestowed on most Latin Americans, just as "gallego" had been imposed on all Spaniards in Cuba and Argentina.[5]

In any event, new arrivals in Spain had to deal not only with high unemployment levels, but with rigid immigration policies dictated by EU membership. This sometimes is used by European governments as a scapegoat for negative economic or social trends, or in order to justify their lack of power in facing the contractual obligations of the common policies of the European Union. In essence, when national governments conveniently claim that their hands are tied by Brussels, hiding the fact that their ministers run the shop once they set foot in the Council of the European Union (previously known as the Council of Ministers), the body that makes new laws and refines old ones. Although immigration policy and border control remain in essence a prerogative of the states – only to be coordinated in pillar three of the EU – , the blaming of Brussels has become as European as in the past when all economic and political ills of Latin America were targeted by the left as directly inflicted by the Pentagon and the CIA.

Rounding up the usual suspects: From '*Madre Patría*' to *Suegra*

It seems that this old-fashioned excuse (sported as a brand name by the Latin American political radicals and most of the intellectual ranks), of blaming the ills of their societies on the United States, has experienced a fascinating shift in rounding up the usual suspects. Now, instead of pointing to the "ugly American," they have discovered the "ugly Spaniard."

This is an apparent parallel with the urgent task of finding an enemy, as experienced by the U.S. political and military establishment once the Soviet Union vanished as a credible threat to the survival of Western civilization. Fortunately for the ones who obviously cannot sleep without the comfort of a nemesis, immediately after the fall of the Berlin Wall, Iraq came to the rescue. A long and dramatic decade later, September 11 generated an "axis of evil," but lacking the termination of Al Queda, Saddam Hussein remained (until his capture) the cause of the ills of today's world, according to the White House. In Latin America, the new economic and social circumstances urgently had to find a new enemy. And they have found it – Spain. Seeking a scapegoat is not the monopoly of one special culture. It is frequently used in the rather confusing climate of the United States in the post-September 11 situation and it was alluded to by German politicians during the legislative campaign. The quickest and cheapest excuse is to place the blame as far away as possible from the actual source of the problems – in this case, the socioeconomic heart of Latin American societies, perennially plagued by inequality and injustice. Ironically, the leftist arguments of the past are not used to explain the new situation.

When Latin Americans witnessed the modest results of II European Union-Latin American Summit held in Madrid in 2002 with no serious progress towards an agreement with Mercosur, rush commentaries alluded to the Common Agricultural Policy (CAP) of the EU as the bête noire of the Latin American interests and the main reason for European resistance to dismantling the tariff structure, especially for agriculture. The endemic lack of political will in the process of Latin American integration is never mentioned as the most formidable obstacle to gaining a competitive edge for the Latin American economies. The depressing absence of a just, balanced, and effective taxation system in most of the Latin American societies is the constant theme of European criticism, a claim that is politely filed away in the desks of Latin American governments. Right and left prefer to take the easy route and point this out to Brussels and the key members of the gang of three, composed of the IMF, the World Bank, and the EU.

Now, in the case of Spain, and most especially in the case study of Argentina, Latin Americans have opted for another brand name: *unanimismo*, as apparently coined by the Argentine sociologist Juan José Sebreli (Gaveta, 2001). Instead of collecting several sources for causes of the present ills, Argentines prefer to concentrate on only one. When the Malvinas war exploded, the "evil" British were to blame. Now it's the turn of the Spaniards.

In the case of the protest against Spanish interests, the task has been helped by the comfort of what in the Hispanic world is natural – a family affair. Harsh words are carefully meditated when they have to be translated into other languages. It is not the same to confront Americans, French, or Germans as it is to face Spaniards. In English, some expressions (gringo) become cliché, while others (to live "in the entrails of the monster") seem incomprehensible or too literary (the duet Ariel-Calibán). In Spanish, all is natural. One only has to speak in a home kitchen in Buenos Aires. "Gallegos, fuera," as a fighting slogan brandished in the Plaza de Mayo may be as extremely effective as a soccer fan song in Boca's "bombonera" stadium. When expressed by sons of *gallegos* this may sound surrealistic, to say the least. However, the fact that expressions like this were heavily used in public is proof of the seriousness of the crisis. Just in case, friendly *porteños* innovatively resorted to warn Spanish visitors not to use traditional expressions such as "vale" or "metro" (for *subte*), in order to avoid unpleasant confrontations.

Another angle that has contributed to the bitterness of some Latin American sectors, especially Argentina, is the fact that Spanish investments were actually, specifically in their first stage in the early 1990s, a sort of transfer of national sovereignty by which an Argentine state property was privatized, placed on the trading bloc, and then bought by a Spanish company whose main shareholder was the Spanish government. For some, this amounted to a switching of flags with considerable loss of national pride. After all, airliners somehow have the image of being modern vessels with all the trappings of state power. It is not by coincidence that *porteños* took to the street and soccer stadiums (even players carried banners) with slogans inspired in old-fashioned political campaigns: "Aerolíneas [as in Malvinas] serán argentines (Goitia, 2001)." Another example is the most personalized rewriting of the classic "Yankies, go home (Vázquez-Rial, 2001)" fighting flag, into an innovative transfiguration of the lyrics of a famous song: "Solo le pido a Dios/ que se vayan todos los Gallegos/ que se vayan para siempre/ Aerolíneas y Austral/ es de la gente (Zarzuela, 2001)." Even more personal, if possible: "González y Aznar, el mismo perro con distinto collar (Montoya, 2001)." And last, but not least, more obscene, in the worst Spanish-Argentine tradition: "Teque, teque, toca, toca,/ Aerolíneas no se toca, díganle a los Gallegos/ que nos chupen las pelotas (Zarzuela, 2001)." Protests against Iberia Airlines of Spain (the

Spanish flag carrier that bought the Argentine companies) became so acute that demonstrations at Buenos Aires airports made the safety of international flights so endangering that American Airlines once suspended service to Argentina (Gualdoni, 2001).

This new "special relationship" between Argentina and Spain became more acute with the election of President Néstor Kirchner. In a populist reaction to the demands from Spanish companies, the Argentine president became entangled in a controversy with the Spanish government and the influential business federation, including the use of the harshest language (Cacho, 2003; C.R.G., 2003; D'Lom, 2003; Egurbide, 2003; Jozami, 2003). The result of a war over an increase in the rates charged in the energy and telephone sectors was a further deterioration of the mutual image of both countries. As a collateral consequence, Brazil, under the new stewardship of President Lula, received the favorable attention of Spanish investors and media analysis (*Cinco Días*, 2003; Díaz-Varela, 2003; González, 2003).

The new Spain: From *bodeguero* to bankers

Part of the explanation for this new trend of the image of Spain in Latin America is the stark contrast to the stereotype of the Spaniard of the past. Long past was the time of the image of the *conquistador,* indelibly enshrined in the mythology of history and popular wisdom in both North and South America. Significantly, Latin Americans often tried to draw a line between their Spanish background (spanning from a couple of generations to colonial times) and the policies of the viceroyalty authorities. At times, it seemed like the family tree of a substantial number of Latin Americans was fond of humble origins. Well-to-do Latin Americans, often direct descendents of Spaniards who had arrived in the new lands fleeing from hunger and political persecution, gladly admitted this background, and converted the experience of their ancestors into a positive accomplishment of the Latin American societies, in a sort of replica of the U.S. dream of upward mobility.

The standard image of the Spaniards was of the political refugee of the Civil War co-opted by the Mexican government, hungry immigrants arriving in the harbors of Buenos Aires and Havana. *Gallegos* were waiters, *bodegueros*, and mom-and-pop store keepers. When visiting Latin America, U.S. tourists would find it normal to be catered to by a Spanish restaurant, flamenco show included, even thousands of miles from the Iberian peninsula. A walk around old town would definitely include a quick photo opportunity in front of the baroque cathedral, the mark of imperial and old-fashioned Spain. The leadership of the church, after all, was fused with political power.

In fact, during most of the twentieth century, imports from Spain also included an extraordinary number of priests and nuns. Without them the selective private education of some countries would not have been the same. They were the teachers of the children of the establishment. In more recent years, without the work of rural nuns and priests, basic education and the roles of the NGOs tending to the needs of the lower echelons of society would have been impossible. Simultaneously, even some Spanish clerics took the causes of the downtrodden as motivation for political activity, reversing the historical trend of siding with the establishment. The ranks of Liberation Theology leaders are full of Spanish (notably Basque) priests, a fact that does not make conservatives very happy, but has contributed to the overall picture of the Spaniards with a more progressive angle.

In the 1980s new visitors arrived – politicians and diplomats trying to help with the Latin American political transitions. They offered well-intentioned, sometimes miraculous solutions for the Latin American ills. They seemed to have lost a golden business opportunity of marketing the Pactos de la Moncloa – the understanding among political parties to consolidate democracy – in bottles (as the San Francisco fog, or the pet rock) in response to the petitions of the moderates to solve the internal wars in Central America. In any event, the political transition of Spain became a model. The visits of King Juan Carlos, Prime Ministers Adolfo Suárez, Felipe González, and José María Aznar became a routine, while members of Congress and scholars were invited to give advice and support. With Spain's membership in the European Community, financial resources became more readily available in the framework of cooperation agreements, incentives for regional integration, and democratization processes. Central America, among all the subregions, received special favor.

Then the ultimate event happened with the arrival of a new personification of Spain, not to be expected. Spanish military and policemen set foot in Latin America, not as new conquistadors, but as agents of peace, trainers in disarmament, and even as counselors and executive leaders of local police forces. The Guardia Civil, historically vilified by the left in Spain and enshrined as a reduplication of the Inquisition by the followers of the Black Legend mythology, after siding with repressive regimes for decades and providing the backbone of the Franco regime, have found a new mission in El Salvador and Guatemala. They trained the local police and advised the military on human rights practices, supplementing the work of nuns and NGOs.

Immediately following, without warning, came the bankers, the managers of communications companies, and the officers of public utilities enterprises. That was news. From the high visibility of the colonial bishops and viceroys, the Latin American perception of the Spaniard had shifted to the modest image of the immigrant and the parish priests and the hospital nuns. Now, back to the past, the new conquistador had arrived, as promised again in the legends of the Aztecs who rightly identified Cortés as the deity announced to come and rule supreme. It was the return of the harsh Spanish image of the empire in Americas, as opposed to the soft, romanticized picture of Andalusian songs (Hernández, 2002).

From the low-key *bodega de la esquina* and the isolated teachings in a university in Mexico, the new Spaniards came to Santiago de Chile with checkbooks in hand, selling portable phones in Lima, and making the water systems of Cartagena de Indias work. They even left replicas of the Font de Canaletes, the public fountain at the head of the Barcelona Rambles. Legend says that the visitor who drinks its water will return sometime to the Catalan capital. It was like a remake of the arrival of gypsy Melquíades to the fictional Macondo of

One Hundred Years of Solitude. All of a sudden, a new literary figure had joined the classical U.S. businessmen who corrupted and manipulated the local political and economic elite in dozens of Latin American novels, from Mr. Danger of *Doña Bárbara* to *El Papa Verde.*

In contrast with the overwhelming power wielded by the old-fashioned U.S. interests and international corporations, the visibility of the new Spanish invasion offered unique features. First, it was mainly anchored in the banking industry and the recently privatized sectors of the economy with direct, daily linkages to the private lives of the citizens, not limited to one social class. Everybody needed to be able to access funds in banks in an era of uncertainty in exchange. All sectors of society went through decades of chaos and corruption in obtaining a decent phone service monopolized by inefficient state enterprises. Increasingly, more strata of the Latin American societies had experienced air travel to overcome the obstacle of distances in large territories. Millions of Latin Americans had access to cars propelled by gas. Banks, phone companies, and airlines became the object of desire of Spanish companies. Then, the unthinkable happened: Spain, with one of the richest soils on earth for the production of olive oil, was orphaned of the modern liquid gold: fosil oil. Selling the most expensive gasoline in Europe, the new oil conglomerate of Spain, REPSOL, the heir of CAMPSA, wanted to have a real oil company, like any good Venezuelan or Saudi Arab potentate. Argentina's YPF became the forbidding fruit.[6] And to manage the new companies came the new *bodegueros*, who did not behave like the former *monjitas.*

In the eyes of Latin Americans, they came in a rephrasing of two well-known perceptive portraits of the experience of World War II. The first is Winston Churchill's depiction of the merit of the Royal Air Force pilot in the Battle of England. The second is the popular British perception of the U.S. soldiers. In a remake, the new Spanish arrivals in Latin America seemed to be "overpaid," they were definitely "over here," and in some specific scenarios (Cuba, more to come on this) they were "oversexed." As a balance to the historical modest and familiar image of the Spanish immigrant, the new trend produced unwanted results in contrast to the extremely positive experiences of the past. Dominican Republic historians love to remember the deep and lasting imprint of the Spanish republicans who briefly stayed in their country at the end of the Civil War: "never have so many owed so much to so few." Six decades later, "never have so few (a handful of corporate officers) done so much damage (bad reputation) to so many (Spain, included)."[7] For many Latin Americans (and U.S. observers in the distance), this change was too much to accept. It was an affront they had to swallow. Resentment remained waiting for a better occasion.

A note on Cuba: From the ugly American to the ugly Spaniard

As a trendsetter, this conference may be unique for not dealing with Cuba, a true novelty in the Miami scene, where one must take sides either for or against the U.S. embargo, and where one's opinions on Castro are heavily scrutinized. To be on the safe side, when judging Spanish investment in Latin American, analysts can easily avoid dealing with Cuba on the basis that actual investments, as considered for the purpose of this paper, are supposed to be executed with all the trappings of a free capitalist society, including acquisition of property, mergers, and transfers with the only limitation imposed by the market and government laws. Actual economic and commercial foreign activities in Cuba may not qualify as investment because they really do not transfer property and are basically concessions of rights in the context of joint ventures.

However, taking into account that Spanish economic activities and trade in Cuba have been the main cause for the development of U.S. polemic measures such as the Helms-Burton law,[8] which in return has generated one of the most serious confrontations between the EU and the U.S. government, a comment is in order to complete the scope of this paper. When dealing with the image of Spain in Latin America in the context of Spanish investment, analysts may find it useful to speculate about the present and, especially, the future image of Spain in Cuba as a result of the impressive volume and scope of Spanish economic activities during the Castro regime. An additional reason for this suggestion is the fact that Spanish investment in Cuba has been implemented in high visibility sectors such as tourism, open to public observation, possibly linking the image of Spain directly with the services rendered by the tourist industry.

Additionally, since the hotel industry employs a notable number of the local work force, this sector of the economy has been targeted as a leader in the diversification of Cuban society into at least two sectors. One is composed of the Cuban population still fully operating under the control of a centralized economy. The other is composed of the privileged citizens who are operating in foreign currencies or have access to external trade and services. In any event, at least in theory, all of the Cuban workforce is paid directly by the government, while foreign companies contract the service of local employees with the central authorities.

This dual system has produced a plethora of negative comments on, first of all, the alarmingly apartheid nature of the tourist industry, essentially out of bounds to ordinary Cubans. Secondly, it has been lambasted by human rights activists on the basis of the discriminatory payment process by which the Cuban government is paid by foreign companies in foreign currency at international level fees, and then the Cuban local employees are compensated at the official salary scales. This system is not different from the one used by the government corporations providing services to embassies and foreign entities. To circumvent this and make it competitive and rewarding, it is a well-known fact that foreign companies establish a system of bonus payments on top of the official salaries, with the end result that employees in this sector are comparatively much better off than ordinary workers. As a consequence, critical evaluation of this dual system includes finger-pointing accusations against Spanish companies engaging in allegedly abusive labor practices in violation of international treaties of which Spain is a signatory.

In addition to this problem of discrimination and favoritism, paternalism is always a risk. Arrogance and condescending attitudes from the Spanish management of these investments are part of the scene. The alleged collateral hyperactivity of Spanish businessmen and tourists in their relations with the opposite sex creates an image (sometimes self-exaggerated) of a Latin macho only interested in a cheap, intense, exotic experience, which matches the stereotype of popular musical, literature and family backgrounds.[9]

In all, a subtle build up of a sort of "ugly Spaniard," as a follow up to the "ugly American," is a present reality that only time can confirm as permanent. Meanwhile, only subjective, scant opinions are available, in the absence of uncontrolled public opinion and credible research. Only time will say if the tourist industry in Cuba contributed to the preparation of capitalistic and democratic practices for the future, or simply contributed to the survival of a repressive and dictatorial regime. The comparison to the opening of the Spanish economy with tourism and investment during the last two decades of the Franco regime is frequently mentioned. But the jury is still out regarding what factor was more important for the apparent miraculous transition process in Spain. The option of giving too much credit to the economic opening of the regime may obscure the resilience of Spanish society and the preparatory work of the political forces in the opposition.

The second intriguing angle of the Spanish investments in the tourist industry is the confrontation generated between the U.S. government (on behalf of the former landowners where some of the new tourist developments are located) and the Spanish companies, most noticeably the leading hotel chains, such as Sol Meliá. Threatened with law suits or application of restrictive measures for their operations on U.S. soil, Spanish companies have been pressured to make deals with former owners in exchange for a promise of not being the subject of retaliatory measures, now or in a future democratic Cuba. In a contradictory claim based on the alleged purpose of Helms-Burton — the democratization and freedom of Cuba — , the U.S. government actually has been promoting a settlement from present Spanish companies, along the lines of the unusual case of ITT and the Italian phone company STET.

As an ironic consequence, this settlement policy actually can be considered as an endorsement of the continuation of the alleged apartheid system and discriminatory labor practices, only justified for monetary compensation. As a result, by stressing a compensatory solution as a relief from potential legal suits, the U.S. pressure might be promoting more investments in Cuba, this time protected from hostile actions. Instead of risking reprisals, companies would prefer to invest safely with a kind of insurance, in the form of a compensation for the former owners. This is exactly the opposite of the publicly announced purpose of Helms-Burton. The actual result never took such form due to a combination of three factors: caution applied by medium-size Spanish companies, flat refusal from important companies to cave in to the demands of the U.S. government, and the obstacles associated with the regulations and intricacies of the Cuban regime. The contradictory claim presented by the law and the invitation for deals remains as a cloud overhanging the alleged purposes of democratizing Cuba. In any event, taking into account all factors, the image of Spain in a future Cuba could be tarnished as a collaborator with the Castro regime, along with the pressures of the U.S. government. Both forces would then be considered as working in unison for the continuation of the regime.

Future prospects: Hope, uncertainties, warning

In view of the damage caused and the level of acrimony perceived at the worst times of the confrontations generated by the protests in cities like Buenos Aires, observers may offer the prediction that this will only be a temporary trend with no lasting consequences (Rojo, 2001). This may be a wishful reaction based on survival of the previous generally good rapport between Latin Americans and Spaniards, regardless of the origin of the former. Well wishers point out that even in the middle of the worst moments of the protests, Latin American citizens rushed to clarify that the harsh commentaries against *gallegos* were only intended against the government officials backing the perceived business culprits causing the financial problems and the rise in the cost of public utilities under Spanish administration. In other words, this distinction seemed to be a mirror image of the standard explanation given by the Latin American left when activating anti-imperialist campaigns explaining that they were geared towards the center of political and economic power of the United States, not against Americans in general. By virtue of the perceived negative management of Spanish investments, Spain was now considered to be at the same level as the United States in the eyes of the Latin Americans.

Warning signs were issued by the corporate officers of Spanish companies in the sense that they would not stay in Argentina "at all costs." This was a confirmation of the statements made by the Spanish government for ending the unrestricted support for the ailing Argentine airline (*ABC*, 2001a; Gómez, 2001; J.M., 2001). Another factor contributing to the hard line attitude of Spain's political leaders is the pressure exerted by the conservative press for the support of Spanish business interests (*ABC*, 2001b). Finally, the Argentine Congress' populist attitude did not help to soften the confrontation; on the contrary, it contributed to worsen it (Rivas, 2002).

Positive signs for hope include the standard declarations of the EU Commission (EU Commission) and the Spanish government pledging support for the efforts made by Latin American governments, specially the Argentine authorities, and its dismissal of criticism aimed at the overall practices of investments in sound sectors. Argentine diplomats have also engaged themselves in dispelling new sources of trouble and the continuation of the negative trend (*El País*, 2001; Lafferriere, 2001). Another factor for confidence in the future is the fact that calls for mass boycotts of Spanish products in Argentina received no noticeable following (ABC, 2001c; De Carlos, 2001; Montoya, 2001; and Relea, 2001). On the other side of the Atlantic, Latin American residents were not the targets of reprisals and their difficulties were a continuation of the regulatory legislation applied under the pressure of illegal immigration from across the strait of Gibraltar. Only time will say if this apparent temporary diagnosis becomes permanent.

Meanwhile, there are some disadvantages for Spain's image in Latin America. The most important one is the slow but inexorable disappearance of the traditional migration of Spaniards towards Latin America. There are no more economic or political immigrants reaching the shores of Cuba or Argentina; in fact, the reverse is the trend, not only of those born in Argentina, but of Spanish immigrants who converted into *retornados*. Forty-eight thousand Spanish emigrants to Latin American returned to Spain in 2001 (Aguirre, 2002; *La Vanguardia*, 2001). A Spanish passport is not only a piece of paper sought by soccer players eager to fill the non-discriminatory EU slots in Spanish teams, but as a right to be fulfilled by children and grandchildren of former Spanish citizens. Spaniards are in essence an endangered species in Latin America. In the not too distant future, Latin Americans will only have as terms of comparison the history books and novels. The only point of reference will be the managers of companies still willing to invest in Latin America.

With the prediction that this trend will continue, only nostalgia will remain of the indelible imprint made by hundreds of Spanish intellectuals who enriched the most productive years of the universities and hospitals of Latin America, as well as the development of literary circles and rural clinics. In the event that business contributions from Spain be perceived with a contradictory or negative balance, the role of Pedroso (as law professor of Carlos Fuentes), Barraquer (as ophtalmology teacher of dozens of Colombian specialists), "el sabio catalán" (as literary mentor of Gabriel García Márquez), and Ellacuría and Casaldaliga (as inspirer of religious activism) will be long missed, as well as the work of thousands of Spaniards who were propelled to Latin America by the will to find a better life or were forced by political circumstances.

The bad press is not only limited to the emblematic case of Argentina but is also detectable in countries like Venezuela and Perú. The unique regime of President Chávez has attracted the wrath of numerous sectors inside the country and the ambivalence of foreign governments, making the activities of investors in that important oil-based economy an example of a difficult mission. It is not surprising then to find out that Spanish banks – especially Banco Bilbao Vizcaya Argentaria, BBVA – have made undercover substantial contributions to both the government political movement of Chávez and parties of the opposition (Ekaizer 2002a; 2002b; 2002c). In the worst moments of the clashes between the government and the opposition that erupted at its maximum level in April 2002 with the apparent resignation of Chávez and his spectacular comeback, Spanish interests appeared to be behind the scenes (*El País*, 2002a). Similar activities were detected in Fujimori's Perú (*El País*, 2002b). The discovery of special expense accounts and investments in "tax havens" used by the leading Spanish conglomerate BBVA caused the downfall of its top corporate officer and the collateral revealing of the bank's under-the-table backing of Latin American political parties and individuals (De Barón, 2002). Spain's business community was not an exception in the overall dark picture of international corruption (Martín and Marcelo, 2001). Spain ranks as No. 11 (out of 21), in the middle of the scale – 5.8, with a perfect score as 10.0 – in a list of countries whose companies are "tempted" or prone to offer bribes for establishing themselves in developing markets (Transparency International; Velázquez, 2002; Viglieca, 2002). On the other hand, Spain's corruption perception ranks with a moderately good rating of 7.1 (out of 10), is No. 22 in the list of 102 countries, from an almost perfect Finland with 9.7 to a dismally corrupt Bangladesh with 1.2 (Transparency International, 2002). As a consequence, on top of the many rational and reasonable explanations for the spectacular level of investment and the considerable risk taken by Spanish companies, besides the affinity of language and customs, now the world could see that some dose of old-fashioned corruption also helped. The failures of Spanish companies and their branches in Latin American caused by mismanagement or fraud seemed to be catching up with the world trend presided over by the Enron format. After all, if Spanish companies were companies at the same level as the U.S. giants, they had to show also that they were also a major-league candidate with all the trappings of white collar crime and management incompetence.

In consequence, the dimension of corruption was added to the image of Spain's new representatives as being arrogant to the old-fashioned establishment and patronizing to the traditional left. Simultaneously, the intellectual sectors, displaced by the technocrats in many functions (from media to publishing houses) focused their critical views on the restrictive immigration policies of the new European Union member, adding this resentment to the never fully masqueraded confrontation between Spanish and Latin American writers over the resounding literary and economic success of the most important masters of the so-called "boom". In the 1990s, to diffuse this potential divorce, the Spanish agencies proceeded to balance the dispensation of awards, among them the prestigious Cervantes Prize for Literature – sort of a Spanish Nobel – equally to Spaniards and Latin Americans. However, economic difficulties have forced the Spanish government to curtail funding of many programs – especially scholarships – that were once generously bestowed to Latin Americans. The result is that in the future the Latin American countries may not have as many government and civil society leaders trained in Spain, as natural allies of Spanish interests able to counteract the negative image of investments.

As a sign of a cloudy future regarding the image of Spain in Latin America with serious consequences for the overall economic and political interests of the Spanish economy and the Spanish government, an apparently insignificant and unrelated development may shed some light and would be worth exploring. It has nothing to do with the Latin American scene but with Morocco and may be a reflection of the potential loss of taken-for-granted Latin American backing of Spain's global diplomatic activities, as in the formation of alliances in the UN. As a hint and an advance of further consequences for the repercussions of the negative aspects of Spanish investments for the image of Spain in Latin America, there is the fact that an apparently unrelated crisis revealed a gap in the overall backing of Madrid's diplomatic actions. When the government of Morocco unleashed a clash over the tiny, uninhabited island of Perejil, the swift reaction of the Spanish government received an overall solid endorsement and understanding from the Latin American press, with a notable exception: a sector of the Argentine press. The trauma of the Malvinas and the recent clashes over the activities of the Spanish corporations investing in Argentina made the difference. Perceptive analysts predicted that this exceptional critical view may reappear in the future. The burden is then placed on the Spanish decision-makers in the field of damage control (Ortiz, 2002).

As briefly mentioned above, the self-inflicted exercise used by the Spanish press in depicting the behavior of Spanish companies in Latin America not only mirrors the best tradition of films and novels in the United States in unearthing the imperfections of U.S. society, but it represents a modern continuation of the ethic energy applied by the domestic critics of Spain's colonial structure and activities. Democracy and freedom of the press have converted Spanish media into one of the most viciously active industries in the world, taking no prisoners when it comes to search and destroy culprits of political or social crimes, as well as in destroying reputations. Feeding on a contemporary Las Casas, U.S., and European competitors of Spain may well exploit the negative perception and cleverly use it for reoccupying the space that Spanish companies may be forced to leave.

In all, damage to the image of Spain caused either by direct actions of Spanish investments, or by manipulation of opinion with populist aims, is a matter of serious concern and should be inserted in an overall government policy. A field that in the past did not receive considerable attention is now being seriously considered in Spain's think-tank community. A solid alliance between government resources and private corporations is not only advisable but a must. Comparative research in the past did not generate results regarding the image of Spain beyond the traditional stereotype. Now, apparently the lack of a distinctive image has been replaced by a partial, in terms of location and time, injury. Before things get worse, the time for action has come.

Notes

1 Survey commissioned by the Real Instituto Elcano to Latinobarómetro 2003. C. Jan, (2003). For a recent evaluation of Spanish investment in Latin America, see W. Chislett, (2003).

2 For an overall analysis of the recent trends of Spanish investment in Latin America, see Arahuetes, 2001.

3 Expression apparently coined in Mexico, as reported by Silva-Herzog (2002).

4 For a sample as reported by BBC:
   http://news.bbc.co.uk/hi/spanish/latin_america/newsid_1740000/1740379.stm.

5 The word may not have come simply as a derivation of "sudamericano", but as a transformation of a distinctive linguistic structure of the porteño Spanish. When an Argentine radio reporter became a novelty in Madrid, people were amused to be asked during on-the-air street interviews: "Y vos, ¿sos de acá?" Madrileños, ready to make fun of anything, immediately coined the "sudaca" umbrella.

6   See chapter 4 of Cechini and Zicolillo (2002).
7   The author takes full credit and blame for the arbitrary parallelism, not inspired in any of the sources used in the chapter.
8   For a review of this law at its consequences, see Roy (2000).
9   For a review of Spain-Cuba relations, see Roy (1999).

References

ABC (2001a), "Aznar considera injustas las críticas a España en el conflicto de Aerolíneas," *Abc,* June 6.
ABC (2001b), "España y la crisis argentina," June 9.
ABC (2001c), "La crisis de Aerolíneas amenaza con abrir una brecha en las relaciones hispano-argentinas," June 2.
Abellán, L. (2001), "El Banco de España se muestra 'preocupado' por el cariz de la crisis económica argentina," *El País*, June 23.
Aguirre, B. (2002), "La crisis latinoamericana hace que el número de retornados a España sea el mayor en 23 años," *El País*, July 29.
A.M.A./C.R.G. (2001), "La crisis de Aerolíneas golpea la imagen de las empresas españolas en Argentina," *Expansión*, June 1.
Arahuetes, A. (2001), "Las inversiones directas de las empresas españolas en América Latina desde 2001 ¿retirada o repliegue?" *Real Instituto Elcano*, http://www.realinstitutoelcano.org/analisis/52.asp (observed July 31, 2002).
Cacho, J. (2003), "Ante el 'estilo K' ", *El Mundo*, July 27.
Cambio 16 (2002), "Los nuevos conquistadores,", July 29.
Cecchine, D. and J. Zicolillo (2002), *Los nuevos conquistadores: el papel del gobierno y las empresas españolas en el expolio de Argentina*, FOCA, Madrid.
Chislett, W. (2003), Spanish Direct Investment in Latin America: Challenges and Opportunities, Real Instituto Elcano, Madrid.
Cinco Días (2003), "Lula garantiza 'buen negocio' ", July 16.
C.R.G. (2003), "las grandes empresas españolas sufren la incertidumbre argentina," *Expansión*, May 20.
De Barón, I. (2002), "El BBVA celebra su primera reunion trasa la crisis de las cuentas secretas", *El País*, September 24.
De Carlos, C. (2001), "El principal sindicato argentino convoca una jornada «antiespañola»" *ABC,* June 18.
Diario 16 (2001), "Ira contra España en América Latina," June 15.
Díaz-Varela, M. (2003), "Más samba y menos tango; Hola Brasil, adios Argentina," *La Vanguardia*, July 20.
D'Lom, L. (2003), "Cuevas acusa a Kirchner de 'poner a parir' a los empresarios españoles," *Abc*, July 18.
Egurbide, P. (2003), "Kirchner acusa a los empresarios españoles de aprovecharse de la Argentina de Medem", *El País*, July 18.
Ekaizer, E. (2002a), "El número 2 del BBVA admite que conocía de los pagos a Chávez," *El País*, June 19.
--- (2002b), "Hugo Chávez ocultó el pago del BBV al Consejo Nacional Electoral", August 29.
--- (2002c), "Las huellas de la corrupción," *El País*, July 15.
El País (2001), "Dos países...," July 3.

El País (2002a), "El Supremo de Venezuela abre el camino para juzgar a Hugo Chávez", June 22.

El País (2002b), "Garzón investiga en Perú", October 9.

EU Commission, http://europa.eu.int/comm/external_relations/argentina/intro/sit.htm.

Gaveta, C. (2001), "De Malvinas a Aerolíneas," *El País*, July 1.

Goitia, F. (2001), "Aterrizaje forzoso en Argentina," *La Clave*, June 8-14.

Gómez, M. (2001), "Fracasa el último intento argentino para conseguir capital español que salve a AA," *El Mundo*, June 15.

González, P. (2003), "Lula entusiasma, Kirchner intimida," *La Estrella*, July 20.

Gualdoni, F. (2001), "American Airlines suspende todos sus vuelos a Buenos Aires por la inseguridad del aeropuerto", *El País*, June 15.

Hernández, A. (2002), "Emilio Lamo de Espinosa," *La Clave*, October, 4-10.

Jan, C. (2003), "España obtiene buenas notas en América Latina", *El País*, 7 November.

J.M. (2001), "El Gobierno español no dará un solo duro más a Aerolíneas Argentinas," *La Razón*, May 30.

Jozami, A. (2003), "Kirchner subordina los intereses de los grupos españoles a la salida de la crisis," *Cinco Días*, July 18.

Lafferriere, R.E. (2001), "Argentina y España: una nueva integración," *ABC,* March 28.

La Vanguardia (2001), "España, objetivo de la emigración argentina," January 2.

Martín, E. and J.F. Marcelo (2001), "Un mundo de corruptos," *La Clave*, September 20-26.

Montoya, R. (2001), "Boicot a los 'gallegos'," *El Mundo*, June 7.

Noya, J. (2002), "The foreign image abroad as a State policy" *Real Instituto Elcano*, (8/10/2002), http://www.realinstitutoelcano.org/analisis/87.asp; "La imagen exterior de España" (3/10/2002), http://www.realinstitutoelcano.org/analisis/82.asp.

Ortiz, R. (2002), "Las miradas de América Latina sobre la crisis hispano-marroquí," *Real Instituto Elcano*, (22/7/2002), http://www.realinstitutoelcano.org/analisis/42.asp.

Patten, C., P. Lamy and P. Solbes (2002), "Information Note to the Commission from Mr. Patten, Mr Lamy and Mr. Solbes on the Argentinean Crisis", European Commission, Brussels.

Petroselli, E. (2001), "Hispanofobia: por qué insultan a los españoles en media Iberoamérica," *Interviu*, 25 June.

Ramonet, I. (2002), talks given on Spanish televisión channels.

Rebosio, A. (2002), "La gran decepción: El fracaso de las privatizaciones en Iberoamérica alimenta el pesimismo de la población y es caldo de cultivo del populismo," *El País*, July 27.

Relea, F. (2001), "Si alguien ha propiciado un boicoteo a lo español, no va a tener ningún eco," *El País*, June 16.

Rivas, R. (2002), "El Congrés argentí apunta a la banca estrangera," *Avui*, August 22.

Rojo, A. (2001), "Los argentinos dejan de confiar en España," *El Mundo*, July 25.

Roy, J. (1997), *The Ibero-American Space*, University of Miami/Universitat de Lleida, Coral Gables/Lleida.

--- (1999), *La siempre fiel: un siglo de relaciones hispanocubanas (1898-1998)*, La Catarata/Universidad Complutense, Madrid.

--- (2000), *Cuba, the U.S., and the Helms-Burton 'Doctrine': International Reactions*, University of Florida Press, Gainesville.

--- (2002a), "Maltratar a Europa: diversión Americana," *El Nuevo Herald*, May 15.

--- (2002b), "Bush facing a more-combative Europe," *The Miami Herald*, May 24, 7B.

Sánchez G. (2002), "González avisa que el BBVA no asumirá 'cualquier coste' por seguir en Argentina," *Cinco Días*, July 10.

Silva-Herzog J. (2002), former Mexican Minister, talk given at the Mexican Cultural Center in Miami, September 26.

Socolovsky, J. (2002), "Exigen explicaciones sobre las cuentas de Menem," *El Nuevo Herald*, January 18.

Transparency International (2002a),
    http://www.transparency.org/pressreleases_archive/2002/2002.05.14.bpi.en.html#bpi; see also a commentary-interview.

--- (2002b), Corruption Perception Index 2002,
    http://www.transparency.org/pressreleases_archieve/2002/2002.08.28.cpi.en.html.

Vázquez-Rial, H. (2001), "¿Tormenta 'antiespañola' en Argentina?: Españoles 'go home,'" *El País*, July 1.

Velásquez, J. P. (2002), "La corrupción es el impuesto más injusto," *El País*, October 17.

Viglieca, O. (2002), "España quemó la plata", *La Clave*, August 30-September 5
    http://www.elpais.es/articulo.html?d_date=20021017&xref=20021017elpepiint_16&type=Tes&anchor=elpepiint.

Yárnoz, C. (2002), "La crisis en Argentina: La UE critica la falta de credibilidad del plan de emergencia de Argentina," *El País*, January 16.

Zarzuela, A. (2001), "España no, gracias," *Cambio 16*, July 2.

Chapter 14

Conclusions:
Challenges and Opportunities of Foreign
Investments in Latin America

Maria-Angels Oliva
Luis A. Rivera-Batiz

Introduction

This chapter examines inward foreign direct investment (FDI) in Latin America and the nature of the major benefits and risks facing foreign investors. The discussion advances the view that the region offers foreign investors substantial benefits from market potential and cost advantages. These benefits are attenuated by macroeconomic vulnerabilities and institutional weaknesses, which represent two broad sources of continuing risks. We derive lessons from past experiences and examine the prospects and opportunities ahead, giving special emphasis to Spanish investments.

The Latin American growth boom of the 1990s gave way to a slowdown during 2000-2003 and a recovery in 2004. Inward FDI flows declined sharply from the high levels attained in the late 1990s but did not stop, staying above the levels of the early 1990s. This decline, but not standoff, is consistent with FDI strategies seeking to exploit long-term market potential and cost advantages. These strategies focus on prospective recovery and potential market expansion driven by Mercosur and the 2005 scheduled inception of the Free Trade Area of the Americas. Strategies based on production sharing focus on production chain efficiency and the exploitation of cost advantages.

A major challenge faced by foreign investors is that, except for Chile, the region currently presents a scenario characterized by opacity, institutional weaknesses, and long-standing macroeconomic vulnerabilities. The analysis suggests that the success of strategies based on market potential hinges on a reorientation toward North American markets or the attainment of stable long-run regional growth. Growth sustainability depends on strengthening institutions, propping up governance, and establishing adequate macroeconomic policy, sound debt management and a reliable exchange rate regime.

FDI in Latin America: Global and regional perspectives

FDI to emerging markets came back with a vengeance in the 1990s and literally boomed in the late 1990s. Latin America was a main recipient of these capital inflows and became the major destination of Spanish investments. Massive Spanish FDI led to a visible regional presence, giving rise to the remark that a reconquest was taking place. Toral (2001) examines the multiple aspects encompassed in the reconquest process.

What gave rise to the wave of FDI toward Latin America? Massive privatization programs, economic liberalization, including liberalization of capital flows, and greater macroeconomic stability supported growing markets with low inflation. A new positive attitude toward openness generated expectations of continuing trade and financial openness. Stable growth with low inflation appeared to be a feasible objective in many countries.

By the late 1990s, Brazil's *plano real* macroeconomic program (making reference to the Brazilian currency, the real) had been able to reinstate growth with low inflation. The Argentinean experiment with a rigid exchange rate regime, the currency board introduced in 1991, had been successful in eliminating hyperinflationary conditions and reigniting growth. Mexico had recovered from the 1994-95 economic crisis and Chile continued to grow. The surge of FDI toward the region during 1996-1999 came to an end with the slowdown that took place during 2000-2002. Figure 14.1 depicts the turnaround of FDI toward Latin America.

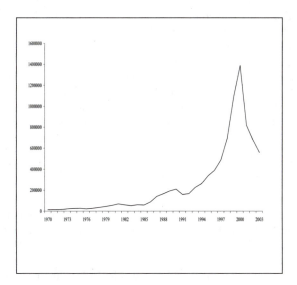

Figure 14.1   FDI in the world (billion %US

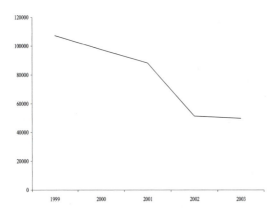

Figure 14.1 (continued)
Source: UNCTAD, World Investment Report 2004

According to UNCTAD (United Nations, 2004) inward FDI flows into Latin America fell from $88 billion in 2001 to $51 billion in 2002 and to $49.7 billion in 2003, a fall of about 43.6% for the region as a whole. This fall followed 9.6% and 9.2% falls in 2001 and 2000. The largest economies experienced huge falls in FDI. Inward FDI flows to Argentina declined by a factor of 4.5 (from $2.2 billion in 2001 to $478 million in 2003), by a factor of 2.5 in Mexico (from $26.7 billion to $10.8 billion) and about halved in Brazil between 2001 and 2003. Inflows to Chile declined by 40% between 2001 and 2003. The experience was heterogeneous rather than uniform across countries. Bright spots included Costa Rica, which experienced a 22% increase in FDI, Peru, and Ecuador.

The special character of the decline of FDI going into the region should not be overemphasized. A slowdown put an end to the booming years of both regional and global FDI. World inward FDI fell by 32% in 2001-2003, which is relatively close to the 44% fall experienced by the Latin American economies. Moreover, the early millennium slowdown did not mean that FDI stopped or that it was low historically. In fact, FDI to Latin America in 2003 greatly exceeded the $21 billion regional average during 1990-95 and remained around the $50 billion received at the start of the investment boom in 1996.

Table 14.1 shows that the behavior of inward FDI at the global level is quite similar to the behavior of inward FDI in Latin America. This association suggests that the decline in Latin America should be viewed from the perspective of a global decline rather than from the perspective of idiosyncratic behavior linked to the region. Latin America's performance as a destination for investment was not worse than performance for the world as a whole. In fact, the percentage of global FDI accounted for by inward investment to Latin America was the same in 2002-2003 and in 1999, which was the historical peak year of FDI in the region.

Table 14.1 Regional distribution of inward FDI flows, 1990-2003

Region	1999	2000	2001	2002	2003	1999	2000	2001	2002	2003
Total South America	69.7	57.9	38.8	26.8	21.3	6.4%	4.2%	5%	4%	4%
Total Latin America and Caribbean	107.4	97.5	88.1	51.4	49.7	10%	7%	11%	8%	9%
World	1086.8	1388.0	817.6	678.8	559.6	100%	100%	100%	100%	100%

Source: UNCTAD, World Investment Report, 2004

What factors led to the decline in FDI? Did the Latin market allure turn sour in 1999? On one hand, the assumption that economic liberalization would take place and would stay put turned out to be accurate. On the other hand, the assumptions of continuing growth and greater stability were not borne out by the events. Financial fragility, currency instability and unsustainable debts showed their ugly face once more. The anticipated continuing boom did not materialize as the region fell into stagnation. Severe recessions hit Argentina and Venezuela, which recovered in 2003 and 2004. Table 14.2 presents country-by-country data on the behavior of FDI to South American countries during 1990-2003. FDI into South American countries declined in steps during 2000-2002.

Table 14.2 Regional distribution of inward FDI flows, 1990-2003

Countries	in billion $						in percentage					
	1990-95	1999	2000	2001	2002	2003	1990-95	1999	2000	2001	2002	2003
Argentina	3.5	24.0	10.4	2.2	0.8	0.5	33%	34%	18%	5.6%	3%	2.2%
Bolivia	0.2	1.0	0.8	0.8	1.0	0.2	1.5%	1.5%	1.5%	2%	4%	0.7%
Brazil	2.0	28.6	32.8	22.5	16.6	10.1	19%	41%	57%	58%	62%	47.7%
Chile	1.5	8.8	4.9	4.2	1.9	3.0	14%	13%	8%	11%	7%	14%
Colombia	0.8	1.5	2.4	2.5	2.1	1.8	8%	2%	4%	6.5%	8%	8.3%
Ecuador	0.3	0.6	0.7	1.3	1.3	1.6	3%	1%	1%	3.4%	5%	7.3%
Paraguay	0.1	0.1	0.1	0.1	0.0	0.1	1%	0.1%	0.2%	0.2%	0%	0.4%
Peru	1.1	1.9	0.8	1.1	2.2	1.4	10%	3%	1.4%	3%	8%	6.5%
Uruguay	0.1	0.2	0.3	0.3	0.2	0.3	1%	0.3%	0.5%	1%	0.6%	1%
Venezuela	0.9	2.9	4.7	3.7	0.8	2.5	8%	4%	8%	9.5%	3%	12%
Total (South America)	10.5	69.7	57.9	38.8	26.8	21.3	100%	100%	100%	100%	100%	100%

Source: UNCTAD, World Investment Report, 2004

The behavior of inward FDI is not uniform across Latin American countries. FDI into Mexico continued to climb until the 2002 slowdown. In relative terms, Brazil has captured an increasing share of the South American pie. Its relative importance as a destination increased from 41% of total South American inward FDI in 1999 to 61% in 2002. Peru, Ecuador and Colombia have also gained greater South American share. By contrast, FDI into Argentina plummeted from 34% to 2.2% of the total from 1999 to 2003.

The increasing Latin American share of FDI into Mexico, the increase of Brazil, Peru, Ecuador and Colombia in total FDI to South America, and the declining share of Argentina and Venezuela are not surprising once we consider that the former countries had a better growth performance than the latter countries. Other things equal, FDI seeking to gain access to local markets is likely to stress fastest growing countries over countries experiencing recession. Moreover, Argentina and Venezuela have experienced enhanced economic uncertainties, institutional weaknesses, and political deadlock compared with the late 1990s. These factors are likely to scare away many potential investors and cause investors to be more cautious in formulating investment plans.

The heterogeneous behavior of economic performance and FDI flows suggests that strengthening the quality of the economic, institutional and political regimes might need to be accomplished in order to reinstate truly solid growth and destination attractiveness in locations experiencing a loss of their share of the foreign investment pie. Past investment poor performance can attract fire sale FDI in the short-term but continuing flows require reinstating adequate performance levels.

The investor strategic setup

The analysis is conducted from a foreign direct investor perspective, stressing market potential and production location advantages. In general, Spanish firms have sought to exploit market potential while the other major regional investor, the US, has sought both market potential and production location advantages such as those provided by Mexico.

The US has traditionally been the major foreign investor in Latin America, and remains so. The major newcomer to the Latin American investment arena is Spain. In the late 1980s, Spanish FDI in emerging markets, and particularly in Latin America, had been reduced to a trickle. Spanish investments in the region represented a mere 4% of the country's total outward FDI. Slow growth, debt difficulties and associated macroeconomic uncertainties had reduced the attractiveness of Brazil, Argentina, Mexico, and other Latin American countries as investment destinations.

Spanish FDI has concentrated in South America and Mexico, with large investments in Brazil, Argentina and Mexico and substantial investments in Chile (see Table 14. 3). The Spanish foreign investing strategy has a long-term perspective and aims to capture growing domestic markets. As a result, investment flows have heavily concentrated in the three largest Latin American markets, Brazil, Argentina and lately in Mexico. Brazil and Argentina have created a common market, Mercosur, promising market growth potential. Mexico is part of the North American Free Trade Arrangement (NAFTA) one of the two largest integrated markets worldwide.

Table 14.3 Spanish FDI flows (million Euros, percentage)

Country/Region	Gross Investment								Net Investment					
	2000	2001	2002	2003	2000 (%)	2001 (%)	2002 (%)	2003 (%)	2001	2002	2003	2001 (%)	2002 (%)	2003 (%)
OECD	29143	34187	32145	18226	36.7	74.9	77.1	74.9	31383	24565	17237	79.2	89.2	86.1
Fiscal Heavens	892	336	266	175	1.1	0.7	0.6	0.7	-169	15	-76	-0.4	0.1	-0.4
Latin America	25223	10965	8739	4101	31.8	24.0	21.0	16.8	8314	2495	1090	21.0	9.1	5.4
Mexico	3983	2045	1119	947	5.0	4.5	2.7	3.9	1629	960	-689	4.1	3.5	-3.4
Argentina	3269	2603	4643	1425	4.1	5.7	11.1	5.9	322	4630	730	0.8	16.8	3.6
Brazil	14533	1552	1798	1421	18.3	3.4	4.3	5.8	1731	-3818	667	4.4	-13.9	3.3
Chile	934	1188	433	92	1.2	2.6	1.0	0.4	1145	228	219	2.9	0.8	1.1
Total	79432	45625	41686	24341	100	100	100	100	39640	27550	20017	100	100	100

Source: Direccion General de Comercio e Inversiones, Spain

The market targeting investment strategy is based on two major premises about Latin America. First, when Spanish involvement started in the mid-1990s the premise was the region had surpassed its longstanding economic instabilities and was bound to take off. This assumption was widely held at the time although one must mention that the US and other investors assumed a cautious "let us see what happens first" approach. In the midst of early millennium stagnation, a premise behind continuing FDI is that recovery will be reinstated in the medium or long term.

Second, a first entry strategy would make more difficult the penetration of markets by late entrants. This preemptive strategy is appropriate to the type of services and utilities in which Spanish firms have invested. The US and other European investors such as Germany and The Netherlands have taken a cautious approach that often precludes an enter-first strategy. US investments are largely part of a globalization of production strategy aiming to achieve low production costs by investing in several low-cost locations. This strategy aims to create competitiveness to face rivals in the source country market and in third markets. Specifically, the production sharing strategy does not rely on capturing host country markets. Host countries play the role of production platforms rather than markets targeted for sales.

The globalization of production approach is quite different from the market targeting approach. The returns from FDI targeting market potential hinge on the size and growth of the host country market. The success of production globalization depends on reliable production linkages, the conditions of host country infrastructure, and export market demand, rather than on host country growth or market size.

FDI motivated by production sharing considerations follows different dynamics from market targeting investment. For instance, FDI to South American countries has been largely a matter of market potential while Mexico has attracted much production sharing activity. Accordingly, even though the amount of FDI going into South American countries declined from 1999 to 2003 due to stagnation,

312 *Latin America's Quest for Globalization*

investment into Mexico continued to climb until it fell sharply in 2002. This fall is associated with the uncertainties and economic slowdown afflicting the United States, the major host country and export market for Mexican exports, in 2003.

Costa Rica's foreign investment strategy is based on attracting foreign investment, largely from the US, to incorporate the country into the production sharing chain of the computer industry and other industries. Larraín, López-Calva and Rodríguez-Clare (1999) and Rodriguez-Clare (2001) examine the Costa Rican strategy and the pivotal role of Intel investments and export markets as opposed to local market demand.

Finally, we must mention the even though market targeting and cost advantage approaches are well establish as analytical tools systematic empirical evidence establishing them over alternative hypotheses is scarce. For instance, the issue of to what extent growth attracts FDI or FDI accelerates growth is still unresolved at the level of country-analysis. Both hypotheses lead to a positive relationship between FDI and growth. De Gregorio (1992), Borensztein, De Gregorio and Lee (1998) and Oliva and Rivera-Batiz (2002) obtain a positive relationship for Latin America in the context of models explaining the determinants of growth. Oliva and Rivera-Batiz conduct causality tests aiming to distinguish empirically between the two hypotheses but the tests are inconclusive. By the same token, wages and other cost factors are often statistically insignificant in empirical studies (see Oliva and Rivera-Batiz, 2002).

The largest markets

In terms of GDP and market size, Brazil, Mexico and Argentina account for most Latin American economic activity. As the largest hosts to FDI in the region, they display distinctive characteristics. Brazil and Argentina have joined Uruguay, Bolivia and Chile (associate member) to constitute the largest integrated market in South America. By contrast, Mexico is a growing market that represents the gateway to the US and Canadian markets.

Brazil: Awakening or dormant giant?

Brazil is by far the largest economy in Latin America. Accordingly, it is the largest recipient of FDI. Table 14.4 shows the share of major foreign direct investors in Brazil in terms of the 1995 and 2000 stocks and the 1996-99 flows. US companies accounted for about a quarter of total flows during the period, a figure that was about the same as the share of US in cumulative FDI up to 1996. US involvement grew as FDI flows expanded but the share of the total remained unchanged. The big newcomers were Spain and Portugal, which together accounted for about 23% of total FDI flows and gained share at the expense of traditional investors such as Germany, Switzerland and Japan. The Spanish share in these years' flows was 16%, much higher than the quite small 0.6% share in the cumulative 1995 FDI stock.

Table 14.4   Brazil FDI flows and stock by home country ($ million and percentage)

Countries	Stock until 1995	%	Flows 1996-99	%	2000 Census (latest data)	%
United States	10,852	25.5	19,138	25.9	24,500	23.8
Spain	251	0.6	11,955	16.2	12,253	11.9
The Netherlands	1,535	3.6	7,422	10.1	11,055	10.7
France	2,032	4.8	5,993	8.1	6,931	6.7
Cayman Isl.	892	2.1	7,960	10.8	6,225	6.0
Germany	5,828	13.7	1,302	1.8	5,110	5.0
Portugal	107	0.3	5,048	6.8	4,512	4.4
Virgin Islands	1,736	4.1	873	1.2	3,197	3.1
Italy	1,259	3.0	1,125	1.5	2,507	2.4
Japan	2,659	6.3	1,086	1.5	2,468	2.4
Switzerland	2,815	6.6	812	1.1	2,252	2.2
Uruguay	874	2.1	259	0.4	2,107	2.0
Canada	1,819	4.3	909	1.2	2,028	2.0
Bermudas	853	2.0	571	0.8	1,940	1.9
UK	1,793	4.2	1,671	2.3	1,488	1.4
Argentina	394	0.9	418	0.6	758	0.7
Total	*42,530*	*100*	*73,812*	*100*	*103,015*	*100.0*

Source: Brazilian Central Bank

What motivated the surge in Spanish and Portuguese involvement in Brazil? The goal of these investments was to gain a large share of privatized industries in the country. Ex ante, it appeared that Mercosur countries and its major member were well positioned to become top recipients of foreign investment into emerging markets. Economic fundamentals appeared to be strong due to the then triumphant real plan (plano real). Superior inflation performance coupled with continuing growth under the currency board established in Argentina in 1991 reinforced the assessment that Brazil's trading partners would continue to grow. Moreover, Mercosur countries advertised a transparent institutional framework, although debt problems at the municipal and provincial levels were scarcely veiled. In fact, the first International Monetary Fund missions focusing on regional problems in Brazil started during the heyday of the *plano real* or real economic program.

The overall perception of Brazil as a foreign investment location is excellent. It ranks 6 in the World Economic Forum index of a pole of attraction for FDI and associated technology transfers. The overall technology perspective is bright. Brazil ranks above average (position 35) in the technology ranking for 80 countries developed by the World Economic Forum (2002). In Latin America, only Chile ranks higher at position 32.

Institutions remain weak. For instance, Brazil falls short in the levels of competition among Internet service providers and in the development and enforcement of legislation for the information and communication technologies sector, leading to higher than competitive prices and under-provision of services (Oliva, 2003). Also, the quality of the labor force admits much improvement while continuous economic growth remains uncertain.

The Brazilian economy was able to face the January 1999 devaluation of the real without large losses in income. Moreover, the short-term conditions of the Brazilian economy became much brighter in 2003, following an election that resolved many uncertainties. The ability to compete for foreign investment in the future hinges on establishing reliable economic growth, realizing continuing improvements in technology and labor force skills, and strengthening the institutional framework.

The Mexican target market and gateway to the north

In the 1990s, Mexico became a veritable showcase of economic growth based on policies formulated to foster trade and attract foreign capital flows. In 1999, Mexico was the 15th destination for FDI worldwide and the third among emerging markets after China and Brazil. In 2001, it became the largest recipient of foreign investment in the region. It received FDI $24.7 billion compared with $22.5 billion in Brazil. Due to the ability to sustain growth while other countries stagnated, Mexico surpassed Argentina in terms of GDP becoming the second largest economy in Latin America.

Who invested in Mexico? In 1996, just after recovery from currency and financial crises, Mexico received an additional $500 millions in FDI, pushing the cumulative FDI total to $4,500 million. There were 1,300 companies with foreign capital, comprising 9.8% of the national total. The origin of this investment by country is impressive, as the US accounts for most FDI.

What are the prospects of FDI in Mexico? The prospects of FDI in Mexico have remained bright due to the access to United States markets, strong macroeconomic fundamentals, consolidated economic reform, trade opening, and a gradually improving institutional framework. Investment liberalization, greater confidence on the legal system, and improved transparency has played a key role in establishing Mexico as a top destination. Moreover, the authorities have negotiated bilateral investment treaties (BITs) with many countries. The investment chapters on the free trade agreements undersigned with 28 countries in North and Latin America, Europe and the Middle East (2000 data), include confidence-building provisions. These factors mean that the country is likely to stay at the top of the emerging market FDI destination list.

Argentina: Twenty-first century Eldorado or gateway to the Americas?

In 2001-2002, Spain became the second foreign investor in Argentina, following closely the US, which was the traditional dominant foreign investor (Table 14.5). Argentina became the main destination of Spanish FDI in Latin America and the third market for Spanish exports in the region.

Table 14.5 FDI in Argentina by country of origin, 1992-2002

	1992	1995	2000	2001	2002
Total (in billion USD)	16,303	27,991	67,770	68,935	34,790
Developed Countries (%)	*78.1*	*75.1*	*85.6*	*86.0*	*81.8*
US	35.3	37.1	30.7	29.8	27.7
Spain	6.0	6.5	27.3	27.6	26.3
France	9.8	7.6	8.1	10.1	9.5
Netherlands	5.0	4.9	3.7	3.6	3.8
Italy	7.7	5.8	5.0	4.7	3.4
Germany	5.5	4.5	3.3	2.8	3.3
Developing Economies (%)	*5.7*	*12.1*	*7.5*	*7.3*	*9.4*
Chile	3.6	7.2	4.9	5.1	4.6

Source: UNCTAD and Argentina's Ministry of Economy, Bureau of International Accounts, 2004

Table 14.6 reviews the destination of Spanish investments in Argentina by sector. Several sectors stand out, namely, gas and petroleum (Repsol), electricity (Endesa), telecommunications (Telefónica), electric energy (Agues de Barcelona), construction (Dragados), and banking services (BBVA). Repsol's acquisition of YPF is the single largest Spanish investment in the country. In addition, growing investments in tourism have concentrated in Buenos Aires city and province.

What are the long-term financial prospects of these investments and their continuation? Given the macroeconomic and financial history of the country throughout the past century, prospects remain uncertain at best. Argentina's institutional and macroeconomic vulnerabilities are well known by now. It suffices to point out that financial and macroeconomic vulnerabilities were the main sources of the large losses experienced by Spanish firms in Argentina but foreign investing has continued. On this account, positioning investments in Argentina represents a high-risk bet. The bright light at the end of the tunnel stems from the recovery in 2003-04, the consolidation of Mercosur and the market expansion brought by the FTAA (Free Trade Area of the Americas), to which Argentina could become a gateway.

Table 14.6 Spanish largest firms in Argentina, by sector

Sector	Spanish Company
Gas and Petroleum	Repsol Endesa Gas Natural
Communications	Telefonica Terra
Electric Energy	Aguas de Barcelona
Construction	Dycasa (subsidiary of Spanish Group Dragados)
Banking Services	BBVA
Insurance	Mapfre Prosegur
Tourism	Sol Melia NH Hoteles

Source: Authors, with data from Companies' Annual Reports

The Spanish reconquest of South America: Eldorado?

The surge in Spanish and Portuguese involvement in South America is a key aspect of what is known as the "reconquest". Even if the reconquest momentary resulted in losses, it did not lead to an FDI standoff. In order to understand why reconquest gave way to losses but not to a standoff, we must recall the market targeting strategic goals of Spanish firms. The decision to concentrate investment efforts in South America, rather than elsewhere, follows a long-term market penetration strategy. This strategy aims to exploit the market expansion promise generated by Mercosur as well as gaining a beachhead into the potential gigantic integrated market resulting from the (FTAA), scheduled to start in 2005.

In order to clarify the evolution of Spanish investments, it is useful to divide recent experience into three sub-periods. The first is the pre 1996-era of moderate investments. The second is the 1996-1999 FDI boom. The third is the FDI slowdown that started in 2000. Many companies incurred large losses from their operations in Latin America during 2001-2002. Frustrated expectations motivated the remark that the Spanish reconquest appeared to have been a venture akin to that fateful 1500s expedition to the Peruvian jungles by Spanish adventurers seeking Eldorado, the legendary city of gold.

Table 14.3 shows the regional distribution of gross FDI flows originating in Spain during 2000-2003. The figures refer to gross flows rather than net flows and are expressed in euros, taking a Spanish perspective. Spanish gross FDI declined from €79 billion in 2000 to €24 in 2003. The largest decline was in Latin America, which fell from €25 billion in 2000 to €11 billion in 2001 and to 4 billion in 2002. The collapse of FDI from 2000 to 2003 represented a 84% decline. By contrast, FDI in OECD countries increased in 2001 to fall back in 2002 and 2003 by 37%, to about 60% of the level prevailing in 2000.

Three aspects of the behavior of FDI should be pointed out. First, Spanish outward FDI flows shifted towards OECD countries and away from Latin America. Second, Spanish FDI into Latin America slowed down but did not stop. Even though Latin America stagnated in the early years of the new millennium, Spanish firms continued to solidify their positions in the region. Third, contrary to the impression given by the multiple troubles faced in Argentina, the Latin American country that lost importance in terms of its share in total Spanish outward FDI was Brazil, not Argentina. The share of FDI going to Brazil fell from 18 to 6% of total Spanish FDI from 2000 to 2003. In fact, the fall of FDI to Brazil from €14.5 billion in 2000 to €1.4 billion in both 2000 and 2003 largely accounts for the collapse of total Spanish FDI to Latin America. By contrast, the share of annual FDI going to Argentina increased from 4% to 6% of total Spanish FDI during the same period. The annual amount invested in Argentina increased from 2000 to 2002. In 2002, Spanish FDI flows to Argentina were almost three times the country's FDI in Brazil and in 2003 these were very similar.

Why is it that global investments in South America were biased toward Brazil and turned away from Argentina during 2001-2003 while Spanish investments were biased toward Argentina rather than Brazil? The striking divergence in location strategy points toward quite different bets on these two countries, the outcomes of which remain to be seen.

Apart from differences in culture, language, and historical interactions, a preference for Argentina can derive from economic considerations. Spanish firms have been able to establish a dominant position in several Argentinean industries, where US and Spanish investment accounted for half of FDI in 2001 (see Table 14.5), but this would have been difficult to establish in Brazil. The United States is by far the major investor in Brazil and there are major investors from France, The Netherlands, Portugal and others (see Table 14.4). The proliferation of competing interests, make it difficult to establish a dominant market position to exploit market power and obtain reliable income flows from basic industries subject to weak competition.

Short-term losses

By 2001, when the Argentinean crisis started, Spanish enterprises had invested a cumulative stock of over $41 billion in Latin America. Even though there were large losses in the region in the early millennium, largely due to the Argentinean crisis, these losses were deemed unthreatening relative to the scale of the enterprises (Latin Trade, 2003). Also, the losses in 2001-2002 followed a stream of benefits received in previous years. Before the Argentinean crisis erupted in 2001, Spanish investments had been highly profitable. Accordingly, the major Spanish investors have taken a long-term perspective. They have moved to position themselves in the region following a long-run strategy that targets the promising Mercosur markets and the emergent Free Trade Area of the Americas (FTAA) markets. Spanish companies have bet on the region and have maintained and even strengthened their investments there.

The ensuing analysis of Spanish companies focuses on the major foreign investors. The largest Spanish investors in Latin America are former government monopolies that were partially privatized in the 1990s and the two leading banks. These are Repsol (oil and energy), Endesa (electricity), Telefónica Española (communications), Banco Bilbao Vizcaya Argentaria (BBVA, banking), and Banco Santander Central Hispano (BSCH, banking). All of them made substantial investments in Latin America, placing a significant proportion of their assets in the region and jointly accounting for the largest Spanish investments there. Other large Spanish multinationals, like Iberdrola, do not have large exposures in the region.

Table 14.7   Spanish MNEs: Net sales, net income and assets ($ million and percentages)

Spanish Firms	Country	Sector	Net Sales		Net Income		Total Assets	
			2003	2002/03	2003	2002/03	2003	2002/03
Repsol YPF	Argentina	Oil, gas	7,153	24	1,564	59	11,256	29
Enersis	Chile	Electricity	3,967	15	21	107	18,099	3
Endesa	Chile	Electricity	1,552	19	132	1119	9,216	2
Telefónica de Argentina	Argentina	Telecom	929	4	137	114	2,808	-1

Source: Economática, individual stock exchanges, Accival, Bear Stearns, Deutsche Bank, IXE Casa de Bolsa, J.P. Morgan, Merrill Lynch, Santander Central Hispano Investment, Smith Barney, Thomson First Call, UBS Warburg, and Latin Trade 2004.

Table 14.7 shows the 2003 sales, gains and assets of Repsol YPF, Endesa and Enersis, the major companies owned by Telefónica Española (Telesp, Telefónica Argentina, and Telefónica del Perú) and CTC, in which Telefónica Española holds a minority interest. Sales, gains and assets went down in all cases except for the reported gains of Repsol YPF.

In 1999, Repsol acquired Yacimientos Petrolíferos Fiscales (YPF), Argentina's largest oil and gas company, to become Repsol-YPF. The operations of Repsol-YPF have generated the largest asset losses of all Spanish-controlled firms in Latin

America. The responses to these losses are examined below. Endesa, which had sales of $4.8 billion in 2002, including $1.3 billion accounted for by Endesa Chile, is Spain's largest energy company. The extensive deregulation of Argentina's electricity sector and the privatization that took place in the 1990s attracted large FDIs into the sector. In 2002, Endesa had more assets in Latin America (43% of the total) than in Spain (41% of the total).

Currency devaluation and economic downturn hit the electricity industry hard. This industry purchases equipment priced in dollars and incurs in dollar-denominated debt but earns its income in local currency. Enersis, the Chilean-based holding company, is the base of Endesa's Latin American operations. In 2002, Enersis reported about $300 million in accounting charges on lost investments in Brazil and Argentina (Latintrade.com, March 2003).

The impact of losses from Argentinean investments on Endesa should not be exaggerated. Even though Enersis had about 20% of its activities concentrated in Argentina, Endesa's overall exposure to Argentina was low, accounting for about 5% of its operating profits worldwide (but one should take into account that the projected profit potential was previously estimated to be higher).

Telefónica Española is Spain's largest communications operator. In the 1990s, it pursued an aggressive investment strategy becoming the largest operator in the telecommunications sector in Latin America. Its largest asset in the region is the 87.42% position held in Telesp (Brazil). In addition, it owns 97.07% of Telefónica del Perú and has a minority position in CTC (Chile). Its main venture in Argentina is 98% of Telefónica de Argentina SA (TASA), the country's largest telecommunications company.

Losses in the Latin American markets, especially the large losses in Argentina, wiped out Telefónica's profits in 2001 and 2002. In 2003, the large investments made in Argentina were not doing well yet. The Spanish group sued Argentina for losses mounting to €3.3 billion (about $3.8 billion at July 2003 exchange rates). These losses were the result of the devaluation of the peso and the freeze in service tariffs charged to users. In June, Fitch Ratings downgraded the foreign and local currency senior unsecured ratings of TASA, as well as the debt rating of its holding company, Compañía Internacional de Telecomunicaciones S.A. (Cointel), to a C rating down from a rating of CC. The downgrading applied to about $954 million in outstanding securities.

In general, Spanish banks have targeted retail operations while US banks have focused on wholesale and specialized operations. The two global banks with heaviest exposure relative to the value of their assets are the two largest Spanish banks. Banco Santander Central Hispano has about 30% of its assets invested in the region and controls Banespa, the third largest private bank in Brazil. Banco Bilbao Vizcaya Argentaria controls BBV Banco Francés in Argentina. In 2002, BBVA and BSCH set aside over $1 billion each to cover the cost of potential losses in Argentina and Brazil.

The impact of the large losses sustained in 2002 (and 2001) on the parent companies should not be exaggerated. First, there were large profits received on account of Latin American operations in previous years. Second, the impact of the losses in the global companies did not threaten their survival. Third, the situation for 2003-04 represents an improvement and the prospects due to the scheduled inception of the Free Trade Area of the Americas in 2005 are bright.

Strategic responses and long-term positioning

How did Spanish firms respond to lowered short-term profits? The required performance and risk analysis might seem to call for an exercise in the application of the dismal science but companies have been able to formulate measured and coherent responses. Spanish firms have continued to expand investments in the region and take advantage of fire-sale investment opportunities. In addition, they sought to offset lower profit margins by increasing market share and moving to the most profitable and stable locations (i.e., Mexico, Chile) and penetrating the large Brazilian market. In some cases, companies have chosen to divest themselves of holdings in the region. This is the case of Iberia's disposition of its control over Aerolineas Argentinas.

The response of Repsol-YPF to the 2002-03 crisis entailed the layoff of thousands of workers, making accounting provisions of more than $2 billion in Argentina, and taking a charge against 2001 profits. To offset the large losses sustained in the region, the company continued a strategy of worldwide expansion. It got a foothold in Brazil by swapping assets with Petrobras, giving the state-run Brazilian giant a share in Argentine retail gasoline and refining business. In July 2003, Repsol-YPF announced that it was planning to invest €17.54 billion globally through 2007, including making large investments in Latin America. Over half of the money invested globally would go into exploration and production projects, taking a long-term perspective.

Enersis' strategic response was cautious. It cleaned up its books and entered into a $100 million deal to increase to 73% its share in Companhia de Electricidade do Rio de Janeiro. Telefónica Española shifted resources into the development of mobile communications in Mexico. Resources devoted to investment on the South American ventures were drastically reduced, thereby generating large cash flows that permitted the repatriation of $1,500 million from Latin America in 2002, through dividends and management fees (Cinco Dias, June 9, 2003).

The banks have sought to consolidate their positions. BBVA lowered profits by expanding banking activity in order to offset lower profit margins. The company has increased its holdings of subsidiaries in Mexico, Argentina and Uruguay and has announced that it seeks to increase market share (Estrategia, February 26, 2003). A key element of this strategy is penetration of the mobile market in Mexico. BSCH merged with Banco Santiago to consolidate its position in Chile.

Strategic responses based on continuing market penetration by means of strategic mergers and acquisitions take an optimistic view of the region. These strategies follow anticipations of continuing growth in Mexico and a wait-and-see attitude toward the reinstatement of good investment performance following economic recovery in Mercosur countries. The strategy also aims to establish a beachhead to maximize the benefits from the Free Trade Area of the Americas (FTAA). Operating profits obtained in the FTAA might turn out to be large, but only if market penetration is deep enough. The free trade area will integrate the Western Hemisphere creating the largest market worldwide, joining countries with a population of 800 people and a combined gross domestic product (GDP) of over $1 trillion.

Macroeconomic and institutional vulnerabilities

Host country macroeconomic instability is the Achilles heel of the market targeting strategic approach to FDI. There are several identifiable sources of macroeconomic instability. A major risk attached to FDI has to do with macroeconomic risks arising from economic, political and institutional vulnerabilities. Among these are

1. Vulnerable currencies.
2. A continuing high or rising debt problem.
3. High interest rates due to high debt levels and lack of credibility concerning both policies and policymakers.
4. Weak institutions as reflected in high measured and perceived corruption and other factors.
5. Political deadlock at the national and provincial levels.
6. Macroeconomic and institutional bases of lack of competitiveness.

In the case of Argentina, the lack of policy flexibility, the difficulties in achieving political consensus about how to face macroeconomic shocks, and the inappropriate use of policy flexibility when it is available, have become chronic maladies. In the 1990s, a rigid exchange rate and a restrictive monetary policy regime under the currency board system setup in 1991, and from the decision to dollarize the denomination of debts and financial contracts, reduced flexibility. In addition, mounting debt threatened to create a catastrophe out of a large devaluation, because it would bring a financial disaster to either borrowers forced to pay in dollar equivalents or lenders subject to borrower default.

The Argentinean debt dilemma led to policy immobility in the face of growing disequilibria. Following the 2001-02 collapse of the currency board system and associated financial crisis, policy immobility continued. For instance, it was not possible to reach an agreement on an economic program to face the crisis. Moreover, the drive to give greater independence to the central bank, an initiative that was supported by the International Monetary Fund, went into a stall due to a bitter dispute about aspects alleged to involve excessive independence.

Institutional environment, opacity and deterred investment

To examine the interaction between FDI and existing economic-politico-institutional variables, Figures 14.2-4 show the relationship between the FDI to

GDP ratio and three elements of institutional quality, measured by Kaufmann's indexes of corruption, rule of law, and institutions. Lower corruption, stronger rule of law, and better institutions are assigned a higher value of the index. The variable institutions is defined as an average of indexes of (1) voice and accountability, (2) political stability, (3) government effectiveness, and (4) regulatory quality. FDI-GDP is an average over 1995-2002 while the indexes are averages for 1996, 1998, 2000 and 2002. The figures show each individual data point as well as the fitted values (shown as triangles) of a linear regression of FDI/GDP as a function of the institutional quality variables. In all cases, there is a positive relationship between the FDI/GDP ratio and the variable measuring the institutional environment.

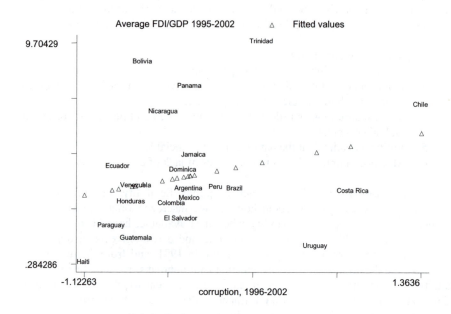

Figure 14.2   Corruption and FDI/GDP
Source: Authors, with data from the World Developing Indicators of the World Bank and
              the Global Competitiveness Report of the World Economic Forum

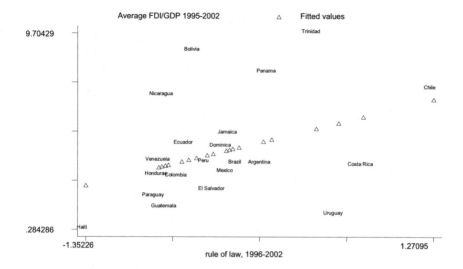

Figure 14.3   Rule of law and FDI/GDP
Source: Authors, with data from the World Developing Indicators of the World Bank and
the Global Competitiveness Report of the World Economic Forum

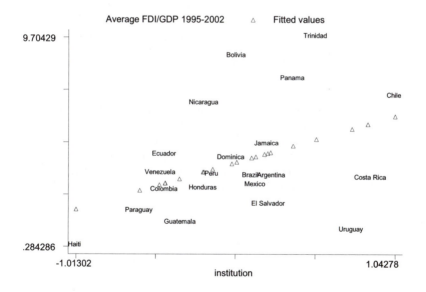

Figure 14.4   Institutions and FDI/GDP
Source: Authors, with data from the World Developing Indicators of the World Bank and
the Global Competitiveness Report of the World Economic Forum

Table 14.8   Deterred foreign direct investment

Country	C	L	E	A	R	O-Factor
Benchmark Countries						
Singapore	13	32	42	38	23	29
USA	25	37	42	25	48	35.5
Chile	30	32	52	28	36	35.6
UK	15	40	53	45	38	
Latin America						
Mexico	42	58	57	29	52	47.6
Uruguay	44	56	61	56	49	53.3
Peru	46	58	65	61	57	57.6
Brazil	53	59	68	63	62	60.8
Colombia	48	66	77	55	55	60.3
Venezuela	53	68	80	50	67	63.4
Argentina	56	63	68	49	67	60.6
Ecuador	60	72	78	68	62	67.9
Guatemala	59	49	80	71	66	64.9
Last Positions						
Indonesia	70	86	82	68	69	75
Russia	78	84	90	81	84	84
China	62	100	87	86	100	87

Note: Larger scores refer to more opacity and lower scores to less opacity
Source: Price Waterhouse Cooper: Investigating the Costs of Opacity:
                Deterred Foreign Direct Investment

Table 14.8 presents several indexes of the quality of the economic environment, as measured by the opacity index, and some estimates of their effects on interest rates and FDI for year 2001. The O-Factor is an opacity index score that controls for 5 variables: corruption C, legal opacity L, opacity in government economic policies E, opacity in accounting standards and information made public A, and regulatory opacity R. The O-Factor for country i is defined as the following weighted average of component factors

$$O - Factor_i = \frac{C_i + L_i + E_i + A_i + R_i}{5},$$

where an O-factor equal to one means greater opacity and an O-factor equal to four means greater transparency.

Table 14.9   Deterred foreign direct investment

Country	O-	Tax-	Opacity Premium	Deterred Lower (%)	Deterred Lower (million)	Deterred Point (%)	Deterred Point (million)
Benchmark Countries							
Singapore	29	0	0	0	0	0	0
USA	35.5	5	0	0	0	0	0
Chile	35.6	5	3	0	0	0	0
UK	38	7	63	0	0	0	0
Latin America							
Mexico	47.6	15	308	53	6.477	70	8.554
Uruguay	53.3	19	452	75	132	100	176
Peru	57.6	23	563	93	1.787	123	2.363
Brazil	60.8	25	645	106	30.267	141	40.261
Colombia	60.3	25	632	104	3.462	138	4.593
Venezuela	63.4	27	712	117	5.275	155	6.988
Argentina	60.6	25	639	105	14.15	139	18.732
Ecuador	67.9	31	826	135	977	179	1.295
Guatemala	64.9	28	749	123	381	162	502
Last Positions							
Indonesia	70	37	1010	164	954	218	1268
Russia	78	43	1225	199	7417	263	9802

Source: Price Waterhouse Cooper, www.opacityindex.com

The tax equivalent measure of opacity for a country i is defined as

$$\frac{\beta_2}{\beta_1}\left[opacity(i) - opacity(Singapore)\right].$$

The coefficients β_1 and β_2 are obtained from a regression of the variable FDI against a source country dummy D, tax levels TAX, opacity levels OPACITY in the host country, a vector X of other characteristics of the host country, and a vector of characteristics Z specific to the source-host country pairs. Formally

$$FDI(k,j) = \sum_i \alpha(i)D(i) + \beta_1 TAX(j) + \beta_2 OPACITY(j) + X(j)\varphi + Z(k,j)\delta + \varepsilon(k,j)$$

The variable deterred FDI is an estimate of the response to the following question. Consider a country that reduces its opacity to the low level displayed by benchmark countries. How much FDI would the country to receive if the other countries' opacity levels remain constant? The benchmark countries are Chile, the UK, the US and Singapore, which have the lowest scores (i.e., best) in the sample. Table 14.8 reports the estimates of deterred foreign investment. The estimates imply that FDI is lost in all the Latin American economies in the sample except Chile due to weak institutions.

Gauging competitiveness

Table 14.10 shows the World Economic Forum (WEF) competitiveness rankings for selected countries, including those achieving the highest and the lowest rankings. The US and Finland shifted positions in the 2001 and 2002 top ranking positions. Zimbabwe and Haiti closed the 2002 growth competitiveness index.

Table 14.10 Competitiveness rankings

Country/Year	Growth Competitiveness Ranking			Current Competitiveness Ranking	
	2004	2003	2000	2004	2000
Finland	1	1	5	2	1
United States	2	2	1	1	2
Canada	15	16	6	15	11
Germany	13	13	14	3	3
Spain	23	23	26	26	23
Chile	22	28	27	29	26
Mexico	48	47	42	55	42
Brazil	57	54	45	38	31
Argentina	74	78	44	74	45
Colombia	64	63	51	58	48
Bolivia	98	85	50	101	58
Ecuador	90	86	58	94	57
Ukraine	86	84	56	69	56
Zimbabwe	99	97	55	82	50

Source: WEF (2004), Global Competitiveness Report 2004-2005, Geneva

The growth competitiveness index measures a number of factors that contribute to sustain medium term growth as measured by the rate of change of real per capita GDP. It aims to help explaining why some countries grow faster than others and permits identifying weaknesses in the economies considered. This growth competitiveness index (GCI) is a composite of

(1) A macroeconomic index capturing the stability of the country's fiscal and monetary policies. In 2002, Singapore appeared on the top of this index and Zimbabwe as the economy with poorest macroeconomic stability.
(2) A technology activity index measuring the capacity to develop new technologies and exploit them. US, Finland and Taiwan headed the list of more advanced technological economies.
(3) An institutional quality index, measuring the efficiency level of the financial system, corruption levels, and legal system development. According to the combined indicator for corruption levels, contracts and law enforcement, Finland and Denmark top the rankings for year 2002.

Chile is the only Latin American economy to be top ranked according to the Growth Competitiveness Index (GCI) and all the sub-indexes of the GCI. Ecuador ranked at the bottom of the 2001 GCI index and ranked just right above Bolivia in the 2002 ranking.

The current competitiveness index attempts to identify those factors sustaining high current productivity levels and economic performance measured in terms of per capita GDP levels. It controls for conditions that permit sustaining high levels of productivity.

The current competitive index is a composite of (following Porter's diamond theory)

(1) Degree of sophistication of company operations and strategy. Firm capacity of innovation, R&D spending, branding policy, product process sophistication, are components of a company's internal situation.
(2) Factor and demand conditions of the markets. This rubric controls for sophistication of inputs and domestic demand.
(3) Country's business environment and competition levels. The extent of domestic and foreign-driven competition is affected government trade policies in place, the quality of institutions, corruption levels, technological advances, and access to latest communication and information devices, among others.

Except for Chile, which is at the same level as industrialized countries, Argentina, Colombia, Brazil, Mexico and other Latin American countries are characterized by relatively slow growth. These economies occupy below-average positions in the indexes on Competitiveness, implying there is ample room for improvement in institutional quality, sound macroeconomic environment and jumping into the technological race.

The global competitiveness index has a close relation to the growth rate. Because better competitiveness is associated with a lower number, a negative relation between the index and growth indicates a positive relation between the competitiveness index and the real per capita growth rate.

Price competitiveness and its instability can also be gauged looking at cost of living indexes expressed in US dollar equivalents. In just one year, Argentina's cost of living collapsed from one of the most expensive countries to live in 2001 to one of the less expensive in 2002-04. Cost competitiveness has been recovered, but at high social and economic costs. This instability in competitiveness is remarkable. At one point the country was artificially and grossly uncompetitive and soon after it was artificially and grossly over competitive in terms of prices.

Lessons: Long-term perspectives and necessary changes

What are the lessons obtained from the recent experience of Spanish involvement in Latin America? First, there are substantial market potential and production sharing advantages from FDI activity in the region but macroeconomic instabilities and institutional weaknesses can nullify these advantages. Macroeconomic instability still afflicting Latin American countries in many aspects can lead to large FDI losses. Recent experiences suggest that bouts of continuing instability might continue to re-appear in the future. The high debt syndrome has not been suppressed and the currencies remain highly vulnerable to shifting capital flows. Unless these problems can be minimized, FDI will remain hazardous.

Second, the debt problem remains a tough one and the underlying difficulty is political. How to implement a Latin version of the Maastrich Treaty or a fiscal deficit pact is difficult to visualize. Third, at the moment, there are four broad alternatives to recurrent currency instability. First, dollarization remains an alternative but it must be systemic, meaning that the major South American countries, Brazil and Argentina, must adopt it to ensure true stability. Second, unilateral dollarization jointly with much intra-regional trade can promote instabilities similar to those recently experienced by Mercosur. Third, flexible exchange rates have worked well in Chile, although it is not obvious that other countries are ready to follow Chile's steps in practice. Fourth, an alternative route is to develop a Latin American currency. For political and economic reasons, this currency will be dominated by Brazil. This alternative remains quite risky at the moment.

Finally, the term reform has a bad reputation in the region even though the data shown strongly suggests that institutional reform, greater opacity and stronger governance remains urgent. In recent elections there have been a tendency to vote against incumbents but there has not been a government policy of retrenchment.

The discussion brings good news and bad news. The analysis suggests that foreign investors encounter good market potential and production sharing opportunities in Latin American countries. Moreover, economic recovery will set in as soon as the world economy reinstates rapid growth and economies should be reinvigorated with the inception of the Free Trade Area of the Americas. These considerations suggest that the rapid growth of cross border investment will be renewed with global economic recovery and the start of the FTAA. The bad news are that the analysis does not suggest that there is a solid basis for a continuing bright macroeconomic perspective and improved institutional environment. We have instead pointed out some alternative routes to the Eldorado dream site. Eldorado has not been found yet, but there is still hope.

References

Borensztein, E.J., J. De Gregorio, and Jung-Wa Lee (1998), "How Does FDI Affect Economic Growth?" *Journal of International Economics*, vol. 45, pp. 115-135.

De Gregorio, J. (1992), "Economic Growth in Latin America," *Journal of Development Economics*, vol. 39, pp. 54-84.

Government of Spain (2003), *Flujos de Inversiones Exteriores. Año 2002*, Dirección General de Comercio Exterior, Madrid.

Kaufmann, D., A. Kraay, and P. Zoido-Lobatón (1999a), "Aggregating Governance Indicators," World Bank policy research paper no. 2195, Washington, D.C.

Kaufmann, D., A. Kraay, and P. Zoido-Lobaton (1999b), "Governance Matters," World Bank policy research paper no. 2196, Washington, D.C.

Larraín, F., L.F. López-Calva, and A. Rodríguez-Clare (1999), "Intel: A Case Study of FDI in Central America," CID working paper no. 58, Center for International Development, Boston.

Oliva, M.A. (2003), "Brazil Competitiveness and Technology," Mimeo. World Economic Forum, Geneva.

Oliva, M-A, and L. A. Rivera-Batiz (2002), "Political Institutions, Capital Flows and Developing Country Growth: An Empirical Investigation," *Review of Development Economics*, vol. 9, pp. 248-262.

PriceWaterhouseCoopers (2002), "Investigating the Costs of Opacity: Deterred FDI," Washington, D.C.

Rodriguez-Clare, A., (2002) "Costa Rica's Development Strategy Based on Human Capital and Technology: How It Got There, the Impact of Intel, and Lessons for Other Countries," *Journal of Human Development*, vol 2, pp. 312-324.

Toral, P. (2001), *The Reconquest of the New World. Multinational Enterprises and Spain's Direct Investment in Latin America*, Ashgate, Aldershot.

UNCTAD (2004), *World Investment Report. 2004*, UNCTAD, Geneva.

United Nations, Comisión Económica para América Latina (2003), *La Inversión Extranjera en América Latina y el Caribe, 2002*, CEPAL, Santiago de Chile.

World Economic Forum (2002), *The Latin American Competitiveness Report 2001-2002*, Oxford University Press, Oxford.

World Economic Forum (2004), *The Global Competitiveness Report 2004-2004*, Oxford University Press, Oxford.

Zellner, M. (2003), "Prosperidad a la Vista: Brasil encabeza la lista de las 100 por su recuperación en 2003," *Latin Trade*, July.

Index